Educating Exceptional Children

FOURTH EDITION

Educating Exceptional Children

SAMUEL A. KIRK
University of Arizona

JAMES J. GALLAGHER
University of North Carolina

HOUGHTON MIFFLIN COMPANY   BOSTON
Dallas   Geneva, Illinois   Hopewell, New Jersey
Palo Alto   London

The authors would like to dedicate this edition to the many, often anonymous, colleagues who pioneered the education of exceptional children in the nineteenth and early twentieth centuries.

Library of Congress Catalog Card Number: 82-83366
ISBN: 0-395-32772-5

Cover design by Jerry Wilke. Cover photograph by James Scherer.
Chapter-opening photo credits: Chapter 1, p. 2, Frank Wing/Stock, Boston; Chapter 2, p. 32, Anestis Diakopoulos/Stock, Boston; Chapter 3, p. 66, © Herb Snitzer 1964, 1965 "Summerhill, A Loving World"; Chapter 4, p. 118, Lionel Delevigne/Picture Group; Chapter 5, p. 180, Ronald Trahan, Perkins School; Chapter 6, p. 230, George Bellerose/ Picture Group; Chapter 7, p. 276, Julie O'Neil; Chapter 8, p. 320, Burk Uzzle/Magnum Photos; Chapter 9, p. 364, Teri Leigh Stratford/Monkmeyer Press Photo Service; Chapter 10, p. 412, © 1980 by Abraham Menashe from the book *Inner Grace* published by Alfred A. Knopf; Epilogue, p. 462, © Marinel M. Johnsen 1982.

Excerpt on pp. 71–74 from James J. Gallagher, *Teaching the Gifted Child*, Second Edition. Copyright © 1975 by Allyn and Bacon, Inc. Reprinted by permission.

Excerpt on p. 81 from M. Wolf, "Talented Search in the Visual and Performing Arts," in I. Sato (ed.), *Balancing the Scale for the Disadvantaged Gifted*, 1981. Printed with permission from the National/State Leadership Training Institute on the Gifted and the Talented, Office of the Superintendent of Schools, Ventura County Schools, Ventura, California.

Excerpt on pp. 204–205 from Susan Jay Spungin (ed.), *Guidelines for Public School Programs Serving Visually Handicapped Children* (2nd ed.), 1981. Reprinted with permission from the American Foundation for the Blind, New York.

Excerpt on pp. 205–206 from Michael Orlansky, *Encouraging Successful Mainstreaming of the Visually Impaired Child*, Project MAVIS Sourcebook 2 (Boulder, Colo.: Social Science Education Consortium, 1979). Copyright Linc Services, 1980. Reprinted by permission of the publisher.

Excerpt on pp. 221–222 from B. Stephens, R. E. Smith, J. R. Fitzgerald, C. Grube, J. Hitt, and M. Daly, *Training Manual for Teachers of the Visually Handicapped*, 1981. Reprinted courtesy of Stoelting Co., 1350 S. Kostner Ave., Chicago, IL 60623.

Excerpt on p. 223 from Irving R. Dickman, *Sex Education and Family Life for Visually Handicapped Children and Youth: A Resource Guide*, 1974. Reprinted with permission from the American Foundation for the Blind, New York.

Excerpt on p. 246 from S. P. Quigley, M. W. Steinkamp, D. S. Powers, and B. W. Jones, *Test of Syntactic Abilities*, 1978. Reprinted with permission from *Test of Syntactic Abilities, Guide to Administration and Interpretation*, Dormac, Inc. © 1978.

Excerpt on p. 308 reprinted with permission of Macmillan Publishing Co., Inc. from *Speech Correction in the Schools* (4th ed.) by Jon Eisenson and Mardel Ogilvie. Copyright © 1977 by Macmillan Publishing Co., Inc.

Excerpt on pp. 345–346 from Ronald E. Galbraith and Thomas M. Jones, *Moral Reasoning: A Teaching Handbook for Adapting Kohlberg to the Classroom*. Copyright 1976 Greenhaven Press, Inc., St. Paul, Minnesota. Reprinted with permission from Greenhaven Press.

Contents

10 Children with Multiple, Severe, and Physical Handicaps   413

Preface

PURPOSE

Educating Exceptional Children, fourth edition, is an introductory text
for those who will work with exceptional children: prospective special and regular elementary and secondary school teachers, counselors, psychologists, inservice educators, paraprofessionals, other
professionals such as rehabilitation personnel, and parents.

The most important development in special education during the
past twenty-five years has been the movement to integrate exceptional children into the regular education program to the greatest degree possible. Federal and state laws have mandated a free, appropriate education for all children in a setting that is as close as possible
to the regular classroom—the least restrictive environment. Special
education is no longer the exclusive province of special educators.
Practically all elementary and secondary school teachers can expect
to encounter exceptional children in their classrooms. The special
needs of these children have become the shared responsibility of regular education teachers, counselors, psychologists, and other members of the educational team including parents of exceptional children. This text is intended to prepare those individuals for their roles
in meeting the needs of exceptional children in modern society.

ORGANIZATION

We have chosen to focus this text on the exceptional child as a
learner. Throughout the book we consider two dimensions that im-

pinge on the educational program developed for an exceptional learner: individual differences and modifications of educational practices.

Knowing full well that each child is unique, we stress the concept of individual differences. Exceptional children differ in some important aspects from others in their age group; they also differ within themselves in their patterns of development. Thus, we discuss both *interindividual* and *intraindividual* differences. In many respects the intraindividual differences—those developmental patterns that cause youngsters to show marked differences within themselves in their physical, intellectual, and social growth—may pose more problems for a teacher and require more adaptations of a child's educational program than the interindividual differences that separate an exceptional child from his or her age mates. By emphasizing intraindividual differences and applying this concept to the various clusters of exceptional children, we attempt to supply an integrating element that gives meaning to both the differences and similarities among children and the suitable adaptations of educational practices which are presented for each cluster within a common framework of curriculum and content changes, skills changes, and learning environment changes.

The first chapter in the text, "The Exceptional Child in Modern Society," offers historical background on the field of special education and an overview of issues and trends that have affected the development of programs for the exceptional learner. Coverage is devoted to the role of the courts, state and federal legislation, the role of parents and families, early education of the exceptional child, mainstreaming, and the recent shift in focus from the medical to the environmental factors that contribute to handicapping conditions. These topics are also discussed throughout the text within the context of specific areas of exceptionality.

The second chapter, "Individual Differences and Special Education," explains in detail the organizing principles for this fourth edition, emphasizing the significance of intraindividual differences and the educational modifications that are necessary to meet the special needs of the exceptional learner. In addition, the chapter covers the controversy surrounding the use of labels and the methods for determining the prevalence of exceptional children.

The fourth edition of *Educating Exceptional Children* continues to provide basic information about the characteristics and distinctive problems of exceptional learners, using the categorical terminology necessary for purposes of communication. Chapters 3 through 10 focus on the various clusters of exceptional children and cover the topics of definition, classification, identification, prevalence, causes, and characteristics as well as the special educational adaptations that might be made for children in each cluster.

FEATURES AND CHANGES IN THE FOURTH EDITION

The text has undergone a thorough revision that reflects improvements in the salient features of previous editions of *Educating Exceptional Children:* an integrated approach that emphasizes intraindividual differences, clearly organized format and highly readable style that promote understanding of basic information about the field, and factual up-to-date coverage of developments in special education.

Each chapter has been rewritten. In particular, chapters focusing on the exceptional child in modern society, individual differences and special education, mentally retarded children, children with learning disabilities, and children with multiple, severe, and physical handicaps have been extensively revised so that coverage is presented in a more cohesive manner. Specifically, the fourth edition covers mental retardation and learning disabilities in one chapter each, combining the two chapters that were devoted to each area in the previous edition. Severely/profoundly retarded children are now discussed in the chapter on multiple, severe, and physical handicaps because educational adaptations for that group correspond to the basic skills approach recommended for the multiply handicapped child. Trends and issues that have had, and continue to have, an impact on special education are now presented in the first chapter and reiterated in the text's epilogue.

At the beginning of each chapter we have added a list of topics to permit students to preview material covered in the text, and we have retained a summary of major ideas at the end of each chapter to help students review material. Within each chapter we have included an article or excerpt from current literature to provide additional insight into particularly important topics and issues that apply to educating exceptional children. For the first time the text includes photographs within the chapters depicting exceptional children in various settings—at school, at home, and in the community.

New end-of-chapter features include annotated bibliographies of items that may be of special interest to readers and sections entitled "Unresolved Issues" that encourage students to discuss and propose solutions for problems which are still at issue in the field of special education.

A glossary of key terms in the text has been retained and bibliographical references for in-text citations are located at the end of the book.

STUDY GUIDE

A Study Guide for the text is also available and, like the basic text, has undergone extensive revision to make it more compatible with students' needs

The new Study Guide for the fourth edition is intended to complement the student's use of the text and class experiences through four types of learning approaches: organizing knowledge, reinforcing knowledge, evaluating knowledge, and expanding knowledge. Thirty to thirty-five multiple-choice questions and true/false statements are provided for each chapter; answer keys appear at the end of the guide so that students may have immediate feedback on their responses to review questions. Other exercises in the guide focus on defining key terms, responding to short answer questions, and extending knowledge through further research of literature in the field and preparation of projects and reports. Appendix A contains case studies that focus on three areas of exceptionality—mental retardation, visual impairment, and learning disability. Exercises for each case study help students summarize and apply their knowledge of the text. Appendix B features a list of commonly available publications related to exceptional children and guidelines for critical reading of periodical literature.

ACKNOWLEDGMENTS

We are grateful to a large group of our colleagues and specialists in various exceptionalities for their criticisms and suggestions during the revision of the text. Those who have provided useful, and in some cases invaluable, assistance include Ruth Barnhart, Iowa State University; Asa Berlin, The Pennsylvania State University; Charles Kokaska, California State University at Long Beach; Marjorie McKee, Northern Michigan University; C. Julius Meisel, University of Delaware; Donald Moores, Gallaudet College; Ouida Fae Morris, University of South Carolina; and John Umbreit, The University of Arizona. Their critical comments and ideas have helped shape and improve our presentation of material.

We also wish to acknowledge the help provided by Ruth Kirkendall whose daily assistance was instrumental in bringing this volume to its present condition. Our families deserve thanks for their tolerance of the necessary time and energy that this text required.

As a final note, we would expect the reader to understand that while our society has come a long way from the placement of handicapped individuals in distant and isolated institutions, we still have a great deal to learn about the best ways to help exceptional children and adults become truly integrated into modern

American society. Judges and legislators can force the exceptional child into physical conjunction and association with children who are not exceptional, but they cannot force understanding, or acceptance, or an effective educational program. That job belongs to all who work with exceptional children. This text tries to faithfully present what is currently known about exceptional children and also what remains to be solved by this and future generations.

Samuel A. Kirk
James J. Gallagher

Educating Exceptional Children

1

The Exceptional Child in Modern Society

Education in any society tends to reflect the political philosophy of that society. Under a democracy as practiced in the United States, where the state is believed to exist for the welfare of the individual, education must be organized primarily to achieve that end. "All men are created equal" has become trite, but it still has important meaning for education in a democratic society. Although it was used by the founders to denote equality before the law, it has also been interpreted to mean equality of opportunity. That concept implies educational opportunity for all children—the right of each child to receive help in learning to the limits of his or her capacity whether that capacity be small or great. Recent court decisions have confirmed the right of all children—handicapped or not—to an appropriate education and have mandated that the public schools take whatever action necessary to provide that education to handicapped children.

Those legal decisions are consistent with a democratic philosophy that all children be given the opportunity to learn, whether they are average, bright, dull, retarded, blind, deaf, crippled, delinquent, emotionally disturbed, or otherwise limited in their capacities to learn. American schools have evolved numerous modifications of regular school programs to adapt instruction to children who deviate from the average and who cannot profit substantially from the regular program. Those modified programs have been designated programs for exceptional children.

WHO IS THE EXCEPTIONAL CHILD?

There have been various attempts to define the term *exceptional child*, and all need considerable elaboration before they can be understood. Some use it when referring to the particularly bright child or the child with unusual talent. Others use it when referring to any atypical or deviant child. The term has been generally accepted, however, to include both the handicapped and the gifted child. For the present purposes the exceptional child is defined as *the child who deviates from the average or normal child (1) in mental characteristics, (2) in sensory abilities, (3) in neuromotor or physical characteristics, (4) in social behavior, (5) in communication abilities, or (6) in multiple handicaps. Such deviation must be of such an extent that the child requires a modification of school practices, or special educational services, to develop to maximum capacity.*

But that is a very general definition and raises many questions. "What is average or normal?" "How extensive must the deviation be to require special education?" "What role does the environment play in the definition?" "What is special education?"

To complicate the picture further, the exceptional or deviating child has been studied by various disciplines—psychology, sociology, physiology, medicine, and education. If we define an exceptional child as one who deviates from the norm of his or her group, then we have many kinds of exceptionalities. A redheaded child in a class would be an exceptional child if he or she differed from the norm of the group. A child with a defective or missing thumb would be exceptional. Actually, such deviations, although of possible importance to physicians, psychologists, geneticists, and others, are of little concern to the teacher. A redhead is not an exceptional child educationally speaking because the educational program of the class does not have to be modified to serve his or her needs. Children are considered educationally exceptional only when it is necessary to alter the educational program to meet their needs. Hence the use of the term *exceptional children* in education may differ from its use in biology, in psychology, and in other disciplines and professions. Children are educationally exceptional if their development deviates in kind and degree to such an extent that they require educational provisions not needed by most children for maximum development.

We group children of like characteristics for instructional purposes (6-year-olds in the first grade). Exceptional children are often grouped to facilitate communication among professionals. The following groupings are typical:

1. mental deviations, including children who are (a) intellectually superior and (b) slow in learning ability—mentally retarded
2. sensory handicaps, including children with (a) auditory impairments and (b) visual impairments
3. communication disorders, including children with (a) learning disabilities and (b) speech and language impairments
4. behavior disorders, including (a) emotional disturbance and (b) social maladjustment
5. multiple and severe handicaps, including various combinations of impairments: cerebral palsy and mental retardation, deaf-blind, severe physical and intellectual disabilities, and so forth

HISTORY OF EDUCATING EXCEPTIONAL CHILDREN

As we look back into history, we find that the entire concept of educating each child to the limits of his or her ability is relatively new. The current use of the term *exceptional* is itself a reflection of radical changes in society's view of those who deviate. We have come a long way from the Spartans' practice of killing the deviant or malformed infant, but the journey was by slow stages.

Historically, four stages in the development of attitudes toward the handicapped child can be recognized. First, during the pre-Christian era the handicapped tended to be neglected and mis-treated. Second, during the spread of Christianity they were pro-tected and pitied. Third, in the eighteenth and nineteenth centuries institutions were established to provide separate education. Fourth, in the latter part of the twentieth century there has been a move-ment toward accepting handicapped people and integrating them into society to the fullest extent possible.

The stages in development of American attitudes toward handi-capped individuals follow a similar pattern. In the early years of our Republic there were no public provisions for the handicapped. Such individuals were "stored away" in poorhouses and other charitable centers or remained at home without educational provi-sions. It was estimated that, as late as 1850, 60 percent of the in-mates of the poorhouses consisted of the deaf, the blind, the insane, and "idiots" (National Advisory Committee on the Handicapped, 1976).

During the period from 1817 to the beginning of the Civil War, a period of nearly fifty years, many states established residential schools for the deaf, the blind, the mentally retarded, the or-phaned, and others, as was being done in Europe. In 1817 a resi-dential institution for the deaf was established in Hartford, Con-necticut, and named the American Asylum for the Education and Instruction of the Deaf. It is now the American School for the Deaf. In 1829 a residential school for the blind was organized in Water-town, Massachusetts, and named the New England Asylum for the Blind, subsequently named the Perkins School for the Blind. In 1859 a residential school for the mentally retarded was established in South Boston, Massachusetts, and called the Massachusetts School for Idiotic and Feebleminded Youth. Thus, the leaders and reformers of that period (Horace Mann, Samuel Gridley Howe, Do-rothea Dix, and others) gave impetus to our second stage, the es-tablishment of residential schools. Those institutions offered train-ing, but equally important was the protective environment, often covering the life span of the individual.

The third stage in the development of provisions for the handi-capped in America was the establishment of special classes in the public schools. The first day class that was created was one for the deaf in Boston in 1869. It was not until 1896 that the first special class for the mentally retarded was organized in Providence, Rhode Island. It was followed by a class for the crippled in 1899 and by a class for the blind in 1900 in Chicago. Since 1900 special classes have been organized in many public schools throughout the nation.

Current American practices and organizations that try to pro-vide an optimum education for exceptional children have been influenced by major ideas and concepts from a number of pioneers who were active in the last part of the nineteenth century and at the beginning of the twentieth century. Sir Isaac Newton once remarked, "If I see farther than others, it is because I stand on the shoulders of giants." Every profession and professional person is dependent, whether recognized or not, on the past contributions of pioneers. The current generation of special educators owes much to a group of creative innovators, some of the most notable of whom are listed in Table 1.1. Although very diverse in background, these

TABLE 1.1
Significant Ideas Influencing American Special Education

Initiator	Dates	Nationality	Major Idea
Jean Marc Gaspard Itard	1775–1838	French	Single-subject research can be used to develop training methods for the mentally retarded.
Samuel Gridley Howe	1801–1876	American	Handicapped children can learn and should have an organized education, not just compassionate care.
Edward Seguin	1812–1880	French	Mentally retarded children can learn if taught through specific sensory-motor exercises.
Francis Galton	1822–1911	English	Genius tends to run in families, and its origin can be determined.
Alfred Binet	1857–1911	French	Intelligence can be measured, and it is amenable to improvement through education.
Louis Braille	1809–1852	French	Blind children can learn through an alternative system of communication based on a code of raised dots.
Thomas Hopkins Gallaudet	1787–1851	American	Deaf children can learn to communicate by spelling and gesturing with their fingers.
Alexander Graham Bell	1847–1922	American	Hearing-handicapped children can learn to speak and can use their limited hearing if it is amplified.
Maria Montessori	1870–1952	Italian	Children can learn at very early ages, using concrete experiences designed around special instructional materials.
Anna Freud	1895–1982	Austrian	The techniques of psychoanalysis can be applied to children to help their emotional problems.
Lewis Terman	1877–1956	American	Intelligence tests can be used to identify gifted children who tend to maintain superiority throughout life.
Alfred Strauss	1897–1957	German	Some children show unique patterns of learning disabilities that require special training and are probably due to brain injury.

creative people had in common an attitude of optimism, of seeking to draw forth a better understanding of the exceptionality and to discover a variety of techniques for maximizing the abilities of the exceptional child. Their contributions remind us that we have been traditionally too pessimistic about exceptional children and consequently find ourselves continually being surprised at what they can do if we are imaginative enough to find better methods and procedures by which to stimulate them.

The fourth stage of development is difficult to analyze at this time. We know that from 1950 to 1980 there was an explosion of provisions for the handicapped, spearheaded by state and federal legislation and appropriations. The next twenty years (1980–2000) will see further developments, especially in a trend toward educating the exceptional child with his or her normal peers to whatever extent feasible.

CHANGING WORLDS—NEW DIRECTIONS

Any textbook must, of necessity, be a static document that portrays the field of special education, or any other topic, at the particular point in time represented by the book's publication date. In this respect, it is like a photograph that faithfully portrays a particular moment in time but often misses the dynamic shifts taking place prior to or after that photograph has been taken. In order to alert you to some of the dynamic forces at work in the field of exceptional children, we will present some of the major trends and issues that are destined to change and modify the future of special education. In this way, you will have an opportunity to see not only the current portrait of those forces but also their potential for influencing the field of exceptional children in the near future.

We have chosen to discuss six of the most important forces now at work in terms of their impact and future implications. They are: (1) a fundamental shift in the view of the causes of exceptionalities, (2) increased interest in the families of handicapped children, (3) legislative action for the handicapped and gifted, (4) court judgments related to exceptional children, (5) the move to mainstreaming and least restrictive environments, and (6) a greater emphasis on early childhood education of the handicapped.

Shift from Medical to Ecological Focus

In the past thirty to forty years, a significant shift in thinking has occurred concerning the causes of handicapping conditions. At one time, the problem of the exceptionality was considered to be inherent within the child, similar to a medical condition that exists when a child contracts a particular disease. If the child were deaf or blind or mentally retarded, then it was accepted that the condition existed entirely within the child and the basic problem was for the professional to find some means to remove the condition or to help the child adapt to the surrounding world.

As programs for exceptional children gradually expanded and included more children with mild handicaps—such as communication disorders, learning disabilities, behavior disorders, and mild mental retardation—it became clear that the definition of *exceptional* involved a mix of the individual's characteristics and the special demands the environment made on that individual. This recognition of the role of the environment in defining exceptionality has been widely referred to as moving from the *medical model*, which implies a physical condition or disease within the patient, to an *ecological model*, in which one sees the exceptional child in complex interaction with environmental forces.

Two examples illustrate this shift from a medical to an ecological focus. Several years ago, the President's Committee on Mental Retardation (1970) published a major report entitled *The Six-Hour Retarded Child*. This report revealed that many children without observable neurological damage appeared to be mentally retarded during the six hours that they spent in school but were not considered retarded either before or after those hours. Essentially, the increased demands for intellectual performance present in the school setting revealed a deficiency on the part of the child that was not considered serious in the child's home or neighborhood environment.

Robinson (1978) reported that predominantly agricultural countries such as China do not recognize the concept of mild mental retardation at all. Only when the demands of the society increase as it becomes more technologically complex do some children reveal problems requiring care. A person's ability to read is a matter of some indifference if the major task in life is planting and harvesting rice. However, in a society such as ours that is committed to advanced technology, the ability to read becomes a critical aspect of social adaptability and the child who cannot read or learn quickly is in substantial trouble in both academic and social settings.

Similarly, the label *juvenile delinquent* carries the implication that the problem of deviant behavior exists within the child and that the solution to the problem rests with the child for changing the deviant behavior to something more acceptable. Many sociologists are outraged by such a concept, which they claim blames the victim for his or her problems (Ryan, 1971). In order to understand

FIGURE 1.1
Special Education Placements of Educable Mentally Retarded by Sex and Race

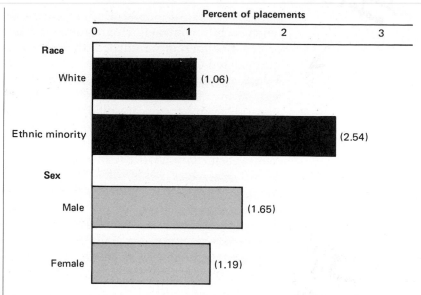

Source: *State, regional, and national summaries of data from 1978 civil rights survey of elementary and secondary schools.* Washington, D.C.: U.S. Office of Civil Rights, April 1980.

the impact of the environment as a contributing factor to exceptional conditions, an analogy can be made between treating disease and dealing with juvenile delinquency. In urban areas, some neighborhoods are disease ridden and the prevalence of childhood illness is far above the average. Two alternative strategies may be taken to meet this situation—(1) individually treat every child who becomes ill or (2) try to correct the environment that causes the illness. In cases of juvenile delinquency, one could attempt to treat or punish each individual child who created a disturbance in a delinquency-prone area, or one could attempt to clean up those dimensions of that environment that seem to predispose some youngsters to deviant behavior.

One of the concerns of special educators, parents, and other observers has been the apparent disproportion of minority group children in special education programs, particularly those programs for the mentally retarded. Figure 1.1 shows graphically the reason for such concerns. Of those students placed in the programs for the educable mentally retarded, approximately 2.54 percent of the total minority population were placed in such programs, as contrasted with only 1.06 percent of the white population. A difference in sex can also be noted in that about 1.65 percent of the available male population was placed in programs for the educable mentally retarded as opposed to only 1.19 percent of the female population.

One explanation for the disproportionate number of minority students referred and placed is the unusually high rate of school failure in minority groups. School failure triggers the special education process of diagnosis, labeling, and treatment. There is the additional suspicion that minority children may be more easily placed in special programs and that sometimes such placement is for the convenience of the educator rather than for the benefit of the student. The otherwise unexplainable sex differences that appear in Figure 1.1 give support to these beliefs. The behavior of male students may be a factor in determining the greater proportion of males placed in special education. It is known that males tend to be more disruptive than females and thus more likely to be identified as lacking necessary social adaptation patterns.

When viewed from an educational perspective, the shift from a medical to an ecological model represents a movement away from the exclusive goal of changing the child toward a broader target of redesigning the child's learning and social environment.

Critical Role of Families

Nonhandicapped people have difficulty understanding what it's like to be handicapped. Blindness, deafness, or physical handicap can be simulated, but there remains for the nonhandicapped person a storehouse of visual, auditory, and motor memories that provide a rich background of recoverable information not available to those who have been handicapped from birth. It is even harder to imagine what it's like to be mentally retarded. Everyone knows how failure feels, but how many have experienced chronic, inevitable failure in almost every task attempted compounded by an inability to even recognize that failure? Imagine what that does to an individual human being.

It is easier to project ourselves as parents of handicapped children because that is an experience that can happen to anyone who has children, regardless of educational background, family status, or financial condition. During the last couple of decades, we have begun to appreciate more fully the pain and the stress that are part of having a handicapped child and to realize the degree of courage and external supports necessary for parents to maintain their equilibrium under such circumstances.

Most parents who must cope with a handicapped child face two major crises. The first is a type of *symbolic death* of the child that was to be. When a woman is pregnant and the parents are looking

minority groups/boys (more) in spec. ed. programs

change environment rather than child....

Parents coping with handicap

forward to having a child, they inevitably think much about the future of their unborn child. Most parents project favorable goals with high aspirations. They want the child to be successful in life, perhaps a leader, certainly well educated and financially secure. They may even have hopes that their child will help them as they grow older. Parents who are ushered into a pediatrician's office and told that their child is handicapped suffer a symbolic death of that child-to-be with the loss of their dreams and aspirations, and many parents react with severe depression under such circumstances (Farber, 1976).

There is a second and quite different crisis faced by the parents and that is the problem of providing daily care. The child who is cerebral palsied or autistic is often very difficult to feed, to dress, and to put to bed, and the thought that the child will not go through the normal developmental process to adult independence weighs heavily on the parents.

During the past thirty years, the increase of organized parent and citizen action in behalf of handicapped people has led to major changes in education. The importance of the more recent parents' movement in the field of exceptional children can hardly be overestimated. In many respects the other changes—legislation, additional professional resources, and court actions—are merely consequences of the forces put into motion by the organized parents' movement.

In the 1940s and 1950s, the parent was often identified as a cause of the problems of the exceptional child and in many cases became the scapegoat for most of the problems. Particularly in cases such as emotional disturbance, professionals often identified the parent as the basic cause of the problem. Such problems with professionals have diminished but have not been eliminated, as can be noted by a recent example of soul searching by conscientious professionals.

Cansler, Martin, and Valand (1975) stated:

Have we as professionals working in a field that traditionally had been child-centered unwittingly cast parents into the role of adversary, object of pity, inhibitor of growth, or automatic misfit, while expecting them to perform in a way expected of no other parents? Have we been too quick to focus on weakness and too slow to recognize the normality of the behaviors we see? (p. 9)

Many parents had attempted to encourage local education authorities to provide some program to aid their handicapped children. Failing in the effort, they formed local programs of their own in church basements, in vacant stores, in any place that would

Parents of Handicapped Children Speak Out

Nonhandicapped people may have difficulty understanding the full impact of what it's like to be handicapped, but most can empathize with the parents of handicapped children and easily imagine the range of emotions experienced by those who must provide for a handicapped child. The following selected quotations from *Parents Speak Out: Views from the Other Side of a Two-Way Mirror* by H. and A. Turnbull convey the sense of often unspoken pain of parents who have "been there."

We don't begin in anger. We start out the way all parents of all children do: with respect, reverence really, for the professional and his skills. The pediatrician, the teacher, the writer of books, and articles on child development, they are the sources of wisdom from which we must draw in order to be good parents. We believe, we consult, we do as we are told, and all goes well unless . . . one of our kids has a handicap. (p. 40)

This friend recommended that I take Jennie to the pediatric neurologist at one of the children's hospitals in Philadelphia. I knew this neurologist and saw him shortly thereafter. He examined Jennie very thoroughly, and when he finished the exam, he looked at me and said, "We may have a problem." At that point, all my hidden fears of the past few months were realized. Even though he had put it in the realm of probability, to me he certified or validated all the nightmares and the fears I had tried in vain to believe were imaginary. It was the start of the year and a half of what I refer to as my grief period. (p. 74)

I remember vividly the details of how I found out that Robin was seriously impaired. Robin was a second child, and from the time he was six months old, I had been questioning my pediatrician concerning his lagging development. For about a year, the pediatrician had been turning aside my questions and delaying any unusual procedures. Finally he agreed to a diagnostic work up at Children's Hospital. When the orderly brought Robin back from one of the procedures, a pneumoencephalogram, he inadvertently left Robin's hospital charts in the crib. I picked them up and read, "Entering diagnosis: Mental Deficiency." Before being discovered, I had read all of the reports. Soon, however, a harried nurse entered and snatched the charts from my hands with a stern admonition that I had no right to read their contents. In no time at all, a small group of white coats and dresses came bustling into the room to talk with me until my pediatrician could be summoned. When he came, they respectfully withdrew and left him with the awesome task of explaining why he had not leveled with me earlier concerning what mental deficiency was, what the prognosis was, and why I shouldn't rush off to Johns Hopkins where I had a pediatrician friend on the staff. The only thing I really remember from that encounter is a garbled explanation of mental deficiency and the doctor saying, "We can't all march in the parade!" (p. 91)

[A] stranger yelled across a restaurant at my husband and me, "What's wrong with that strange little boy?" When we tried to ignore him, he kept pressing, "I asked you why that little boy looks and acts so strange." Other persons in the restaurant looked back and forth between him and us, waiting for a response. My husband told him that nothing was wrong and for him to mind his own business. The stranger replied, "That little boy can't talk for himself. You are an insincere man, and you have a strange little boy." The stranger left the restaurant. My husband and I were in a state of shock. (p. 137)

SOURCE: H. Turnbull & A. Turnbull (Eds.), *Parents speak out: Views from the other side of a two-way mirror.* Columbus, Ohio: Charles E. Merrill, 1978.

Parental participation in early intervention treatment programs has produced favorable results in overcoming some of the developmental deficits in children with moderate and severe handicaps. (Photo: Copyright © Betty Medsger 1979.)

parents counselling other parents.

house them. Those local organizations, loosely formed by parents around the common needs of their children, often provided important informal help and assistance to new parents who struggled to find aid for their handicapped children. In many respects, the parents who counsel other parents provide a base of confidence that the problem can be dealt with and that other people understand and share the anxieties that often accompany the discovery that one's child has special problems.

The parents quickly realized that fundamental changes were needed in the allocation of resources at local, state, and federal levels. No casual or haphazard approach was going to provide much permanent assistance for them or their exceptional children. Accordingly, in the 1940s and 1950s, they were able to form large parents' groups as exemplified by the National Association of Retarded Citizens, the United Cerebral Palsy Association, and, later in the 1960s, the Association for Children with Learning Disabilities.

The parents' organizations have successfully obtained legislation providing for additional trained personnel, research, and a variety of other programs that brought the handicapped to the attention of the general public and also attracted more qualified people into the field to provide a stronger professional base (Cain, 1976). Organized parents' groups for gifted children have only recently been formed and have not yet shown the same influence as those concerned with handicapped children.

Another major step in the changing role of parents took place when the parents themselves began to participate meaningfully in the treatment programs. Such participation grew as more information was gained. Turnbull and Turnbull (1978) listed several reasons for a movement toward a parent-professional partnership based on mutual respect and decision making:

1. experimental evidence that parents can positively influence the development of their children through teaching them at home
2. encouraging results of early intervention in ameliorating some of the developmental deficits associated with moderate and severe handicaps
3. success of parents in bringing litigation to establish the educational rights of their children
4. federal legislation, notably PL 94–142, the Education for All Handicapped Children Act, that sets forth clear standards for parental involvement in the educational process

The parents are now, if not partners with professionals, at least vigorous participants in decision making that affects programs and policies.

State and Federal Legislation   Ever since the turn of the century, states have been involved in a limited way in subsidizing programs in public schools for children with severe handicaps—blindness, deafness, physical impairments. Some states helped local school systems organize and support classes for children who were mentally retarded and behaviorally disordered.

It was not until after World War II that states made a major thrust to financially support special classes and services for all types of handicapped children in local schools. This expansion created an emergency in the late 1940s and early 1950s because of the short supply of professional educators and the lack of knowledge about the education of exceptional children.

Although traditionally education has been a local matter, after much debate, the federal government between 1957 and 1963 acceded to supporting small efforts directed toward research and training of professional personnel in fields of the handicapped. Public Law 88–164 provided for training of professional personnel and authorization of research and demonstration. It represented a strong initiative by President John Kennedy whose interest was heightened by the presence of a mentally retarded sister in his own family.

Since the passage of the Elementary and Secondary Education Act in 1965, the federal government has become involved in public education in a significant way. It still contributes less than 10 percent of the total cost of education, while the state and local governments contribute over 90 percent of the cost of public education from kindergarten through twelfth grade.

Federal legislation in support of handicapped children was not easy to obtain. Parents' groups had organized and with the aid of other interested citizens convinced Congress that they needed help. The arguments that they used were compelling, as was the intensity of feeling that accompanied them. Why should handicapped children and their parents be penalized through the accident of birth in a particular state or a particular region of a state? Were not American citizens (in this case the parents of handicapped children) entitled to equal treatment anywhere in the United States? Should they, in addition to the special burdens of having a handicapped child, be forced to move their family to another community where special education resources were available or to send their child to some institution far away from home and family because no local resources existed? The manifest unfairness of the situation called out for special attention.

The United States Congress was responsive, but the initial reaction was fragmentary and limited in nature. The Congress first passed a variety of special legislation to improve the research and training efforts to help the deaf and mentally retarded. Later legislative changes included funds for demonstration projects and stimulation grants to the states and extended coverage to all areas of handicapping conditions. At the end of the 1960s the federal initiatives included

special grants to states to encourage new programs for handicapped children

support of research and demonstration projects to seek better ways to educate handicapped children

establishment of regional resource centers to help teachers develop specific educational programs and strategies

extension of provisions for training leadership personnel to head training programs and administer programs for handicapped children

establishment of a nationwide set of centers for deaf-blind children to aid multiply handicapped children

a requirement that some funds for innovative programs in general education would be reserved for special projects for handicapped children establishment of a Bureau of Education for the Handicapped within the Office of Education to administer these and other provisions for handicapped children

That flood of provisions served notice that the federal government was beginning to accept responsibilities to provide support resources for the handicapped and to encourage and aid the states in carrying out their basic responsibilities.

Ten years after this initiative, programs for handicapped children had dramatically increased across the country. States began putting a much greater share of their educational dollars into educating the handicapped, increasing their contributions by almost 300 percent (Gallagher et al., 1975).

One major area of continued dissatisfaction was that some states were still not assuming responsibility for providing services for many of their handicapped children. This led to the next major legislative initiative: PL 94–142, the Education for All Handicapped Children Act, passed in 1975 to take effect in 1977, whose stated purpose is:

to assure that all handicapped children have available to them . . . a free, appropriate public education which emphasizes special education and related services to meet their unique needs, . . . to assist states and localities to provide for the education of all handicapped children, and to assess and assure the effectiveness of efforts to educate handicapped children. (Pelosi and Hocutt, 1977, p. 3)

To that end the federal government authorized the spending of up to $3 billion by 1982, promising much larger sums of money to aid the states than had previously been provided from the federal level. In return for this aid, states are required to provide evidence that they are doing their utmost to help handicapped children receive needed services. Following are some of the specific requirements with which the states must comply:

1. State and local educational agencies must insure that all children who are handicapped and in need of special education and related services are to be identified, located, and evaluated.
2. Parents are provided a number of procedural safeguards that protect the handicapped child's right to a free and appropriate education. Some of these safeguards are:
   a. Parents have the right to review the educational records of their child.
   b. They can obtain an independent evaluation of the child.

c. They are to receive a written notice before the school initiates a placement process.

d. They have the right to request a hearing before an impartial
officer to challenge the placement of their child if they so desire.

3. A comprehensive educational assessment is required. This assessment goes beyond single IQ tests. It requires the attention of
a multidisciplinary team and should include teacher recommendations, data relating to sociocultural background and adaptive
behavior, in addition to standard school measures. Also, a re-
evaluation is required at least every three years.

4. A written individualized education plan (IEP) is to be developed
and annually updated. The IEP documents the child's current
performance, the long- and short-term educational goals, and
the specific procedures and services to be provided to the child,
plus a means for evaluating the success of the plan.

5. Children must be placed in the *least restrictive environment* compatible with their handicap. This means that if they can receive
an effective program in a regular setting they should not be
placed in a special class; if they can receive their education in a
special class they should not be placed in an institution. In
Deno's cascade of educational services (see p. 57), the philosophy is to move as close to the normal setting as feasible for that
particular child.

These requirements place substantial pressure on public school
systems and require a good deal more in the way of assessment,
parent contact, and evaluation than many school systems have
been accustomed to providing. Not surprisingly, many educators
have protested the heavy burdens that such requirements place on
them and consequently the law and its regulations are currently
under review. Nevertheless, the regulations represent a goal that
most special educators would endorse for an effective ongoing program.

Abeson and Zettel (1977) explain that this legislation was never
intended as a mandate that all handicapped children must be educated in the regular classroom. For many moderately to severely
impaired children and multiply handicapped children, the normal
classroom would clearly be inappropriate, but many such youngsters were brought back into the orbit of the public schools, receiving attention that was previously denied them.

Although individualization of instruction has long been one of
the key concepts in special education, the design and formalization
of the individualized education plan (IEP) has been a new and

One of the requirements of PL 94–142 is that an individualized education program must be developed and updated annually for each exceptional child by a multidisciplinary team of professionals. (Photo: Sybil Shelton from Peter Arnold, Inc.)

complicated experience. The law itself specifies in some detail that the IEP should include:

1. a statement of the present levels of educational performance of each child
2. a statement of annual goals, including short-term instructional objectives
3. a statement of the specific educational services to be provided to each child and the extent to which such child will be able to participate in regular educational programs
4. The projected date for initiation and anticipated duration of such services and appropriate objective criteria and evaluation procedures for determining . . . whether instructional objectives are being achieved

In two decades the federal government has moved from a position of little concern or involvement to become a major partner with the local and state public education programs for the handicapped. These major changes are not without their problems or their detractors. Such requirements place new burdens on local school systems, and many educators worry about the intrusiveness of federal regulations on local programs.

Gifted children, alone among the exceptional children, are not included in this cornucopia of legislation and remain without meaningful assistance from federal sources, though some small beginnings have been made. The federal government in 1980 expended over $5 million on special education programs for the gifted student, less than 1 percent of that spent on those children with handicapping conditions.

Role of the Courts   Since World War II individuals and groups interested in the education of handicapped children have appealed to governmental sources at the local, state, and federal levels to gain assistance. Only since the early 1970s, however, has there been a sustained effort to use the courts to bring additional resources to these children and their families.

As our society has matured enough to reject the option of physically removing the handicapped from view (out of sight, out of mind), many persons have begun to review the legal status of the handicapped in the society itself. If handicapped persons are citizens, are they not entitled to all the rights and privileges of ordinary citizens? It is out of this type of self-examination that another major trend has emerged—namely, the deliberate attempt to translate these abstract rights into tangible societal actions.

Handicapped citizens are playing an increasingly active role in reaffirming their rights and in convincing members of Congress of the need to address inequities. (Photo: Owen Franken/Stock, Boston.)

Minority groups have used the courts to establish their rights as individuals beginning with the classic school desegregation case of *Brown* v. *Board of Education* in 1954. Since that time, courts have reaffirmed the rights of minority citizens in a wide variety of settings. Those interested in the rights of the handicapped have watched these cases and have seen that a similar situation applies to the handicapped whose rights as citizens need to be reaffirmed.

One of the most vigorous actions has focused on seeking court decisions to support the rights of the handicapped to an appropriate education. Most state constitutions include statements to the effect that "every child has a right to a free public education." An example of the early promise to educate all children at public expense is found in Article X, Section [1] of the Wisconsin Constitution adopted March 13, 1848, which stated: "The legislature shall provide by law for the establishment of district schools which shall be free to all children between the ages of four and twenty years" (Melcher, 1976). Seizing on the phrase *all children have a right to education,* various interested groups have brought legal suits against states to compel them to provide special education that would fulfill the stated promise.

Class action law suits have been influential in changing the status of handicapped children in the United States. A class action suit provides that legal action taken as part of a suit applies not only to the individual who brought the particular case to the courts but applies equally well to all members of the particular class to which that individual belongs. Thus the rights of all mentally retarded children and emotionally disturbed children can be reaffirmed by one case involving one exceptional child.

The following rulings in recent court cases are among those that reaffirmed the rights of the handicapped:

A handicapped child cannot be excluded from school without careful "due process" and it is the responsibility of the schools to provide appropriate programs for children who are different. (*Pennsylvania Association for Retarded Children* v. *Commonwealth of Pennsylvania*, 1972; *Goso* v. *Lopez*, 1974; *Hairston* v. *Drosick*, 1974)

The presumed absence of funds is not to be used as an excuse for failure to providing educational services to exceptional children. If there are not sufficient funds, then all programs should be cut back. (*Mills* v. *Board of Education*, 1972).

Handicapped children committed to state institutions must be provided a meaningful education in that setting or their incarceration is to be considered unlawful detention. (*Wyatt* v. *Stickney*, 1972)

Children should not be labeled handicapped or placed into special education without adequate diagnosis that takes into account different cultural and linguistic backgrounds. (*Larry P.* v. *Riles,* 1979)

These court decisions create an expectation that something will be done but do not guarantee it. Just as laws have to be enforced, and money promised has to be appropriated, so court decisions have to be executed. The class action suits that affect large numbers of citizens have been implemented very slowly.

It is now clear that merely passing a law or getting a court decision is no guarantee that something will be done. In reviewing the results of the court decisions and their implementation, Kirp, Kurloff, and Buss (1975) concluded:

Court decisions

1. Legal mandates do not fulfill themselves; they must rely on others for implementation.
2. The mandates most readily implemented are those that require a minimum amount of organizational change.
3. Resistance to such mandates comes not so much from resentfulness and malevolence as from a perceived threat to the current institutional and social structure and to the people who are functioning comfortably within that structure.

affirmative action for the handicapped

According to Hobbs (1975), full implementation of the laws and court decisions would require (1) intense and lasting pressure together with systematic incentives, (2) court-appointed overseers to help direct and encourage implementation to completion, (3) the provision of some additional resources to pay for what has been mandated, and (4) the strong commitment of institutional administrators (that is, school superintendents, state education officials, and others).

The financial and psychic cost of closing down state institutions, reorganizing the public schools, or providing special services to every handicapped child does amount to substantial change and markedly increased financial investment. It is still up to the American people, as a whole, to determine the degree to which they wish to live up to the theoretical ideas of equality that were placed in laws and constitutions many years ago.

Court decisions and legislation related to the handicapped can be linked together. The series of court decisions that reaffirmed the states' responsibility to provide education for all handicapped children caused great dismay among many state executive and legislative leaders who wondered aloud where the additional money would be found. As a result, state and local leaders increased pressure on the Congress to pass the Education for All Handicapped Children Act, which would compel the federal government to help pay for the requirements that the courts had placed on the schools.

Mainstreaming and Least Restrictive Environments

Court decisions and legislative actions in the 1970s have accelerated the movement toward *mainstreaming,* which is an effort to provide special services for exceptional children in the *least restrictive environment.* Mainstreaming means that the exceptional child (1) will be placed with his or her normal peers, (2) will receive special services while enrolled in the regular classes (not special classes), and (3) will interact as much as possible with his or her normal peers in a least restrictive environment. To understand this movement it is necessary to trace its development and to analyze the social forces leading to its implementation (Gottlieb, 1981).

Several forces have come into play to bring about this significant social movement. They will be discussed in more detail in subsequent chapters and are mentioned briefly here.

1. Many children were misclassified as mentally retarded.
2. Special classes showed few beneficial results.
3. Special classes became classes for problem children instead of remedial centers.

Dunn (1968) was one of the first to urge special educators to stop being pressured into "a continuing and expanding special education program (special classes) that we know now to be undesirable for many of the children we are dedicated to serve" (p. 5). Gallagher (1972) pointed out that "special education too often was an exclusionary process masquerading as a remedial process" and added that there was precious little evidence that special education was returning a significant number of children to the regular class. His comments were particularly true of the educable retarded. Once they were identified and placed as *educable retarded,* such children were often in the special education stream for the balance of their school careers.

The criticisms leveled against special classes served as the impetus for the mainstreaming movement. Those forces have come together to create a powerful surge within the public schools toward abandoning special class programs for exceptional children and replacing them with regular class programs, which would be supplemented by special remedial or special educational services provided by a resource or itinerant teacher (Reynolds and Birch, 1977).

The goal of special education programs for preschool exceptional children is to prevent the potential handicap from emerging in its most troublesome form or, if necessary, to prepare the child to adapt to the handicap.
(Photo: © Lionel Delevigne/Picture Group.)

Early Education for the Handicapped

The final trend to be noted is the movement toward establishing programs for preschool handicapped children. This trend, like the others noted in this chapter, stems from many different forces: research evidence on child development, models of successful performance, and the observations of lay persons and experts. Implementation of the general principle "the younger we start, the better" is not easy primarily because there is no single social institution, like the schools, through which programs can be directed.

The importance of early intervention to provide a proper developmental start for exceptional children has been known for many years. Leadership for such programs can be found in the field of the deaf where children need assistance to develop communication

systems from the earliest age possible. Other exceptionalities such as cerebral palsy are quickly brought to the attention of professionals at, or shortly after, birth. They receive attention from multidisciplinary teams who plan multifaceted treatment programs in such dimensions as physical therapy, speech and communication, and cognitive development at the earliest time in the child's life.

It has not been lack of awareness of the importance of early childhood that has been a problem but rather securing the resources to support the programs and the commitment of such social institutions as the public schools to take the responsibility for implementing programs for these children. Also, parents and the community often overlook the condition of mildly handicapped children (learning disabled, educable mentally retarded, behaviorally disturbed, or developmentally delayed) until they reach the public schools. The schools apply standards for development that parents and neighbors rarely expect at preschool age. Only then are these problems of developmental delay or inappropriate social adaptability revealed.

The studies of Skeels, Kirk, Heber, and Ramey on mentally retarded children reported in Chapter 4 and Hunt's influential review of what was known about the relationship of intelligence and experience (1961), among many others, led the way to an acceptance of the rich possibilities of early intervention. Hunt commented, "The assumption that intelligence is fixed and that its development is predetermined by the genes is no longer tenable" (p. 342). "It might be feasible to discover ways to govern the encounters that children have with their environments especially during the early years of their development, to achieve a substantially faster rate of intellectual capacity" (p. 363).

Karnes and Teska (1975) reviewed the growing literature on the effect of intervention programs on young children and reached the following conclusions:

Can the developmental status of children be changed through deliberate programming? The answer to that from the available research is "yes." It is possible to move groups of children from one-half to one standard deviation higher on measures of intellectual ability. There is substantial evidence that many children will lose the temporary gain in intellectual ability as measured by standard tests, but will keep achievement and motivational gains for a longer period of time. There is substantial evidence to support the general principle, "the earlier the instructional program is begun, the better." (p. 219)

Stedman (1977) reviewed over forty longitudinal intervention research programs for children "at risk" for developmental problems and concluded:

The manner in which a child is reared and the environment into which he is born have a major impact on what he will become. The family's method of establishing social roles leaves little doubt that early family environment has a significant impact on the child's development before he reaches his second birthday. Where access to children can be gained in the early years, preferably during the language emergent years (one to two years of age), intervention programs will be more effective than those begun at later ages. There is evidence that the effects of early intervention programs for children are strengthened by the involvement of the child's parents. (pp. 2–3)

A recent review by Kirk (1982) reached substantially the same conclusions.

The development of special education programs for preschool handicapped children has resulted in many program changes from the traditional special education program, changes that are having their influence on the issue of how to aid exceptional children. Some of the more important changes are discussed in the following paragraphs.

Less Emphasis on Classification

The child with developmental problems at the preschool level is likely to have a wide variety of difficulties. The categorization of such children, or pigeonholing them, by use of such definitive terms as *mentally retarded* and *speech handicapped* becomes less important than the need to identify the developmental problems of these children and to provide special programs for them.

More Emphasis on Multidisciplinary Approaches

The problems of the young handicapped child are likely to include the domains of health, education, and social psychological issues. No single profession could lay claim to all the expertise necessary to provide all the help that the child and his or her family will require. This has resulted in bringing together many different disciplines to work in a single setting so that the family can have the range of expertise needed to develop a comprehensive treatment program.

Parent Education

The parent remains the primary caretaker of the child at the preschool age. Most programs at this level include the parents in the total treatment program, as noted earlier in this chapter. Although parents often leave much of the care and education of their child to the schools when the child reaches 5 or 6, they are quite often prepared and ready to take responsibility for some of the training program for their child before that age. Many parents also appreciate the opportunity to do something constructive with their child who has often been a puzzlement and a source of great frustration to them. The professional community finds itself using more and more of its time and effort teaching parents rather than providing the service to the preschool handicapped child directly.

Child Find

Quite often the handicapped child at school age identifies himself or herself through inadequate adaptation to the expectations and demands of the school program. The necessity for embarking on a major search for such children is not often a key objective for the school unless forced to it by governmental requirements. At the preschool level, however, it becomes important to search out those children in need of help, whose problems may be hidden or not realized until the child reaches the classroom. A substantial effort has been made to develop procedures for screening children to find those in need of special help. This means developing more sophisticated measures for evaluating or assessing the child's progress during that period.

Frankenburg (1977) presented important criteria for using screening as a technique, since it obviously was beyond professional capabilities to screen all children for all conditions.

1. The condition should be treatable or controllable.
2. Early treatment should help more than later treatment.
3. Screening should be done while distinctive treatment is still possible.
4. A firm diagnosis should be possible in the screened child to differentiate that child from a nondiseased or nonhandicapped individual.
5. The condition sought should be relatively prevalent.
6. The condition should be serious or potentially so.

The field of early education for handicapped children brings the professions of medicine, public health, family counseling, psychology, and education together for a common purpose—the more effective adaptation of the handicapped child to the society. The goal is to prevent the potential handicap from emerging in its most troublesome form or, if necessary, to prepare the child to live with the handicap in the most effective style possible.

SUMMARY OF MAJOR IDEAS

1. The exceptional child is one who deviates from the average child in ways that require changes in school practice for the child to reach full potential.

2. The major categories of exceptionality within the field of special education include: mental deviations—unusually rapid or slow mental development; visual and auditory handicaps that interfere with the processing of information; communication disorders, including learning disabilities and problems in expression; behavior disorders that interfere with social adaptation; and multiple and severe handicaps.

3. Attitudes toward exceptional children have moved from rejecting and isolating the handicapped to integrating exceptional children as much as possible into society.

4. A number of major social trends have influenced much of what we now do to and for exceptional children. At present, each exceptionality is defined by special conditions within the individual that interact with special demands of the environment. At one time, professionals believed that the exceptionality existed totally within the individual.

5. Families play a critical role in the life of a handicapped child, with parents first adjusting to the symbolic death of their dreams for the future of their child and then coping with the constant pressures of daily care.

6. Parents of exceptional children have organized to become a potent political force, influencing legislatures to provide resources to educate their children and petitioning the courts to reaffirm their rights to equity.

7. During the post–World-War-II era gains in services have been achieved through the actions of state and federal legislatures, thereby confirming society's desire to provide equity to families of the handicapped.

8. Courts have taken a series of actions to guarantee a free public education for handicapped children, but implementation of the court rulings has often been neither sure nor swift.

9. Mainstreaming has been encouraged as a desirable objective—namely, to integrate the handicapped child as fully as possible with normal society while providing an effective educational program.

10. Early education for exceptional children, starting as soon as possible after birth, is considered desirable but is still not often available.

UNRESOLVED ISSUES

Every generation leaves as its special gift to the new generation some unusual problems for which solutions have not been found. There are many issues in the field of special education that the present generation of professionals has been either unable or unwilling to resolve. The end-of-chapter sections entitled "Unresolved Issues" provide brief descriptions of several widely debated issues as a beginning agenda for the current generation of students who will face those problems in their professional careers.

1. Special Education and Regular Education. The design of special education has been based on the assumption that a competent educational program exists in the regular school program. Children who are not able to respond to that program would be identified as exceptional students needing special help.

But what if the regular program falls short of basic competence and is not able to provide a stimulating or even appropriate educational environment for all the students? What is the role of special education then? Too often such a situation has resulted in flooding the special education program with borderline students who should, under more favorable circumstances, fit into a competent regular education program.

2. Handicapped Infants—A Shortage of Service. Strangely enough, federal legislation provides financial support for the education of handicapped children starting at age 3, but not before. Yet psychologists say that years 0–3 may be critical to later development, particularly with exceptional children. Clearly, the public schools have been reluctant to start educational programs for handicapped children under 3 because they find it uncomfortable and awkward to cope with such young children. The problem of providing needed services and resources for exceptional children between birth and age 3—the period during which both parent and child form their attitudes about one another—is still largely unsolved.

3. Personal Fears and Anxieties. Dr. Edwin Martin, former director of the Office of Special Education in the Department of Education, recently gave his view of the reason for the reluctance of the non-handicapped to meet directly the needs of the handicapped.

[T]he basic problem faced by the disabled, historically, is that they have made us afraid. As human beings evolved, we have learned certain cautions. One is to be afraid of the unknown, of the strange, of the different. In a primitive world full of possible dangers we did not know what dangers lurked in strange places, in the dark, or in the hearts of strangers.

Perhaps, most specifically of all, as humans we do not know what lies behind life itself. As human beings we are finite, not immortal, we become old, ill, and we die. For many of us these are frightening thoughts and we do not wish to dwell on them; we do not wish to face these truths. If disabled persons symbolize or represent our finiteness, if they stir in us these suppressed fears, then it is not surprising that we have excluded them from our tribes, from our schools, our places of work and leisure. . . .

In our stories, in our public statements, in our television advertisements, and in other information media, we have tried to present new images of disabled people. We have presented images of independence, not dependence; images of involvement, not isolation; images of learning, not being treated for a sickness; images of work, not inactivity. These images expressed values we hoped would replace the old fears, would change the unknown into the known. (Martin, 1981, pp. 3, 6)

How can we recognize and conquer our own fears so that we can feel more comfortable in close relationships with the handicapped?

REFERENCES OF SPECIAL INTEREST

Gliedman, J., & Roth, W. *The unexpected minority: Handicapped children in America.* New York: Harcourt Brace Jovanovich, 1980.

A report from the Carnegie Council on Children, which views the problems of handicapped children as a civil rights issue, points out that the handicapped are a hidden minority group in our society, possessing many characteristics of other minority groups. The authors urge parents to greater activism in controlling services, both educational and vocational, for their handicapped children.

Meyen, E. (Ed.). *Basic readings in the study of exceptional children and youth.* Denver, Colo.: Love, 1979.

An excellent compilation of articles and papers that provide readings in each of the areas of exceptional children. In addition, the book contains articles and papers on current perspectives in special education and in instructional planning.

Turnbull, H., & Turnbull, A. (Eds.). *Parents speak out: Views from the other side of a two-way mirror.* Columbus, Ohio: Charles E. Merrill, 1979.

A series of personal experiences by professional families, each of whom has had a handicapped child. The parents discuss the frustrations of coping with a handicapped child and the conflicts and difficulties they have had as parents dealing with other professionals. It gives a good sense of the anger and despair felt by many such parents.

Weintraub, F., Abeson, A., Ballard, J., & LaVor, M. (Eds.). *Public policy and the education of exceptional children.* Reston, Va.: Council for Exceptional Children, 1976.

A comprehensive presentation of state and federal initiatives designed to provide more extensive resources for the education of exceptional children. Written by legislative aides and professional activists, it provides a current portrait of how legislation has changed the educational world of exceptional children, both handicapped and gifted.

2

Individual Differences and Special Education

Organizing Principles
To Classify or Not to Classify
Individual Differences
Interindividual Differences
Interindividual Differences in Academic Performance ♦ *Interindividual Differences in IQ Scores*
Intraindividual Differences
Individual Differences in Exceptional Children
Individual Differences in a Gifted Child ♦ *Individual Differences in a Retarded Child*
Prevalence of Exceptional Children
Defining Prevalence
Determining Prevalence
Estimating Prevalence by Category
Number Served vs. Estimated Prevalence
Special Education Adaptations
Content
Skills
Learning Environment
Teacher Consultant ♦ *Itinerant Personnel* ♦ *Resource Room* ♦ *Part-Time Special Class* ♦ *Self-Contained Special Class* ♦ *Special Day School* ♦ *Residential School* ♦ *Hospital and Homebound Services*
Regular Education and Special Education

One of the proudest claims of American society, and justifiably so, is its support of education for all citizens. Every child, regardless of family background, income, or personal characteristics, is entitled to a basic education and is clearly expected to continue that education well into adolescence.

Americans accept as necessary and desirable that the educational system retains almost all children of a given age group much longer than many other cultures do. Ours may be one of the few societies to call youngsters who leave school before completing the twelfth grade "dropouts." The desire to retain students in school until their late teens along with the extraordinarily diverse cultural background of families in the United States create very special problems for U.S. education.

The introduction of compulsory education laws in the latter part of the nineteenth century in the United States was a prime factor in directing the attention of schools to individual differences among children. They found that not all children learn at the same rate, move at the same rate, react emotionally in the same way, and see and hear equally well. Prior to compulsory education,

Every child, regardless of family background, income, or personal characteristics, is entitled to a basic education. (Photo: Alan Carey/The Image Works.)

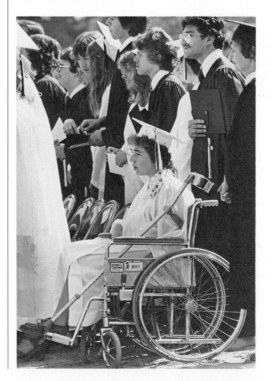

handicapped children dropped out of school because they could not compete with normal children and the schools were not organized for them. Today in the United States, as well as in Western European countries and the Soviet Union, provisions for the education of exceptional children are almost universal. Virtually all countries that have established universal and compulsory education have found that general programs for the ordinary child have to be modified for the exceptional child.

ORGANIZING PRINCIPLES

In any complex subject, as in the study of exceptional children and special education, it is easy to be overwhelmed by the wide range of apparently unrelated facts about each type of child and the many educational options that are available. We, the authors, wish to propose several organizing principles to help you integrate that information into a more coherent whole.

The first set of concepts involves the dimensions in which exceptional children differ from nonexceptional children—the *interindividual differences.* We will also discuss the uneven physical, social, and mental development—or "split growth"—within the exceptional child, a concept we shall speak of as *intraindividual differences.* This concept portrays the pattern of differential development or the product of the exceptionality as it appears within individual children.

The second set of organizing principles stems from the educational program itself. A remarkable set of modifications has been proposed for various groups of exceptional children. Those adaptations will be considered within a common framework of *curriculum and content changes, skills changes,* and *learning environment changes.* By discussing the modifications in each area of exceptionality, the patterns of educational adaptations for exceptional children may become more evident.

The major focus of this book, then, is on individual differences and the strategies for adapting educational programs to different clusters of children.

All children not only differ from each other (interindividual differences) but also have differences in abilities and disabilities within themselves (intraindividual differences). The degree of deviation and the constellation of differences vary with each child. Even within a group of so-called normal or average children, no two children have the same constellation of differences. But there are minor differences that are accepted in the rubric of "normal" because a high percentage of the population differs to that extent. Outside that larger group we find clusters of children who differ from the majority in one or more learning characteristics. Those children have similarities in characteristics such as are found in clusters of auditorily or visually impaired children, in other clusters of children with problems in interacting with their peers, or in those with significantly slower learning ability. The similarities *within* each cluster do not eliminate individual differences.

In any book on education the focus or organization of the text can be centered around one of three major dimensions of the education process: (1) the learner, (2) the teacher-learner interaction (that is, instruction), or (3) the learning environment.

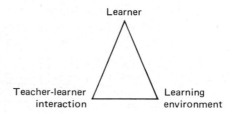

If we focus on the *learner*, then we will discuss and describe individual children or clusters of children. If we focus on the *teacher-learner interaction*, then we must organize the book around various teaching techniques such as the stimulation of language development or social skills. If we focus on the *environment*, then the book would be organized around various environmental modifications such as special classes, resource rooms, and itinerant teacher programs.

We have chosen the first of those three approaches—the exceptional child as a learner—as a way of organizing this book. It is important to give a portrait of the exceptional child as a human being. Starting from the vantage point of the individual child, it is easier to select the most suitable learning environment and the most suitable teacher-learner interaction strategies.

Despite the obvious fact that no one child or adult is the same as another, we generally group or cluster people together as a convenient form of reference. Mothers, quarterbacks, bankers, carpenters, and friends are all terms that allow us to consider how an individual relates to large numbers of other individuals with similar characteristics or functions. So it is with exceptional children. Those children are grouped together in various categories through classification to allow for the organization of special remedial programs. That we have chosen to study and discuss exceptional children according to subgroups or clusters does not indicate that we would keep them separated from other children in all areas of instruction or in daily living.

Starting from the vantage point of the exceptional child as a learner, it is easier to select the most suitable learning environment and teacher-learner interaction strategies. (Photo: Alan Carey/The Image Works.)

Educational authorities have long recognized that exceptional children do not always fit into neat, well-defined categories with uniform characteristics. They have recognized that mentally retarded children, even with a narrow range of IQ scores, are not homogeneous in characteristics and that not all deaf children learn at the same rate. One deaf child might learn speech reading, while another does not. One child may be classified as cerebral palsied but may also be mentally retarded, while another cerebral-palsied child may learn adequately in school or may even be intellectually gifted.

TO CLASSIFY OR NOT TO CLASSIFY

One of the current controversies in special education is whether to classify or categorize exceptional children into subgroups (that is, the mentally retarded, emotionally disturbed, and others). Some feel that: (1) classification leads to misclassification and mislabeling, particularly in low-income families; (2) categories do not lead to educationally relevant programs; and (3) categories and labels are detrimental to the self-concept of children so labeled.

Those who advocate the use of classification systems state that: (1) the purpose of classification is to bring the child with special

children with special
needs into contact with specially trained personnel who will provide a special educational program in a special learning environment; (2) categories have aided in focusing the attention of lawmakers on the problems of exceptional children, thereby aiding in obtaining legislation to support special programs; (3) categories allow us to pursue the causes of the handicapping conditions; and (4) categories, when used properly, aid in communication.

In recent years attempts have been made to abolish the labels and categories used with exceptional children. The major reason for the rejection of labels is that they have little educational relevance. Telling a teacher that a child is dyslexic, brain injured, or mentally retarded does not help the teacher organize an instructional program. A label is sometimes used in place of the more important assessment of the child's educational needs.

Another reason given for decreasing the emphasis on labels and categories is that many children are mislabeled and miscategorized. To call a hard-of-hearing child "deaf" is to mislabel, or to call a child blind or legally blind when some vision remains is to mislabel. Although such errors are often cited by critics of classification as a primary reason for abolishing labels, the attacks should instead be directed toward the *mis*labeling.

One troublesome issue intruding on decisions to use labels is their potential effect on the exceptional child. In order to receive special assistance under current procedures, the child must usually be given a classification and label. For example, if a state will give additional money to a local school district that agrees to establish a program for the mentally retarded, then it will clearly wish the local school district to demonstrate that the child in question is, in fact, mentally retarded. In the process the child acquires a label.

In 1972 the question of "to label or not to label" became acute. The then Secretary of Health, Education, and Welfare (Elliot Richardson) requested a task force to study that question and selected Nicholas Hobbs of Vanderbilt University to serve as its chairman. The task force studied and analyzed the benefits of classification and labeling as well as the harmful effects. Hobbs (1975) summarized the conclusions and recommendations of the task force by stating that labels have both detrimental and beneficial effects. His task force registered its concern for the negative effects of labeling but noted its useful elements as well. Special educators are currently seeking ways for minimizing labels while retaining the beneficial results.

Because of the inherent dangers in labeling and the possibilities for damaging children's personalities and self-concepts, it is vital that certain precautions be taken if labeling is to be used. Although the Hobbs report did not recommend the abolition of labels, it rec-

[handwritten: all benefits to those in control]

Pros and Cons of Labeling

Proponents of labeling note the following:

1. It tends to identify the child and thereby serves as a basis for further diagnosis and treatment.
2. It serves as a basis for further research into etiology, prevention, and treatment.
3. It serves as a basis for differentiated treatment, often opening up opportunities that children might not experience in other programs.
4. It allows local schools to establish eligibility for additional resources through state and federal legislation.
5. It serves as a rallying point for volunteer groups that espouse one group or another and are often influential in securing financial and other assistance.
6. It facilitates passage of legislation.
7. It serves as a rational structure for governmental administration.
8. It serves as a shorthand for communication, making it possible to focus on one relevant characteristic.

Opponents of labeling note the following:

1. Labeling may tranquilize diagnosticians into reaching closure by applying labels (such as *autism* or *minimal brain dysfunction*) rather than outlining differentiated programs of treatment.
2. It allows misdiagnosis of minority-group children who show superficial abnormalities resulting from lack of experience.
3. *[handwritten: ✳]* It delays needed social reform by focusing on the individual rather than on social and ecological conditions.
4. It allows practices and policies to deprecate individuality and diverse cultural backgrounds.
5. It serves as a means of social control by eliminating undesirables from the mainstream. It has been used as "an exclusionary process disguised as a remedial process" (Gallagher, 1976). ✓
6. Once labeled, a child often remains in an inappropriate program in spite of changing conditions.
7. It blinds people to the rapid and irregular growth patterns of childhood and may allow a child to remain in a program that he or she has outgrown.
8. It denies many children the normal experiences of childhood and wholesome community life.
9. It allows some children to be placed in inadequate, uncaring programs that "legitimize mistreatment" (Hobbs, 1975, p. 8), such as poorly staffed institutions.
10. In communication, it allows bias and stereotyping because of the incompleteness of the label.

[handwritten: IMPROVING LABELLING] ommended a reduction of the harmful effects of their use by "(1) improvements in the classification system, (2) some constraints on the use of psychological tests, (3) improvements in procedures for early identification of children of developmental risk, (4) some safeguards in the use of records, and (5) attention to due process of law in classifying and placing exceptional children" (pp. 232–233).

INDIVIDUAL DIFFERENCES

Interindividual Differences

One of the major reasons for the emergence of special education has been the great diversity of abilities and school performance among students of a similar age and grade level. Although regular elementary school teachers are expected to "individualize" their curriculum and lessons to meet the needs of each student, the problems inherent in developing a program of individualized instruction are rarely acknowledged. Planning for special education programs creates significant instructional difficulties because exceptional students may differ so greatly from average students. As pointed out by Bailey and Harbin (1980), "Children are not usually referred for evaluation on a teacher's whim. A referral indicates a significant educational problem that is unlikely to be remedied without some form of additional intervention with the teacher or child" (p. 595).

Most of the tests that have been developed in psychology and education (intelligence, reading, spelling, arithmetic, and so forth) measure interindividual differences. They are used primarily for classification of children and for placement purposes. Teachers use educational tests and ratings to group children in clusters with similar achievements. Likewise, children with low IQ scores will often be placed or grouped for instructional purposes in a group different from that of those who have very high IQ scores. The main purpose of tests that measure achievement level or global scores of intelligence is to help place the child in the group in which he or she will most likely get appropriate instruction. Such tests do not tell the teacher what specific program each child needs.

Interindividual Differences in Academic Performance

An illustration of the range of academic performance is given in Figure 2.1. The graph results represent the performance of all sixth-grade students in the state of North Carolina on the California Achievement Test. All students in North Carolina are required to take the same achievement test at grades 3, 6, and 9 as a means of charting overall student performance in the state. Since the North Carolina mean or average performance matches rather closely the national norms for the test, the findings are likely to appear in student populations in most states.

About 90,000 North Carolina students took the California Achievement Test in the sixth grade. Figure 2.1 gives grade equivalent scores[1] obtained by the students for both reading and mathematics.

---

[1]A grade equivalent score means that the student has obtained a raw score equal to the average performance of that grade. Although such scores have some serious statistical problems, they communicate useful information to teachers and are used descriptively here.

Figure 2.1 shows that in reading, approximately 29 percent of the students scored within one grade level, plus or minus, to their grade status at the time of the examination. Another 16 percent scored between one and two grade levels below norm, and a similar percentage scored between one and two grade levels above norm. Taken as a whole, then, 61 percent of the sixth-grade students scored between −2 and +2 grade levels of their assigned grades in reading. However, this also means that, in reading, 39 percent of the students were performing more than two grades above or below their grade level.

Actually, 5 percent of the sixth-grade students in North Carolina were progressing so slowly in reading skills that they scored more than three grades below grade norm, indicating a rather serious need for special educational attention. Another 10 percent of the sixth graders scored between two and three grades below norm, indicating a need for the teacher to significantly modify the programs, lessons, and assignments intended for youngsters performing at the sixth-grade level.

It is also interesting to note that 8 percent of the sixth-grade students were performing between two and three grades above their grade level and over 16 percent scored more than three grades

**FIGURE 2.1
California Achievement
Test Results for
North Carolina
Sixth-Grade Students**

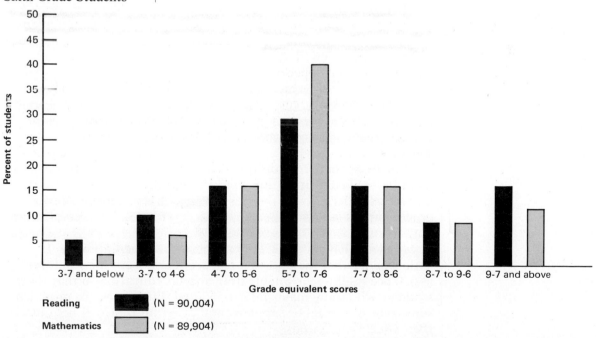

Reading	⬛	(N = 90,004)
Mathematics	⬜	(N = 89,904)

Source: Data reported in *Annual testing program.* Raleigh, N.C.: Department of Public Instruction, Division of Research, 1981.

above their expected level. Moreover, 3 percent of the students performed so well on the California Achievement Test that they ran off the scale at the twelfth-grade level. Thus, at the same time that 15 percent of the students were operating more than two grade levels below norm, one in every four students was performing more than two grades above norm. Surely this creates another type of problem for the teacher who must devise a more sophisticated and complex set of assignments to challenge the above-average student.

A similar result can be found for mathematics in Figure 2.1, except that students tended to group more around the middle scores with fewer students scoring at low and high extremes. About 40 percent of the North Carolina sixth-grade students scored between −1 and +1 grade levels in mathematics. As in reading, 16 percent of the students scored between one and two grade levels below norm and another 16 percent fell between one and two grade levels above norm. Altogether, 72 percent of the students obtained scores in the middle range between −2 and +2 grade levels.

This still left 28 percent of the students performing more than two grades below or above their expected grade level performance. In this case, 8 percent of the students performed more than two grades below norm, with 2 percent scoring more than three grades below norm. Students who scored more than two grades below their expected level of performance are strong candidates for some type of adaptive or remedial program in which basic mathematical skills would be taught or reviewed. At the same time, 20 percent, or one out of every five students, performed more than two grades above norm in mathematics, thus creating another problem for the teacher, since these students have already clearly mastered the basic skills expected of them for their grade level and have the potential for being bored or disruptive unless appropriate lessons can be found for them.

Without introducing additional variables, such as motivation for learning, social abilities, and so forth, that further complicate the individual differences in the class, the teacher clearly has three very different groups of students to deal with: students performing around expected grade level, those who are well below grade level, and students who are well beyond grade level performance. It is little wonder that the harassed teacher reaches out for whatever assistance might be available from special education so that those students who show major interindividual differences are provided some type of special or supplemental program that will help meet their educational needs.

Interindividual Differences in IQ Scores

Another measuring instrument that yields a wide range of individual differences is the intelligence test. Those tests usually include items that assess various aspects of cognitive development as follows:

Mental Operations	Sample Items
Memory	Who was the first president of the United States?
Association	Glove is to hand as shoe is to _____.
Reasoning	If Paul is taller than Sam and Sam is taller than Tom, then Tom is _____ than Paul.
Classification	Which of the following do not belong? chair sofa table red

These mental operations are crucial to academic performance. Any serious problem or delay in development can create significant school problems.

Intelligence tests assume a reasonably common experience base for most American children and are clearly inappropriate for children for whom English is a second language or for those who have had atypical early childhood experiences. The results of intelligence tests are usually reported in IQ scores that compare the child's performance with that of other children the same age. For the vast majority of American children tested, the results arrange themselves in a Gaussian curve or normal distribution, as shown in Figure 2.2. This means that when a large sample of the population is examined on almost any common characteristic, we find most members of the group clustering near the average with fewer and fewer members spread out to the extremes. Figure 2.2 shows the distribution of IQ scores and illustrates the normal dispersion for a test such as the Wechsler Intelligence Scale for Children.

FIGURE 2.2
The Theoretical Distribution of IQ Scores

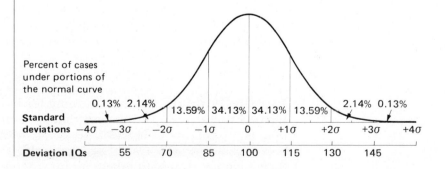

Percent of cases under portions of the normal curve

| | 0.13% | 2.14% | 13.59% | 34.13% | 34.13% | 13.59% | 2.14% | 0.13% |

Standard deviations −4σ −3σ −2σ −1σ 0 +1σ +2σ +3σ +4σ

Deviation IQs 55 70 85 100 115 130 145

Wechsler Intelligence Scale

From Figure 2.2 the following facts will be noted:

1. Sixty-eight percent (68.26 percent) of the children fall into the range of -1σ IQ points (minus one standard deviation) to $+1\sigma$ IQ points (plus one standard deviation). That means, in terms of the Wechsler scale IQ scores, that 68 percent of the children fall between an IQ score of 85 and an IQ score of 115. Children in that range are considered normal or average.
2. Nearly 14 percent of the children are in the -2σ to -1σ IQ scores point range, or between Wechsler IQ scores of 70 and 85. Likewise, 14 percent of the children are between $+1\sigma$ and $+2\sigma$, or between IQ scores of 115 and 130.
3. Approximately 2 percent are between -3σ and -2σ, or between IQ scores of 55 and 70, and approximately 2 percent are between $+2\sigma$ and $+3\sigma$, or between IQ scores of 130 and 145.

Those distributions represent a theoretical curve of the ranges of intelligence among children based on an intelligence test. When we measure reading, writing, spelling, height and weight, or even the length of the little finger, we find that the distribution follows approximately the theoretical normal curve shown on intelligence scores.

The intelligence test has come under severe attack in recent years. The attack stems from strong disagreement as to what the IQ score actually means. It has been used in the past

Uses

1. to indicate innate intellectual potential
2. to predict future academic performance
3. to indicate present rate of mental development of this child compared to others of the same age

Of those uses, the first has received the severest criticism. Extensive discussions in recent years leave little doubt that intelligence tests should never be used to buttress simplified discussions of whether one or another ethnic or racial group is innately superior to others. The tests are clearly not pure measures of genetic potential. However, the predictive value of the intelligence test and its ability to fix the current rate of mental development remain powerful; the test is still used professionally for those purposes.

Intraindividual Differences   Another meaning for individual differences, and the one that is dominant in special education, is the concept of *intraindividual differences*; namely, the differences in abilities within a particular child. This comparison, rather than a comparison with other children, determines intraindividual

A teacher must know an exceptional child's unique pattern of strengths and weaknesses as well as how those characteristics compare with other children. (Photo: © Meri Houtchens-Kitchens 1982.)

differences and provide information to help develop a program of instruction for an individual child.

In general the concept of *interindividual* differences is used for classification and for grouping children in special classes or ability groups. The concept of *intraindividual* differences, on the other hand, is used to organize an instructional program for a particular child in conformity with strengths and weaknesses, without regard to how he or she compares with other children.

Exceptional children differ from nonexceptional children in many characteristics. They may be intellectually superior, they may not see or hear as well, they may not have the mobility of the average child, they may not have the facility or skill in language or speech of the average child, or they may be deviant in interpersonal relationships. To a teacher it is just as important to know a child's unique pattern of assets and deficits as to know how those average out in comparison with other children.

The teacher needs to know how to organize a program for a particular child. What are his or her discrepancies in development? What can the child do and what is difficult for him or her to do? Does the child read at the first-grade level and do arithmetic at the third-grade level, showing a discrepancy in achievement? Such variance has led many to say that the exceptional child is a normal child who has exceptionalities or deviations only in some characteristics. In other words, they feel that the similarities in characteristics of the exceptional child and the average child far exceed the differences.

Individual Differences in Exceptional Children

To illustrate (1) how the exceptional child differs from the average and (2) how the exceptional child grows unevenly, the following discussion will present two profiles of intellectually exceptional children—a gifted child and a mentally retarded child.

Intellectually gifted and intellectually retarded (mentally retarded) children represent the upper and lower groups on the intelligence scale. Figure 2.2 shows that children with an IQ score below 70 (−2 standard deviations) constitute 2 percent of the population studied and represent the group generally labeled mentally retarded. The right-hand portion of the curve shows children with IQ scores above 130 (+2 standard deviations) and represents 2 percent of the population. Those children are generally labeled very superior or gifted.

The unique characteristics and educational programs of the intellectually accelerated and the mentally retarded will be discussed in later chapters. Here we will take a look at the development of those two kinds of exceptional children to see how they deviate from the norm (interindividual differences) and how they are affected by deviations within themselves (intraindividual differences).

Figure 2.3 shows the discrepancies in growth of an *intellectually gifted child* and of an *intellectually retarded child*. Both children are 10 years of age; both are in a fifth-grade class; both have normal hearing and vision. But the similarities stop there. They differ markedly from the average child in many characteristics and, in addition, have variations in growth within themselves. The history and status of those two children, typical of their types of exceptionality, can best be illustrated by a description of their characteristics and development and by the profile in Figure 2.3. The profiles are reported in age scores for descriptive purposes.

Individual Differences in a Gifted Child

John, the gifted child, was the older of two children. His father was employed as a teacher in the local high school. John's developmental history showed that he learned to talk at an earlier age

**FIGURE 2.3
Profiles of an
Intellectually Gifted
Child and a Mentally
Retarded Child**

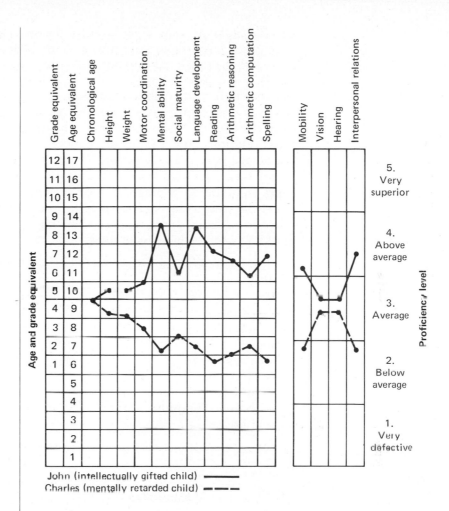

John (intellectually gifted child) ———
Charles (mentally retarded child) ― ― ―

than most children and that he walked at the age of 10 months. He became interested in books and at the age of 5 1/2 was reading some books and simple picture stories.

On entering school at the age of 6, he quickly learned to read, and by the end of the year he was a fluent reader in third-grade material. He was not allowed to advance in school beyond his age group, and by the age of 10 he was in the fifth grade. At that time a series of examinations was administered to him.

Test results are given in various forms. For example, John obtained an IQ score of 140 and a mental age equivalent of 14 years. His height age was 10-8, meaning that his height was similar to that of an average boy of 10 years, 8 months, even though John was only 10 years of age (10-0). On a reading test he obtained a grade equivalent score of 7-7, meaning that his reading level was similar to the average of children in the seventh month of the seventh grade, even though John was in the fifth grade. His reading score, when translated into an age score, was 12 years, 7 months (12-7).

Other individual characteristics cannot be stated in terms of age scores. For example, vision and hearing are reported in deviations from the average. John's vision and hearing were average. Interpersonal relations do not necessarily increase with age; hence, there are no age norms. In the profile, those characteristics are represented on a five-point scale: (1) very superior, (2) above average, (3) average, (4) below average, and (5) very defective.

On the various tests given to John, the scores were translated into ages or points on a scale so that they could be readily compared. His scores were as follows:

Chronological age	10-0
Height age	10-8
Weight age	10-8
Motor coordination age	10-11
Mental age	14-0
Social age	11-6
Language age	13-10
Reading age	12-7
Arithmetic reasoning age	12-2
Arithmetic computation age	11-4
Spelling age	12-4
Mobility	above average
Vision	average
Hearing	average
Interpersonal relations	above average

Figure 2.3 shows John's growth patterns at the life age of 10. Note that there are some points on the profile showing John to be like other children of his age. In vision and hearing he is like other children with normal sense organs, neither superior nor inferior. His height, weight, and motor coordination are slightly superior to those of most children, but not abnormally so. His mental age, however, deviates very markedly from the average of other 10-year-olds as it is four years beyond his age and grade placement. His social age, which is accelerated by a year and one-half, is not as advanced as his mental age. His achievements in school vary but in general are more accelerated than the physical factors, though not as far as is the mental-age level. Note that language, spelling, and reading are more advanced than arithmetic computation—a fairly common finding among intellectually advanced children.

On the scaled portion of the profile, John shows above average mobility, average hearing and vision, and above average interpersonal relations. He presents a developmental picture different from that of a child who is average in many respects. On that scale, an average child would show only minor deviations from a straight line.

Not only does John differ from the average child in many characteristics, but he also varies within himself in some characteristics. In this respect he is said to have *discrepancies in growth* or, more precisely, *intraindividual differences*. Because of those deviations, he will require certain adaptations of educational practices—to be described in later chapters.

Individual Differences in a Retarded Child

Charles, the intellectually retarded child whose developmental pattern is shown in Figure 2.3, yields a profile markedly different from that of John, the gifted child. The profiles are very nearly mirror counterparts of each other. Charles was the second child in a family of four children. His father worked as a machinist. During infancy Charles was a sickly child and at the age of 1 year had a very high fever, diagnosed as encephalitis and later assumed to have had neurologic effects fundamental to his slow mental development. Charles developed at a slower rate than the other children. He walked at 16 months but did not talk in sentences until he was 3 years of age. (On the average, children begin to talk in sentences at 2 years of age.) He was admitted to the first grade at the age of 6 and, in spite of his inability to learn, was promoted year by year until at the age of 10 he, like John, was in the fifth grade. The school system in which he was enrolled believed that children should be neither held back in school nor accelerated. The philosophy of the school held that the teacher should adapt instruction to wide individual differences among children.

In the fifth grade Charles was given a series of examinations. He obtained the following ratings:

Chronological age	10-0
Height age	9-2
Weight age	9-1
Motor coordination age	8-5
Mental age	7-0
Social age	8-0
Language age	7-4
Reading age	6-8
Arithmetic reasoning age	7-0

Arithmetic computation age	7-5
Spelling age	6-6
Mobility	below average
Vision	average
Hearing	average
Interpersonal relations	below average

When those age scores and ratings are plotted in Figure 2.3, we find that Charles, with an IQ score of 70, presents a reversal of the picture shown by John. Although both boys are 10 years old and have normal hearing and vision, their growth patterns in other characteristics are very different.

As with most intellectually retarded children, Charles's profile indicates that he can be considered normal or near normal in height, weight, mobility, motor coordination, and in vision and hearing. But he is exceptional in other areas of development. He differs from the average child in social, mental, and educational characteristics. His mental age is 7-0, and in the academic subjects of reading, spelling, and arithmetic, he tests at educational ages of 6-8, 6-6, 7-0, and 7-5; that is, after four years in school his educational accomplishments are at the first- and beginning second-grade level. His deviation from the majority of children in the fifth grade in mental, social, and academic abilities, in spite of his similarity to the other children in physical characteristics, again requires a special adaptation of school practices.

PREVALENCE OF EXCEPTIONAL CHILDREN

Defining Prevalence One of the fundamental questions in the field of special education, and one of the most difficult to answer, is: How many children are exceptional? Such a question is stimulated by more than intellectual curiosity. The answer will determine how many special teachers and other resources are needed to meet the special educational needs of those youngsters. Two different indices are traditionally used by epidemiologists or specialists interested in population statistics of varying conditions. One is the incidence rate and the second the prevalence rate. *Incidence* refers to the number of *new* cases occurring in a population during a specific interval of time. The incidence rate will answer the question, "How many youngsters were born with cerebral palsy in the United States in 1980?" *Prevalence* refers to the number of children in a given category present in a population group during a specified interval of time (for example, the number of learning disabled children who are of school age this year). Prevalence rate is determined by finding the number of youngsters with a certain condi-

tion and dividing that figure by the total population for that same age range. Only prevalence figures are reported in this text because they are most relevant to educational planning.

Determining Prevalence   At first thought, determining prevalence might seem to be relatively easy. But it is not, and it is worth noting why it is not. If you were given the task of finding the number of mentally retarded, learning disabled, gifted, or emotionally disturbed children in this country, how would you go about it? Perhaps you could put an item on the United States Census asking people to check a box if they have children with those exceptional conditions. But this procedure could have many errors. First of all, some parents might not wish to say they have an exceptional child, and others might not know they have an exceptional child.

Perhaps teachers could be asked to identify all exceptional children within their current experience. Here again, you would face problems. A teacher might not know that a child is exceptional if the case is mild and not easily observable, or a teacher might not wish to report mild handicaps.

Another possible approach would entail contacting existing special education programs and counting the number of exceptional children enrolled in those programs. That tally would provide the number of children currently being served but would not account for those exceptional children not receiving service, those who have not even been correctly identified, or those children who may not even be in school.

As you can see, a problem that may have at first seemed easy to solve is actually quite difficult to answer. Instead of precise figures, prevalence rates represent rough estimates based on small samples of children identified at a local or a regional level that are then projected to a national level. Determining the prevalence of exceptional children is further complicated by disagreement among professionals on issues of identification, such as the dividing point between an emotionally disturbed child and one having temporary adjustment problems or the extent to which a child must be developmentally delayed in order to be classified as mentally retarded. Determining whether a child is exceptional or going through a phase is not always a clear-cut process, since the dividing line between the two is sometimes imperceptible, just as yellow fades into orange which fades into red in a gradual flow of color in the rainbow. The dividing points between yellow and orange and orange and red are always hard to draw and somewhat arbitrary. So it is with the schools and their identifying procedures for exceptional children.

Identification Problems

All the preceding factors tend to make us cautious about the actual number of exceptional children in the various classifications that exist in the United States. So we make general estimates for communication purposes without trying to defend them at this point. Each chapter in this text will discuss the issue of prevalence as exceptionalities are reviewed.

Estimating Prevalence by Category Table 2.1 shows the projected number of children in each of the major categories of exceptionality based on a population base of 46.9 million children between the ages of 5 and 17 in the United States in 1978. The category of gifted and talented has a conservative estimated prevalence of 2 to 3 percent that would yield, in that age range, anywhere from 938,000 to 1,407,000 children. Each of the other exceptional categories is listed similarly in Table 2.1. One can note that categories such as mental retardation, learning disabilities, and emotional disturbances make up a very substantial number of youngsters, whereas visual handicaps, orthopedic handicaps, and hearing handicaps represent a much smaller percentage.

Allocation of funds for special education programs is based on prevalence estimates of children in each category. According to the lowest and the highest estimates in Table 2.1, between approximately 3.8 million and 7.5 million children are exceptional; they represent between 8.2 percent and 16.2 percent of children in the

TABLE 2.1
Estimated Prevalence of Exceptional Children by Category[1]

Category	Estimated Prevalence (by Percent)	Estimated Number of Exceptional Children
Giftedness	2.0–3.0%	938,000–1,407,000
Mental retardation	1.0–3.0	469,000–1,407,000
Learning disabilities	1.0–3.0	469,000–1,407,000
Emotional disturbances	1.0–2.0	469,000– 938,000
Visual handicaps	0.1–0.2	46,900– 93,800
Hearing handicaps	0.3–0.5	140,700– 230,450
Speech handicaps	2.5–4.0	1,172,000–1,876,000
Orthopedic handicaps	0.3–0.5	140,700– 230,450
Total	8.2–16.2%	3,845,300–7,589,700

[1]A base of 46.9 million children in K–12 age range in United States.

Source: Statistics of public elementary and secondary day schools. Washington, D.C.: National Center for Education Statistics, Fall 1979.

Note: The school-age population has been decreasing in recent years. The number of exceptional children would be expected to decrease proportionately.

5–17 age range. Those figures indicate the importance of exceptional children in the total scheme of American education because at least one in every twelve children has an exceptionality and needs some special attention. The problem, as we shall see as we proceed through the text, is that this large number of children is really subdivided into many smaller categories, each with its own unique needs and special educational adaptations.

Number Served vs. Estimated Prevalence

How many exceptional children currently receive special services? If, by law, each exceptional child should receive an appropriate education, then, ideally, all children are being served.

Figure 2.4 shows a comparison between the number of exceptional children enrolled in public schools in 1978 and those enrolled in 1958. These years were chosen to contrast post–World-War-II program development with rather extensive programs that have recently become available. During that time, remarkable increases have occurred in the number of exceptional children served in some of the major categories.

Figure 2.4 reveals the extremely uneven distribution among the categories of exceptional children served. The visually handicapped, hearing handicapped, and orthopedically handicapped represent the lowest numbers of exceptional children served within the public schools; those figures have changed very little since 1958. Many sensory handicapped children are still educated in special schools for the blind and the deaf that may be administered by state Departments of Mental Health and are not included in the public school count.

In contrast to the steady-state figures in the handicapping conditions noted previously, there have been dramatic increases in public school enrollments of children with mild or moderate handicaps, particularly in the domains of speech problems, mental retardation, and emotional disturbances. Here the numbers of children receiving services in the public schools in 1978 have doubled or quadrupled since 1958. Those increases are indicative of the major social changes brought about by legislation and court actions at both the state and federal level (see Chapter 1).

Perhaps the most striking increase in enrollments has been in the category of learning disabilities, which did not even exist when the data were collected in the 1950s and has vaulted into the most prevalent category in public school enrollment. Where were these children in 1958? One would have to assume either they were not

FIGURE 2.4
Public School
Enrollments of
Exceptional Children
(1958 and 1978)

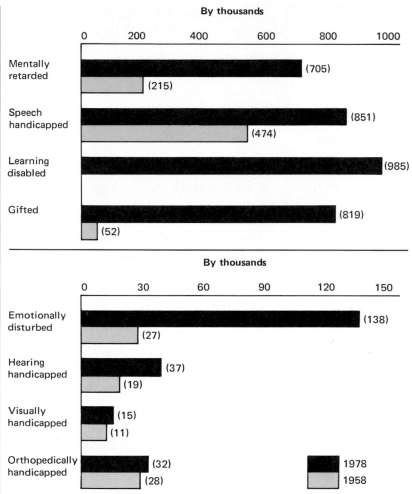

Source: Data for 1958 from R. Mackie and P. Robbins, Exceptional children in local public schools, *School Life*, 1960, *43*, 15.
Data for 1978 from *The condition of education.* Washington, D.C.: U.S. Department of Education, National Center for Education Statistics, 1981.

served or they were served under the categories of mental retardation or other handicapping conditions, since children with learning disabilities had not been differentiated from the categories of exceptional children that existed two decades ago.

Another dramatic increase is apparent in enrollments of gifted children. Educational programs for the gifted have grown substantially as a result of increases in state funds that provide stimulation for local programming.

Although the 1978 figures clearly represent a major movement within the public schools to provide services for exceptional children, the figures still fall short of the estimated prevalence of exceptional children in the society and suggest that many children who presumably need services are not currently receiving them.

SPECIAL EDUCATION ADAPTATIONS

The nature of special education is to provide special services not available in the regular education program for exceptional children. Special education differs from the regular program in that it tries to take into account those interindividual and intraindividual differences described earlier in this chapter. Regular education teachers, who are responsible for providing general instruction for all children, cannot be expected to respond fully to the special needs of exceptional children. It is important to note that special education does not exist because regular education has failed. The basic premise of special education is that the individual differences of some children are too great for the regular education teacher to deal with unassisted. Special education is built on the assumption that the majority of the students are provided with an appropriate educational program in the regular school setting.

Three major types of modifications can be made in the standard educational environment to adapt instruction to interindividual and intraindividual differences found in exceptional children. Changes can be made in the actual content of the lessons, the specific knowledge that is taught. The types of skills that a teacher wants a student to acquire can be adapted or increased according to the needs of the exceptional child. The learning environment can be modified to create an appropriate setting for special education to take place. The areas in which modifications can be made will be described generally in the following sections and discussed at length in subsequent chapters as they apply to each category of exceptionality.

Content   The instructional needs of some exceptional children may require modifications in the content of the curriculum originally intended for average students. Such adaptations apply most often to those children who deviate in intellectual development— the intellectually gifted and the mentally retarded.

Content for the gifted may be accelerated by providing more advanced lessons or different kinds of learning experiences not generally available to the average student. Courses in biogenetics, computer design, or the study of artificial intelligence are examples of special content developed for students who may have mastered the regular requirements with ease. For mentally retarded students, content may be modified to teach lessons that relate to their immediate experiences about things close to their homes, families, and neighborhoods. Instead of studying the civilizations of the past or far-distant lands in Asia or South America, mentally retarded students are likely to learn about their own towns and cities. In this way, not only is the pace of lessons changed to fit the needs of the children, but the actual content may be modified to make the lessons more appropriate. Mentally retarded students can learn about specific job placement opportunities as part of their vocational training in secondary school, while gifted students can study material that will help them adapt to higher education.

Skills   Most educational goals and objectives focus on the mastery of certain well-recognized skills—for example, reading and arithmetic. The first three years of school for the average student are generally spent trying to master basic skills. Those academic skills are often presented in ways that encourage practice of other skills—punctuality, attentiveness, persistence, and so forth—that can lead to better social adaptation. In the case of exceptional children, some special kinds of skills are taught that the average student is likely to master without special instruction. A blind person's ability to find his or her way from one place to another is a major skill that the average student does not need to focus on. Special communications systems, such as the mastery of braille for the visually handicapped or sign language for the deaf, represent very specific skills that some exceptional children need for adequate communication of ideas. Practically all types of exceptional children are provided with some kind of special skills training.

Learning   Special or different types of learning environ
Environment   ments may be necessary to make instruction more conducive to helping the exceptional child master content and skills. Unlike modifications in content and skills, which in most instances the teacher can adapt without affecting anyone outside the immediate classroom, changes in the learning environment cause reverberations throughout the entire educational system. Perhaps more attention is paid to environmental modifications than to the other two because changes in the learning setting involve both special educators and regular educators. When youngsters are removed from the classroom to a resource room for an hour a day, space must be allotted in the school for special instruction to take place. The regular teacher has to modify

his or her instruction to accommodate those students who will be gone for part of the day. Moreover, a whole battery of special services and special personnel have to be brought into the system to identify eligible children and to carry out the special services. The variations or modifications of the learning environment are very extensive.

Figure 2.5 presents graphically some of the most common learning environments that are worthy of careful study. The width of the section for each learning environment indicates symbolically the number of exceptional children likely to be found in a particular setting. Starting at the bottom of Figure 2.5, the expected number of exceptional children served in each learning environment increases as the settings move closer to the regular classroom at the top of the diagram. The philosophy of *least restrictive environment* advocates providing special instruction for a child in a setting that is as close to normal as possible and that enables a child to master

FIGURE 2.5
Special Learning Environments for Exceptional Children

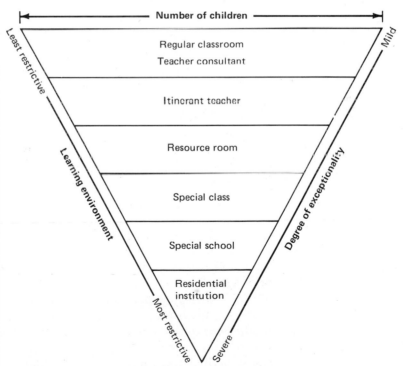

Note: Hospital and homebound services provided for handicapped children who may be confined for long periods of time fall within the realm of the residential institution on the scale of special education learning environments.
Source: Adapted from Special education as developmental capital by E. Deno, *Exceptional Children*, 1970, 37, 229–237. Copyright 1970 by The Council for Exceptional Children. Reprinted with permission.

content and skills. That is, children who can be served effectively in the resource room do not need to be assigned to a special class; children who can prosper in an itinerant teacher arrangement do not need to be in the resource room, and so on. The goal of special education is to move exceptional children in the direction of the least restrictive environment, as shown in Figure 2.5.

Of course, the ultimate *least restrictive environment* is for exceptional children to be in the regular program without specialized help and assistance—at which time they would not be classified as exceptional. The variety of special settings are described briefly below, so that you may begin to understand the options available in the educational system.

Teacher Consultant

To facilitate the education of exceptional children remaining in the regular grades under the *mainstream* philosophy, school systems may provide consultant services to regular teachers through the use of a specially trained, and often more experienced, teacher consultant. The consultants are available to regular teachers when they have questions about a child or when they need advice concerning special materials and methods of instruction.

Itinerant Personnel

Speech-language pathologists, social workers, school psychologists, remedial reading teachers, learning disability specialists, and other special educational personnel may deal with exceptional children on an itinerant basis. They may serve several schools and travel over a considerable area, visiting the exceptional children and their teachers at regular intervals or whenever necessary. Thus, the youngster spends the most time in the regular classroom and is taken out of the room only for short periods for tutorial or remedial help. A speech-language pathologist, for example, may work with the speech-impaired child several times a week for short periods, while an itinerant teacher for the visually impaired child might visit only once a week to bring special materials and to consult with the regular teacher in the use of the materials. In both cases the primary responsibility for the general education of the exceptional child rests with the regular classroom teacher.

The school social worker and psychologist may interview and confer with a child, the parents, and the teacher and may generally assist in the adjustment of the behaviorally disturbed child in the home and school. They may counsel a child consistently over an extended period of time or only occasionally.

The itinerant special teacher program is particularly valuable in rural areas where exceptional children are few and scattered over a wide area. Thus one teacher may serve several schools. That program is also well suited to certain types of exceptionality, such as defective speech or partial vision, that require limited services or materials. Often one of the itinerant teacher's primary roles will be that of a consultant or resource person for the classroom teacher. Itinerant teachers also provide homebound and hospital services.

Resource Room

Wiederholt, Hammill, and Brown (1978) define a *resource room* as "any instructional setting to which a child comes for specified periods of time, usually on a regularly scheduled basis" (p. 13). The usual setting for a resource room is a small classroom to which a special teacher is assigned and to which the children come during the day for brief periods of special work. The resource room teacher also consults with the regular teacher, and together they develop a program that is intended to eventually eliminate the need for resource room assistance.

Part-Time Special Class

The part-time special class accepts children who require more special instruction than the short period in the resource room. The programs for the children in those classes are the responsibility of the special class teacher. Children in such classes may spend a half-day in the special class and are assigned to regular grades or classes in areas in which they can compete. In junior and senior high schools this practice is used for exceptional children who are unable to respond to standard class requirements.

Self-Contained Special Class

It is sometimes advisable to assign the more severely handicapped children to self-contained special classes where the special teacher assumes the major responsibility for their programs. In the past this kind of class was the most common for all degrees of mental handicaps. It has been replaced, especially for the more mildly handicapped, with resource rooms, itinerant teachers, and part-time special classes, but the self-contained special class still plays a role in a total program for exceptional children.

Special Day School

Some school systems have organized special day schools for different kinds of exceptional children, especially those who are behaviorally disturbed, crippled, trainable mentally retarded, and multiply handicapped. In general there is a trend toward reducing the number of special schools, at least for certain types of handicapping conditions. Physically handicapped and mild mentally retarded children can make appreciable adjustment with normal children. It is also felt that contact with average children provides atypical children with a better preparation for future life. There are still a number of special day schools, particularly for children with severe behavior disorders, for the severely handicapped, and for the multiply handicapped.

Residential School

All the states of the Union have residential schools or institutions for various types of handicapped children, including the mentally retarded, delinquent, blind, deaf, crippled, and emotionally disturbed. Such institutions are sometimes privately administered, but they are usually administered by a state agency. Historically, residential schools are the oldest educational provision for exceptional children. They tended to be built away from population centers and too often became segregated, sheltered asylums with little community contact. In recent years those faults have been recognized and reforms have been attempted.

Disadvantages of a residential school include removal of the child from home and neighborhood, emphasis on the handicap, and the rigidity of institutional life. This is not to say that such a program no longer meets the needs of certain exceptional children, for it does indeed. In a sparsely populated area no other provision may be feasible, especially for a condition like deafness, which requires extensive equipment and special training on the part of the teacher. In some cases the condition itself demands professional attention for more than a few hours a day. Often with young deaf-blind children specialized treatment, stimulation, and education are carried out in the dormitory or cottage of the residential school during the children's waking hours. Situations within the child's home may require that, for the welfare of the family, he or she be placed in a residential school, at least for a time.

There is no reason to believe that any of the types of programs discussed will disappear in the immediate future; they will continue to supplement each other. A changing role may, however, be seen for many residential schools. As special education programs in public schools expand and enroll more exceptional children, the residential schools may emphasize programs for severely and multiply handicapped children.

Hospital and Homebound Services

Sometimes physically handicapped children are confined to hospitals or to their homes for long periods of time. To avoid educational retardation, itinerant teachers specially prepared to teach the homebound go to the hospital or home and tutor those children during their convalescence. Usually the local school system assigns the teachers of the homebound to help such children for an hour or more a day if the youngster's condition permits. The teacher's case load varies according to the type of disabilities and the amount of academic help needed. In larger children's hospitals such classes are taught by full-time teachers. In some cities two-way telephone

Some hospitals provide full-time teachers to instruct physically handicapped children who may require long periods of hospitalization. (Photo: © Christopher Morrow/ Stock, Boston.)

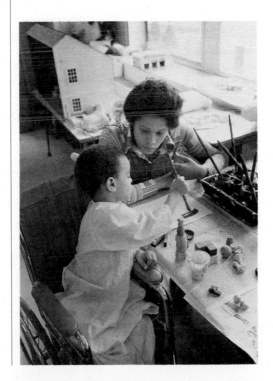

communication can be established between the child's home and the classroom so that the child can listen in on the class discussion and make a contribution.

REGULAR EDUCATION AND SPECIAL EDUCATION

A school that does not meet the needs of its students is likely to refer more children to special education programs. A number of research projects have been conducted recently to determine the characteristics of schools that effectively educate all their students. Are there factors that appear consistently in those schools identified as doing a superior job of educating their students?

The research studies have revealed similarities in the educational philosophy of effective schools, including the following standards: (1) all students are expected to master basic skills, (2) all students are expected to achieve and are encouraged and motivated by the high expectations of their teachers, and (3) teachers are expected to maintain an orderly learning environment with predictable discipline (Brookover et al., 1977). Interestingly enough, Rutter and his colleagues (1979) studied schools in London and reported similar findings, noting that the following variables are most related to a school's effectiveness: (1) an orderly environment, (2) high level of teacher involvement and caring for the students, and (3) high expectations for behavior and academic achievement.

The students in the schools identified as effective understand the reasons for rules, believe that the teachers care about them, and are allowed to take more responsibility for themselves. Whereas some children may be classified as exceptional and referred for special education partly because of the inadequacy of a regular education program, many borderline youngsters enrolled in effective schools may find an appropriate learning environment within the framework of the regular program.

SUMMARY OF MAJOR IDEAS

1. Adaptation of instruction to individual differences in children is made necessary, in part, by the establishment of universal and compulsory education.
2. This book is organized with a focus on the individual differences in exceptional children and the special educational adaptations that can be made to provide for the learning needs of children in each category of exceptionality.

3. Labeling of exceptional children is the subject of much debate among professionals in the field of special education. Legitimate cases can be made for and against the practice of classifying children. Attempts are being made to de-emphasize labels.

4. Measures of academic performance (achievement tests) and cognitive ability (intelligence tests) indicate a wide range of differences between children (interindividual differences). Planning instruction to effectively accommodate those differences places extreme pressure on teachers.

5. Careful analysis of the developmental profile of an exceptional child shows major differences in abilities within a particular child (intraindividual differences). In planning special educational programs, teachers need to take into account each child's pattern of intraindividual development.

6. A reasonable conservative estimate shows that exceptional children constitute between 8 and 16 percent of the general school-age population in the United States. The number of exceptional children between the ages of 5 and 17 ranges from 3.8 million to 7.5 million.

7. Enrollments of exceptional children in the public schools have increased dramatically during the last two decades due to important legislative and judicial initiatives. Increases are most striking in the areas of mild handicaps —mental retardation, communication problems, and learning disabilities.

8. In adapting instructions to the needs of exceptional children schools can modify three major educational domains: content, skills, and learning environment.

9. The content of lessons can be modified so that a child who differs markedly from the average student is required to master material that corresponds to his or her abilities.

10. The types of skills that a teacher wants a student to acquire can be adapted according to the needs of the exceptional child.

11. Modifications in the learning environment are important in blending the regular education program and the special education program. Alternative learning environments range from consultation between regular education teachers and special education personnel to placement in special residential schools. The purpose of modifying the learning setting is to provide special instruction for a child in the *least restrictive environment* that is as close to normal as possible.

12. For special education to be effective the regular education program must be effective as well. Research on effective schools reveals common elements of an orderly environment, high ex-

pectations for student achievement on the part of teachers, an understanding on the part of students as to what they are expected to do, and a feeling of optimism that they are capable of performing these goals.

UNRESOLVED ISSUES

1. The Use of Labels. In order to facilitate allocation of funds for special programs, governmental regulations require schools to identify those youngsters in need of help according to category of exceptionality. Labeling is thought by many educators to have detrimental effects on the exceptional child's adaptive behavior. At present, professionals in the field of special education have not agreed on a way in which to provide special services without the intermediate step of classifying children as exceptional.

2. Geography and Special Education Services. One of the most consistently frustrating problems for both special educators and regular educators is providing services for exceptional children who live in rural areas. Most of the commonly used methods for delivering services are often inappropriate when exceptional children, who constitute approximately one out of every twelve students, are scattered over a wide geographic area. Although a variety of program options are available, they have not proved entirely satisfactory in meeting the needs of rural children; some new creative ideas are needed.

REFERENCES OF SPECIAL INTEREST

Abroms, K., & Bennett, J. (Eds.). *Issues in genetics and exceptional children.* New Directions in Special Education (Vol. 7). San Francisco: Jossey-Bass, 1981.

A series of chapters is presented providing updated information on genetic influences for a number of exceptionalities. Mental retardation, giftedness, visual impairment, and affective disorders are among the topic areas reviewed. A useful chapter introduction is presented as a primer in genetics to orient those who have a meager background in this field.

Hobbs, N. (Ed.). *Issues in the classification of children* (Vols. 1 & 2). San Francisco: Jossey-Bass, 1975.

These two volumes include thirty-one chapters, each exploring a different aspect of the classification of children and written by outstanding experts in their own fields. The topics range from the classification of conditions such as behavior disorders and mental retardation to the special effects of classification on minority group children, the effects on parents of labeling children, and the issue of the legal rights of those children who have been classified. This work is a major baseline from which to start on the topic of classification.

McLoughlin, J., & Lewis, R. *Assessing special students: Strategies and procedures.* Columbus, Ohio: Charles E. Merrill, 1981.

This book successfully combines clinical observations and testing procedures in developing a model of assessment for special students. The authors cover the nature of assessment and its technical aspects. Much of the book focuses on the application of assessment to school problems and how tests are used in team decision making.

3

Gifted and Talented Children

In all societies and times, observers have noted that some children seem to learn faster, remember more, and solve problems more efficiently than others. In current terminology, those children are called *gifted and talented*.

Society has a special interest in gifted and talented children both as individuals and as potential contributors to the society's well-being. As individuals they have the same right to opportunities for full development as do all children. In addition, many of the leaders, scientists, and poets of the next generation are likely to come from the current group of gifted and talented children, and few societies can long afford to ignore or scorn that potential.

Children of all the other groups described under the label *exceptional* have deficits in one or more areas of development. The gifted are the only group of exceptional children with a surplus of abilities or talent. As this chapter will show, that very surplus of abilities creates some distinctive educational problems for the typical school system.

WHO ARE THE GIFTED AND TALENTED?

Each culture defines giftedness in its own image and fixes the nature of the gifted person for that culture. From that definition we learn something about the values and lifestyles of the culture. The person called *gifted* in a primitive society may be very different from one so designated in an advanced technological society. Ancient Greece honored the orator, whereas Rome valued the engineer and the soldier.

The earliest definition of the gifted in the United States was tied to an IQ score, and particularly to the Stanford-Binet Intelligence Test that was developed by Lewis Terman shortly after World War I. Those children who scored above a certain point—an IQ score of 130 or 140 or whatever was agreed on—were declared gifted.

During the past two decades, attempts have been made to broaden the concept of giftedness by including other dimensions of ability. One of the more popular definitions currently accepted was proposed by former U.S. Commissioner of Education Sidney Marland (1972). The following definition has been used in federal legislation, and although subsequent efforts have modified it, this definition covers the territory well.

Gifted and talented children are those identified by professionally qualified persons who, by virtue of outstanding abilities, are capable of high performance. These are children who require differentiated educational programs and services beyond those normally provided by the regular program in order to realize their contribution to self and society.

Children capable of high performance include those with demonstrated achievement and/or potential ability in any of the following areas:

1. General intellectual ability
2. Specific academic aptitude
3. Creative or productive thinking
4. Leadership ability
5. Visual and performing arts (p. 10)

The purpose of such a definition was to recognize youngsters who possessed a diversity of talents, rather than to restrict the definition to the more linguistically facile child, as had been done in the past. Despite this effort to go beyond the strictly cognitive domain, a strong emphasis is still placed on intelligence tests for identifying gifted children because (1) they are well-developed and proven instruments and (2) they tap those intellectual operations so crucial to high performance in school-related activities.

Table 3.1 shows some of the intellectual operations expected of school children. Gifted students perform much better than their agemates in all those dimensions. Some operations seem more dependent on experience than others, and IQ scores clearly depend

TABLE 3.1
Intellectual Products and Operations (Adapted from Guilford, 1967)

Intellectual Operations		Questions or Test Items	Presumed Cultural Influence
Memory	Short-term	Repeat what I say: 3–7–2–9–6	Only requires paying attention to task.
	Long-term	What is a giraffe?	Must have had prior experience with the concept as well as remembering.
Relations		Foot is to shoe as hand is to ____.	Relies partly on experience and partly on basic thinking processes.
Classification		Name the one that doesn't belong: Horse Whale Cow Flounder	Concepts are most often taught. Ability to understand clusters or groupings appears fundamental.
Reasoning	Convergent	If Sam is taller than Pete and Sam is shorter than Joe, then Pete is _____ than Joe.	Little influence of culture. Basically an internal intellectual process.
	Divergent	What would happen if oil was suddenly not available?	Number and kinds of answers given depend on past experience—also self-confidence and freedom from inhibitions.
Evaluation		Who is the stronger president, Washington or Lincoln?	The criterion of "stronger" is learned but the ability to match or compare seems to be a basic thinking process.

not only on native ability but also on the opportunity to experience those ideas. You cannot *remember* what a giraffe is if you have never seen or heard of one! The IQ tests have generally been criticized for focusing too much on memory, association, and convergent reasoning and too little on divergent reasoning and evaluation. New tests, to be described later in this chapter, try to compensate for that imbalance.

We have become increasingly aware of the role of the environment in the definition of giftedness. Feldman (1979) pointed out that even Einstein's remarkable achievements were as much a function of the state of the field of physics at a particular point in history as they were a function of Einstein's own talent. Feldman concluded, "Thus, early prodigious achievement should be seen as the occurrence in time and space, by a remarkably preorganized human being, born during perhaps the optimal period and educated in the precise manner most likely to enable the individual to interact optimally with a highly evolved field of knowledge" (p. 342). The coincidence or the conjunction of person and environ-

Gifted and talented children need a fertile environment in which to display their abilities. (Photo: © Herb Snitzer Photography.)

ment yields the product of gifted performance. Stephen Vincent Benét wrote a short story on what would have happened to Napoleon if he had been born twenty years later: His enormous military talents, made useless by an era of peace, caused him to become a disgruntled retired colonel living out his life in an old-soldiers home. The implications for the education of the gifted seem clear. We not only need to stimulate the individual talents of children but also to create a fertile environment in which they can display their talents.

Although not everyone agrees on the usefulness of distinguishing between *gifted* and *talented*, the term *talented* generally refers to a specific dimension of skill (that is, musical or artistic talent) that may not be matched by a child's more general abilities. In most children there is a substantially positive relationship between intellectual giftedness and talented performance. Occasionally a child may have an unusual talent in one area and limited abilities in other areas.

The direction in which gifts and talents emerge in a gifted individual depends on many factors, such as experience, motivation, interest, emotional stability, hero worship, parental urgings, and even chance. Many intellectually gifted individuals might also have been successful in another area had their interests and training focused on that direction.

Even though superior intelligence is only one factor in determining success, achievement, or contribution to society, it still remains a basic ingredient of giftedness. We do have gifted children who are not outstanding in creativity; we do have gifted children who are using their talents in socially unacceptable ways. But the common denominator is intellectual superiority.

talented implies existence of intraindividual differences.

CHARACTERISTICS OF GIFTED CHILDREN

Developmental Profiles

Although we often discuss gifted children as a group when addressing topics such as characteristics, the teacher usually encounters such children one at a time. Figure 3.1 shows the developmental portraits of two gifted children described by Gallagher (1975). The profiles illustrate the characteristics that puzzle and frustrate teachers as well as the intraindividual differences within each child, with development proceeding at different rates. Following is the description that accompanies the profiles:

Cranshaw is a big, athletic, happy-go-lucky youngster who impresses the casual observer as the "all-American boy" type of youngster. He seems to be a natural leader and to be enthusiastic over a wide range of interests. These

**FIGURE 3.1
Profiles of Two
Gifted Students**

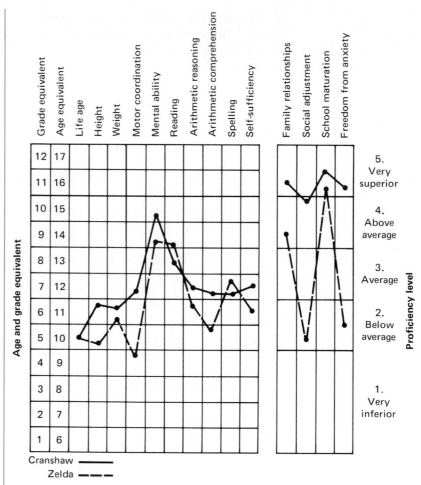

Cranshaw ⎯⎯⎯
Zelda ⎯ ⎯ ⎯

Source: J. Gallagher, *Teaching the gifted child* (2nd ed.). Boston: Allyn and Bacon, 1975, p. 22. Copyright © 1975 by Allyn and Bacon, Inc. Used with permission.

interests have not yet solidified. One week he can be fascinated with astronomy, the next week with football formations, and the following week with the study of Africa.

His past history in school has suggested that teachers have two very distinct reactions to Cranshaw. One is that he is a joy to have in the classroom. He is a cooperative and responsible boy who can not only perform his own tasks well but be a good influence in helping the other youngsters to perform effectively. On the other hand, Cranshaw's mere presence in the class also stimulates in teachers some hints of personal inferiority and frustration, since he always seems to be exceeding the bounds of the teachers' knowledge and abilities. The teachers secretly wonder how much they really are teaching Cranshaw and how much he is learning on his own.

Cranshaw's family is a well-knit, reasonably happy one. His father is a businessman, his mother has had some college education, and the family is reasonably active in the community. Their attitude towards Cranshaw is that he is a fine boy and they hope that he does well. They anticipate his going on to higher education but, in effect, say that it is pretty much up to him what he is going to do when the time comes. They do not seem to be future-oriented and are perfectly happy to have him as the enthusiastic and well-adjusted youngster that he appears to be today.

Zelda shares similar high scores on intelligence tests to those manifested by Cranshaw. Zelda is a rather unattractive girl who is chubby, and wears rather thick glasses that give her a "bookish" appearance. Her clothes, while reasonably neat and clean, are not stylish and give the impression that neither her mother nor Zelda have given a great deal of thought to how they look on this particular child. Socially, she has one or two reasonably close girl friends but is not a member of the wider social circle in the classroom and, indeed, seems to reject it.

Teachers respond to Zelda with two generally different feelings. They are pleased with the enthusiasm with which Zelda attacks her school work and the good grades that she gets. At the same time, they are vaguely annoyed or irritated with Zelda's undisguised feeling of superiority toward youngsters who are not as bright as she is; they tend to repel Zelda when she tries to act like an assistant teacher or to gain favors that are more reserved to the teacher.

Zelda and her family seem to get along very well with each other. The main source of conflict is that the family, itself, has values that Zelda has accepted wholeheartedly but that are getting her into difficulty with classmates. Her father is a college professor and her mother has an advanced degree in English literature. They seem to value achievement and intellectual performance almost to the exclusion of all other things.

Their social evenings are made up of intellectual discussions of politics, religion, or the current burning issue on the campus. These discussions are definitely adult-oriented and Zelda is intelligent enough to be able to enter into such conversations occasionally. This type of behavior is rewarded much more by the parents than is the behavior that would seem more appropriate to her age level.

Figure [3.1] shows the range of abilities in different developmental areas for Zelda and Cranshaw. If all the points on the scale were at the same height as their mental ability, there would be little trouble in placing them educationally. Cranshaw shows a wide variation from the physical development of an average 11-year-old to the mental abilities of an average 15-year-old. This means that any standard placement at any [grade] level will displace Cranshaw physically, academically, or socially.

Zelda has an intellectual and academic profile similar to Cranshaw's. Both are doing as well as might be expected on the basis of these measurements. Zelda is slightly inferior to Cranshaw in arithmetic. However, it is in the personal-social area where real differences are apparent. While Cranshaw's adjustment here has the same superior rating as his academic record, Zelda has social difficulties. She is not accepted by her peers and worries about it. . . . Her inability to understand how her own behavior causes antagonism is also apparent—*and quite important*. (Gallagher, 1975, pp. 20–21)

Some of the basic challenges to teachers of students such as Cranshaw and Zelda include interesting Cranshaw in reading-related subjects when his mental ability is four years ahead of his age level and encouraging Zelda to try areas of less interest to her, such as mathematics. Her attitudes and unhappiness have to be a matter of concern as well.

The Terman Longitudinal Study

Gifted children have been the object of interest of numerous investigators. Many studies on the characteristics of gifted children, however, are short-term ones and tend to confirm the results of one major longitudinal study covering a period of a half century by Lewis M. Terman. Since Terman's research is considered the magnum opus of all such studies of the characteristics of the intellectually and academically gifted, it is reviewed here.

Following his revision and publication of the Binet-Simon tests of intelligence in 1916, Lewis M. Terman, a distinguished professor of psychology at Stanford University, became interested in gifted children. He devoted much of the rest of his life to the study of 1,528 gifted children whom he had identified in 1920. He followed the group for thirty-five years, until his death in 1956. During that period he was instrumental in designing and supervising the research that led to a set of five volumes entitled *Genetic Studies of Genius* (1925–1959).

Terman's search for gifted children was conducted in the public schools of California. Teacher nominations and group intelligence tests were used as screening procedures. (That procedure is now considered to limit the findings since it tends to eliminate gifted children who underachieve or whose behavior teachers may find obnoxious.) The final selection of most subjects was based on an IQ score of 140 or above on the 1916 Stanford-Binet Intelligence Scale. The average IQ score for more than one thousand children selected by the Binet test was 151.

Those gifted children came from homes that were notably in the higher socioeconomic levels. Their parents averaged four to five years more schooling than was typical for the United States, and the median family income was more than twice the California average. There was a low incidence of broken homes. It may be that some of the differences that Terman found between the gifted children and the comparison groups were due to their superior homes as much as to their measured high intelligence.

Physical Characteristics

In physique and general health the high-IQ children surpassed the standards for American children. Height and strength were superior. Medical examinations revealed that the incidence of sensory defects, dental caries, poor posture, malnutrition, and so forth was below that usually reported in medical surveys of school populations in the United States. At the average age of 44 their mortality rate was four-fifths that of the general population.

Intellectual and Educational Characteristics

In 1940 Terman's subjects were retested on a difficult adult intelligence test. At that time no subject had regressed to the intelligence level of the average adult, and no more than 10 percent were below the 85th percentile rank. Terman concluded that the bright child remains bright.

Nearly one-half of the Terman sample had learned to read before the age of 6. Terman and Oden (1947) stated, "It is a conservative estimate that more than half . . . had already mastered the school curriculum to a point two full grades beyond the one in which they were enrolled, and some of them as much as three or four grades beyond" (p. 28).

The rates of college attendance (90 percent for men and 86 percent for women) were eight times those of the general population in California. This superior group participated in extracurricular activities to a greater than average extent. Surprisingly, however, 8 percent of the men and 2 percent of the women "flunked out" of college (although half of those re-entered and graduated).

Interests and Preoccupations

These gifted children were interested in abstract subjects such as literature, debate, and ancient history; they were less interested in "practical" subjects such as penmanship and manual training. Gifted and comparison children were equally interested in games and sports.

The gifted appeared less sociable in their interests. They showed a stronger liking for playing with just *one* other person than did the controls.

Character Tests and Trait Ratings

A battery of seven character tests showed gifted children above average on every rating. They were less prone to make overstatements and to cheat. They scored above average on an emotional stability test. On all seven subtests combined, 86 percent of the gifted boys and 84 percent of the girls scored above the mean for the comparison groups.

Mental Health and General Adjustment

One of the areas investigated in the 1947 follow-up report was mental health and adjustment. At that time approximately 80 percent showed "satisfactory adjustment," about 15 percent had "some maladjustment," and 5 percent had "serious maladjustment." The rate was slightly lower than the national expectancy for serious maladjustment. The delinquency rate was far below that of the general population. Terman concluded that the superior emotional adjustment seen in childhood was maintained in adulthood.

Marriage, Divorce, Fertility

The marriage rate for the gifted group as adults was about the same as that for the general population (84 percent) while the divorce rate was somewhat less than that for the general population.

A total of 1,525 offspring of the gifted group have been tested. The mean IQ score is 132.7. About one-third scored above 140 and only 2 percent below 100.

Vocational and Occupational Status

The occupational status of the gifted men reported in 1955 showed about eight times as many men in the professions as was true for the general population. The incomes for the gifted group were considerably higher than the national average. The most successful gifted men were compared with the least successful gifted, and many striking differences were found. Terman and Oden (1951) state, "Everything considered, there is nothing in which the A [most successful] and C [least successful] groups present a greater contrast than in drive to achieve and in all-round social adjustment" (p. 37). Success for the gifted was associated with well-balanced temperament and freedom from excessive frustration.

Oden (1968) concluded: "All the evidence indicates with few exceptions the superior child becomes the superior adult. . . . Two-thirds of the men and almost as large a proportion of the women consider that they have lived up to their intellectual abilities fully or reasonably well" (pp. 50–51).

The Stanford *Genetic Studies of Genius,* under the direction of Lewis Terman, stands as a monumental investigation of one kind of exceptional child and thus far is unsurpassed by any other study in the field. It will remain as a monument to its brilliant author, who contributed so much to our knowledge of intelligence.

Special Groups   Although the general findings of Terman are still valid for most of the upper-middle-class suburban children with high IQ scores, there has been growing interest in various subgroups that differ in important ways from this positive portrait. They include the gifted underachiever, culturally different gifted, children with extraordinarily high intellect, and gifted women.

The Underachieving Gifted

One of the many myths surrounding the gifted has been referred to as the Cannonball Theory. The idea, simply put, is that a gifted child can no more be stopped from achieving his or her potential than a cannonball can be diverted from its path once it has been fired. Like most simplistic ideas regarding human beings, the notion turns out to be incorrect. Its popularity in the face of contrary evidence may be accounted for on the basis that if it were true, we would be relieved of any special responsibility for those children.

The fact is that a substantial proportion of gifted children, perhaps as many as 15 to 20 percent, never achieve the level of performance that their high scores on intelligence tests would seem to predict for them. The longitudinal study by Terman and Oden (1947) yielded information on those underachievers. In the study a group of men were identified who had not achieved to the level of their apparent ability. The men were compared with other men who had done well. In their own self-ratings and in ratings by their wives, four major characteristics separated the underachievers from the achievers. The underachievers had *more feelings of inferiority, less self-confidence, less perseverance,* and *less of a sense of their life goals.* Even more striking was an examination of teacher ratings made on those men twenty years earlier while they were in school. Even at that time, teachers were rating the underachieving men, then boys, as lacking in self-confidence, foresight, and desire to excel.

Later studies by Shaw and McCuen (1960) have confirmed that it was possible to identify underachieving boys as early as the third grade and underachieving girls by the sixth grade. So, underachievement is a condition that is fairly permanent and not significantly influenced by any temporary set of environmental circumstances. Those facts answer one of the major questions about underachievers: Does the problem exist mainly within the child or is it a product of a poor educational system? Although poor schooling can always be a contributing factor, there is little doubt that certain behavior patterns seem to predispose some gifted children to school underachievement.

One factor that predicts underachievement is substantial family conflict, often between father and son in the life of the underachieving boy. It is not certain whether it is part of the cause of the child's problems or merely a secondary result of the child's chronic poor performance, far below the standards of the father.

Perkins (1965) studied the actual classroom behavior of some underachievers and found that psychological withdrawal or lack of commitment was the most prominent feature of their behavior. The underachievers were observed more often than the achievers to be working in an academic area other than the one they were supposed to be attending to or to be engaged in nonacademic behavior. In short, the day-to-day classroom behavior of the underachiever more or less guaranteed a continuation of the problem condition. Gallagher (1975) summarized the situation in this fashion:

One way to look at the underachiever is that he is in the middle of a circle of barbed wire . . . and all of his environment has contributed to the building of that wire circle—his family, his friends, his school, and, most important, himself. Any movements that he attempts to get out of the barbed wire are going to be painful to him. Sometimes it is more comfortable to sit quietly in the middle of his trap and bemoan his fate than to risk getting scratched trying to get out. (p. 353)

There are two major ways out of that barbed wire. One is counseling, which will allow the underachiever to explore attitudes toward self and others with a sympathetic and skilled listener and then to reorganize those attitudes that cause continued difficulty for the underachiever in the school setting. An alternative strategy for educators is to provide some systematic modifications in the classroom environment that might cause the underachiever to modify his or her characteristic patterns. One such strategy would be to deliberately place the child with a warm, accepting, and flexible teacher who would provide a sympathetic source of identification (Raph, Goldberg, and Passow, 1966).

Remedial programs have yielded limited effects, which seem to confirm the hypothesis that chronic underachievement is a total lifestyle and one that can be modified only under the most persistent and intensive type of educational and personal attention.

Whitmore (1980) has reported a positive result for gifted underachievers emerging from an intensive special class experience in the primary grades in which the teacher focused on the building of self-concept and the fostering of motivation to take risks and to try to achieve. She believed it to be very important to begin in the early grades before the patterns of resistance in the underachiever became too ingrained.

The Culturally Different Gifted

Gifted and talented students who come from subcultures different from the standard American culture constitute another special area of interest. There are two important pieces of information available from past research. The first is that high-level intellectual ability can be found in every ethnic and racial group (Adler, 1963; Jenkins, 1948; Martinson, 1972; Terman and Oden, 1947). The second is that there are demonstrable differences in the percentages of children from various racial and ethnic groups who fall into the category of gifted (Adler, 1967; Barbe, 1955). Social scientists generally believe that certain cultural advantages accrue to the favored groups, advantages that allow the gifted among them to maximize their cognitive development and that favor the kinds of talent found important in the standard American culture.

The notion that certain value systems seem more inclined to maximize intellectual talents than others is given further support by the generally high proportion of gifted children from Jewish (Terman and Oden, 1947) and Oriental families (Coleman et al., 1966). Both cultures encourage the pursuit of intellectual activities and honor the role of "scholar" in the family and community.

Special programs for the culturally different gifted focus on two major problem areas: first, how to identify effectively the culturally different gifted youngsters and, second, how to design special programs that would seem particularly relevant.

Several different approaches have been used to identify culturally different gifted students. Each approach recognizes the limitations of many gifted students from cultural groups in which emphasis is not placed on those verbal concepts that seem so central to traditional assessment of giftedness and to the mastering of educational content.

Mercer and Lewis (1981) have proposed an identification technique known as the System of Multicultural Pluralistic Assessment (SOMPA), which uses traditional measures of intelligence but weighs the results according to the social and family characteristics of the child. Thus, a child with an IQ score of 111 can, when

Jewish and Oriental
- value the scholar

Problems: - how to identify
- how to design relevant
programs

Verbal concepts
de-emphasized

SOMPA
System of Multicultural Pluralistic Assessment

compared with children from similar sociocultural backgrounds, obtain an estimated learning potential score of 134, placing the child in the top 1 percent of children *in that sociocultural group.* According to Mercer and Lewis, the learning potential scores are indicators of ability that would have been demonstrated if the child had received equal opportunity.

Torrance (1979) has taken a different approach. In his view, each cultural group has major strengths to bring to the society, and the identification of these strengths can be made through instruments such as the Torrance Tests of Creative Thinking (which provide stronger evidence of minority group gifted performance than standard intelligence tests do) as well as through careful observation by teachers and others of characteristics valuable to leadership and creativity. Examples of some characteristics follow:

Ability to Express Feelings and Emotions
Observations of behavior in discussions, classroom meetings, role playing, sociodrama, creative dramatics, dance, creative movement, music, and rhythm.

Enjoyment of and Ability in Visual Arts
Experiences real joy in drawing, painting, and sculpture.
Communicates skillfully through drawings, paintings, sculptures, and other visual arts.

Enjoyment of and Skill in Group Problem Solving
Produces original and useful ideas in small groups.
Influences other students to engage in projects he or she initiates.

Originality and Inventiveness
Produces stories that have unusual and surprising plots and endings.
Comes up with inventions to solve problems. (Torrance, 1979, pp. 26–55)

According to Torrance, students who rate highly on those characteristics (and fourteen others he has linked to creativity) would qualify for special program attention.

Wolf (1981) uses a similar approach to identify urban minority students for advanced work in the visual and performing arts. The identification process consists of two stages. First, the top 15 or 20 percent of the student body is selected based on performance on standard tests (for example, Torrance Tests of Creative Thinking and Differential Aptitude Tests), then enrolled in a theater techniques program that emphasizes expressive and communication skills. The second stage takes place at the end of that program. The staff rates the students along a number of dimensions and those who rate highly can graduate to an independent study and seminar program of the Educational Center for the Arts, which provides training in music, dance, theater arts, and graphic arts.

The theater techniques program thus becomes an opportunity for a selected group of students to show special abilities. Following are the extreme ratings for some of the dimensions along which students are judged on a seven-point scale after the theater techniques program:

Communication

Makes no effort to communicate ideas, directions, and feelings to others.

Highly effective in communicating ideas, directions, and feelings to others (like a successful playwright).

Leader-Follower Flexibility

Is extensively inflexible in leader-follower roles, needing to dominate others or needing to be dominated by others or vacillating between the two extremes.

Is highly flexible in taking the lead in a course of interaction when it is appropriate and following the lead of others when that is appropriate (like a good actor).

Perception of Others' Behavior

Is unattending to the behavior of others or often misses its significance.

In a group context is exceptionally perceptive of the significance of the behavior of others (like a good actor).

Body Command

Exhibits either very tense or very uncontrolled behavior so that the body is not used as a well-directed resource.

Shows exceptionally free and agile body command (like a good gymnast).

Completion of Activities

Gives up on most tasks at an early stage.

Is exceptional in the capacity to stay with a task until it is successfully completed (like a good novelist). (Wolf, 1981, pp. 110–111)

Clearly we are still in the initial stages of finding constructive answers to the educational problems of the culturally different gifted child.

Children of Extraordinary Ability

It is now generally accepted that superior intellectual ability predicts a good academic future and superior personal adjustment, but doubts linger about those youngsters of extraordinary ability—the 1 in 100,000 level of a von Braun or Einstein. There have been some spectacular failures, such as William Sidis who showed early brilliant performance in mathematics as a teen-ager only to end up as an anonymous accountant. Much more likely, however, is the result described by Montour (1977) who reported on a brilliant student, identified early, who has already accomplished much and still has much of his career ahead of him.

Dr. Charles L. Fefferman, the first recipient of the National Science Foundation's Alan T. Waterman Award at 27, is a precocious professional on the order of mathematicians like Lagrange and Hamilton. At the University of Chicago in 1971, as a 22-year-old, Fefferman became the youngest college professor in the United States and became the youngest full professor in Princeton University's history when he was named a professor of mathematics there in 1974. He began showing an interest in mathematics by the age of 9 and was already taking a course at a University of Maryland campus near his home at 12. He was 14 when he became a full-time student at Maryland and graduated there in 1966 at 17. (p. 277)

Hollingworth (1942), who studied twelve youngsters with IQ scores over 180 (one in a million students), found them to have some adjustment problems and pointed out the following five major problems to overcome.

1. to find enough hard and interesting work at school
2. to suffer fools gladly
3. to keep from becoming negativistic toward authority
4. to keep from becoming hermits
5. to avoid the formation of habits of extreme chicanery (p. 299)

It is unrealistic to think that any educational system is going to reorganize its program to fit children like those who may appear once in a lifetime. Nevertheless, the potential impact of such children on society is so great that some degree of attention, such as individualized tutoring and apprenticeship to other talented individuals, may be called for.

Feldman (1979) conducted an individual study of extraordinarily precocious youngsters who performed remarkable feats in chess and music at the elementary school age level. According to Feldman, no matter how talented the child, he or she will require intensive education over several years to reach full potential as a master practitioner. In looking at these children and their tutors, Feldman observed:

1. The children are taught by remarkable teachers, such as a master of his field and a master teacher.
2. Each teacher has a distinctive style; the styles are different, but there is a coherence to how each teacher carries out his plan of instruction.
3. All curricula (in chess, music, and I believe in mathematics as well, although I have had less experience in the latter field) recapitulate in some sense the history of the field. For example, in chess both masters guide

Tutors can provide the type of intensive instruction needed for a gifted and talented child to reach full potential. (Photo: © Herb Snitzer Photography.)

their students through the games of all the world champions of chess, often going back 150 years.

4. The teachers are at least as passionate and committed to the field in which they work as are their pupils; they are also enormously dedicated teachers, reflective and vigilant about their instruction.

5. None of the teachers was a child prodigy himself. (p. 343)

The realization that tutors are important to the emergence of such ability can only make one speculate on the number of talented children not fortunate enough to match up with the type of teachers or tutors previously described.

Gifted Women

The "consciousness raising" of the women's movement has caused educators to pay special attention to that subgroup. Gifted girls and women have characteristically differed from gifted boys and men on a number of dimensions that appear related to the less assertive role of women in our society. Two major elements of that traditional "women's role" have been that women were expected to take fewer risks than men and that there were certain areas of interest (for example, athletics and mathematics) that they were expected to avoid, for those areas were clearly marked for males only. The research literature has confirmed that many gifted and talented girls learned their "social lessons" well. For example:

1. In a secondary physics program, girls were more conforming, docile, uninterested in risk taking, and intellectually unassertive (Walberg, 1969).
2. In classroom interaction in twelve classes of gifted students, across a variety of content fields, girls were eight times less likely to quarrel with the opinions of their peers or with the teacher as were boys (Gallagher, Aschner, and Jenne, 1967).
3. Girls who were creative or who had ideas off the beaten track were less well accepted by their peers than were boys with similar characteristics (Torrance, 1959).
4. In six biology classes of talented students, boys were observed to talk significantly more in class despite evidence of the girls' having relatively equal intellectual ability (Gallagher, 1967).

What has the emphasis on traditional sex roles done to hinder the gifted girl and woman?

1. In junior high school, girls do less well in mathematics and science and perform better in artistic and social subjects, paralleling the expected role for them in society (Astin, 1972).
2. Girls begin to reject toys with masculine identifications, such as fire engines and doctor kits, even before school age (Torrance, 1959).
3. Girls choose occupations in the area of nurturance, such as nursing and teaching, while only a few choose science (Gowan and Groth, 1972).
4. In a talent search for extraordinarily talented students in mathematics, boys appeared with much greater frequency than girls. The top forty-three students, as measured by tests of mathematical aptitude, were all boys (Keating, 1974).

The revolution in thinking about the appropriate role or roles of women in a modern society is probably changing many of those findings in favor of a freer and more productive intellectual life for gifted women. Although some outstanding women have overcome the prejudices and restrictions of the earlier culture, there is little doubt that the old order has taken its toll on many.

The barriers that need to be stripped away in order that gifted girls receive full opportunity to develop in mathematics and science have been described by Fox (1977):

1. Sex role stereotypes held by parents that lead them to have different expectations and aspirations for daughters than for sons. This is most noticeable in the area of mathematics achievement and professional goals;
2. Sex role stereotypes held by educators that lead them to discourage rather than encourage intellectual risk taking and the taking of advanced courses in mathematics and science;
3. Sex role stereotypes held by the adolescent peer culture, particularly males, that discourage female creativity, intellectual risk taking, and achievement, particularly in mathematics and science;
4. Sex role stereotypes reinforced by the media and in textbooks that portray females as passive and engaged in nonintellectual pursuits, reinforcing the idea of mathematical and scientific pursuits as masculine and social and nurturing activities as feminine. (pp. 11–12)

One encouraging note is that, despite such barriers, a number of gifted women in the recent past have done well. Sears and Barbee (1977) have reported on the career and life satisfactions among Terman's gifted women. Many of the women used their superior intellectual ability to cope successfully with the task of living independently because they were divorced, widowed, or unmarried. Those women appeared to get much satisfaction from their chosen employment, which their high intellectual ability allowed them to attain and maintain.

Sears and Barbee (1977) used other samples of women as comparisons to the Terman women and found no differences on factors such as divorce, health status, and so forth. The difference that set the Terman women apart from others was that two out of three obtained a college degree at a time when only one out of ten women in the general population finished college. That difference in education translated into more advanced job status and a high degree of satisfaction from their chosen occupations.

FACTORS CONTRIBUTING TO GIFTEDNESS

Where does giftedness come from? Why is it that some youngsters are substantially more advanced than others in their ability to remember, solve problems, or create?

When intelligence tests were first developed, their originators often assumed that they were measuring the basic genetic capacity of students. They assumed that the test items were within the experience of practically all children of a given age range. If that were true, then the children's ability to remember, cluster ideas, or reason would reflect that basic learning capacity. Unfortunately, such assumptions, we now know, are not true. The diverse cultural backgrounds of families in the United States suggest that not everyone has equal opportunity to learn, and certainly some children have many more experiences than do others to master some of the concepts and ideas on the tests.

The scientific study of giftedness and its origin began over a hundred years ago, in 1865, when Sir Francis Galton first started publishing articles in England on the topic of hereditary genius. Galton had observed, on the basis of biographies and direct inquiry, that outstanding abilities appeared to run in families. Galton evaluated the performance of eminent men in the society and found that the abilities and performance of close relatives of the eminent men were also quite noteworthy. (Plomin, DeFries, and McClearn, 1980, p. 27).

We cannot say that giftedness springs entirely from genetic background, but it is just as foolish to contend that the genetic background has no effect at all. In addition to the evidence provided by the high relationship of IQ scores between identical twins, there is the emergence of prodigies—at ages 3, 4, and 5—in whom no set of experiences or combination of activities could conceivably yield the fabulous results observed. The prodigy offers the clearest evidence that some aspect of inherent constitutionality influences the development of the gifted child (Feldman, 1979).

We are left then with an interesting mix of genetic and environmental influences that combine in some not-well-understood way to yield the final product identified in our educational programs as *giftedness*. It is, as has been said, native ability married to opportunity that represents the giftedness discussed here.

FINDING GIFTED CHILDREN

Before gifted children can be engaged in special educational programs, they have to be found. That task is often more difficult than the average citizen supposes. In every generation many gifted children pass through school unidentified, their talents uncultivated. Prominent among those undiscovered are children from low socioeconomic backgrounds or subcultures that place less stress on such characteristics as verbal ability. There are, in addition, those who have to drop out of school for economic reasons and those whose emotional problems disguise their intellectual abilities.

There is a general expectation that the teacher will spot those children and do something for them, but various studies have shown that teachers are not effective in recognizing the gifted child, even those with academic talent. They may fail to identify from 10 to 50 percent of their academically gifted students.

As one example, W. D. Kirk (1966) found that kindergarten teachers failed to take chronological age (CA) into account and

Gifted Pupils: Many Are Unidentified, Underserved

When she reached fifth grade, Carol, a student from East Hartford, Conn., was placed in a program for "gifted and talented" students. Admission to the program was based largely on IQ scores; students with IQs below 130 were not admitted. Carol, with an IQ of 133, was accepted.

But the following year, after Carol's family moved across the river to West Hartford, her parents learned that in the new district, only students with IQs of 135 or higher were classified as "gifted." Hence, Carol would not be able to take part in the program.

Carol's experience, according to Joseph S. Renzulli, is one of many such cases. It points, he said, to one of the most serious problems in education for the gifted and talented: defining what "gifted" means and identifying students who meet that definition.

Mr. Renzulli, a psychologist at the University of Connecticut and a pioneer in the field of education for gifted students, was one of several experts on the subject who spoke at a special symposium on "New Directions for Gifted Education" at the annual meeting of the American Psychological Association (APA).

Among the major points of the discussion:

Many bright children are wasting up to half the time they spend in regular classes. And the available data suggest that fewer than half of all gifted students have been identified and placed in special programs attuned to their needs.

Educators too often define a "gifted" child as one who attains exceptionally high scores on tests of academic aptitude and achievement. But, the panelists noted, many children have unusual talents and intangible qualities that are not readily measured on standardized tests.

The special programs that are developed rarely suit the widely varying needs and interests of very bright children.

Many of the methods of measurement and evaluation are "characterized by unsophisticated and often inaccurate data collection," said Donald J. Treffinger, an educational psychologist at the State University of New York College at Buffalo. Many districts adopt a "matrix" approach, in which "incomparable data are thrown together" in an effort to create a numerical index of "giftedness." Such indices, he said, defeat the purpose of gathering a wide range of information about the student.

Furthermore, the tests that students take to qualify for a special program may not be an appropriate measure of "giftedness," according to Mr. Treffinger. "There is widespread misuse of tests for purposes for which they were not developed and for which they are not appropriate."

Some school officials rely too heavily on total test scores to establish cutoff points, Mr. Treffinger said. In doing so, he added, they are ignoring the margin of "standard error" that is built into virtually all standardized tests.

The use of standardized tests to identify gifted students is problematic in other ways, Mr. Renzulli said. There are two kinds of giftedness, he believes. The first, "schoolhouse giftedness," is found in those students who are "good test takers or lesson learners." The majority of public school students classified as "gifted" probably fall into this category, Mr. Renzulli said.

But these talents alone offer no guarantee that a student will achieve success. "History does not remember people who merely learn their lessons well," he said.

The processes of identifying students and developing programs for them should be interrelated, Mr. Treffinger said. Psychological and educational assessments should provide useful information, but test scores alone are not the principal source of such information. "We need a broader profile of students," he said.

The programs themselves, although created with good intentions, are often inadequate, the speakers agreed. Many offer only a few supplemental activities in which all gifted students, regardless of their particular talent, participate.

These programs are premised on the notion that "all gifted students can be treated identically or benefit from a single program," Mr. Treffinger said.

"One of the great paradoxes is that we build programs on the rationale that students have unique talents, then expect the same program to suit them all."

Other speakers, however, questioned whether the public schools have the resources to create effective programs for gifted students.

A recent study by the educational theorist Benjamin S. Bloom found, according to John F. Feldhusen of Purdue University, that many parents with gifted children give up on the public schools and seek special instruction elsewhere. In some cases, school-board policies preclude rapid promotion, and bright students become extremely bored.

Moreover, Mr. Feldhusen said, the gifted are tremendously diverse. "No single program could come close to meeting all their needs. Any notion that we can come up with some single program is unrealistic."

SOURCE: Susan Walton, "Gifted Pupils: Many Are Unidentified, Underserved," *Education Week*, September 1, 1982, p. 6. Reprinted by permission.

tended to select older children as being bright. Seventy percent of the children selected as bright were mistakenly identified and had a mean IQ score of only 102.5. The teachers failed to identify 68 percent of the children with IQ scores of 116 and above. When the teachers were given guidelines for selection and an adjustment was made for CA differences, twice as many correct identifications were made, and the teachers missed only 30 percent of the eligible children.

On the basis of those and other studies on identification, it is clear that subjective evaluation, such as teacher judgment and parent referral, needs to be checked by more objective measures of ability, such as standardized tests. Any program for identifying the gifted children in a school system should include both subjective and objective methods of evaluation. Some types of behavior are best observed informally, some by more controlled methods.

Classroom behavior, for example, may point up children's ability to organize and use materials and reveal their potential for processing information better than a test can. Many aspects of creativity and verbal fluency are also best observed in a classroom or in informal experiences. However, the classroom seldom challenges a gifted child to the limit of his or her ability, as can be done in a test situation.

When the areas of creativity, leadership, and visual and performing arts are considered, identification procedures somewhat different from those used for academically gifted children may be employed. Some special "creativity" tests may be used to identify the creatively gifted (sample items: How many different ways can you think of for improving a toy dog? What would happen if annual rainfall was reduced by half?). Moreover, actual finished products, such as essays, poems, or art work, may be used, along with teacher ratings, to find the creative student.

In the case of leadership, observation of performance, along with ratings (based on past research on leadership qualities), may be used. The characteristics most often associated with leaders in a variety of situations are: (1) a strong drive for responsibility and task completion, (2) vigor and persistence in the pursuit of goals, (3) venturesomeness and originality in problem solving, (4) self-confidence and sense of personal identity, (5) the willingness to absorb interpersonal stress, (6) the willingness to tolerate frustration and delay, (7) the ability to influence other persons' behavior, and (8) the capacity to structure social interaction systems to the purpose at hand (Arnold, 1976). In leadership it is particularly clear that we are not describing inborn characteristics but instead the cumulative capabilities that youngsters demonstrate as a result of some intermix of constitutional ability and experience.

In the field of visual and performing arts, talent is still predominantly determined by a consensus of expert judges and often in an audition setting. Experts in the arts are not enthusiastic about the use of tests of artistic ability or musical aptitude. They trust their own judgment more, although such judgment is as susceptible to bias and limitations as is that of the traditional teacher rating.

Table 3.2 provides some sample items from an observational check list that teachers find useful and convenient in identifying gifted children. Later testing of intelligence shows that children who achieve high ratings on such an observational check list are often shown to be gifted. Such a scale, however, cannot protect against teacher bias or just plain dislike of certain children and a subsequent downgrading of them.

Most schools have test scores available from group intelligence tests or group achievement tests. Those can serve as a starting

**TABLE 3.2
Sample Scale Items:
Teacher Ratings for
Behavioral
Characteristics of
Superior Students**

Learning characteristics	1. Has unusually advanced vocabulary for age or grade level; uses terms in a meaningful way; has verbal behavior characterized by "richness" of expression, elaboration, and fluency. 2. Is a keen and alert observer; usually "sees more" or "gets more out of" a story, film, poem, etc. than others.
Motivational characteristics	1. Strives toward perfection; is self-critical; is not easily satisfied with own speed or products. 2. Is quite concerned with right and wrong, good and bad; often evaluates and passes judgment on events, people, and things.
Creativity characteristics	1. Displays a great deal of curiosity about many things; is constantly asking questions about anything and everything. 2. Displays a keen sense of humor and sees humor in situations that may not appear to be humorous to others.
Leadership characteristics	1. Is self-confident with children his own age as well as adults; seems comfortable when asked to show work to the class. 2. Tends to dominate others when they are around; generally directs the activity in which he is involved.
Visual and performing arts characteristics	1. Incorporates a large number of elements into art work; varies the subject and content of art work. (Art) 2. Is adept at role playing, improvising acting out situations, "on the spot." (Dramatics) 3. Perceives fine differences in musical tone (pitch, loudness, timbre, duration).

Source: J. Renzulli, L. Smith, A. White, C. Callahan, and R. Hartman, *Scales for rating the behavioral characteristics of superior students.* Mansfield Center, Conn.: Creative Learning Products, 1976.

point in selecting candidates for a special program, but certain pitfalls are widely recognized in using group tests:

1. Group intelligence tests are not as reliable as individual tests.
2. They seldom differentiate abilities at the upper limits.
3. Some children do not function adequately in a timed test situation.

Group intelligence tests, however, are practical for screening purposes because it is financially prohibitive to give all children individual examinations. Those children who are near the cutoff point or for whom the group test is not representative can be given individual examinations.

Achievement tests are even less discriminating; the same criticisms hold for them as for the intelligence tests. In addition, they will detect only children who are achieving well academically. Emotional disturbance, family problems, peer-group standards of mediocrity, poor study habits, a foreign language background, and many other factors may affect a child's ability to perform academically. There are some children who, because of family pressures, good study habits, or intense motivation, achieve at a higher educational level than is consistent with their other abilities or their apparent mental level.

Another approach used to identify gifted students is to start from the particular program one wishes to undertake and find youngsters with the particular abilities that would match that program. Stanley (1979) used this approach to initiate a talent search through his *Study of Mathematically Precocious Youth.*

In a field such as mathematics, in which the curriculum content can be organized in a sequential fashion, it is possible for bright students to move quickly through the content. Stanley's program provides for accelerating the student in mathematics courses and even for awarding college credit to children 12 to 14 years of age. Stanley described one such student:

Sean, who at 12 1/2 years of age, completed four and one-half years of precalculus mathematics in six 2-hour Saturday mornings compared with the 810 forty-five or fifty-minute periods usually required for Algebra I through III, plane geometry, trigonometry, and analytic geometry. . . . [D]uring the second semester of the eighth grade he was given released time to take the introduction to computer science course at Johns Hopkins and made a final grade of A. . . . While still 13 years old, Sean skipped the ninth and tenth grades. He became an eleventh grader at a large suburban public high school and took calculus with twelfth graders, won a letter on the wrestling team, was a science and math whiz on the school's television academic quiz team, tutored a brilliant seventh grader through two and one-half years of algebra and a year of plane geometry in eight months, played a good game of golf, and took some college courses on the side (set theory, economics, and political science). (Stanley, 1979, p. 175)

All this work allowed Sean to enter Johns Hopkins University with thirty-four credits and sophomore status at the age of 14. Stanley reported a number of cases in which the academic careers of youngsters with extraordinary talent in mathematics could be shortened through accelerating the content, and, in some cases, the student.

Aptitude tests in mathematics, such as the Scholastic Aptitude Test, are used to screen students who are extraordinarily capable in mathematics. Other characteristics, such as motivation and academic efficiency, determine the type of special attention suitable for those who score at the highest level on the aptitude test. Most special education programs for gifted students now use a combination of aptitude tests, teacher ratings, nominations, and past scholastic record to help identify eligible students.

The reasons for going through the process of identifying gifted children in the first place are complex. It is hoped that such identification will serve as the opening step to a differentiated program, but it can also be used to determine eligibility for financial aid from the state Department of Public Instruction or to satisfy state or federal guidelines.

Sometimes it seems as if we spend more time designing identification procedures than designing the special programs the students are supposed to receive. Martinson (1972) places a needed perspective on such activity:

Identification per se does not improve learning. Children who are identified and placed in regular programs show no change. . . . Identification cannot reduce the impact of malnutrition, restricted learning opportunities, poor parent-child relationships, lack of interpersonal relationships, and other negative factors. But if a well-planned program reduces these or other defects, performance and achievement of a gifted child will considerably improve. (p. 135)

EDUCATIONAL ADAPTATIONS FOR THE GIFTED

The basic issue for special education concerns the major changes or modifications in content, skills, and learning environment needed to meet the special needs of students. Passow (1982), representing an eight-member curriculum council established by the National/State Leadership Training Institute for the Gifted, listed seven major curriculum principles that the council believed should be included in any comprehensive program for gifted children. The educational applications that follow from those principles (see Table 3.3) indicate that major changes would be expected in all three areas of the educational program for gifted students: content, skills, and learning environment. The basic goal of the modifications is to provide experiences of sufficient complexity to challenge the advanced intellect of gifted children while helping them practice special skills that will increase their capabilities for self-initiative in problem solving and problem finding.

Content   Since the gifted child understands ideas and abstract concepts at an advanced level well beyond his or her classmates, it makes sense to design special content experiences that allow the child to fully exercise that ability.

TABLE 3.3
Applications of
Curriculum Principles to
Education of Gifted and
Talented Students

integrate systems of thought

rethinking knowledge

exploring new knowledge

use of resources

self-initiation self-direction

finding oneself in the scheme of things

EVALUATION in accordance with above principles.

OBJECTIVES

Principles of Curriculum	Educational Applications
The content of curricula should focus on and be organized to include more elaborate, complex, and in-depth study of major ideas, problems, and themes that integrate knowledge with and across systems of thought.	Special programs should emphasize systems of ideas such as physical theories, historical generalizations, economic principles, etc. that are within the capabilities of students.
Curricula should allow for the development and application of productive thinking skills to enable students to reconceptualize existing knowledge and/or generate new knowledge.	The students should be taught techniques of research and how to generate new ideas so that they become able to process knowledge without depending on teachers.
Curricula should enable students to explore constantly changing knowledge and information and develop the attitude that knowledge is worth pursuing in an open world.	Share with students the limitations of current knowledge and provide them with intellectual tools to explore the frontiers of knowledge.
Curricula should encourage exposure to, selection, and use of specialized and appropriate resources.	Students should be taught to use fully resources such as libraries, computers, the collection and processing of data, etc.
Curricula should promote self-initiated and self-directed learning and growth.	Problem recognition may be more important than problem solving. Students should gain experience in locating significant questions.
Curricula should provide for the development of self-understanding and the understanding of one's relationship to persons, societal institutions, nature, and culture.	The role of self in society should be approached directly to allow the students to see how they fit into their culture.
Evaluations of curricula should be conducted in accordance with prior stated principles, stressing higher-level thinking skills, creativity, and excellence in performance and products.	The test of program effectiveness is whether students have the special knowledge and skills noted above, not simply high performance on standard achievement tests.

sounds like Graduate school

asking questions

Source: A. Passow, *Differentiated curricula for the gifted/talented*. Proceedings of the First National Conference on Curricula for the Gifted/Talented. Los Angeles: National/State Leadership Training Institute on the Gifted and Talented, 1982, pp. 7–10.

When educators say they are "enriching" the curriculum for gifted children, *that* is what they generally mean. The child is presented ideas and concepts at his or her level of intellectual understanding, not at several levels below. However, unless the administrators and teachers have a clear vision of their objectives, enrichment turns out to be merely a flood of more and more facts, rather than the synthesis and unification of complex ideas.

Table 3.4 shows some suggested modifications of standard curricula based on the ability level of students. In the area of history, the slow-learning youngsters who learn best through direct experience would seem to respond better to specific discussions on how their local government works and how it influences their daily lives. Local affairs are of lesser complexity than descriptions of the abstract nature of government at the state and federal levels. Such specific discussions also have the advantage of dealing in the present rather than in the historical past, which is an abstraction level difficult for many slow-learning youngsters to handle.

On the other hand, average youngsters at about the middle grade or junior high school level are fully ready to begin understanding the nature of our government and the way in which decisions that affect them are made. They should learn the nature of our country's heritage.

However, the bright or gifted youngster is able to climb higher on the abstract conceptual ladder and to begin considering historical patterns of governance across time and across space. Such a child is able to link together important ideas that stretch across physical space and historical eras.

Similarly, in the field of nutrition (Table 3.4), while slow-learning youngsters seem best able to grasp the concept of a good diet for themselves and their families, the average youngster is able to understand the broader and more abstract concepts such as the building blocks of nutrition—carbohydrates, proteins, fats, and so on. The bright youngster is able not only to understand those concepts but to interrelate the system of nutrition with the body's ability to transform food into energy. They may even grasp the complex agricultural system that exists to bring adequate supplies of various foods to the public. Placing the slow-learning child in a curriculum program designed for the bright youngster can be a disaster, but so is placing a bright youngster in a program that is

able to begin to consider the history of ideas

TABLE 3.4
Curricular Levels of Abstraction by Ability Levels

Ability Level	History	Nutrition
Bright	Patterns of governing in cultures across time and national boundaries	The biochemistry of food and the translation of food into energy
Average	The beginnings of American government—our historical heritage	Understanding of nutrition; classification of carbohydrates, proteins, fats, etc.
Slow	How local government works and influences me	Kinds of nutritious foods to buy; samples of balanced meals

Source: J. Gallagher, *Teaching the gifted child* (2nd ed.). Boston: Allyn and Bacon, 1975, p. 78.

too simple for his or her own advanced intellectual level. Such a placement can cause the gifted child to develop long-lasting bad habits based on the lack of intellectual challenge.

Some of the ways in which curriculum content can be expanded for the gifted include the following: (1) emphasizing the structure of the concepts and basic principles of subject matter fields rather than memorizing individual facts, (2) placing emphasis on *how* information is derived instead of on *what* is derived, and (3) expanding the curriculum in breadth and depth.

Curriculum Reform in the 1960s

In the late 1950s the Russian development of space technology shocked Americans and caused them to re-evaluate their school programs, particularly those in the areas of mathematics and science (Bruner, 1960). Major efforts to reform curricula were begun by calling on scholars in the content fields to focus new curricula on the fundamental concepts and systems of ideas at the heart of the content discipline. (This is exactly what Passow is now urging in his curriculum principles in Table 3.3.)

With unaccustomed but welcome financial aid, the curriculum designers in mathematics and science began to organize their programs around the themes of teaching basic constructs and helping students learn to think scientifically by performing experiments and processing data. The physical scientists were soon followed by other scholars in the social sciences and the humanities, who began to develop more basic curricula in which individual facts became less important than the structure or the basic principles and theories underlying each content field.

Gifted children, with their readiness to absorb new knowledge and see relationships, seemed to respond well to these new curricular programs. By creating situations in which the child must follow some problem-solving method, these programs made a deliberate effort to help the child learn to think and to evaluate by using the same procedures and processes as the scientist and the scholar. Rather than memorizing facts and figures, gifted children were asked to derive the information themselves, to delve for answers themselves, and to act like scientists and scholars. They were learning not only facts but also how to acquire facts—to fit facts together to derive more fundamental generalizations (see Table 3.3).

The curriculum reform movement gradually faded out as the funds ran out and attention shifted to other educational problems, but the two goals of teaching the basic ideas of the discipline and teaching the student to think in a scientific or scholarly mode are still central themes in many secondary curricula today.

[margin notes:]

concepts, principles rather than facts

how info? instead of what info?

1960's:

Problem-solving method

learn to think independently

two goals

Expanding Contemporary Curricula

Educators face the current challenge of creating a modern analogy to the 1960s curriculum efforts (Maker, 1982). An interesting exercise in teaching basic concepts in recent times comes not from the classroom but from public television. Several series have tried to present key concepts and ideas, illustrating them and showing applications. Among the more prominent are "Civilization," "The Ascent of Man," "Connections," and "Cosmos." The limited program time available forced the producers to strip away nonessential, although interesting, facts in favor of core ideas and concepts—again, those concepts remaining well within the range of the preadolescent gifted child.

Consider the plight of Bronowski (1973), the originator of "The Ascent of Man" series, who had to take mankind from nomads tending their sheep to modern civilization in twelve one-hour programs. Examples of some key generalizations from that series give the flavor of the integrative nature of the presentations:

War, organized war, is not a human instinct. It is a highly planned and cooperative theft. And that form of theft began ten thousand years ago when the harvesters of wheat accumulated a surplus and the nomads rose out of the desert to rob them of what they themselves could not provide. (p. 88)

The horse and the rider have many anatomical features in common. But it is the human creature who rides the horse, and not the other way about. There is no wiring inside the brain that makes us horse riders. Riding a horse is a comparatively recent invention, less than five thousand years old. And yet it has had an immense influence, for instance, on our social structure. Plasticity of human behavior is what makes that possible. That is what characterizes us in our social institutions, of course, and above all, in our books, because they are the permanent products of the total interest of the human mind. (p. 412)

Another current emphasis on content is to help gifted children understand the emotions and feelings of themselves and others. Gallagher and his colleagues (1982) have provided a curriculum unit on leadership that attempts to sensitize gifted and talented students to the worries of *leaders*, whether captain of the football team, conductor of a symphony orchestra, director of a local citizen group, or governor of a state. What do leaders worry about? Following is a list of some topics that came forth when discussion focuses on the worries of leaders (each one of which could be extended into a topic for study and for further interchange):

Will I make a serious mistake and ruin the entire enterprise?
Will I represent my group well in the inevitable conflict, crisis, or
    competition the group will meet with?

Do I have sufficient authority to carry out the responsibilities I have?

Do I have the time I need to get the job done?

Who will follow me in this position? Will he/she undo what I have done?

How will my leadership performance be viewed now or in the future? (Gallagher et al., 1982)

As you can see, such questions apply to all of the leaders noted previously. Preadolescent students, or those moving into adolescence, are often preoccupied with their own feelings, anxieties, and worries. They rarely consider the worries of others, particularly adults; but focusing their attention on the hopes and fears of others can aid them in coming to grips with their own self-concept.

Providing for adequate or significant content remains a serious task. Many of the current lessons for gifted and talented students may be questioned, not because they are inadequate, but because they occupy precious time that could be used for the presentation of more significant ideas.

Skills in Productive Thinking It is not just the accumulation of knowledge that is important but also how that knowledge is used to generate new ideas and solutions. Gallagher (1975) has provided some observations:

The ability to generate new information through the internal processing of available information is one of the most impressive and valuable skills of mankind. . . . It is the ability to recombine the bits of this information into new meanings that sets mankind apart from the animals. It is the ability to perform these thinking processes well that sets the gifted student apart from the student with average ability. (p. 201)

Thus, another major instructional goal for the educator of the gifted is to enhance those thinking skills that allow the child to be creative; that is, to produce a unique product (from the child's point of view) from the available data or information. One manifest special education goal is to help gifted children develop those skills that will eventually make them autonomous thinkers, not dependent on adults or teachers, but possessing the tools and ability to seek knowledge on their own.

During the past decade, educators have been influenced greatly by two theoretical models, each of which provides a necessary structure to allow teachers to organize style and level of thinking processes as an objective for their classes.

The first model is referred to as Bloom's Taxonomy of Educational Objectives (Bloom, 1956), which has six levels of thinking

Changing perspective -- looking through another's eyes.

gathering, recombining, processing bits of information

complexity and through which teachers can shape questions or problems that stress those levels. Some examples of those levels and educational triggers for the thinking processes follow:

Knowledge: List the major causes of World War I as stated in Jones's text.
Comprehension: Explain the concept of détente and give an illustration of détente in action.
Application: If the temperature rises and the amount of gas pressure increases, what would be the stress impact on the metal container?
Analysis: What are the major components of a book? Compare and contrast their importance to the reader.
Synthesis: Using the concepts of gerontology, describe an ideal pattern of behavior in old age.
Judgment: Using standards of literary criticism, critique Jones's essay on modern education. (Feldhusen and Treffinger, 1977, p. 34)

Although all levels of thinking processes can be used to master a given topic, the dimensions of application, analysis, synthesis, and judgment would be expected to appear more often with gifted classes or resource groups.

By far the greatest amount of curricular effort has centered about the work of the psychologist J. P. Guilford, who developed the second theoretical model under discussion. Guilford devised a model of thinking processes (Figure 3.2) called the *structure of the intellect* (Guilford, 1967). He was able to divide human abilities into three major dimensions: *content, product,* and *operation.* Productive thinking requires the use of many if not all of these intellectual operations, products, and content in the Guilford system. The full model is too complex to be dealt with here. It is important for educators of the gifted because it focuses attention on two thinking processes not often measured in standard intelligence tests: *divergent production* and *evaluation.* Divergent thinking (the ability to produce many different answers to propositions such as "What would happen if everybody was born with three fingers and no thumb?") was supposed to be linked to creative abilities and thus was a legitimate skill to encourage with specific educational exercises.

Extensive analysis of classroom recordings suggests that divergent and evaluative thinking questions by teachers are rare compared with memory and convergent thinking questions (Gallagher, Aschner, and Jenne, 1967). Table 3.5 shows how different thinking processes can be stimulated by varying the types of questions asked in a discussion of *Hamlet.* Any topic can be explored in a similar fashion.

One of the more common devices used to increase *fluency,* or the number of responses that a child or adult can give to a problem, is

FIGURE 3.2
Structure of the Intellect Model

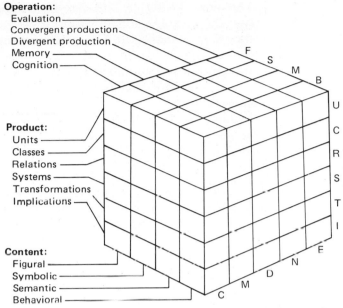

Operation:
Evaluation
Convergent production
Divergent production
Memory
Cognition

Product:
Units
Classes
Relations
Systems
Transformations
Implications

Content:
Figural
Symbolic
Semantic
Behavioral

Source: From *The nature of human intelligence* by J. P. Guilford. Copyright © 1967 McGraw-Hill Book Company. Used with permission of McGraw-Hill Book Company.

brainstorming (Parnes, 1966). Using that technique, a group of people or a whole class discusses a particular problem (for example, how to improve local government), trying to suggest as many answers as possible. There are important ground rules that they must follow:

1. **No criticism allowed.** Nothing smothers the free flow of ideas like the sharp, critical remark—or an even sharper guffaw of scorn—of a peer or of a teacher. The temptation to point out faults in an answer is very strong and needs to be quickly checked. The students need to know in advance that no critical comments will be entertained for the moment. Evaluation comes later.

TABLE 3.5
Guilford System by Intellectual Operations

Operation	Example
Memory	Whom did Hamlet kill by mistake?
Convergent thinking	Explain why Hamlet rejected Ophelia.
Divergent thinking	Name some other ways Hamlet might have accomplished his goals.
Evaluative thinking	Was Hamlet justified in killing his uncle?

Source: J. Gallagher, *Teaching the gifted child* (2nd ed.). Boston: Allyn and Bacon, 1975, p. 238.

2. **The more the better.** The students can accept the proposition that the greater the number of ideas presented, the more likely the chances that a good one will be among them. A premium could be placed on unusual or unique ideas.
3. **Integration and combinations of ideas welcomed.** The students can be alerted to the possibility of combining or adding to previous ideas.
4. **Evaluation after all ideas have been presented.** The teacher can judge when the fluency or inventiveness of the class is lagging. At that point evaluative thinking should be encouraged on the part of the students.

After all the ideas are produced, the group can pick those that seem most likely to help solve the problem. Thus the "storming" part requires divergent thinking, while the judgment part is more evaluative.

Another example stressing complex thinking processes comes from a large collection of exercises by Williams (1970):

The class was asked to use their imaginations and think ahead to the year 2000, to think of how old they will be then, and to try to predict as many changes as they can that will have come about by then. They were asked to discuss in detail how their lives would be affected by changes in food, clothing, automobiles, transportation, places to live, work, leisure activities, etc. After they had made their predictions, they were to test these against the facts by establishing some basis or evidence for their predictions. (p. 107)

Detailed attribute listing is another device used to encourage the student to think about how things could be different or better. This method forces students to perceive the characteristics of many common objects in a different light and prepares the way for product change or improvement. Table 3.6 by Callahan (1978) gives a full roster of ways of looking at an object from a screwdriver to a washing machine, or an automobile, or a social organization (like the Boy Scouts or the League of Women Voters). Try using an attribute review—you'll be surprised at the novel thoughts that come forth.

The true value of thinking exercises may be in creating a more receptive learning atmosphere for intellectual risk taking and for uncommon and unconventional ideas. Studies of creative people (MacKinnon, 1978) clearly suggest that the more creative individuals in our society are those who have a strong self-concept, are not swayed by the crowd, and seem strongly motivated to produce their own unique ideas regardless of the opinions of others. Evidence now available indicates that such skills are quickly learned by gifted (and other) students and that the students can quickly in-

TABLE 3.6
Attribute Listing

Attributes	Questions
Other uses	Can it be put to other uses as is? Can it be put to other uses if it is modified?
Adaptation	What else is like it? What other ideas does it suggest? What could you copy? Whom could you imitate?
Modification	What new twist could be made? Can you change the color, size, shape, motion, sound, form, or odor?
Magnification	What could be added? Can you add more time, strength, height, length, thickness, or value? Can you duplicate or exaggerate it?
Minification	Can you make it smaller, shorter, lighter, or lower? Can you divide it up or omit certain parts?
Substitution	Who else can do it? What can be used instead? Can other ingredients or materials be used? Can you use another source of power, another place, or another process? Can you use another tone of voice?
Rearrangement	Can you interchange parts? Can you use a different plan, pattern, or sequence? Can you change the schedule or rearrange cause and effect?
Reversibility	Can you turn it backward or upside down? Can you reverse roles or do the opposite?
Combination	Can you combine parts or ideas? Can you blend things together? Can you combine purposes?
Transformation	Can you change its form in any way? Can you burn it, punch a hole in it, paint it?

Source: C. M. Callahan, *Developing creativity in the gifted and talented child.* Reston, Va.: Council for Exceptional Children, 1978, p. 30–31.

increase their ability to use them on tasks similar to those on which they were trained (Mansfield et al., 1978). It is less clear whether the students can transfer such skills into their content courses, such as English, math, and history, and improve their performance as a result.

Learning Environment The first two broad areas of program modification, content and skills, involve changes in the teacher's approach to the child. Changes in the learning environment require administrative decisions, which are usually made by the school system or at a higher level in the educational hierarchy. Because changes in the learning environment reverberate through the entire school system, they have often received more attention at the district level than have changes in content, which remain primarily a classroom issue.

The basic reason for changes in the learning environment for gifted students is that some modification is necessary to accomplish the instructional goals of differential content and skills development. Environmental modifications such as special classes and resource rooms allow any special education program to be applied more easily. When gifted students are clustered together for part or all of a day, specially trained teachers can be assigned to the program, rather than expecting the classroom teacher to challenge those children. The classroom teacher must direct the regular program as well as face the time-consuming problem of dealing with students who need remediation. For this reason, a wide variety of learning environment adaptations have been tried to assist the teacher and to provide a program for the gifted student.

[handwritten margin note: separate them out (opposite goal)]

Special Grouping

To adapt and enrich the curriculum for gifted children in the regular school, various forms of grouping have been used. They include: (1) grouping the children within a regular class in the elementary school, (2) organizing special sections in the subject matters (for example, English, science, mathematics, and social studies) in the upper elementary school and in the secondary school, (3) offering advanced courses for superior students in secondary schools, and (4) offering honors courses for superior students in college.

More controversial is the establishment of special schools for gifted children or self-contained special classes within the regular schools. Four forms of such organization have been used: (1) resource room and itinerant teacher, (2) special classes, (3) special schools, and (4) out-of-school programs.

RESOURCE ROOM AND ITINERANT TEACHER PROGRAMS The resource room allows the gifted and talented children to be removed from their regular classes and their agemates for a portion of the day in order to engage in special activities focused on their talents. Sometimes the program is content related (for example, accelerated mathematics), and sometimes it is a broad general program. That approach, a type of mini–special class, tries to keep the child with his or her social peers for much of the day, but it still gives some degree of special stimulation.

A variation on that theme is the itinerant teacher who works with the gifted children individually, or in small groups, in the regular classroom and who also gives guidance to the regular teacher on how to plan more effectively for the gifted in the regular program. Both of those approaches depend heavily on the quality of the special teachers and their training.

SPECIAL CLASSES The grouping of gifted children into special classes is practiced in a few urban school systems. The children are grouped in grades and progress from one grade to another in a curriculum adapted to their interests and abilities. An example of such classes is found in the major work classes in Cleveland, Ohio, which have been in operation as a part of the Cleveland public school system since 1921. They admit children with measured IQ scores of 125 and above. The purpose of those classes in the elementary school is to enrich the program but not to accelerate the child. Gifted children graduate from the elementary school at the same age as do other children. Here the gifted learn with other gifted children but participate with all children in such school activities as safety patrol and physical education and in other general school programs. At the secondary level, "college bound" sections and honors courses accomplish the same goal.

SPECIAL SCHOOLS There are only a few special public elementary schools for gifted children. The Hunter College Elementary School is a special school admitting only gifted children, ages 3 to 11. In that school, children are grouped by chronological age and work independently but participate in unit topics and study themes. In addition to special schools, there are some neighborhoods in which the majority of children in the school are gifted. They constitute a natural, more homogeneous group of superior children. In some such schools and classes, as in the specially selected class or school, the average IQ scores may be 120 or 125.

A residential school for gifted and talented students at the high school level in science and mathematics was established in North Carolina in 1979 (Eilber, 1981). The North Carolina School of Science and Mathematics is currently the only residential school for gifted and talented students supported by taxpayer monies. Three hundred carefully selected students take an advanced program in secondary science and math that also includes an emphasis on the humanities.

OUT-OF-SCHOOL PROGRAMS One of the troublesome problems facing educators trying to plan for gifted children is what to do with highly talented and competent secondary school students. In

Itinerant teacher works with students, guides regular teacher

many instances those gifted youngsters may have exhausted the intellectual and academic resources of their high school by the time they are sophomores or juniors and have nothing of academic consequence to look forward to until they attend college. For such youngsters a mentor program has been suggested in which the student spends a part of the time in the community being tutored by an outstanding adult in some area of interest to the student, whether it be art or science or commerce.

when resources of high school are exhausted.

Acceleration

The second major concern that stimulates the recommendations of changes in learning environment is the length of the educational program itself. As more and more must be learned at the highest levels of the professions, talented and gifted students find themselves in school almost until the age of 30. Whereas a skilled worker may have begun earning a living and starting a family ten to twelve years earlier, the gifted student has been in a role of semidependence for a good deal of his or her young adult life. The procedure of acceleration, or methods to shorten the time that the student spends in the total educational program, is therefore a clear educational objective related to gifted children.

lessen long term dependence

All of the administrative procedures noted below are designed to cut down the time a person must remain in school.

EARLY SCHOOL ADMISSION Age of admission to kindergarten or first grade is a matter of law in most states. The age is generally set at 5 years for kindergarten and 6 years for first grade, with a few months' leeway for each. In programs of early school admission, the gifted child who is socially and intellectually mature may be allowed to enter in advance of the normal age.

SKIPPING GRADES Skipping grades, another form of acceleration, refers to completely eliminating one grade or one semester in school. Contrary to current belief, and as evidenced by the Terman study and others already cited, children who have skipped grades have shown social, educational, and vocational adjustment superior to, or comparable to, that of equally intelligent nonaccelerated children. Nevertheless, skipping grades is an unpopular and a decreasingly used form of acceleration because of its potential for creating temporary adjustment problems for the gifted student.

TELESCOPING GRADES Since skipping a grade sometimes leaves a gap in a child's experiences, some school systems have established programs that enable a child to cover the same material that is offered in the regular curriculum but in a shorter period. The ungraded primary program is a good example. In that program children may progress through the first three grades as rapidly as they are able. Some may finish in two years, some may take four years, and a few even finish three grades in one year. Occasionally seventh and eighth grades are combined in order to accelerate a group of capable students at that level.

ADVANCED PLACEMENT AND EARLY COLLEGE ADMISSION One of the more popularly used devices for acceleration, requiring little administrative change in the school, is the advanced placement program. In that program students will take courses in high school for which they will receive college credit. As much as a half-year of college courses can be obtained by talented students in many high schools, thus reducing the length of their college careers. Other programs have allowed gifted youngsters to enter colleges and universities at the age of 16 or 17 with little observable negative effect when the students are properly screened for social and emotional adjustment as well as for academic talent.

enter college early

The program of radical acceleration in mathematics and science carried out by Stanley (1979) found children who were remarkably precocious in mathematics and were enrolled at the ages of 13–15 in Johns Hopkins University. These students appear to be adjusting quite well socially and intellectually, performing at an honors level in their college classes.

EVALUATION OF ACCELERATION EFFECTS Plowman and Rice (1967) reported on the results of the acceleration of more than five hundred pupils in ten separate programs in Project Talent, a state program for the gifted in California. Those students had high ability, high achievement, and advanced physical and social adjustment. Only nine of the children were reported to have serious problems, and they were doubful participants in the first place.

Those findings continue an unbroken string of positive results reported in the educational literature. From early admission to school (Braga, 1971; Reynolds, 1962) to early admission to college (Terman and Oden, 1947), the research studies invariably report that those children who were accelerated made adjustments as good or better than did the comparison children of similar ability. Despite the favorable findings, some parents and teachers continue to have strong negative feelings about the practice, while some educational administrators dislike the awkwardness of dealing with those children as special cases. The result is that many gifted students have been consigned to spend the greater part of their first three decades of life encased in an educational system in a relatively unproductive role, to the detriment of themselves and their society.

The major objection to the acceleration of students, whether by early admission, skipping, or telescoping, has been a fear that acceleration displaces gifted children from their social and emotional peers and thus affects their subsequent social adjustment.

Weiss (1978) tried to find gifted individuals who, as adults, would look back on their experience of acceleration and comment on their feelings of how it affected them. A sample of 586 professors was drawn from five university faculties. The majority of those found that the acceleration helped them enter their careers earlier with no serious accompanying problems. Nevertheless there were some who reported social problems:

Skipping seemed desirable at the time, an honor; in retrospect, it was probably unwise to skip, as it led to feelings of insecurity due to physical and social immaturity.

In the long run, it was not worth it because I was too socially immature. (pp. 127–128)

The most positive responses were reserved for the advanced placement program and some of the reasons can be noted in the following comments:

Superb. A combination which did not isolate all the gifted from the rest.

It was a great joy and also intellectually stimulating to be exposed to peers and teachers who found the same excitement in learning that I did.

The class was one of the best I had in high school. I learned skills which were valuable to me in college and, in fact, from which I still benefit. (pp. 129–130)

When one reflects that many gifted children entering first grade now will not finish their educational program until well into the twenty-first century, we can understand the continuing efforts to shorten the one-third of a lifetime that our strongest students spend in formal education.

Program Variation and Innovation

The traditional strategy for organizing a program for gifted students has been to identify the gifted children and then develop an instructional program to meet their needs. However, an alternative strategy, which has been receiving increased interest and trial, is to create a program that would be stimulating and attractive to gifted students and to ask all students who are interested to volunteer for the program. That strategy avoids the major problem of

Volunteer

prior identification because it allows the gifted youngsters to identify themselves through their performance in the special coursework. By providing a special trial period for the youngsters, it also opens the opportunity for students who have hidden potential but have not revealed that potential through test performance. Alternatively, a student may have one area of special skills that matches the special coursework but not have unusual talent across the board; as a result the student would not be picked up in a general intelligence screening program.

One such approach receiving attention is the revolving door procedures designed by Renzulli (1979). Renzulli's plan allows a large number of students of above average ability, perhaps 20–25 percent of the student population, to participate in the program as their own interests and motivation dictate. Unlike the more traditional programs for gifted students, these students are neither permanently in nor out of the program but can apply for special consultation and additional time to work on a special project of their own choosing.

Renzulli claims that this approach brings the regular class teacher into more active participation in the program and also allows students to understand they must earn the right to participate in the program by showing high motivation and task commitment. In this program, then, the resource teacher is no longer just another special teacher but a consultant in the true sense of the word. In Renzulli's words:

The resource teacher helps the student to focus or frame the area of interest into a researchable problem; suggests where the students can find appropriate methodologies for pursuing the problem like a professional inquirer; helps the youngster to obtain appropriate resources (persons, equipment, reference materials, financial support); provides critical feedback, editorial assistance, encouragement, and a shoulder to cry on; and helps the child find appropriate outlets and audiences for his or her creative work. (Renzulli, 1979, p. 34)

In another variation of traditional practice, Renzulli (1977) proposed a three-step sequence of activities that he calls the *enrichment triad*. The purpose of the three steps is to lead the gifted student through a series of experiences that culminate in activities in the society in a variety of content fields. The basic philosophy of the program maintains that the prospective scientist, artist, or fledgling historian can derive great satisfaction from the realization that he or she can, as a young student, have an impact on the adult world and, further, that teachers can organize experiences so that students can start to participate while in the upper elementary grades.

Activities in the enrichment triad expose gifted students to a series of experiences in a variety of content fields. (Photo: © Herb Snitzer, 1972 "Today Is for Children.")

Phases in the ① enrichment Triad

(TEACHER)

②

Phase I in the enrichment triad consists of general exploratory activities that are designed to bring the learner in touch with topics or areas of study in which he or she may be interested. A variety of activities are provided to introduce the learners to particular fields. Renzulli suggests establishing interest centers in the classroom that would have as their focus social studies, physical and life sciences, mathematics and logic, music and performing arts, writing, philosophy, ethics, and social issues. In addition to learning about history, students would learn about how history is developed. He suggests posing the following kinds of questions to the students:

1. Why do we study history?
2. Where does the historian look for evidence?
3. What qualifies as a historical document?
4. How does the historian move from raw data to conclusions and generalizations?

Once a student becomes intrigued with a particular area of study, he or she can move forward into Phase II of the triad: group training activities. Renzulli refers to the training exercises as warm-ups for the intellect, analogous to the physical exercises done by athletes before a contest. Brainstorming exercises that stimulate flexibility and originality in the content fields fit that type of activity. Assignments that free up the intellect and imagination are encouraged—for example, students imagine that they are members of a crew on a starship who have found an alien race and are expected to find out all they can about the aliens: their dress, their art, their science, their communication, and so forth.

In Phase III of the triad, individual and small group investigations of real problems are undertaken. Renzulli suggests that the student is now ready to engage in a project that will be meaningful to him or her and to the society. He maintains that the process of adding new knowledge involves the organization of raw data or unorganized bits of information, synthesizing the conclusions of others who have dealt with the field in the past, and the use of methods of inquiry that allow one to generate new information. The role of the teacher in this situation is to provide students with meaningful reference material and the opportunity to go outside the school environment to use their interests and their skills. Renzulli provides the following examples of Phase III behavior.

1. Students in the biology department at Bronx High School of Science in New York City have for several years published the *Journal of Biology*, a scholarly journal that reports the research findings of biologists attending the school.
2. A group of young historians have summarized the battles of the American Revolution fought in the Carolinas. An attractive battle map, pictures of soldiers in regimental uniforms, and an informative narrative are printed on placemats that have been purchased by many restaurants in the area.
3. A twelve year-old student lectures twice a week on ancient Egypt to persons who visit the St. Louis Art Museum. He is also assisting the museum by translating the Egyptian *Book of the Dead* from the original hieroglyphics.
4. The research of two thirteen-year-old students at the Tallcott Mountain Center in Avon, Connecticut, regarding wind flow patterns over a proposed new highway route, was submitted to a citizens action group. This data, contradicting the findings of professional climatologists, showed that the proposed highway was potentially hazardous to a major water reservoir because of automobile emissions. The results of the students' research were instrumental in stopping construction of the highway. (Renzulli, 1977, p. 51)

Although Renzulli would agree that such projects can be helpful for all students, the gifted students respond most readily because they already have absorbed a large part of the skills and knowledge that are a necessary foundation for such investigations.

Magnet Schools for the Gifted

The concept of *magnet schools* is another strategy for providing a learning environment conducive to gifted students. Essentially this approach sets up an alternative education system within the regular education system, featuring a wide variety of educational opportunities in which parents and children can volunteer to participate. The idea is to create exciting opportunities for creativity, for participation in the performing arts, and for more fundamental basic education in the learning skills. Entire schools in a district may be identified as focusing on creativity and aesthetics while other schools are committed to a strong emphasis on learning the basic skills of reading, mathematics, writing, and so forth. Parents and children can choose the school that fits their special interests (Marks and Nystrand, 1981).

By volunteering for special courses, the students commit themselves to significant tasks and identify themselves as "outstanding" through their performance on the tasks rather than on tests (just as an audition tends to identify those with musical talent). Originators of the concept hope that by providing a variety of educational emphases, students will elect to participate in important experiences and go into greater depth on issues of their choice.

In the Basics component, children receive instruction in heterogeneously grouped classes in reading, math, science, and social studies. In the Aesthetics component, children and their parents, in cooperation with teachers, choose exploratory learning experiences from the following areas: art, creativity, dance, drama, foreign language, futuristic studies, language arts/social studies, leadership, math/science, music, philosophy and logic, physical arts, contemporary institutions, and film. In the Creative I Component the child has the opportunity to do something about a specific experience, to apply knowledge in a new way, to dream, or to pursue an idea in great depth and breadth. In this dimension of the program, a child can receive private music lessons, design and carry out a special community project, or receive small group instruction in a foreign language. If special proficiency is shown, students are scheduled individually into a personalized program. (Marks and Nystrand, 1981, p. 117)

The minicourses noted in Table 3.7 are examples of the variety available to students interested in this approach, which uses many individuals from the community as instructors. Gifted students, as described in this text, would quickly move through the introductory phases into in-depth study in an area of their choice. Individualization of program offerings enables gifted students, as well as other students, to find ways to develop their own particular skills. Such an approach is obviously not for all school districts as it places a heavy managerial burden on school leadership. It is, however, a concept worthy of further exploration.

TABLE 3.7
Special Minicourses for
Gifted Students

Course Title	Course Description
The Cradle of Civilization	Sail down the Nile and explore the dynasties of ancient Egypt. We'll look into the mummy's tomb, pyramids, hieroglyphics, and much more. For those of you who missed King Tut during his visit to our area, don't miss this chance to meet the famous boy king. (12–15 students; grades 3, 4, 5)
Great Inventors	Studying great inventors such as Ben Franklin, Thomas Edison, Alexander Graham Bell, and Granville T. Woods will provide students with role models to design inventions of their own. Patents, advertising, marketing, corporations, and stockholders are areas to check out. Students will design a blueprint (and a working model if applicable) of their invention(s) and follow through the process to advertising and marketing. (12–15 students; grades 3, 4, 5)
Philosophy and Logic I	Join Harry Stottlemeir, a fictional fifth-grade philosopher, who ponders such questions as why the sentence "all cucumbers are vegetables" is true, but "all vegetables are cucumbers" is false. If you like to debate issues, share concerns, enjoy being inquisitive, or want to improve your reasoning, then this course is for you. (10–12 students; grades 4, 5)
Geometry	This course will introduce the child to the basic skills and tools used in geometry. It will provide opportunities for creativity through activities and projects, such as line designs, curve stitching, and string art. (12–15 students; grades 3, 4, 5)
Insect Study	Eight of every ten animals on earth are insects. This course introduces the student to the world of insects and their kin. There will be opportunity to collect, observe, and investigate the common insects found in our area. Students will learn about beneficial and harmful insects and the role they play in the environment. (14–16 students; grades 3, 4, 5)
The Wonderful Story of You!	One of nature's miracles is the human body. This course will introduce children to the different systems of the body and show how they work together. Is your blood really blue? How does your body warn you of danger? These and other related topics will be explored. (14–16 students; grades 3, 4, 5)

Source: W. Marks (Ed.), *Gifted and talented magnet schools: Model program guide, grades 3, 4, 5.* Raleigh N.C.: Wake County Public Schools, 1982.

Evaluation of Special Programs

Do special programs result in a positive change? Do they also produce unfavorable side effects? Those are questions to which parents and the general public want answers. Although the availability of full-scale and careful evaluation of programs is limited, there is evidence to support the usefulness of special grouping *whenever the program includes content and skills changes* as well as administrative modifications. Some fragmentary findings follow:

Students in the California Project Talent program who attended special class programs where content changes were stressed showed significant gains in achievement over comparison groups not in such programs (Robeck, 1967).

A major review of studies on the training of productive and creative skills concluded that such skills are trainable but there is a lack of evidence for the generalization of these skills to other content fields (Mansfield, Busse, and Krepelka, 1978).

Advanced placement programs in ten southeastern states found a savings of $19 million through college credits earned by over 17,000 students (Southern Region Education Board, 1981).

Classes for gifted students reveal a wider range of thinking processes than in ordinary classes and there is a greater freedom to encourage creative and reflective thinking on the part of the students (House, Kerins, and Steele, 1969).

A carefully designed special class program organized for chronic underachievers has demonstrated success in improving academic and behavioral skills (Whitmore, 1980).

Much of the evaluation of programs for gifted and talented students remains poorly designed and depends on unsupported feelings and attitudes of participants. In this regard, they resemble most educational programs, few of which have placed a premium on careful evaluation of their results.

Choosing a Program for a Gifted Child

No single plan is appropriate for the education of all gifted children. Efforts to properly educate all those children by only one specific plan, such as acceleration, special classes, or enrichment in the regular grades, will surely be inadequate for some gifted students.

Decisions on where to place a gifted child, how to organize his or her education, and what teaching techniques and materials to use depend largely on the pattern of development of that particular child and on the provisions for all children in the school system. It is therefore necessary to evaluate a gifted child in terms of abilities, interests, habits, home environment, and community values. The educational program for the child can be better determined on the basis of that evaluation than by setting up a special educational program and trying to fit all gifted children into it.

Following are some adaptations and adjustments that should be taken into consideration:

1. When a child's patterns of growth in physical, social, mental, and educational areas are all accelerated beyond the chronological age, as indicated by Cranshaw and Zelda in Figure 3.1, acceleration in grade placement should be considered.
2. When the physical, social, and emotional areas are equal to the chronological age but the educational achievement is advanced, a special class or resource room can be considered.
3. When the school system is too small (not providing sufficient numbers of gifted children of a particular kind for a special class), enrichment, tutoring, or itinerant teachers for the gifted children in the regular classroom may be necessary.
4. When the class in which a gifted child is placed contains a preponderance of children of superior intelligence, even though it is not designated as a class for the gifted, enrichment of the program is probably more desirable than special classes or acceleration, neither of which may be necessary.
5. When the child is gifted but underachieving, special attention to social and emotional problems or to possible areas of weakness is called for. Intensive counseling and parent education or even remedial instruction may be more important for the child than the type of classroom placement.
6. When inner discrepancies in growth are quite marked, as we often find in children with extremely high IQ scores, a tutorial or individualized method of instruction may be necessary, especially when the child is unable to adjust to existing educational situations.
7. When school systems feel that enrichment in the regular grades is the most feasible plan, a coordinator for gifted children is critical. Many feel that it is unrealistic to expect every teacher to furnish enrichment in the regular grades. Teachers need the help of a specialist or consultant to provide materials, inservice training, and community resources to aid that teacher.

Societal Values Influence Gifted Programs

What each community and the collective American society decide to do about providing special educational experiences for gifted children probably depends more on societal attitudes and values than on educational evaluations. Gallagher (1976) identified four broad forces that have influenced action in the past:

1. **Egalitarianism.** There is a strong belief in the need to give all citizens equal treatment and equal opportunity and a determina-

tion that there be no special privileges for special people. Such attitudes, narrowly applied, can hinder special provisions for gifted children, especially since "equal education" often gets translated into "identical education."

2. **Universal education.** The commitment of the United States to full education for all children through high school has retained many children of limited ability in school. That situation has created a range of talents and achievement at junior and senior high school ages that is difficult to manage within a single classroom. Much of the pressure for special provisions for the gifted is a recognition of extraordinary student diversity and the problems it creates for the conscientious teacher.

3. **Decentralization of educational decision making.** When each separate school district makes its own major educational decisions, the need for special education for the gifted does not seem as pressing as other more immediate needs. At the state and federal levels there is greater opportunity for taking a longer-range perspective. The program stimulus for the gifted often comes from those levels.

4. **Sense of societal confidence.** As long as there is overconfidence in the ability of the United States to conquer any obstacle or solve any problem as it arises—to muddle through if necessary— then the pressure to provide special educational help for the talented is quite low. When some of that overconfidence is lost, then there is increased pressure to build programs that would enhance the education of the most talented students in the society.

Recognition of the social forces that influence or determine our educational policies is the first step toward understanding the otherwise curious reluctance of the society to do more for the gifted student.

SUMMARY OF MAJOR IDEAS

1. Gifted children are currently defined as those showing outstanding abilities in a variety of areas, including intellectual ability, academic aptitude, talent in creative thinking, leadership ability, and skills in visual and performing arts.
2. The identification of gifted children has traditionally been accomplished through a combination of procedures, including intelligence tests, past achievement in school, peer referral, and teacher identification. Additional measures of creative and productive thinking are being tried on an experimental basis.
3. The prevalence of gifted children in any community depends on the criteria used to identify them and the socioeconomic status of the community. It could range from 1 percent of the

school population to 15 or 20 percent in a community of high socioeconomic level.

4. The studies on gifted children, particularly the longitudinal research of Terman, have indicated that the academically gifted are:
   a. superior in physical and health characteristics
   b. advanced two to four years beyond average in school subjects
   c. able to maintain their intellectual maturity into adulthood
   d. superior in mental health adjustment
   e. less prone to serious maladjustment and delinquency
   f. eight times more likely to be in the professions

5. Attention is now being directed to special subgroups of intellectually gifted children who have their own unique sets of characteristics and educational problems. They include the underachiever, the gifted child who is culturally different, children with extremely high IQ scores, and gifted women.

6. Enrichment within the regular classroom for gifted students is viewed with skepticism by many who believe that more tangible help in the form of special materials, training, and auxiliary personnel is needed to make a meaningful difference.

7. Changes in content focus on emphasizing the structure and basic concepts of subject matter fields. Interest has also been shown in adding special content areas not usually included, such as the teaching of logic and ethics.

8. Skills instruction for gifted students emphasizes stimulation of their productive thinking and creative skills. These are attempts to develop autonomous thinkers and to encourage maximum productive thinking. Two theoretical models—Bloom's Taxonomy of Educational Objectives and Guilford's Structure of the Intellect—have greatly influenced educators and each has provided a basis for teachers to organize thinking processes in lessons for their students.

9. Changes in the learning environment may vary from one community to another; they include resource rooms, summer classes, special classes, special schools, and various forms of acceleration when appropriate.

10. New approaches to creating learning environments to attract gifted students together with other above-average students (such as *magnet schools, enrichment triad,* and *revolving door programs*) are gaining in popularity.

11. Evaluations of special programs for gifted children, though few in number, have generally reported positive results.

12. Values in the society, such as egalitarianism and universal education, have a determining influence on the type and amount of special programs provided for gifted students.

UNRESOLVED ISSUES

1. The Mystery of Selective Precocity. Lest we deceive ourselves that we know all that needs to be known about the rapid development of giftedness in some children, we may reflect on the questions posed by Feldman (1979), emerging from his own study of extremely precocious children.

How could it be that a child cannot only comprehend and discuss, but can *produce* original compositions of the subtlety and complexity of a mature composer, yet find Piaget's five chemicals problem to be difficult to solve? How can a chess player who regularly wins tournaments against mature adult players show moral judgment and reasoning typical for that of an eight- or nine-year-old child? (p. 350)

These extraordinary intraindividual differences remain as much a mystery today as they did when Mozart was writing his compositions before the age of six.

2. Equality and Excellence. The simple concept of equality that "all children should be treated alike" has hindered the development of programs for gifted and talented students in many schools and communities. Although special instruction and programs for those talented in athletics or in the performing arts are easily accepted, there is less acceptance for the same type of stimulation for students who excel intellectually or academically. Some people feel that having special abilities is in itself unfair and unjust and that the schools should not compound the problem by giving greater advantages to such students. How can education deal with the issue of *equal* versus *appropriate* education for gifted students?

3. Special Teachers and Classroom Teachers. A largely undiscussed but well-understood problem facing special educators has been the often difficult relationship that develops between the classroom teacher and the special education resource teacher. Theoretically, they should work together as a team to aid the exceptional child; however, there are personal problems of professional status, turf, and authority that have often caused a chasm to exist between two professionals who are both interested in the well-being of the gifted child. What is the nature of the personal and administrative adjustments needed to encourage more cooperation and support?

REFERENCES OF SPECIAL INTEREST

Karnes, F., & Collins, E. *Handbook of instructional resources and references for teaching the gifted.* Boston: Allyn and Bacon, 1980.

A detailed guide for helping teachers find or adapt materials to enhance the learning experiences of gifted students. Includes check lists to help evaluate materials, a comprehensive list of publishers, professional references games and puzzles, and a general overview of the special needs of the gifted.

Maker, C. *Curriculum development for the gifted.* Rockville, Md.: Aspen Systems Corporation, 1982.

A book designed primarily for practitioners interested in providing differential curricula for gifted students. It includes general principles of curriculum development, suggestions for the reader's own program development, and four examples of how such curricula can be implemented.

Passow, A. (Ed.). *The education of the gifted and talented: Seventy-eighth Yearbook of the National Society for the Study of Education.* Chicago: University of Chicago Press, 1979.

Twenty-seven chapters present an up-to-date statement on what we know about gifted and talented children and special attempts to educate them. In addition to standard topics of identification and special content adjustment in mathematics and social studies, chapters cover special subgroups such as gifted women, culturally different gifted, and extreme giftedness.

Torrance, E. P. *Discovery and nurturance of giftedness in the culturally different.* Reston, Va.: Council for Exceptional Children, 1977.

A cohesive summary of the work done over the past two decades on special identification methods for gifted children from minority groups and some of the special instructional adaptations that seem particularly appropriate. Also contains an annotated list of biographies and autobiographies of successful culturally different people for young readers.

Whitmore, J. *Giftedness, conflict, and underachievement.* Boston: Allyn and Bacon, 1980.

A comprehensive portrait of one type of giftedness that is often overlooked—the gifted student who does not perform well. A detailed description of one effective program is provided.

The search for solutions. Film series by Phillips Petroleum Co. New York: The Search for Solutions Booking Center, 1981.

This series attempts to illustrate the various stages of problem finding and problem solving that scientists follow when in a creative and productive mode. Well produced, attractive, and based on sound professional information.

4

Mentally Retarded Children

Just as we have always been aware that some children learn more quickly than others, so we have known that some children learn more slowly than their agemates and, as a consequence, have difficulty adapting to the social demands placed on them. Organized professional attempts to help slow-learning children began less than two hundred years ago with Jean Itard, a French physician, who tried to educate a young boy found wandering in the woods outside Aveyron. Although Itard felt that his attempts to teach the Wild Boy of Aveyron had failed, one of his students, Edward Seguin, developed Itard's approaches much further and became an acknowledged leader of the movement to help mentally retarded children and adults. Seguin came to the United States in 1848 because of political turmoil in Europe. This country's efforts to provide education for mentally retarded children were enhanced by Seguin's work. Care and education of the mentally retarded in the United States has moved gradually from large state institutions to special class provisions in the public schools to the current philosophy of integrating mentally retarded children as much as possible into society—the *least restrictive environment* policy (Crissey, 1975).

This chapter will review definitions, causes, characteristics, and current educational practices that apply to mental retardation. Three levels of mental retardation are commonly used to indicate the educational implications of the condition: *educable, trainable,* and *severely and profoundly retarded*. These levels represent different causations and implications for social adaptation. The first two groups, educable and trainable, will be discussed in this chapter; severely and profoundly mentally retarded children will be discussed in Chapter 10, "Children with Multiple, Severe, and Physical Handicaps."

DEFINITION

There have been numerous attempts to define *mental retardation*. Many professional disciplines—medicine, psychology, social work, and education among them—have been concerned with mentally retarded children and adults and each looks at the condition from its own perspective. This text emphasizes the educational standpoint.

Definitions of all the exceptionalities in this book are not static, but tend to be modified and refined as more experience and evidence become available. The definition of mental retardation is a good example of such modification. In recent attempts to define mental retardation, emphasis has shifted significantly from a condition that exists solely within the individual to a condition that represents an interaction between an individual and a particular environment.

The most commonly used definition is one devised by key members of the American Association on Mental Deficiency (AAMD) (Grossman, 1977). Following is the AAMD definition along with an explanation of how that definition translates into practical terms:

Definition	Explanation
Mental retardation refers to significantly subaverage general intellectual functioning	Defined as a score on standard intelligence tests that would be lower than that obtained by 97 to 98 percent of persons of same age.
existing concurrently with deficits in adaptive behavior	Meeting standards of independence and social responsibility expected of age and cultural group (that is, learning basic academic skills, participating in appropriate social group activity).
and manifested during the developmental period. (Grossman, 1977)	Should be observable during childhood. Problems of a similar nature manifested only in adulthood would likely be classified as mental illness, not mental retardation.

A key distinction between the current AAMD definition and many previous efforts is the emphasis on adaptive behavior combined with intellectual subnormality, which are discussed in more detail in the following paragraphs.

Intellectual Subnormality No definition, no matter how comprehensive, is worth much unless there are ways to translate its abstract concepts into some form of practical action. The *intellectual subnormality* dimension has traditionally been determined by performance on intelligence tests, which were, in fact, originally developed by Alfred Binet for the express purpose of finding children who were *not* capable of responding to the traditional education program in France at the turn of the twentieth century. The performance of mentally retarded children on such tests resembles a mirror image of the performance of gifted students as described in Chapter 3. Mentally retarded children are markedly slower than their agemates in using memory effectively, associating and classifying information, reasoning, and making adequate judgments.

Figure 4.1 shows the theoretical distribution of scores on a test similar to the Wechsler intelligence scales. A standard deviation is a statistical measure of variance or spread from the center or mean of the distribution, in this case an IQ score of 100. Students whose scores fall between an IQ score of 85—minus one standard deviation (-1σ)—and an IQ score of 70—minus two standard deviations (-2σ)—are often referred to as *borderline intellectually subnormal.* They are often found at the low end of the typical class but are able to perform there if given an appropriate educational program. Those students who score between minus two standard deviations and minus three standard deviations (IQ scores between 55 and 70) would be termed *educable mentally retarded* if social adaptation was also low. Students falling below minus three standard deviations but who still are capable of responding to the test would be consid-

**FIGURE 4.1
Relative Prevalence
of Intellectual
Subnormality**

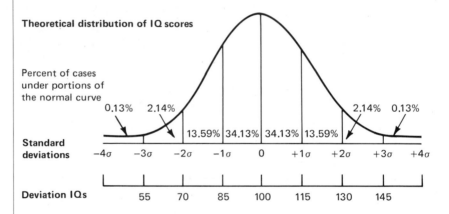

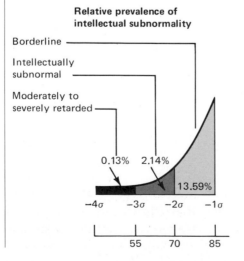

ered in the *trainable* range. Although we no longer place uncritical faith in such intelligence tests, they still possess strong power in predicting who will achieve academic goals.

Adaptive Behavior

Edgar Doll medical model

Adaptive behavior depends partly on factors outside the child—the environmental envelope in which the child exists. Contrast that position with Edgar Doll's (1941), which places the burden squarely on the constitutional nature of the individual. Doll defined mental deficiency as: (1) social and occupational incompetency with inability to manage affairs at the adult level, (2) mental subnormality, (3) intellectual retardation from birth or early age, (4) retardation at maturity, (5) a result of constitutional origin through heredity or disease, and (6) essential incurability.

With the inclusion of adaptability in the AAMD definition, the condition becomes contingent not only on intellectual performance but also on the individual's ability to respond to the demands of the society.

environment

If one particular environmental setting creates more demands than another, we face the unsettling truth that a child can be mentally retarded in one community but not in another, in school but not in the neighborhood, at one time in his or her life but not in another. Although controversy exists over whether the development of intellectual performance can be modified, there is universal acceptance of the proposition that, through training, the adaptive behavior of mentally retarded children can be influenced. Thus, it may be possible in some instances to "cure" mental retardation, if not intellectual subnormality, through educational programming or modification of the social environment.

CLASSIFI-CATION

Although there have been many different ways to categorize mentally retarded individuals, including the terms *mild, moderate,* and *severe* used by the American Association on Mental Deficiency and suggested by the President's Committee on Mental Retardation, we will focus on terms that carry specific educational meaning and implications. These terms are noted in Table 4.1 as *educable, trainable,* and *severe/profound.*

Educable Mentally Retarded

An educable mentally retarded child (corresponds to the mildly retarded child in the AAMD classification) is one who, because of subnormal mental development, is unable to profit sufficiently from the regular program of the school but who is considered to have capacity for development in three areas: (1) educability in academic subjects at the primary and advanced elementary grade levels, (2) educability in social adjustment to a point at which a child can eventually get along independently in the community, and (3) occupational adequacies to such a degree that the child can be partially or totally self-supporting as an adult.

In many environmental settings during infancy and early childhood, the educable mentally retarded child is not recognized as retarded. Most of the time retardation is not evident because expectations for the child are not heavily weighted with intellectual content during the preschool years. The educable retarded child may be first identified by the school when learning ability becomes an important part of social expectations. In most instances there are no obvious pathological conditions to account for the retardation.

Trainable Mentally Retarded The trainable mentally retarded child (corresponds to moderately retarded in the AAMD classification) has been defined as one who has difficulty: (1) learning academic skills to any functional level, (2) developing total independence in social adjustment at the adult level, and (3) attaining vocational adequacy at the adult level sufficient for total self-support without supervision or help. The trainable person is capa-

**TABLE 4.1
Levels of Mental
Retardation**

	Educable	Trainable	Severe/Profound
Etiology	Predominantly considered a combination of genetic and poor social and economic conditions	A wide variety of relatively rare neurologic, glandular, or metabolic defects or disorders that can result in moderate or severe retardation	
Prevalence	About 10 out of every 1,000 persons	About 2–3 out of every 1,000 persons	About 1 out of every 1,000 persons
School expectations	Will have difficulty in usual school program; need special adaptations for appropriate education	Need major adaptation in educational programs; focus is on self-care or social skills; limited effort on traditional academics	Will need training in self-care skills (feeding, toileting, dressing)
Adult expectations	With training can make productive adjustment at an unskilled or semiskilled level	Can make social and economic adaptation in a sheltered workshop or, in some instances, in a routine task under supervision	Will always need continued custodial care

ble of attaining: (1) <u>self-help skills</u> (such as dressing, undressing, using the toilet, and eating); (2) the ability to protect himself or herself from common dangers in the home, school, and neighborhood; (3) social adjustment to the home or neighborhood (learning to share, respect property rights, and cooperate in a family unit and in the neighborhood); and (4) <u>economic usefulness</u> in the home and neighborhood by assisting in chores around the house or working in a sheltered environment or even in routine jobs under supervision. In most instances such children will be identified as retarded during infancy and early childhood. The retardation is generally noted because of known clinical or physical stigmata or deviation or because the children are markedly delayed in talking and walking.

Severely and Profoundly Mentally Retarded

Most severely and profoundly mentally retarded children (corresponds to severely retarded in the AAMD classification) have multiple handicaps that often interfere with normal instructional procedures. For example, in addition to being mentally retarded, the child may have cerebral palsy and a hearing loss. The goal of training procedures for such severely handicapped children is limited to establishing some level of social adaptation in a controlled environment. Those training issues are discussed in Chapter 10, "Children with Multiple, Severe, and Physical Handicaps."

IDENTIFICATION

The identification of mentally retarded children is done by using agreed-upon procedures to measure *intellectual subnormality* and *social adaptation*. The individual intelligence test still remains the instrument most often used for determining intellectual subnormality, although some doubts have been raised about its appropriateness in all cases. A student whose scores fall below those of 98 percent of his or her agemates (two standard deviations below the average) is considered intellectually subnormal. However, that is just half of the definition. The other dimension, social adaptation, is a much less definitive concept (although more and more attempts have been made to measure it). The Education for All Handicapped Children Act (PL 94–142) has required a comprehensive educational assessment that includes measures of both adaptive behavior and intelligence.

Two measures of adaptive behavior are currently in major use. Although similar in many respects, they have important differences. The first is the AAMD Adaptive Behavior Scale—Public School Version (Lambert et al., 1975). The scale is an extension of an earlier scale developed by the American Association on Mental Deficiency that was designed for mentally retarded populations. It is divided into two parts, the first of which contains ten competence domains, including independent functioning, physical development, language development, and vocational activities. The second part contains twelve domains of maladaptive behavior, including antisocial behavior, untrustworthiness, withdrawal, inappropriate manners, unacceptable or eccentric habits, and hyperactivity. This scale is usually completed by a teacher and has been standardized on a sample of over 2,600 children, including normal children as well as children identified as educable mentally retarded, trainable mentally retarded, and educationally handicapped.

The second instrument, the Adaptive Behavior Inventory for Children (ABIC), is a subsection of the System of Multicultural Pluralistic Assessment (SOMPA) developed by Mercer and Lewis (1978). The instrument contains over two hundred items organized into six competence areas: family, community, peer relations, non-academic school roles, earner/consumer, and self-maintenance. The scale has been standardized on a sample of over two thousand children divided among black, Hispanic, and white groups.

The difference between the two is that the AAMD scale focuses on behavior within the school setting whereas the ABIC focuses on behavior outside of school. It is possible, therefore, that a child could get a reasonably average score on adaptive behavior outside of school on the ABIC and still receive a low adaptive behavior score on the AAMD scale because of inappropriate behavior within the school setting.

In many instances the assessment of social adaptation still remains the judgment of the teacher and other educational personnel who have had direct experiences with the child.

PREVALENCE

How many mentally retarded children are there? Numerous surveys to determine the prevalence of children with low intelligence have shown a wide range of estimates. The figures for the prevalence of severely/profoundly and trainable mentally retarded children generally agree from one population to another, whereas the figures for the number of educable or mildly mentally retarded vary widely from place to place. There are a number of reasons why researchers obtain different prevalence figures, among which are:

1. **Different IQ cutoff points are used for intellectual subnormality.** Farber (1968) reported on studies by Akkeson in Sweden and Lofthus in Norway. Akkeson used an IQ score of 70 as the limit and found 1.8 percent mentally retarded, while Lofthus used an IQ score of 75 as the limit and obtained 3.8 percent.

2. **Different ways of determining adaptive behavior.** If a number of intellectually subnormal children (IQ score below 70) are adapting to their communities' expectations, then they may or may not be included in the sample of "mentally retarded." A good example of the difference that makes is illustrated by Birch et al. (1970). Those investigators picked Aberdeen, Scotland, as a city for study because that school system routinely uses intellectual screening for all of its 7-year-olds, thus providing an opportunity to get a count of the entire population at a given age. After screening, the children were examined individually by psychologists and medical officers. They found that about 1.3 percent of the children were eligible for special class placement. In their study less than half of the children whose IQ scores were low were identified by the total clinical process as mentally retarded.

3. **Different locales have different proportions of social classes.** One of the most clearly associated factors to mild mental retardation, although we are still not sure what it means, is lower social class. The majority of educable mentally retarded children come from the lower social classes. A section of a large urban area that has a high percentage of lower class families will be expected to produce a higher prevalence of mental retardation. A community with a high percentage of upper middle class or upper class families would produce proportionately fewer cases of mental retardation (Robinson and Robinson, 1976, p. 153).

4. **Different prevalence at different ages.** Tarjan et al. (1973) have observed, as have many others, that prevalence of mild mental retardation differs at various age levels. It is low at the preschool level, high at the school-age level, and then declines during late adolescence or young adulthood. These different prevalence figures seem clearly due to the differences in the environmental demands for intellectual performance at the various ages, with school age being the period of maximum adaptive problems.

The President's Committee on Mental Retardation (1970) observed in its report entitled *The Six-Hour Retarded Child* that some children are retarded (nonadaptive) only between the hours of 9:00 A.M. and 3:00 P.M., while they are in school. The school's activities, requirements, and expectations create an environment in which the child is retarded, but in family or neighborhood settings the child may be adapting adequately and is not considered retarded before 9:00 A.M. or after 3:00 P.M.

Mercer (1973) pointed out that it is no longer possible to anticipate the percentage of children who will be mentally retarded. Although we can estimate with substantial accuracy the number of intellectually subnormal children in a given population, we cannot know what proportion of them will lack sufficient levels of adaptability affecting their ability to function in average environments.

CAUSES OF MENTAL RETARDATION

Is the human brain capable of understanding the human brain? It is more complex than the most advanced computer and much of its function and development still remains a mystery. Yet astonishing advances have been made during the past few decades in the neurosciences, genetics, and biochemistry. Although many advances have been made in the study of neural systems in lower animals, the advances that have made the most difference in our current understanding of the physical causes of mental retardation have been in genetics and biochemistry (Begab, 1981).

Nine major groupings have been identified as causal agents for mental retardation by the American Association on Mental Deficiency (Grossman, 1977):

infection and intoxication
trauma or physical agent
metabolism or nutrition
gross brain disease
unknown prenatal influence
chromosomal abnormality
gestational disorders
retardation following psychiatric disorder
environmental influences

We will discuss only a few of these categories here.

Genetic Disorders

Impressive advances in research in the field of genetics during the past decade have revealed much regarding the mechanisms by which chromosomes and genes influence or determine mental retardation.

The genes are blueprints for the assembly and regulation of proteins, the building blocks of our bodies. Each gene is responsible for a code for a specific sequence of amino acids that the body assembles to form a protein. If even the smallest part of this chain is altered, the entire protein can malfunction. (Plomin, DeFries, and McClearn, 1980, p. 7)

Do certain patterns of genes predetermine certain types of behavior? Are we unwitting automatons moving through life driven by mysterious bursts of chemicals? Not really. No particular gene or protein forces a person to raise a whiskey glass to his or her lips, but some people have a genetic sensitivity to ethanol that may tip the scales in the direction of alcoholism for a frequent drinker. The paths between genes and behavior travel very complex routes and the environmental influence on the final result is almost always an important factor.

The more one learns about the mechanisms of heredity the more remarkable the transmission of genetic material becomes. It seems astonishing that a father and a mother each contribute 23 chromosomes with hundreds of genes resting in just the right location on each chromosome and performing just the right chemical process to produce a new human being. It is not surprising that in many cases the process goes awry. According to Plomin, DeFries, and McClearn (1980), human genetic abnormalities are quite common, involving as many as half of all human fertilizations. These are not noticed in the general population because most genetic abnormalities result in early spontaneous abortion. About one in two hundred fetuses with genetic abnormalities survives until birth, but many of these babies die soon after they are born. The result is that while many deviations from the "normal" pattern occur, most are never seen.

Two specific genetic disorders of the over one hundred that have been identified are noted here. Fortunately, most of these are relatively rare in the society.

Down's Syndrome

One of the more common and easily recognized conditions is *Down's syndrome*. This condition, previously referred to as mongolism because of a superficial resemblance to the Oriental race, was one of the first to be linked to a genetic abnormality (Lejeune, Gautier, and Turpin, 1959). People with this condition have forty-seven chromosomes instead of the normal forty-six. A picture of the abnormal chromosome is shown in Figure 4.2. The *karyotype* or prepared picture of chromosomal patterns indicates the presence of an extra chromosome in pair 21. Such a condition leads to moderate or mild mental retardation, along with a variety of hearing, skeletal, and heart problems. The presence of Down's syndrome is also related to maternal age, with the incidence increasing significantly in children born to mothers 35 years of age or older. According to current figures, over 50 percent of Down's syndrome children are

FIGURE 4.2
Karyotype of a Down's (Trisomy 21) Female

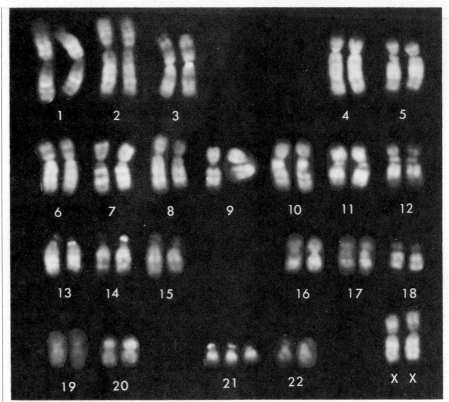

Source: Courtesy of Dr. Irene Uchida, McMaster University Medical Centre, Ontario, Canada.

born to mothers over 35. The exact reason why advancing age should be related to this condition is not clearly known at this time. It should not be concluded, however, that the mother is the exclusive cause of the extra chromosome. The father contributes the extra chromosome in 20 to 25 percent of the cases (Abroms and Bennett, 1980).

Another form of chromosomal abnormality causing Down's syndrome results from *translocations*; the child has 46 chromosomes, but a pair of one is broken and the broken part is fused to another chromosome. A third type is called *mosaic Down's syndrome*. The latter two kinds of chromosomal abnormalities account for only 4 to 5 percent of Down's syndrome in children (Lilienfield, 1969). The incidence of Down's syndrome is 1 to 2 births out of 1,000.

Until the last decade the diagnosis of Down's syndrome, as well as a wide variety of other pathological conditions, was not made until the birth of the baby or later. The development of a new diagnostic technique, amniocentesis, has opened the possibility of much earlier diagnosis. *Amniocentesis* is a procedure for drawing some of the amniotic fluid from the pregnant woman. Since cells from the fetus are found in that fluid, the cells can be analyzed for chromosomal abnormality by karyotyping. Thus, high-risk parents can know early in a pregnancy that they will or will not have a handicapped child.

The medical procedures described in the preceding have generated a moral issue of major consequences. Should the individual parents have the right to terminate a pregnancy, given the information that they will have a handicaped child? The controversy over that issue has resulted in limited use of the amniocentesis procedure.

Phenylketonuria

Another condition caused by genetic irregularities is *phenylketonuria (PKU)*, which is a single gene defect that can produce severe retardation and has been responsible for about 1 percent of institutionalized mentally retarded individuals. Extensive biochemical studies have revealed that in children with PKU mental retardation is caused by the inability of the gene structure to break down a particular chemical, *phenylalanine*, which is accumulated at high levels in the blood, resulting in severe damage to the developing brain. Although this condition is clearly a result of a genetic disorder, it is now possible to prevent mental retardation if a diet low in phenylalanine is provided early in the developing years of the child. We have, therefore, the phenomenon of a genetic problem in which the more disastrous consequences of the condition can be prevented by an environmental intervention.

Polygenic Inheritance

While the single gene effect has a dramatic impact on the development of the individual children, many human traits such as skin color, hair color, height, and general body build are controlled by the action of many genes operating together. Those results that merge from the interaction of numerous genes are called *polygenic* inherited characteristics. Intellectual development is generally assumed to be the result of complex polygenic inheritance, which, when combined with certain environmental conditions, can result in mental retardation. Since environmental conditions are involved, many professionals have tried to change the environment in order to affect mental development, as we shall see later in this chapter.

Toxic Agents and Infectious Diseases

Toxic agents ingested by the mother during pregnancy or by the child may disturb the internal biochemical balance. Viruses or germs in the form of infectious diseases can invade the body and cause long-lasting damage to the central nervous system beyond the course of the original disease.

Fetal Alcohol Syndrome

Heavy drinking by the mother during pregnancy has been identified as a possible cause of mental retardation. Although a precise threshold of safety cannot be specified, as little as three ounces of pure alcohol can be harmful to the fetus (Nitowsky, 1979). There is no doubt that alcohol crosses the placental barrier, remains in the fetus's bloodstream, and depresses central nervous system functioning in the fetus. Whether the actual damage is caused by the alcohol itself or in combination with other risk factors (such as smoking) is not clear (Streissguth et al., 1980).

Lead Poisoning

Lead that is found in some paints, particularly in poor housing areas where the paint is flaking, can also cause mental retardation in young children who often place the paint in their mouths. Apparently the lead can cross from the blood into the brain, thus resulting in mental retardation.

Viruses

Rubella, or German measles, can cause mental retardation if the mother contracts the disease during the first three months of pregnancy. *Encephalitis* is caused by a virus that produces high fever and possible brain cell destruction with long-term effects. These conditions are merely illustrative of a large number of other conditions, fortunately rare, each of which has the potential for producing mental retardation.

Environmental Factors

For many years we have known that there is a close association between poverty or membership in the lower social classes and the prevalence of mild mental retardation. Understanding that this relationship exists is one thing; explaining the reason for it is something else. Many investigators and observers have suggested that the limited environmental opportunities available to minority group or lower class youngsters are partly responsible for the developmental delays noted. But Shonkoff (1982) has indicated that poor and minority group children are not only the victims of social discrimination; they also carry a disproportionate burden of biological vulnerability that is largely related to the increased health risks of poverty. The brain, regardless of its genetic potential, is subjected to a variety of potentially damaging influences throughout its prenatal, perinatal, and postnatal development that can have adverse effects on its ultimate functioning. Shonkoff noted that malnutrition, lead intoxication, fetal alcohol syndrome, and other factors occur with greater frequency among poor and minority populations. Birch and Gussow (1970) commented that "almost every complication of pregnancy, labor, delivery, and the perinatal period which is potentially damaging to children is excessively prevalent among economically depressed populations and particularly among those further handicapped by ethnic or racial differences" (p. 46).

We have come to recognize more and more that some of these environmental factors operate in combinations to the detriment of the child. The presence of illness by itself may not be a serious problem, but illness combined with environmental limitations can, and often does, become a problem. Malnutrition and otitis media—an infection of the middle ear—or even the presence of certain unfavorable temperamental variables in the child can be negatively compounded when they occur in an impoverished environment (Sameroff and Chandler, 1975).

DEVELOP-MENTAL PROFILES

Figure 4.3 shows the typical developmental patterns of an educable mentally retarded child and a trainable mentally retarded child. Bob and Carol are both 10 years of age and the patterns revealed in the figure are not unusual for children of their intellectual development, although there are great individual differences from one child to another within this group.

In the case of Bob, the educable mentally retarded child, his physical profile, represented by height, weight, and motor coordination, does not differ markedly from others in his age group and would not set him apart from his peers. However, in the areas of academic ability—reading, arithmetic, and spelling—Bob is performing between the second- and third-grade level, falling more

**FIGURE 4.3
Profiles of Two
Mentally Retarded
Children**

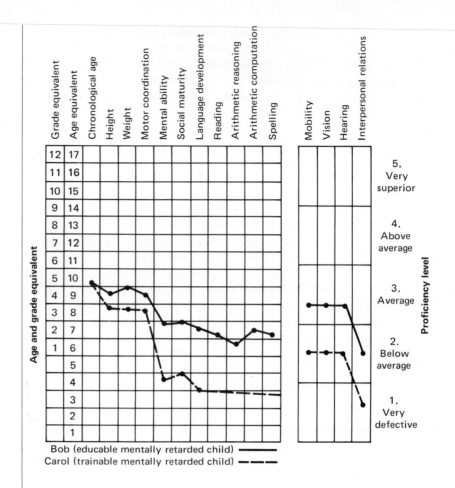

Bob (educable mentally retarded child) ————
Carol (trainable mentally retarded child) — — —

than two grades below his age group. Depending on the rest of the class and the levels at which they are performing, Bob would fall either at the bottom of the regular class group or would be set apart as a truly different youngster for his low performance. Bob's vision, hearing, and mobility are average, but he is having problems with his interpersonal relationships. He is quick to take offense and fights on the playground. In the classroom he has a tendency to interrupt other children at their work and, at times, wanders aimlessly around the classroom when given an individual assignment. All of these characteristics add up to a situation where Bob has few friends, although he is tolerated by his classmates. With special help he is able to maintain a marginal performance within the regular class.

Carol, the trainable mentally retarded child, has a much more serious adaptive problem. In addition to having the mental ability level of a 4-year-old (IQ score in the 40s), Carol shows, as is typical of a Down's syndrome child, poor motor coordination and also some minor vision and hearing problems that tend to complicate an already difficult set of problems from an educational standpoint. Although Carol does not have an unpleasant personality and is generally even-tempered, her physical appearance and her slowness in thought have resulted in her not being well accepted by her agemates. The developmental pattern in Figure 4.3 shows that Carol's academic performance is well below first grade level; indeed, at maturity Carol's reading and arithmetic skills are not likely to exceed the level of first or second grade. This is not to say that Carol is unable to learn some important skills or concepts in an educational setting; rather, that the standard academic program is clearly inappropriate for her and some very special kinds of experiences presented by a trained teacher are indicated if Carol is to develop her existing abilities to their maximum potential.

CHARACTERISTICS OF MENTALLY RETARDED CHILDREN

Educable Mentally Retarded Children

The nature of the special programming for the educable mentally retarded child should be shaped in some fashion by the characteristics those children reveal that distinguish them from their agemates. The key distinguishing feature of educable retarded children is that they are failing in their school work. The academic performance of educable mentally retarded children such as Bob can lag by two to five grades, particularly in language-related subjects such as reading and language arts. The question often asked is whether other intellectual, social, or physical characteristics besides the slow rate of academic learning may complicate the picture. The literature on this topic has not been totally consistent and reflects the diversity of children within this category.

Family Background

It is relatively easy to obtain reliable information on an individual mentally retarded child such as Bob but much more difficult to obtain a general portrait of mentally retarded children. How can we be sure that our observations are representative of a general group of children? Because of these concerns, studies that view the entire landscape of mental retardation rather than a select corner are highly valued.

Richardson (1981) described a study in which a group of investigators attempted to find all of the mentally retarded children in a major city in Scotland. Of course, the study was limited by whatever the unique characteristics of Scotland may be. However, Richardson and his colleagues were not content to study only those retarded children found in the special education program, but gave group IQ tests to all youngsters ages 7 through 9 and followed up with an individual assessment of intelligence for those who scored low on the group test. In this way, they were able to obtain a reasonable portrait of all mentally retarded children in one age group within that city. From that information Richardson tried to discern particular characteristics of families with a mildly retarded child that set them apart from other families in that community and neighborhood who did not have retarded children. The mildly retarded children were overrepresented in families with the following characteristics:

environmental factors

1. five or more children
2. living in the least desirable housing areas in the city
3. living in more crowded homes as measured by a person:room ratio of two or more
4. the mother's occupation before marriage was a semiskilled or unskilled manual job

In ways still not fully understood, those combinations of characteristics are more likely to produce a mildly mentally retarded child. Richardson also found that, as was true in earlier studies, when the mildly retarded children grew to young adults they often were able to survive in the community with little or no special services.

Physical and Motor Abilities

A few studies have been conducted on the motor proficiency and physical education achievements of the educable retarded. These studies (Francis and Rarick, 1960; Rarick and Widdop, 1970) indicate that in motor proficiency the average scores on physical tests of mentally retarded children are inferior to the average scores of children with average IQs. Studies on the effects of physical education programs in improving motor proficiency have shown positive results (Soloman and Pargle, 1967). In height and weight most educable retarded children resemble normal children. Remember that we cannot generalize from group results to individual children. In height or weight some mentally retarded children are superior to some average and gifted children.

Since educable mentally retarded children have a slightly higher incidence of vision, hearing, and neurological problems, some tendency to poorer physical and motor abilities would be expected, although, as indicated, individual mentally retarded children might show outstanding physical and athletic skills.

Memory and Attention

Since limited intellectual development defines the category of mental retardation along with maladaptive behavior, it is no surprise that retarded children perform less well on a major component of intellectual behavior such as *memory*. However, it is important for educators and scientists to probe more deeply to understand the nature of the memory defect. Poor recall is the beginning of the puzzle, not the end. For example, is poor memory in the retarded child attributable to an inability to attend to objects or ideas, or hold information in short-term memory, or transfer information from short-term memory to long-term memory, or use effective strategies to recover the appropriate information from the memory storage?

Available research information indicates that the inability to pay attention and an inability to transfer from short-term to long-term memory are most important.

One of the factors influencing memory is the ability to pay attention, to stay on task. Unless the student maintains a focus on the task at hand, he or she will have trouble learning, retarded or not. Krupski (1979) designed a study to test whether educable mentally retarded students between the ages of 9 and 12 remained on task as well as a comparison group of children matched for age and sex but not ability. The mentally retarded children were in two special classes and the children of average ability were in the regular classroom. All the children were observed during periods when they were expected to work on their own. The results of the comparisons indicated that the retarded students did indeed spend more time off task, primarily through peer interaction and out-of-seat behavior, than did the comparison group. Many believe that such inattention may stem from progressive failure in academic tasks and consequent discouragement and dislike for those tasks.

These results, taken in the natural classroom setting, confirm laboratory results and indicate a special problem for the teacher in getting mentally retarded students to focus on their lessons.

deficiencies:
a) attention span
b) short-term to long-term.

inattention because of failure.

Language Acquisition and Use

One characteristic commonly regarded as typical of mentally retarded children is delayed language development. We do not know how much of the language delay is due to, or how much is a result of, low cognitive abilities. Does the development of language in the mentally retarded follow the same sequence of development as in normal children but at a slower rate, or are there qualitative differences in the development of language in the mentally retarded? There appears to be enough evidence to support both positions, in part.

Semmel, Barritt, and Bennett (1970) studied institutionalized and noninstitutionalized educable mentally retarded subjects and compared their linguistic performance with two groups of average children. They found that the educable mentally retarded children with average IQ scores of 70 were lower in language skills than normal children, even when mental age was taken into account. That is, a mentally retarded child of 10 with a mental age score of 7 years was still not performing as well in language development as the average 7-year-old. The researchers concluded that there may not be only a difference in rate but a qualitative difference as well.

Cromer (1974) reviewed the studies on receptive language of the mentally retarded and concluded that (1) retarded children develop language at a slower pace; (2) subnormal children are more delayed in language age than in mental age; and (3) poor cognitive abilities, such as limited short-term memory span, may be responsible for the linguistic delay.

A clue as to how the issue may be resolved is shown by another study that revealed a rate difference in language development at early ages and a qualitative difference at later ages. Naremore and Dever (1975) collected five-minute speech samples of normal and retarded children at each age level from 6 to 10. The samples were analyzed for such linguistic properties as subject elaboration, subordination index, and relative clause index, as well as for such basic linguistic items as the number of words, sentences, pauses, repeats, and so on. The retarded children were most deficient in using complex clauses and subject elaboration. That is an important communication deficit because it limits the kind and amount of information the retarded child can communicate to others, particularly when sequences of activities are called for.

An example of the differences between the expressive language of normal children and that of educable retarded children is given in the following samples as two 10-year-old children describe the same TV program that they saw (Naremore and Dever, 1975):

weak in complex clauses and subject elaboration.

Normal 10-year-old

Every time he tried to start something they all started to play their instruments and wouldn't do anything so Lucy said that they needed a Christmas tree, a pink one, for the Christmas queen, but when Charlie Brown went out he found that there were lots of them that were pink and green and blue, but there was just one little one.

Educable retarded 10-year-old

Charlie Brown didn't seem to have the Christmas spirit *and* so Linus said he should get involved *and* there's this little doctor place *and* Charlie Brown went over there *and* that's what Lucy told him to.

The retarded child's production is not only sparser than the normal child's, with limited content, but is also meager in syntactical form. The retarded child depends heavily on *and* as a connective and lacks the ability to economically impose temporal or hierarchical structure on events, unlike the normal child.

Personal and Social Characteristics

Retarded children often show special problems in personal and social characteristics. Such problems relate, in part, to the reactions of others to their condition and also to their history of past failure to reach the level of performance expected by others. Characteristics such as limited attention span and low frustration tolerance can be ascribed to the previous lack of success experienced by the mentally retarded individual. Whether the intellectual limitations of the mentally retarded child and adult also limit their social adjustment is still uncertain.

personal characteristics reflect history of frustration.

The progressive way in which experience influences behavior is summarized by Kauffman and Payne (1975):

1. Mentally retarded individuals typically experience more failure than normal children and therefore develop greater generalized expectancies for failure. The predisposition to expect failure tends to cause retarded children to avoid situations where failure is likely.
2. Retarded children enter novel situations with performances that are usually depressed even below their mental ability.
3. Retarded children have fewer tendencies than normals to increase their output following a mild failure. (p. 164)

Those findings are encouraging to the educator because if some experiences can create the problem, then other experiences can help reduce it. If one can reduce the number of failure experiences, create novel experiences in which the child succeeds, and present successful models of behavior, one can improve the poor attitudes that progressively prevent the mildly retarded child from making full use of his or her limited abilities.

Vocational Adjustment

There is a widespread belief that young adults who are mildly retarded, once released from the intellectual demands of the school, can be marginally self-sufficient in the community through a variety of unskilled, semiskilled, and service positions. Numerous follow-up studies have suggested as much. When mildly retarded adults, who as children were subjects in research studies, were found in their communities, many were adapting at least at a marginal level. The results of these investigations have led to the following conclusions regarding possible occupational adjustment:

1. The educable mentally retarded can learn to do unskilled and semiskilled work at the adult level.
2. Any failure in unskilled occupational tasks is generally related to personal, social, and interpersonal characteristics rather than to inability to execute the task assigned.
3. Employment records of the educable mentally retarded show that approximately 80 percent eventually adjust to occupations of an unskilled or semiskilled nature and partially or totally support themselves.

However, these studies (Channing, 1932; Kennedy, 1948; Charles, 1953; Baller, Charles, and Miller, 1966) are twenty to fifty years old and more current information is needed that is relevant to a rapidly changing and shrinking job market.

Brickey and Campbell (1981) have reported on a major project to employ retarded youth and adults in fast-food establishments. McDonald's restaurants normally expect an annual employee turnover rate as high as 300 to 400 percent when they typically hire high school or college students. McDonald's participated in a job-training program of the mentally retarded in which seventeen retarded young adults were placed. They found that the majority of such employees could successfully handle most of the tasks required of fast-food help. The turnover rate for these employees was only 40 percent, compared to the turnover rate of 175 percent for regular employees. According to Brickey and Campbell, the project demonstrated that McDonald's profited from their hiring of mentally retarded adults, who provided the restaurants with reliable employees and a lower than average turnover rate. In addition, the mentally retarded youth experienced natural feelings of accomplishment and a sense of independence that accompanied their successful employment.

Another report by Foss and Peterson (1981) has revealed the most relevant characteristics to job tenure according to the reports of job placement personnel. Those elements receiving the highest ratings were following supervisor's instructions, responding appropriately to supervisor criticism or correction, refraining from exhibiting bizarre or irritating behavior, cooperating with coworkers on the job, and working independently of direct supervision. Items considered less relevant were maintaining a sense of humor and interacting appropriately with coworkers in off-task settings. It is obvious from such ratings that part of the training program that can be effective with mildly or moderately mentally retarded individuals is their ability to work in harmony with the supervisors and coworkers.

A review by Brickey, Brauning, and Campbell (1982) has shown encouraging success in competitive job placements for mildly mentally retarded students. They found that 48 percent of those who were in a Projects With Industry program were subsequently placed in competitive jobs. One of the key elements to success in this program appears to be the degree to which the job is sufficiently structured by the employer so that retarded students understand what is expected of them. Sowers, Thompson, and Connis (1979) found a 70 percent success rate for mentally retarded individuals when the employer had a written job description and a zero percent success rate when the employer did not have one. The intelligence score within the mentally retarded range did not seem to mean as much for eventual job success as did other factors relating to the structure of the job itself and the ability of the employee to work cooperatively with the supervisor.

Trainable Mentally Retarded Children   There are numerous differences in the general characteristics of children who are labeled trainable mentally retarded, as opposed to those who are educable mentally retarded. One of the most fundamental differences is that practically all children who are trainable mentally retarded have had a biological insult that has created the condition of retardation, whereas in educable retarded children a combination of polygenic heredity factors and limited environmental stimulation appear to be the fundamental cause. According to current standards, the *lowest* intelligence test score that can be obtained by a child who has no direct injury to the central nervous system is in

primarily biological cause.

the range of 50 to 60 IQ. Any score less than that automatically causes specialists to think of metabolic disorders, central nervous system damage, and many different genetic anomalies. The wide variety of causes and side effects that appear in trainable mentally retarded children contribute to a great diversity of characteristics in these children.

Family Background

The previous section on the characteristics of the educable retarded child identified a high proportion of lower socioeconomic levels in the family background. However, the variety of accidents that can cause metabolic and genetic or neurological injury indicate that the condition of trainable mental retardation could happen to anyone. Much of the strength of the parents' movement to support programs for the mentally retarded has come from relatively well-to-do and well-educated parents who have had these accidents occur in their families.

In addition to developmental delays that can be observed in young retarded children, there is some indication (Morgan, 1979) that in some children the delay increases at a sharper rate when the child reaches school age. In other words, the IQ score of a retarded child may be in the 50s during the preschool years, but will often drop to the 30s or 40s when the child reaches school age, thereby suggesting a continued deceleration of development. This may be due in part to the increasing tendency of IQ tests to measure verbal and language concepts when the child reaches school age. Unlike preschool measures of intelligence, IQ tests for school-age children do not emphasize simple perceptual matching and grouping—tasks that may be easier for the trainable retarded child to master.

Physical and Motor Abilities

Since the majority of children who fall within the trainable range of mental retardation share some form of central nervous system disorder or damage, problems involving coordination, gait, and fine motor skills can be expected (see Rie and Rie, 1980). A high prevalence of motor problems in children with various metabolic disorders has been noted as well. Even when a definitive neurological diagnosis of cerebral palsy may not be possible in many cases, children who are trainable mentally retarded appear to be awkward and clumsy and to walk with a stiff, robotlike gait.

Programs like the Special Olympics, designed to encourage participation of mentally retarded children and youth in sports and a variety of physical activities, have indicated that even where retarded children have identifiable physical and motor problems, practice and encouragement can significantly upgrade skills in these areas (Shriver, 1980).

Language Acquisition

Damage to the brain can have a devastating effect on a child. Even if the development of a child is only one-half of normal (scoring at a level of age 3 on tests while having a life age of 6), language development may be more seriously impaired. *Aphasia* is the name for an absence of language presumably due to injury to the language centers of the cerebral cortex. Few children have such an extreme disorder, but there are suspicions that partial damage to the brain can negatively influence the development of language skills in many cases.

In addition to brain injury, there are other associated handicapping conditions that can affect language development. Downs (1980) reported finding an unusually high percentage of Down's syndrome children with mild hearing loss presumably associated

aphasia - injury to language centers - absence of language.

Programs like the Special Olympics help mentally retarded children improve their physical and motor skills. (Photo: Courtesy of Special Olympics, Inc.)

with a susceptibility to otitis media, an infection of the middle ear. Such problems may contribute to the poor language shown by many Down's syndrome children.

Personal and Social Characteristics

Many of the characteristics of the trainable mentally retarded, in terms of social and behavior traits, would seem to stem rather directly from the cognitive problem or from the basic cause of the condition in the first place. If the child has limited language capabilities and has consequently failed in response to expectations, then his or her behavior is likely to be inflexible and repetitious with a certain amount of passivity. This condition may reveal a relatively simple or uncomplicated emotional life characterized by rapid swings to the positive or negative side depending on circumstances. The possibility that central nervous system damage has created the retardation in the first place may tend to explain a certain propensity to hyperactivity and impulsivity and regression to earlier more childlike behaviors in stressful situations (Rie and Rie, 1980).

Another major influence on social behavior of trainable retarded children can be the nature of the environment in which they find themselves. Many of these children are found in institutions or group homes, environments that are powerful shapers of social behavior. Today there is a belief that some of the atypical behavior often associated with the condition of mental retardation may be caused, in fact, by the special environments of the institution itself.

Suppose you were raised in a bedroom with one hundred other individuals, had a rotating list of adult caretakers (none of whom is present more than eight hours), and never had the experience of going to the store, exploring a neighborhood, or doing many of the things that young children do. You might have difficulty adapting to the community outside the institution. The inability of such youngsters to adapt to their community can be partly attributed to the environment rather than to the condition of mental retardation.

In summary, the child who is moderately retarded is likely to have specific problems across a broad spectrum of developmental characteristics. In some cases, the family or social environment tends to make these problems more severe.

environment has influence on progress

PREVENTION OF MILD MENTAL RETARDATION

While the causes of moderate and severe mental retardation are generally attributed to a variety of neurological and metabolic insults, there has been a growing acceptance of the idea that mild mental retardation might be partially due to poor environmental conditions. Many psychologists and educators have reasoned that if environmental conditions can create mental retardation, then perhaps changing and improving the social and learning environment can prevent mental retardation or lessen its more severe effects. A second assumption—intervention at an early age would facilitate the prevention process—guided the work of many persons trying to help potentially retarded children. These two assumptions set in motion a collection of studies attempting to improve the intellectual and social development of young children; some of the major studies and their findings are noted briefly here.

Skeels + Dye

One of the earliest studies was done by Skeels and Dye (1939) who took youngsters identified as mentally retarded from an orphanage and placed them in a state institution for the mentally retarded where each was assigned to a different ward with the older patients. The children received a great deal of individual attention from the older retarded women and the attendants. These children consequently showed a remarkable gain in intelligence test scores—on the average of twenty-seven points. At the same time, a comparison group from an orphanage, where little attention was provided, dropped an average of twenty-six IQ points.

Skeels (1966) followed these children twenty-one years later. This was an important step because it was necessary to discover whether the children in the experimental group would be able to maintain the gains made at an early age or if they would lapse back into a retarded pattern of development when the special experience was concluded. Skeels was able to find all twenty-five subjects from the experimental and comparison groups and reported the following results:

1. The thirteen children in the experimental group were found to be self-supporting, and none were wards of any institution, public or private.
2. In the contrast group of twelve children, one died in adolescence following residence in an institution for the mentally retarded, and four were wards of institutions.

✳
AMAZING

3. The median grade in school completed by the thirteen experimental children was twelfth grade. The median grade for the contrast group was less than third grade.

The results of the studies were provocative and encouraged others to pursue this issue. In a series of studies on young mentally retarded children, Kirk (1958, 1965) found similar results. In one study, fifteen institutionalized children who received special training were compared to twelve children in the institution who received no special training. The children who received the training improved substantially in mental and social maturity. The control group during the same time showed decreases in their rate of intellectual development and social adjustment. In a similar experiment in the community, twelve children from inadequate homes who attended a special community preschool for the mentally retarded were also compared with their siblings living in the same home but without the benefits of preschool education. While two out of three of the children in the experimental group showed gains in their rate of mental development, the majority of children in the control group only maintained or dropped in their rate of social and mental growth. These studies indicated that when compensatory education was provided increases in the rate of social and cognitive development could be observed.

In another study called the Milwaukee Project (Heber and Garber, 1975; Heber, 1977), the investigators chose families who lived in the most economically deprived neighborhoods and whose mothers had measured borderline intellectual ability. This time intervention began during the child's first year of life and the mother also received some occupational training and strengthening of academic skills. Children in the program who had been predicted at risk for mental retardation were still performing at an average or above average level at age 9 and substantially above the performance of the comparison group after age 9.

A similar all-day stimulation program which was conducted in North Carolina started with the birth of children from low-income families in rural and small town settings. Children from these families were randomly assigned to experimental and control groups. Both groups received nutritional supplements, but only the experimental group received systematic educational stimulation. Significant differences were found in measured intelligence at age 5 between the group treated and the comparison group (Ramey and Haskins, 1981).

One of the limitations placed on the significance of such studies is whether, in the long developmental processes, gains start to erode. A major attempt to answer that question was made by researchers who followed the progress of children from twelve of the most famous preschool intervention projects, five years or more after the projects were completed (Lazar and Darlington, 1982). The majority of the children were 3 or 4 years of age when first studied. From their synthesis of follow-up results, the authors drew the following conclusions:

1. Children from all types of preschool programs (home-based, center-based, and so on) surpassed their control groups for up to

three years after the end of the program on measures of cognitive abilities. After that, the experimental and control groups no longer showed major differences.

2. Fewer experimental than control children were assigned to special education classes at a later date.
3. Fewer experimental children were held back a grade or more, compared to the control children.

Thus, while cognitive gains were less visible over time, increased academic efficiency would seem to remain.

Susan Gray, from the perspective of twenty years of experience, summarized the early overenthusiasm of educators and the realization of the important role played by the social environment in which the child is immersed (Gray, Klaus, and Ramsey, 1981):

In 1962, when we began the study, we thought naively that it was possible to design a program that would be strong enough to offset the early handicaps that these children experienced. Our naivete was short-lived. It became readily apparent that the best we could hope to do was to provide a basis on which future schooling could build. . . . We could do little to help meet the pressing demands of living in poor housing with large families, low income, and all the associated ills. . . . Preschool is not an inoculation whereby the individual is rendered forever after immune to the effects of an adversive environment. (p. 216)

The message now seems clear. Projects with strong staff and clear objectives can make a difference in intellectual and social growth. Such programs are not, as Gray appropriately noted, a cure-all for children in the face of continuing poverty, hunger, and social disorganization.

EDUCATIONAL ADAPTATIONS FOR EDUCABLE MENTALLY RETARDED

Bob, the educable mentally retarded child described in the earlier part of this chapter, and students like him are now the subject of major concern in the public schools of the United States. This concern focuses not so much on *how* Bob is to be taught or what he is to be taught as it does on *where* he is to be taught. *Mainstreaming*, the placement of exceptional children in the regular classroom, has become a major issue. Vigorous discussions continue regarding whether Bob should be placed in the regular class program, in some kind of special program apart from the regular classroom, or in some combination of the two such as in the part-time resource room placement.

Wherever Bob is, he has problems that will require the school to make some major program adaptations. You will recall from Figure 4.3 that Bob is two or three grades behind in reading and arithmetic and is having some interpersonal adjustment problems. Regardless of where he is placed, Bob's special goals might resemble the following:

Goals

1. to learn the basic skills taught in the elementary school, including reading, writing, arithmetic, language arts, and manual skills, to the limits of the child's capacity
2. to develop habits of physical hygiene through a practical program of health and sex education
3. to become socially competent—to get along with peers through programs of social experience
4. to become emotionally secure and independent in the school and home through the organization of instruction that includes successful experiences and a positive self-concept
5. to become an adequate member of the home and community through a curriculum designed to emphasize home and community membership
6. to develop wholesome leisure-time activities through an educational program that teaches enjoyment of recreational and leisure-time pursuits
7. to develop occupational competence through prevocational, career, and vocational training and guidance as a part of the school experience so that the individual may eventually become partially or totally self-supporting in some productive activity

One of the major legislative initiatives mentioned in Chapter 1 was the Education for All Handicapped Children Act (PL 94–142). This law has had an important effect on the education of educable mentally retarded children in the public school system. It has proposed a number of standards that local and state educational agencies are required to meet regarding the placement and education of educable and trainable mentally retarded children, and has stated that mental retardation is to be defined in terms of intellectual functioning, adaptive behavior, and school performance.

Learning Environment

Mainstreaming

A major shift in emphasis on where children like Bob are educated has occurred in the past decade in the direction of keeping Bob and children like him in the regular class program, if at all possi-

Panel Cautions Against Misplacing Minority Pupils in Special Education

Racial imbalance in special education programs, which has fueled charges of discrimination in many school districts, does not by itself pose a major problem unless the disproportion results from improper assessment procedures and inadequate instructional practices, according to a panel convened by the research branch of the National Academy of Sciences.

The panel's report was commissioned by the Education Department, which has repeatedly documented the overrepresentation of minority groups in special education.

In 1978, for example, the department's office for civil rights (OCR) found that black children represented 38 percent of the students in classes for the educable mentally retarded, although they represented only about 16 percent of all elementary and secondary students.

The academy's Panel on Selection and Placement of Students in Programs for the Mentally Retarded based its conclusions on a review of the biennial OCR surveys, other existing research, and its own case studies.

In a published account of its three-year study, entitled *"Placing Children in Special Education: A Strategy for Equity,"* the panel argues strongly for the improvement of current assessment procedures and educational services, rather than "remedies that would directly eliminate disproportion in placement rates." To reduce educational practices that may contribute to racial imbalance in special education, the panel recommended that school districts adopt teaching approaches tailored specifically to the needs of students.

The purpose of student assessments, the panel contends in its report, is to improve instruction and learning. "We believe that better assessment and a closer link between assessment and instruction will in fact reduce disproportion, because minority children have disproportionately been the victims of poor instruction," the report says.

The panel also recommended that OCR alter its biennial survey of school districts to include less ambiguous questions and more precise information about special education enrollments.

The panel's recommendations have not been formally reviewed by OCR, which is responsible for monitoring school districts' compliance with civil rights laws.

Since 1970, OCR's national surveys of elementary and secondary schools have shown high minority representation in classes for the educable mentally retarded (EMR).

The survey's findings have often resulted in discrimination charges against school officials because of the disproportionate numbers of minority children and males in special education classes.

At the center of the controversy has been the use of IQ tests, which civil rights groups and other advocacy organizations have termed racially biased.

In its review of the OCR surveys and other studies, the academy's panel found insufficient evidence to support such charges and questioned the wisdom of abandoning both IQ tests and EMR classes. The panel concluded that such action would not solve the problem of educational failure or unequal treatment of minority children.

"Simple solutions that lead only to the reduction of ethnic or sex disproportion are misdirected," the panel warned in its report. "The focus should be on fundamental educational problems underlying EMR placement—on the valid assessment of educational needs and on the provision of appropriate, high-quality service."

Turning its attention primarily to the over-representation of minorities in EMR classes, the panel noted that such classes are "perceived as programs offering few valid educational services, channeling students into tracks that impede their return to regular programs while isolating them from the regular classroom peers."

By contrast, the panel pointed out that the disproportion of minority children in compensatory education programs has not been challenged because the remedial services are designed to help them achieve levels attained by students in regular programs.

In reaching its conclusion that OCR should revise future survey questionnaires, the panel noted a need to gather more information on special education programs in small school districts and in those located in the South-east, where high degrees of racial imbalance have consistently been reported.

Wayne H. Holtzman of the Hogg Foundation for Mental Health at the University of Texas, who chaired the fifteen-member panel, said that the changes recommended for the OCR questionnaire would lead to "less distortion in interpreting disproportion and the quality of education as it exists in local school districts."

Instead of relying solely on IQ tests, according to Mr. Holtzman, school districts should use intelligence tests in combination with other instruments to determine appropriate placement and instruction.

Referring to the complexity of the federal law protecting handicapped children, Mr. Holtzman said that many school districts are having difficulty "matching the letter of the law." He said the law was "well thought out" when it was drafted but difficult to put into effect because some school districts lack the resources.

The panel's report can be purchased for $18.95 from the National Academy Press, 2101 Constitution Avenue, N.W., Washington, D.C. 20418.

SOURCE: Susan Foster, "Panel Cautions Against Misplacing Minority Pupils in Special Ed.," *Education Week*, August 25, 1982, p. 9. Reprinted by permission.

ble. Two major reasons for this shift are (1) the lack of evidence for the advantages of special classes and (2) the identification of many minority children as educable mentally retarded with consequent concern for a type of racial segregation that might appear in special classes for the retarded.

Budoff and Gottlieb (1976) compared the achievement of educable mentally retarded pupils in a special class and those in a regular class who had resource room help. No differences in reading and arithmetic achievement were found between the groups after one year. Similar nondefinitive results were obtained in studies by

Walker (1972) and Bradfield et al. (1973), leading to a conclusion that mainstreaming, at least, does not seem to harm the mentally retarded student in a cognitive or academic sense.

Does mainstreaming facilitate social acceptance for the mildly retarded? The earlier studies on the relatively poor social acceptance of mentally retarded children in the regular class (Johnson and Kirk, 1950) seem confirmed by the mainstreaming literature. Generally speaking, the retarded student is not well accepted by nonretarded students, whether they are in the special class or the regular class (Gottlieb, Semmel, and Veldman, 1978). Comments from educable mentally retarded pupils indicate that those who are integrated have a more positive attitude toward school and a higher self-concept than segregated children (Budoff and Gottlieb, 1976). The integrated class setting also seems to result in better prosocial behavior and less random behavior (Gampel, Gottlieb, and Harrison, 1974).

However

Gottlieb (1981) completed a review of the mainstreaming data on the mentally retarded with the following summary comments:

N.B.

> More disturbing is the lack of clearly conceptualized and articulated goals for mainstreaming education. At this particular time, special educators are more involved with placing children in the least restrictive environment than with educating them in the least restrictive environment. . . . The assumptions that propelled special education professionals away from segregated classes and toward mainstreamed education have not, for the most part, been realized. There is little evidence that EMR [educable mentally retarded] children's social adjustment is superior in mainstreamed settings or that children achieve more in mainstreamed classes. (pp. 121–122)

At the present time, there is little reason to believe that placement of the educable mentally retarded student with his or her agemates in a regular education setting without detailed special programming will produce favorable results.

Despite some current unhappiness about mainstreaming and its difficulties, it is highly likely that for the foreseeable future at least part of the education of the educable mentally retarded student will take place in the regular classroom.

Special Classes

Over the past forty years a number of studies have attempted to document whether it is more effective to place mildly retarded children in special classes or to leave them in the regular grades. This was done primarily by comparing the relative growth and achievement of educable retarded children assigned to special classes with a similar group of retarded children remaining in the regular grades. The results of such studies are not clear and, in some cases contradictory, but the basic findings seem to be as follows.

INTELLIGENCE There seems to be little evidence to suggest that educable retarded children placed in special classes improve their IQ scores when compared to similar children in the regular program (Goldstein, Moss, and Jordan, 1965; Cegelka and Tyler, 1970).

EDUCATIONAL ACHIEVEMENT There is some evidence to suggest that educable mentally retarded children in the lower IQ range of that category (60–70) tend to make better educational progress in special classes, while those at the upper levels of the category (70–80) tend to make better educational progress in the regular grades. Heller (1982) has summarized the literature as follows:

The academic achievement of children in special classes was found to be lower than the achievement of children remaining in regular classrooms, whereas social adjustment was often lower for children remaining in regular classrooms. (p. 264)

SOCIAL ADAPTABILITY Educable retarded children seem to be isolated and rejected by normal peer groups in the regular classes. However, those retarded children who remain in the regular grades have higher self-concepts than the retarded children who are placed in segregated classes. At the secondary level the youngsters in the classes for the educable retarded become increasingly conscious of their lower status within the school system and become resentful of the class itself (Jones, 1972).

SELF-ADJUSTMENT There is a moderate amount of evidence to suggest that the educable retarded child is under less tension in the special class than in the regular grades (Welch, 1967).

Overall the advantages that accrued to the children in the special classes in these studies were less than special educators hoped for. The studies also have revealed that special classes gradually became the dumping ground for problem children from the regular classes. Finally, there was the strong suggestion that special classes for the retarded were being used as a disguised form of segregation of minority group children. A strong movement in the late 1960s and early 1970s to do away with special classes and to return children to the regular grades was sparked by Dunn (1968), who stated, "A better education than special class placement is needed for socioculturally deprived children with mild learning problems who have been labeled educable mentally retarded" (p. 5). Gallagher (1972) also pointed out that "special education too often was an exclusionary process masquerading as a remedial process" and added that there was little evidence that special education was returning to the regular class those children who had been placed in programs for the educable retarded.

The conjunction of all these forces has led to a movement away from special classes at the present time. The success of the mainstream movement will depend in large measure on identification of those factors that lead to a successful adjustment in the mainstream regular classroom.

Institutions

Before World War II many educable mentally retarded children were found in large state residential institutions. Today less than one in ten of such children would be found there (Scheerenberger, 1976). It would take combination of unusual circumstances—for example, sexual and criminal delinquencies or other behavior disorders—to warrant placement of an educable retarded child in an institution instead of some community living arrangement.

Gunzberg (1974) has commented on the limitations of the institution as a training center for teaching social adaptation to mentally retarded children: "How would they learn that houses are numbered odd and even on opposite sides of the street, that a round-trip ticket may save money, how to shop in a grocery store, or how to have comfortable relationships with the opposite sex?"

Curriculum Content

The curriculum for the educable mentally retarded is similar to a curriculum of the elementary school. It includes reading, writing, language, arithmetic, science, aesthetics, physical education, recreation, and related topics leading to personal adequacy and social and occupational competence. However, modifications of the instructional procedure and curriculum are needed to fit the slower-learning and less abstract-thinking characteristics of the mentally retarded.

The Unit Approach

The unit approach is one strategy identified by Heiss and Mischio (1972) that may be used in designing instructional activities for educable mentally retarded students. This approach tries to integrate the mastery of a variety of skills with a particular topic of interest

The curriculum for the educable mentally retarded child is similar to that of the elementary school, with modifications made to fit the slower-learning characteristics of the mentally retarded child. (Photo: Meri Houtchens-Kitchens.)

to retarded students. As an example, a unit on community helpers would offer specific knowledge of workers who provide services to the community (mail carrier, firefighter, and so on). Reading, arithmetic, writing, and spelling skills would then be woven into the general topic. The topics tend to be highly motivating because they are practical and within the direct experience of the child. With the movement toward mainstreaming, the popularity of the unit approach has declined because it is better suited to a special class setting. However, a mainstreaming plan that features a resource room pull-out program where the retarded students spend an hour or so away from the regular class may still use the unit approach to provide content for the resource room activities.

An example of a more integrated set of concepts was presented in a special curriculum program developed by the Biological Sciences Curriculum Study (Mayer, 1975). This team of biologists, teachers, and writers were originally organized to improve curriculum for high school biology classes. They scaled down information on important biological concepts to the reading and intellectual levels of mildly retarded junior and senior high school students. In this way, the retarded students were taught significant ideas at a level and in a format that they understood (see Table 4.2). Reports of field-test evaluations confirmed that mildly retarded students can master even relatively complex material if vocabulary and sen-

TABLE 4.2
Science Content of the BSCS Projects Designed for Mildly Retarded Students

Me Now	Me and My Environment	Me in the Future
Digestion and circulation	Exploring the environment	Metrics
Respiration and body wastes	Self as an environment	Agribusiness
Movement, support, and sensory perception	Transfer and cycling of materials	Natural resources
Growth and development	Energy relationships	Construction
	Water and air	Manufacturing
		Personal services
		Public services
		Transportation
		Sports
		Nature

Source: W. Heiss, Two models for developing curriculum materials. In H. Goldstein (Ed.), *Curriculum development for exceptional children.* San Francisco: Jossey-Bass, 1981, p. 27.

tence structure are simplified and concrete illustrations and exercises are provided.

Sex Education

One of the special curricular areas in social adaptation that merits consideration is the area of sex education. The degree to which mentally retarded youngsters are vulnerable to exploitation has sensitized parents and educators to the need for adequate training. Various studies suggest that the mentally retarded individual generally has a very incomplete understanding of intercourse, pregnancy, and childbirth. Over a decade ago Goodman, Budner, and Lesh (1971) conducted a study with parents of educable mentally retarded children and reported the following results:

1. Parents had made only minimal efforts (or none at all) to give sexual instruction.
2. Parents showed marked anxiety over the dangers facing their retarded children in this area.
3. Parents themselves often had limited knowledge of sexual function and felt inadequate in giving their children sexual information.
4. Parents showed much greater concern in this area and showed more readiness to participate in a sex education program with their retarded child than with their normal children.
5. Parents were strongly in favor of a sex education program, not only for the retarded, but for themselves as well. (p. 44)

Applying Learning Principles

The primary characteristic of mentally retarded children is that they do not learn as readily as others of the same chronological age. They lack the ability to master abstract ideas and are usually unable to learn material incidentally, without instruction, as the average child learns it. Much of the knowledge and skills acquired by the average child is learned without specific instruction by the teacher. But for the retarded child instruction needs to be systematically presented without too much reliance on incidental learning. Learning should be programmed in sequence and presented in such a way that the child will learn at a rate compatible with his or her development. Systematic instruction in every area requires time, planning, and insight, the essentials in a special education program for the educable mentally retarded child.

To implement systematic instruction it is necessary to apply sound principles and techniques that will facilitate learning. Some of the principles that facilitate learning and make teaching more profitable follow.

1. **Let the child experience success.** Organize materials and use methods that lead the child to the right answer. Provide clues where necessary. Narrow the choices in responding. Lead to the right answer by rewording the question or simplifying the problem. Never leave the child in a failure, but carry him or her along to success.

2. **Provide feedback.** The child should know when he or she has responded correctly. Learning is facilitated when the child has knowledge of whether the response is correct or not. If the response is incorrect, let the child know it, but let it be only a way station in finding the correct response. Lessons should be so arranged that the child obtains immediate feedback on the correctness of answers. This is one of the principles used in any good programmed learning procedure. If a child is learning to write the word *dog*, for example, he or she covers the model, writes the word, then compares the response with the model, thus getting feedback.

3. **Reinforce correct responses.** Reinforcement should be immediate and clear. It can be either tangible, as in providing tokens or food, or it can be in the form of social approval and the satisfaction of winning a game.

4. **Find the optimum level at which the child should work.** If the material is too easy, the child is not challenged to apply the best effort; if too difficult, he or she faces failure and frustration.

5. **Proceed in a systematic way.** Lessons should proceed in a step-by-step fashion so that the more basic and necessary knowledge and habits precede more difficult material.

6. **Use minimal change** from one step to the next to facilitate learning.

7. **Provide for positive transfer of knowledge from one situation to another.** This is facilitated by helping the child generalize from one situation to another. By having the same concept presented in various settings and in various relationships, the child can transfer the common elements in each. Itard, for example, when training the Wild Boy of Aveyron, noted that the boy learned to select a particular knife from a group of objects in response to the written word *knife* but that when a knife of a different shape was substituted, he could not respond. The child had not generalized the concept of *knife;* he had failed to transfer the understanding of the label to knives in general.

8. **Provide sufficient repetition of experiences to develop overlearning.** Many teachers have said, "Johnny learns a word one day but forgets it the next day." In such cases Johnny probably had not had enough repetition of the word in varying situations to ensure overlearning, that is, learning to the point at which he will not forget it readily. Mentally retarded children seem to require more repetitions of an experience or an association in order to retain it.

9. **Space the repetitions of material over time** rather than massing the experiences in a short duration. When a new concept is presented, come back to it again and again, often in new settings, not as drill but as transfer to a new situation.

10. **Consistently associate a given stimulus or cue with one and only one response in the early stages of learning.** Do not tell the child, "This letter sometimes says *a* and sometimes says *ah.*" Teach one sound at a time until it is overlearned and then teach the other sound as a different configuration in a new setting. If the child has to vacillate between two responses he or she will become confused.

11. **Motivate the child toward greater effort by:** (a) reinforcement and the satisfaction of succeeding, (b) variation in the presentation of material, (c) enthusiasm on the part of the teacher, and (d) optimal length of sessions.

12. **Limit the number of concepts presented in any one period.** Do not confuse the child by trying to have him or her learn too many things at one time. Introduce new material only after older material has become familiar.

13. **Arrange materials with proper cues for attention.** Arrange materials in a way that will direct the pupil's attention so that he

or she will learn to attend to the cues in the situation that will facilitate learning, and to disregard those factors in the learning situation that are irrelevant.

14. **Provide success experiences.** Educable mentally retarded children who have faced failure may have developed low frustration tolerance, negative attitudes toward schoolwork, and possibly some compensatory behavior problems that make them socially unpopular. The best way to cope with those problems is to organize a *day-to-day* program presenting the child with short-range as well as long-range tasks in which to succeed. The self-concept and the self-evaluation of the child are dependent on how well he or she succeeds in work assignments. Thus a teacher must be very careful to see not only that the child does not fail but also that he or she experiences positive success and knows success. Although that principle is applicable to all children, it is particularly necessary with children who are retarded. They face enough failures in school and in life without having to repeat them over and over again in a classroom situation.

One of the serious management problems facing many teachers who are trying to integrate retarded children into the regular classroom is how to deal with the often unacceptable behavior of these children. In addition to the problem of delayed intellectual development, the teacher must also cope with special problems created by inappropriate talking, lack of attention, wandering in the classroom, and sometimes aggressive behavior. Gresham (1981) has reviewed a number of techniques to cope with the social behavior problems of retarded children. Following are some of the techniques that have been found useful, mainly within the framework of special classes:

1. **Differential reinforcement.** This approach follows the basic behavior modification procedures by rewarding those behaviors that are appropriate and ignoring the target behavior, for example, aggressive behavior. A variation of this direct reinforcement is to provide positive rewards if the student can increase the time periods between displays of unacceptable behavior. If the child is showing a great deal of talking-out behavior, then the teacher can reward a ten-minute period of acceptable behavior that reflects an increase in the elapsed time between earlier unacceptable behavior.

2. **Time out.** Time out represents the physical removal of a child from a reinforcing situation for a period of time, usually immedi-

ately following the occurrence of an undesirable response. If the child has shown unacceptable aggressive behavior in the classroom, the child may be asked to leave the classroom or be removed to a section of the classroom in which he or she is left alone with some reading or work materials and essentially isolated from the group for a period of time. Such procedures have proven to be extremely effective in decreasing disruptive, aggressive, and inappropriate social behaviors in a number of studies.

3. **Contingent social reinforcement.** A number of teachers dealing with young handicapped children have used a token system to teach appropriate social behavior. Tokens are administered according to the appropriate use of certain social skills, such as greeting another child, borrowing a toy in an acceptable manner, and so forth. If the child displays unacceptable behavior, such as self-abusive activities or repetitive physical movements, then tokens would be taken away. Such reward and cost programs appear to be effective in controlling social behavior within groups of handicapped children and, to some extent, within the context of a mainstream class.

4. **Modeling.** One of the essential arguments for mainstreaming handicapped children is based on the assumption that multiple models of appropriate behavior will be available for the handicapped child to imitate within the regular classroom setting. However, the information concerning the circumstances under which children will imitate one another's behavior is more complex than originally assumed, and there is no guarantee that the retarded child will imitate the appropriate behavior of models. Gresham concludes, "The evidence to date does not support the assumption that handicapped children will automatically attend to or retain the social behaviors of their nonhandicapped peers" (p. 160).

Another approach described completely in Chapter 8, "Children with Behavior Problems," is the cognitive control approach, identified with Meichenbaum (1977). These techniques ask the child to go through a series of responses that are essentially self-reflective in nature before acting. It encourages the children to think first and act later and to remind themselves about their own tendencies toward aggressive or destructive behavior. In the process of such reminding, the child gains greater self-control over his or her own responses. Although such techniques have worked effectively with behavior disordered youngsters, they have received limited use with retarded youngsters, possibly because of lower verbal facility in these children.

Skills   The educable mentally retarded student has often had great difficulty mastering the academic and social skills that allow for program adaptation in later vocational and community environments.

The Social Learning Approach

The social learning approach, designed to develop critical thinking and independent actions on the part of the mentally retarded, has been identified mainly with Goldstein (1974). This approach builds lesson experiences around psychological needs such as self-respect and mastery, physical needs such as sensory stimulation, and physical maintenance and social aspects such as dependence and mobility. For example, lesson experiences based on achieving economic security could include the following objectives: (1) to choose a job commensurate with skills and interests, (2) to locate and acquire a satisfactory job, (3) to maintain a job, and (4) to manage effectively the financial resources gained from a job.

Goldstein (1974) has developed a comprehensive social learning curriculum that encompasses both behavioral and conceptual goals. Like the unit approach, it includes the teaching of arithmetic, writing, and reading skills. Unlike the unit approach, it orders and sequences the concepts and content. In his social learning curriculum, Goldstein emphasizes the use of inductive questioning when presenting instructional activities—drawing forth from the children information about the event or situation that they are studying. There is a five-stage process in this model that works as follows:

1. **Labeling.** Questions that elicit the identities of what is to be studied or explored. (What is in that picture? It is a big dog.)
2. **Detailing.** Questions that elicit the specific characteristics in the event. (What can you tell me about the dog? It is a big brown dog and it has a wagging tail.)
3. **Inferring.** Questions that elicit a conclusion based on available characteristics. (Why is the dog's tail wagging? His owner is going to feed him.)
4. **Predicting.** Questions that elicit responses about the inference, given more information. (What would happen if the owner didn't give him the food? The dog would get mad and bark and bite him.)
5. **Generalizing.** Questions that elicit responses applying a general rule based on available information. (How should we treat dogs? We shouldn't tease them, especially if they are big.)

Instrumental Enrichment

For many years the conventional wisdom in the field of education of the mentally retarded has been that if major changes in cognitive development are to occur, they would take place early in the preschool years. Moreover, if the youngster remains mentally retarded into adolescence, then the major task of the educational system is to help the youngster adapt to his or her cognitive shortcomings as best as possible. Reuven Feuerstein, an Israeli psychologist-educator, has recently challenged these ideas. Feuerstein (1980) has maintained that the problem of the retarded individual is not so much the inability to understand as it is failure to know how to solve problems. According to Feuerstein, developmentally retarded children are characterized by impulsiveness and the failure to make associations or comparisons. He proposed a training program (Feuerstein et al., 1980) that focuses on *instrumental enrichment*, which means training in how to solve problems and in the recognition of patterns in the environment. The instrumental enrichment program consists of a series of exercises in which a task is analyzed and a plan of attack is worked out. Feuerstein's ideas are currently being tried out in the United States to see if ideas developed with the *disadvantaged* child in Israel may have relevance here for the mildly retarded.

Prevocational and Work/Study Skills

As the mildly retarded child reaches the secondary level, the objectives of the program turn to the development of those skills necessary for the world of work. The skills may be directly related to some occupation such as an assembler for transistor radios or may involve role playing and other activities that stress the importance of worker cooperation, punctuality, and persistence.

The specific content for the preadolescent retarded child often takes the form of prevocational experience—lessons focusing on knowledge that forms the base for vocational competence. Following are some examples of prevocational skills that might appear in an individualized education program (IEP):

Given a road map, the student can demonstrate the route to be taken from one point to another.

Given an assigned work task involving two or more students, they will work together until the task is completed.

Given a newspaper, the student will demonstrate that he can find specific information when requested to do so. (Kolstoe, 1976)

Such specific and observable behaviors often form the essence of the IEP that provides teacher and student with tangible and reachable goals.

Vocational training focuses on a number of dimensions beyond the job itself, such as banking and using money, grooming, caring for a car and obtaining insurance, interviewing for jobs, and using leisure time. Adjustment to the world of work involves adapting to the demands of life as well as a specific job (Kolstoe, 1976).

Halpern (1978) explored the usefulness of work/study programs for mentally retarded students in secondary programs in Oregon. He found that those completing a full program were more successful than those receiving only partial training. However, training does not help much when the economy is in difficulty; mentally retarded citizens then become a part of the surplus population, a group larger than the work slots available in the social machinery. Halpern concluded:

1. When the level of community unemployment is high, it will be very difficult for mentally retarded persons who are new to the job market to find jobs.
2. When community economic conditions deteriorate, mentally retarded workers are not necessarily in jeopardy of losing their jobs.
3. Mentally retarded persons who are assisted by well-structured vocational training programs have a good chance of finding jobs, regardless of the level of general community unemployment. (p. 23)

Table 4.3 provides a brief summary of the major special education adaptations for educable mentally retarded students.

TABLE 4.3
Summary of Educational Adaptations for Educable Mentally Retarded Students

CONTENT

A greater emphasis on concrete and "hands on" experiences to match special cognitive limitations. Practical work experiences and learning about home and community are stressed.

SKILLS

A heavy emphasis on social adaptation skills linked to successful vocational experience. Emphasis on cooperative behavior, understanding the feelings of self and others, punctuality, etc.

LEARNING ENVIRONMENT

A goal of mainstreaming with special assistance, or, at most, a resource room program at the elementary level, is current style. Programs often include other mildly handicapped, learning disabled, and emotionally handicapped students, as schools attempt to abide by the least restrictive environment concept.

EDUCATIONAL ADAPTATIONS FOR TRAINABLE MENTALLY RETARDED

As a trainable retarded 10-year-old, Carol faces a situation that is very different from Bob's. Carol's level of development hasn't reached the first grade level so the standard school curriculum is not appropriate and a specially designed program is needed to provide her with the knowledge and skills appropriate to her level of ability. Some of the objectives for Carol include reading signs and recognizing simple words (for example, *stop, women, bus*), learning a code of social behavior, and developing work habits of punctuality and persistence.

In virtually all other handicapping conditions discussed in this text, the ultimate educational goal is self-sufficiency and the educational program is geared to that objective. However, complete self-sufficiency is highly unlikely for most trainable mentally retarded children to attain. The goal of the program then becomes training the child to cope, within a state of limited dependency, in self-help and self-care, in economic usefulness, and in social adjustment in the home and neighborhood (or in a sheltered environment).

Family Influences

The trainable retarded child may be found in a wide variety of families and social backgrounds. Carol's parents are well educated and the news of her retardation came as a shock to them. The wide range of metabolic and genetic accidents that can cause handicaps such as Down's syndrome do not seem closely related to family income or social status. Consequently, the family of the trainable retarded child may be able to bring more personal and financial resources to bear in aiding their child's program than can the family of the educable retarded child.

Farber (1975) has pointed out that families of moderately to severely handicapped children have special problems—the handicapped child has arrested the normal family cycle and the difficulties the family faces change over time but do not necessarily ease as the child grows older. The family must face several difficulties: the decision of whether to institutionalize the child, the realization that the child may never be self-sufficient, and the problem of what will happen to the child when the parents die. The full realization of the complex and continuing issues that the family of a handicapped child must face has led to much greater emphasis on family counseling and special programming for the family as well as for the child.

Rynders and Horrobin (1975) have described a home-training program in which parents were given specific lessons on strengthening the communication skills of their Down's syndrome infants. The basis of the program for parents is to specify, in sufficient detail, procedures that the parents can follow to carry out the lessons as games with their child. Too often, parents who are frustrated with the slow development of their handicapped child may give up, and the child then does not even have a chance to develop to the best of his or her limited capabilities.

The principles that the program lists as fundamental to the activity represent well-accepted ideas:

1. Each activity should engage the child and parent in affectionate, focused, sensory-motor interaction.
2. Each activity should engage parent and child in sensory-motor activity and require, at the same time, that the parent talk with the child about the activities.
3. The program teaches parents to use a hierarchy of teaching strategies.
4. A child should be exposed systematically to the fact that three-dimensional objects, photographs of the objects, and their printed labels have related meaning.
5. One of the crucial considerations in a parental tutoring program is to ensure that sufficient structure guides the parent's activity in the execution of curricular principles but at the same time does not stifle the unique style of the parents.

The authors reported that the children in the program showed gains in concept formation and expressive language compared with Down's syndrome children who were not enrolled in the program. This is not to say that those youngsters improved to the point of becoming normal or average children. What it does mean is that the children exhibited significant improvements in their attitudes, their learning capabilities, and their approach to the world—improvements that will prepare them for further training toward self-sufficiency in adulthood.

The "parent as teacher" model has become extremely popular as a result of growing recognition that the trainable retarded child will have much more time to interact with the parent than with the professionally trained specialist. A second consideration is to prevent the parents from concluding that their child can do little or nothing and from avoiding interaction with the child, thus compounding an already difficult situation and keeping the child from reaching his or her potential.

There have been many manuals produced to help the parent in this teaching role. An example from England stresses parent understanding of the importance of creating a good learning environment and of following basic teaching strategies such as:

1. **Work from the known to the unknown.** Start something the child can do and work to the next stage that he cannot do.
2. **Know exactly what it is you are trying to teach.** If you don't know what you want the child to do, how can he know what it is you want him to do? (Cunningham and Sloper, 1980, p. 122)

All of these programs stress a careful statement of objectives, short steps to achieve these objectives, and some means of collecting data on the child's performance. The gradual and systematic approach illustrated by many programs (for example, Hanson, 1977; Karnes, 1975) provides the parent with detailed directions on how to achieve the instructional objectives. The child is given a realistic chance for success and the data collection allows the parents to see the progress that is taking place because the parents, who may be often depressed, need positive reinforcement as much as the child does.

When the general practice was to send moderately or severely handicapped children to an institution, the effects on the rest of the family were not well documented. Now that families tend to keep handicapped children at home, there is concern about the effects on other family members, including siblings. Simeonsson and McHale (1981) reviewed the available literature on the handicapped child's effect on siblings. According to the review, the presence of the handicapped child, as expected, often results in problems of adjustment for siblings, but siblings of handicapped children may also benefit from their experiences and are often well adjusted. Among the factors that seem to predict a better adjustment for siblings are (1) the family is large, (2) the sibling is older than the handicapped child, (3) the child's handicap is mild, and (4) the sibling is a boy. However, much research is needed to trace the important family transactions that result in a favorable adaptation.

Lillie (1974) has summarized the general objectives of working with parents of moderately to severely handicapped children:

1. **Social and emotional support.** To reduce anxieties caused by guilt feelings and feelings of inadequacy in the family, and to provide socially stimulating activities which increase positive feelings about the family unit as well as the parents' feelings about themselves as competent parents.

2. **Exchanging information.** (a) Providing parents with an understanding of the rationale, objectives, and activities of the program in which their child is enrolled; (b) developing an understanding of the continuous growth and development of the child as they apply to the child's interactions in the

home; and (c) providing the project personnel with background information on the child to facilitate the effectiveness of the Center program.

3. **Parent participation.** The assumption is that by productively utilizing the parents in activities such as being a teacher aide, the parents' feelings of self-worth will be enhanced, their understanding of children will increase, and a larger repertoire of experience and activity for the parents to draw upon for interaction with their own child will be developed.

4. **Child interactions.** Training parents to become more effective child rearers. To facilitate parent-child interaction, your program should provide opportunities for parents to develop skills in (a) general child rearing practices; (b) promoting and fostering social and emotional development; (c) utilizing and optimizing everyday experience; (d) fostering and encouraging language growth; and (e) utilizing effectively the community resources available to assist the child in learning activities. (pp. 4–5)

Learning Environment

Residential Institutions

The enrollment in institutions is decreasing. Fewer trainable mentally retarded children are being sent to institutions. This does not mean that trainable mentally retarded children have been completely removed from institutions or that some residential care may not be appropriate for some trainable retarded children. Generally, training programs in institutions emphasize the development of techniques of self-care: dressing, washing, feeding, and using the toilet.

Institutions, however, provide few opportunities for the modeling of appropriate behavior and chronic staff turnover can often lead to wariness or unwillingness on the part of the retarded individual to establish any permanent social contacts or relationships. When those disadvantages are added to the widely held view that institutions demand and enforce a conformity that fits the child or adult for institutional living but ill prepares them for any adjustment outside the institution, it is easy to see why institutions are viewed with concern.

To match the public school concept of mainstreaming, a philosophy known as *normalization* has been developed. It contends that the life environment of the mentally retarded should be as "culturally normative as possible in order to establish or maintain personal behaviors and characteristics which are culturally normative as possible" (Wolfensberger, 1972, p. 28).

Community Programs

GROUP HOMES One alternative to the institution is provided by group homes. In some communities small units have been established that operate as much on the family concept as possible. The purpose of the group home is to create an environment for the mentally retarded adult that is more homelike than that of a large institution, and a setting in which the variety of skills necessary for effective living can be mastered. Permenter (1973) has made available the report of a young student who for one week impersonated a retarded girl in a group home for six girls. The report of her experience provides an interesting description of life in a group home.

After we returned home in the afternoon (from a sheltered workshop) our time was our own. On a typical evening all of us went to our living area to change clothes. We sat around and talked while folding laundry or putting away clothes. Mary was absorbed in soap operas, Pam and Julie played with Robby, the little boy, and with the family dog. Later, Julie, Pam, and I went to help Ann prepare the evening meal while we talked about incidents at work. Soon some of the others came in and set the table or helped with the final stages of the meal. Everyone was together, sometimes in the kitchen, but more frequently in front of the television. While one group did the dishes, the rest managed to get our things ready for the next day. (pp. 20–21)

After a week in the situation, during which neither the houseparents nor the other girls were aware of her true identity, the student observer summed up her experiences.

The members of this cohesive family did a great deal more than just share the same roof, they helped and cared for each other. Conflicts such as those revolving around Mary (a manipulating and disruptive girl) became "family" problems requiring each member to adjust her behavior for the good of the group. The group home became more than just a training ground and residence, it became "home" to the girls. They had a strong sense of belonging—a source of strength when difficulties arose and a contributing factor to their seemingly healthy adjustment. (p. 41)

The group home is one of the settings that is used to encourage *deinstitutionalization*, bringing retarded adolescents and adults into a semiprotected setting where they can function outside an institution.

SHELTERED WORKSHOPS Sheltered workshops have been organized in the larger communities since the majority of trainable

Through sheltered workshops, trainable retarded adults can become partially self-supporting. (Photo: Anestis Diakopoulos/ Stock, Boston.)

retarded citizens are unable to be regularly employed. The workshops enroll adolescent and adult mentally retarded individuals, train them to do routine tasks, contract with industries for piecework, and also develop and make salable products.

In well-established workshops, the mentally retarded come to work, or are transported to work, on a full-day basis and are paid wages for their labor. Thus these trainable adults become partially self-supporting. Besides the remuneration that is received from contracts and the sale of products, the sheltered workshops are also supported financially by parents' organizations, foundations, community funds, and donations. In some of the larger cities, the community center working with people at this level of mental retardation may include a diagnostic center, a preschool program, a sheltered workshop, and a recreation center.

Public Schools

Prior to the enactment of the Education for All Handicapped Children Act (PL 94–142), a series of court cases reaffirmed the rights of retarded children to receive an "appropriate education" in the public schools. Those cases have clearly indicated the responsibilities of the schools.

In the early 1950s school boards resisted organizing programs for trainable children in the public schools. Today, after the court cases following Section 504, a basic civil rights provision of Public Law 93–112, and Public Law 94–142, federal legislation requires all public schools to provide education for all children. The organization throughout the country involves special schools and classes, and they are considered least restrictive environments compared with institutionalization. Mainstreaming is practiced with young retarded children in Head Start and in kindergarten in public school. Generally, however, school-age trainable children are educated primarily in special classes or special schools with contacts with other children when feasible.

Curriculum Content and Skills

In defining an educational program for any group of children, it is necessary to identify the general objectives of the curriculum and then to give the specific elements required in a course of study. The general objectives of the curriculum for a trainable mentally retarded child are inherent in the definition of this category: (1) developing self-care or self-help skills, (2) aiding the child's social adjustment in the home and neighborhood, and (3) developing economic usefulness in the home or in a sheltered environment. They constitute the broad goals of the educational program for trainable mentally retarded children.

Self-Help Skills

The major characteristic that differentiates the trainable mentally retarded from the severely and profoundly mentally retarded is self-care. If a child can (1) learn to dress and undress, (2) eat properly, (3) take care of himself or herself in the bathroom, and (4) follow sleep routines, he or she is not dependent on someone else for personal needs. The child becomes independent in a restricted sense as far as taking care of simple routines is concerned. Although such independence is common among normal children after age 4 or 5, the trainable retarded child needs to be educated about those elements of self-care.

Social Adjustment in the Home and Neighborhood

Trainable mentally retarded children are not expected to become totally independent in the community or to be in charge of their affairs outside of the home. They are, however, expected to get along in the home and in their immediate neighborhood. That particular learning achievement includes sharing with others, waiting their turn, obeying, following directions, sensing the feelings of others, and coping with other aspects of interpersonal relationships, especially those concerned with daily associations. Social adjustment is not a subject that is taught like chemistry or physics. It is an intangible type of development that comes about through rewarding group experiences in recreation and play, singing, dramatics, and working and living with others.

Economic Usefulness

The term *economic usefulness* is applied to the trainable mentally retarded child to differentiate that ability from occupational or vocational activities within the capacity of educable retarded children. The trainable retarded child is expected to be helpful in the home, in the school, in a sheltered work environment, or in a routine job under supervision in either the community or institution. In the home, economic usefulness means helping with housework and yardwork. Those activities can be developed in the classroom more successfully with older trainable children than with younger ones through many of the programs requiring care of the room, cooking, washing and wiping dishes, arts and crafts, woodworking, and the ability to complete simple tasks under minimum supervision.

Basic Skills

In addition to the three preceding goals, there are basic skills that are offered in every class. In teaching those skills, the educator must recognize the equivalent developmental ages in classes for trainable retarded children, which usually range between 3 and 7 years. At this developmental level, an academic program of the type prescribed for the educable mentally retarded or for normal children is not warranted. The following paragraphs discuss the expected performance levels for trainable mentally retarded children.

MODIFIED READING In general, trainable retarded children do not learn to read beyond the first-grade level. Their ability is limited to recognizing their names, isolated words and phrases, common words used for their protection, such as *danger, stop, bus, poison, wet paint, men,* and *women,* and other signs that they encounter in a community. Some trainable retarded children with special abilities can learn to read at a slightly higher level. Most who learn to

For the trainable retarded child, economic usefulness in the home can mean helping with housework. (Photo: © Elizabeth Crews.)

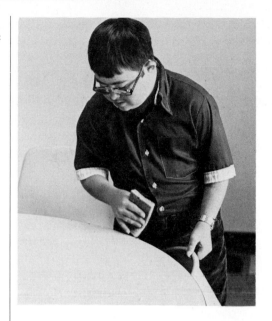

read, however, are probably educable mentally retarded children, misdiagnosed as trainable, or children with wide *intra*individual differences.

ARITHMETIC Trainable retarded children are not taught the formal arithmetic presented in the primary grades. They can learn some quantitative concepts, however, such as more and less, big and little, and the elementary vocabulary of quantitative thinking. They can be taught to count up to ten and to identify quantity in small groupings. The older trainable mentally retarded children can learn to write numbers from one to ten, and some of them can learn time concepts, especially the sequence of activities during the day, telling time by the clock, and possibly an elemental understanding of the calendar. Some can recognize and remember telephone numbers, their own ages, and some simple money concepts. In general, the arithmetic that is taught is related to everyday living.

WRITING Trainable mentally retarded children can learn to write their own names, addresses, and telephone numbers and certain words that they learn in reading for their own protection.

LANGUAGE This program includes the development of speech and the understanding and use of verbal concepts. It includes communication skills, such as listening to stories and roll calls, discussing pictures, and other activities familiar to the children in the classroom.

SOCIAL STUDIES The important area of study is the home and the way it participates in the community. This includes learning about holidays, transportation, and church and knowing the months and days of the week, as well as contributions to home life.

DRAMATIZATION Classes for trainable retarded children use considerable dramatization such as acting out a story or a song, playing make-believe, shadow play, and using gestures with songs, stories, and rhymes.

ARTS AND CRAFTS Activities in this area include coloring, drawing, painting, simple woodworking, pasting and cutting, and making simple craft objects. Such activities may help in developing motor coordination, an appreciation of color and form, and the ability to complete a task.

PHYSICAL HYGIENE The routine of a classroom includes snacks and juice or milk, and discussions about the kinds of food eaten at different meals, the care of the teeth, body cleanliness, clothing, safety, and posture. Health habits usually need to be fostered both in the school and at home.

PRACTICAL ARTS Included under practical arts are cooking, sewing, dishwashing, cleaning, gardening, setting the table, chores around the classroom, preparing foods, and learning to help with home activities. This program is best limited to older trainable children, although even at a young age, trainable children may be exposed to such activities.

MOTOR DEVELOPMENT Motor development is best stimulated through games, recreational activities, various manipulative skills, playing, outdoor diversions, and similar activities.

MUSIC Music is a medium through which trainable children can learn many things. Singing, rhythm bands, musical games, and other activities help release energy and also serve as a form of expression and a socializing influence. Language is sometimes fostered through putting words to music and through group choral experiences. The concepts of sequence and memory can also be developed through music.

One of the interesting consequences of the increased educational attention to trainable children is that such programs may yield better results than anticipated. There has been a widely held view that Down's syndrome children have a limited range of intellectual ability and that the vast majority will be able to function only at the trainable level of mental retardation. Such results, however, have been challenged by Rynders, Spiker, and Horrobin (1978). In a major review of programs that teach Down's syndrome children, the researchers have found a substantial number of children who fall within the educable or higher range of measured intellectual performance. Conclusions based on the researchers' data and those from other projects indicate that physicians who see parents of Down's syndrome children should tell them:

1. There is a possibility that their children could be educable on a psychometric basis.
2. There is a great deal of variability in Down's syndrome children's early developmental progress.
3. The limits of Down's syndrome children's educability are virtually unknown.

Strategies for Teaching Skills to the Trainable Mentally Retarded

BEHAVIOR MODIFICATION The special problems of the trainable mentally retarded child have stimulated a number of special teaching techniques, including the principles made popular by the American psycholoist B. F. Skinner and further developed by Bijou (1966) and by Neisworth and Smith (1973). Those principles have had a multitude of applications in the training of retarded children in the last decade. Since those techniques do not necessarily require language skills or communication in order to work, they are especially valuable for noncommunicative children. The basic principle of *operant conditioning,* as proposed by Skinner, is that the child's behavior is determined by how the environment responds to it. Behavior that is rewarded will be repeated. Behaviors that do not receive positive reinforcement will gradually drop out of the response repertoire of the child (Skinner, 1953).

The educational strategy is to arrange the environment so that the particular behavior the teacher wishes the child to repeat will occur. When the desired behavior does occur, then it receives a positive reward in terms of food, praise, a token, or some other symbol of recognition. The teacher should not respond to the undesirable or even actively obnoxious behavior if at all possible.

There is a rather natural tendency to scold the child for whining or clinging to an adult, but the correct response according to Skinnerian theory is to pay no attention to the behavior that the teacher does *not* wish the child to show in the future, while giving attention and other reinforcement to desirable behavior. In most instances, even the disturbed or moderately retarded child begins to respond with more socially constructive behavior if such procedures are followed consistently by the caretaker or teacher.

The applied analysis of behavior (behavior shaping and behavior modification) is used extensively in shaping or modifying habits of self-help. Detailed programs on how to teach toilet training, dressing, undressing, eating, and sleeping have been developed. The teaching of language and other skills for the retarded is developed effectively through the use of behavior modification (operant) techniques. The techniques are available through many publications.

TASK ANALYSIS In the past few years advances have been made in developing special instructional techniques drawn from learning theory that teach trainable retarded children complex tasks previously assumed to be beyond their grasp.

Gold (1973) has been successful in developing a number of assembly tasks that retarded individuals can perform through the process of breaking down the tasks into their individual parts. He comments, "The decision to teach or not teach any task to the severely/profoundly handicapped must be based on whether or not that task can be analyzed into teachable components rather than some general feeling about the difficulty of the task."

Zider and Gold (1981) reported on the ability of two retarded individuals to learn driving skills in a Link-Singer simulator in a driver education program at the University of Illinois. Under such simulated conditions, moderately retarded students with IQ scores in the 40s were able to start the engine, maintain speed and braking, and effectively control the simulator in turning and passing. Each of these skills was learned through a very specific breakdown of the step-by-step process by which the skill is carried out. While this type of training is no guarantee that such drivers could perform effectively in traffic, it does demonstrate that the ability to teach complex tasks to the retarded depends as much on the careful analysis of the task by the teacher as it does on the capabilities of the retarded individual.

Zane, Walls, and Thvedt (1981) have reported a successful training program in which trainable retarded adults learned complex behaviors connected with assembling a carburetor, a bicycle brake, a dishwasher pump, and a lawn mower engine (see Figure 4.4). Using techniques such as *backward chaining* (going step by step backwards from the finished product, placing the last part, then the last two parts, and so forth) and *prompts* (verbal suggestions or demonstrations and reinforcement for successful performance), Zane, Walls, and Thvedt were able to demonstrate that twelve moder-

FIGURE 4.4
Apparatuses Assembled by Trainable Mentally Retarded Adults (including nine parts each of, from top to bottom, a Carter truck carburetor, a Schwinn bicycle brake, a Perry dishwasher pump, and a Briggs and Stratton lawn mower engine)

Source: T. Zane, R. Walls, and J. Thvedt, Prompting and fading guidance procedures: Their effect on chaining and whole task teaching strategies. *Educating and Training of the Mentally Retarded*, 1981, *16*, 125–135.

ately to severely handicapped adults (ages 19 to 45) successfully learned to assemble various parts of machinery in a sheltered work situation.

SOCIETY'S VIEW OF THE MENTALLY RETARDED

We have spent much of this chapter on the adaptation problems that mentally retarded individuals face. Undoubtedly one of the most serious problems is the way in which they are viewed by the nonhandicapped majority. They are often shunned and feared. When a group home for the mentally retarded is proposed in a community, the great disturbance that often takes place reflects a good deal more of the neighbors' personal feelings than the often-used fear of a drop in real estate values. Much of our future progress in social integration will depend on overcoming the fears and attitudes of the nonhandicapped majority rather than on improving the skills of the retarded citizen.

SUMMARY OF MAJOR IDEAS

1. The current definition of mental retardation includes two major components: intellectual subnormality and adaptive behavior. A definition of mentally retarded depends, in part, on the characteristics of the child and also on the demands of the social environment.
2. Mentally retarded children have been classified according to three groups for educational purposes: (a) educable mentally retarded, (b) trainable mentally retarded, and (c) severely/profoundly mentally retarded.
3. Procedures for measuring intellectual abilities and ratings of social adaptation have been developed and are used to identify those children who are mentally retarded.
4. Estimates on the prevalence of mental retardation vary widely. Conservative estimates of prevalence in the child population, according to current concepts and definitions of mental retardation, indicate that approximately 0.25 to 0.5 percent are trainable and profoundly mentally retarded and that approximately 0.5 to 1.5 percent can be classified as educable mentally retarded.
5. The causes of mental retardation are many and varied. They include factors within the general categories of genetic disorders, toxic agents and infectious diseases, and environmental influences.
6. The families of the educable mentally retarded child are, in most instances, economically limited and possess few resources to contribute to the total educational program. The families of the trainable mentally retarded child come from all socioeconomic levels.
7. The general characteristics of mentally retarded children that call for special programming are (a) a tendency for poorer physical and motor abilities, (b) a limited memory and a limited capability for rehearsal of ideas, (c) a lessened capability to use language and to describe temporal or causal relationships, and (d) a short attention span and a limited frustration tolerance developed in some measure from a long history of failure.

8. The importance of the early environment on the young child has led to expansion of preschool programs designed for prevention as well as remediation of mental retardation. Such programs have contributed to better academic performance in retarded children at a later age.

9. The learning environments in which the educable mentally retarded are usually placed include mainstreamed regular class programs, resource rooms, and part- or full-time special classes.

10. The curriculum for educable mentally retarded children who are mainstreamed generally follows the program of the regular grades, with supporting help in the academic subjects.

11. In the special class or the resource room, the program emphasizes social learning and prevocational skills and explicitly teaches life experiences, such as the need for social cooperation, in addition to the academic subjects.

12. Work/study programs for secondary level educable mentally retarded youngsters seem to help them prepare for independent or semi-independent community work. Moreover, educable mentally retarded youth have demonstrated abilities to succeed in and retain jobs of a routine nature not desired by high ability individuals, such as working in fast-food restaurants.

13. Educational goals for the trainable mentally retarded include self-care, social skills, and some degree of economic usefulness.

14. A wide variety of available placements for trainable mentally retarded children include: (a) residential institutions, (b) community-based programs such as group homes and sheltered workshops, and (c) public school programs.

15. Parents have been included much more frequently in the treatment programs for trainable mentally retarded children through counseling and direct instruction on how to teach their child at home.

16. Specific learning procedures, based on task analysis and operant conditioning, have been of much value in teaching basic skills to trainable mentally retarded children. Breaking down complex tasks into their simplest parts have helped trainable retarded individuals learn economically useful work, often in sheltered workshop settings.

UNRESOLVED ISSUES

1. The Culture of Poverty. We are still not sure what factors within the culture of poverty are responsible for the slow development of mildly retarded children. Until we can determine the nature of the problem (lack of motivation, poor language, inattention and hyperactivity, lack of effective adult models, and so forth), it is difficult to design efficient methods for preventing it.

2. The Changing Job Market. The future of educable mentally retarded students depends as much on the nature of the social envelope in which they live as on their education and training. The increasing complexity of modern society and the tendency for jobs to require a great amount of education casts a shadow over the goal in independence for the mildly retarded child. Is there a place in a shrinking job market for the mentally retarded or will they be part of a "surplus" population?

3. The Resilient Family. Some families are able to adjust to the problem of having a child who is moderately to severely handicapped and to continue a productive and healthy existence. Other families faced with the same problem are shattered by it. Where are the wellsprings of strength that allow some families to maintain themselves under this stress? There are two diametrically opposed approaches to the families of the handicapped—one wishes them to be teachers of their handicapped children, the other stresses respite care to allow periodic relief from the daily burden of caring for the child. Which approach is more appropriate for which families?

4. Continuum of Services. Special education has brought additional resources to some children needing help in the educational setting. There are many other students (for instance, borderline retarded or slow learning students) who also need help within the framework of the traditional education program. Schools need to design a continuum of services to match the continuum of student needs instead of giving special help *only* to those eligible for special education with little additional help to those with problems not severe enough to qualify for the special education program.

5. The Proper Learning Environment. Over the past thirty years professional opinion on the best setting for effectively educating mildly retarded children has fluctuated widely. Proponents of mainstreaming and advocates of special classes are both hard put to generate impressive evidence in favor of their choice. Secondary education represents a rarely studied educational level for maximizing educational opportunity for the educable retarded student. The optimum solution to this problem awaits more detailed evidence on the conditions of success for the alternative approaches.

REFERENCES OF SPECIAL INTEREST

Feuerstein, R., Rand, Y., Hoffman, M., & Miller, R. *Instrumental enrichment*. Baltimore: University Park Press, 1980.

The book details the techniques used by an Israeli team of psychologists and educators to train retarded children and youth in problem-solving activities. It assumes that once trained in basic approaches of how to solve problems, the retarded child can become more adaptable in society.

Hobbs, N. *The futures of children*. San Francisco: Jossey-Bass, 1975.

A clearly written review of the major study on the classification of exceptional children that spanned over two years and involved over seventy citizens and scientists who explored the various aspects of the need to classify children and the possible consequences of such classification to them and their families. It is a bench mark from which other discussions on this topic should begin.

Mittler, P. (Ed.). *Frontiers of knowledge in mental retardation;* (Vol. 1) *Social educational and behavioral aspects.* (Vol. 2) *Biomedical aspects.* Baltimore: University Park Press, 1981.

An excellent compendium of chapters providing up-to-date information on advances in the social and biological sciences and dealing with mental retardation in professional fields extending from sociology to genetics. Volume 1 pays particular attention to educational and community issues.

Ogbu, J. *Minority education and caste: The American system in cross-cultural perspective.* New York: Academic Press, 1978.

This book presents the viewpoint of an anthropologist on the pervasive effect of race bias on the development of the minority child in the United States. Ogbu believes that the perception of lack of opportunity reduces the minority child's motivation to work hard on academic interests. This argument is relevant to the concern expressed by many about the overrepresentation of minority children in prevalence figures of mental retardation.

Kirk, S., Kliebhan, J., & Lerner, J. *Teaching reading to slow and disabled learners*. Boston: Houghton Mifflin, 1978.

A comprehensive text detailing special procedures for reading instruction to meet the needs of children who are developmentally delayed. Both early and advanced stages of reading are given special attention. The book discusses formal and informal methods of student assessment and provides a detailed review of exisitng research on slow and disabled learners.

Children with Visual Impairments

Educational activities depend heavily on the sense of vision. Learning colors, watching hamsters in a cage, observing expressions on people's faces, using workbooks and readers, sensing distance perception—all are restricted for children whose vision is impaired. Their horizons must retract to the immediate vicinity where they can touch and hear stimuli. Walk around blindfolded, or even sit behind a clouded glass, and some sense of their restricted environments and limited perceptions will be evident.

This chapter will discuss the special needs of children who are labeled blind or partially sighted and the educational adaptations that must be made for them.

DEFINITIONS AND CLASSIFICATIONS

As is true with other handicapping conditions discussed in this text, the definition of the visually impaired is more complicated than the individual with casual interest might suppose. In general, children with visual impairments are classified in two major groups: (1) the blind and (2) the partially sighted or low-vision children.

The general shift of emphasis from personal characteristics of the exceptional child to how those characteristics intersect with the environment is seen again in a modification of the definition of children with visual handicaps. Previously, the definition focused on a rather abstract standard of visual efficiency. Although these standards remain in use and will be reported here, it has become increasingly popular to use a functional definition—one that stresses the effects of visual limitation on the critical skill of reading.

Lowenfeld (1973) has noted: "During the past decades, educators have recognized that the functional visual efficiency, the way in which a child utilizes his vision, is more important than his measured visual acuity. Therefore, a functional definition of blindness . . . is being sought" (p. 31).

The terms used by Barraga (1976) to differentiate three types of visually impaired children represent a step in that direction. Barraga considers children *blind* when they have only light perception or have no vision and must learn "through braille and related media without the use of vision" (p. 14). She considers children as having *low vision* when they "have limitations in distance vision but are able to see objects and materials when they are within a few inches or at a maximum of two feet away" (p. 14). Barraga considers a third group of children with *limited vision*. These children are considered sighted if their vision can be corrected.

Bateman (1967) defined the blind and partially seeing in terms of the method they use in learning to read. She states, "Educationally speaking, *blind* children are those visually handicapped children who use braille, and *partially seeing* children are those who use print" (p. 258).

The standards of visual acuity that still carry legal weight are noted in the *National Society for the Prevention of Blindness Fact Book* (1966).

Blindness is generally defined in the United States as visual acuity for distance vision of 20/200 or less in the better eye, after correction, with acuity of more than 20/200 if the widest diameter of field of vision subtends an angle no greater than 20 degrees.

The partially seeing are defined as persons with a visual acuity greater than 20/200 but not greater than 20/70 in the better eye with correction. (p. 10)

Figure 5.1 shows the difference between 20/20 vision and 20/200 vision in views of the same scene.

IDENTIFICATION

School systems show great diversity in approaches to detecting visually handicapped children. In some schools, children are referred directly to an ophthalmologist or an optometrist when visual problems are suspected. Other school districts screen youngsters routinely to determine those who might have vision difficulties. Children who fail to pass the school screening are then referred for more comprehensive assessment.

The standard school screening instrument used is the *Snellen chart*, which consists of rows of letters of descending size that the children are asked to read at a distance of twenty feet. A variation of the Snellen chart, consisting of capital *E*s pointing in various directions, is useful for screening young children and people who do not know how to read. The child is asked to indicate the direction in which the legs of the *E* are pointing. Scores are based on how accurately the child is able to identify the rows of letters (or direction of the *E*s), using one eye at a time. A reading of 20/70 in the left eye means that the child can see at twenty feet what a person with normal vision can see at seventy feet. These screening techniques are very crude indicators of visual problems and do not address special problems in depth perception, near vision, or fusion.

FIGURE 5.1
Contrasting Visual Acuity
Top: View as seen by person with 20/20 vision. Not only can most of the letters be read, the person holding the chart and the background objects are sharp and distinct.

Bottom: View as seen by person with 20/200 vision. All the letters except the top one are indecipherable. Although objects in the background are distinguishable, much of the detail is lacking.

Source: From Marvin Efron, *Who is the visually impaired child?* Project MAVIS Sourcebook 1. Boulder, Colo.: Social Science Education Consortium, 1979. Copyright LINC Services, 1980. Reprinted by permission of the publisher.

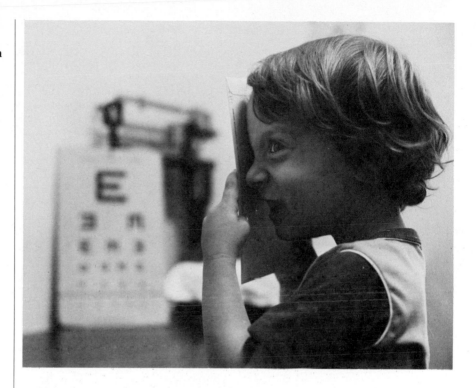

The Snellen E chart is useful for screening the vision of young children and people who do not know how to read. (Photo: Michael Weisbrot and Family © 1982.)

More extensive tests, using elaborate equipment such as the Keystone Telebinocular or the Bausch and Lomb Orthorater, measure vision at far point and near point and test other characteristics such as muscle balance, fusion, and usable vision. Although these devices provide sophisticated diagnostic information, their use in most school systems is limited because they are expensive and special training is required to interpret the test results.

The two major professional points of referral for vision problems are an *ophthalmologist*, who is a physician specializing in diagnosis and treatment of defects and diseases of the eye, and an *optometrist*, who examines, measures and treats certain functional vision defects by methods requiring no physician's license.

Once a vision problem is discovered, additional testing can be conducted to identify the extent of the problem using the Program to Develop Efficiency in Visual Functioning (Barraga, 1980). This scale was designed to assess the level of visual functioning through the presentation of a series of increasingly smaller and less visible objects using words and sentences as well as pictures. The purpose of this test is to determine the extent to which the child is able to use his or her vision with some efficiency, such as ability to read a sentence, even though the vision is impaired.

TABLE 5.1
Identifying Children in the Classroom with Vision Problems

Observe	Ask	Experiment
Can he/she read the chalkboard from the seat or does he/she need to walk up to it?	Read the cumulative record—any information about physical restrictions, medication, or the need for vision aids (magnifiers, lamps, etc.) should be noted on the eye report.	Try different lighting—is dim light or bright light better?
Does he/she squint when reading a book?		Try different seating—does he/she respond better if close or far away from the board or from you when you're talking to the class?
Does visual skill vary in different situations—on the playground, in reading group, at the desk?	Ask the parents—does the student like to watch T.V.? Where does he/she sit—close or far away?	Try different ideas—how does he/she do when lessons are taped?
	Ask the student what he/she sees outside the window, in the picture, in the book, on the board, etc.	

Source: J. Todd (Ed.), *Visually impaired students in the regular classroom.* Columbus, Ohio: Ohio Resource Center for the Visually Handicapped, 1979, p. 30.

Just as the pediatrician is the first line of identification of handicapped children in the preschool years, so the teacher is the prime source of identification of mild handicaps in the school-age group. Efforts have been made to sensitize classroom teachers who may have received minimal training in identifying exceptional children. Table 5.1 provides some hints from the Ohio department of education on what to look for or how to spot a child with visual problems.

Until recently, visually impaired children were grouped in school according to the classification devised for medical and legal purposes. Such groupings provided one program for blind children and one for partially sighted youngsters. Research has demonstrated that there is not a one-to-one correspondence between visual acuity and educational performance. Optometrists are also concerned with visual efficiency, and for teachers visual efficiency may be the most important factor for educational planning.

PREVALENCE

The number of children who are visually handicapped is strikingly less than the number of children who are mentally retarded or learning disabled. Only one out of one thousand children is visually handicapped. (Remember, if an eye problem can be corrected by glasses, then the defect is not considered a visual handicap in an educational sense.) According to *Facts about Blindness* (1976) issued by the American Foundation for the Blind, Inc., 1,750,000 persons in the United States are severely visually impaired. This figure includes 400,000 who have no usable vision. Of these, 4 percent are under age 25, about 33 percent are between the ages of 25 and 64, and over 65 percent are over the age of 65. It is anticipated that the number of blind people over 65 will continue to increase as the average life span increases.

Klineman (1975) pointed out that the number of multiply handicapped children with visual problems increased in the early 1970s. Periodic epidemics of maternal rubella have yielded large numbers of multiply handicapped blind and deaf-blind children. Major advancements in medicine have helped many high-risk babies survive, but not without multiple disabilities. When a child with cerebral palsy is also blind, serious educational issues arise as to how curriculum and educational objectives can be adapted to meet the problem of two or more handicaps existing at once. Chapter 10 discusses in depth the problems of multiply handicapped children.

THE HUMAN EYE

In order to understand functional defects in vision, it is helpful to know how a healthy eye operates. The human eye is a complex system of interrelated parts (Figure 5.2). Any part may be defective or become nonfunctional through disease, accidents, hereditary anomalies, and other causes.

The eye has been likened to a camera for the brain. Like a camera, the human eye has a diaphragm, the *iris*. This is the colored muscular partition that expands and contracts to regulate the amount of light admitted through the central opening, or *pupil*. Behind the iris is hung the *crystalline lens*, which is an elastic biconvex body that focuses onto the *retina* the light reflected from objects in the line of vision. The retina is the light-sensitive, innermost layer of tissue at the back of the eyeball. It contains the neural receptors that translate the physical energy of light into the neural energy that results in the experience of seeing. The process of visual interpretation as summarized by Barraga (1976) is presented in Figure 5.3.

As can be seen in Figure 5.2, many other protective and structural elements in the eye can affect vision. The *cornea* is the transparent anterior portion of the tough outer coat of the eyeball. The *ciliary muscles* control changes in the shape of the *lens* so that the eye can focus on objects at varying distances from the individual. In the normal, mature eye, no muscular effort is necessary to see

FIGURE 5.2
The Human Eye

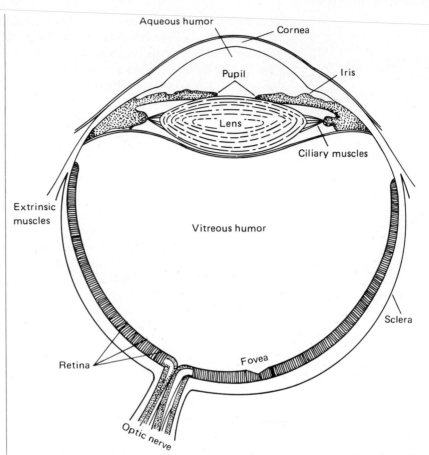

Source: From P. Lindsay and D. Norman, *Human information processing.* New York: Academic Press, 1972.

FIGURE 5.3
Process of
Visual Interpretation

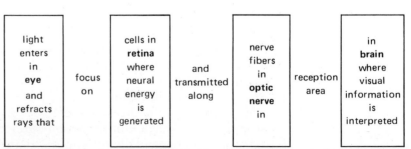

Source: Redrawn from *Visual handicaps and learning: A developmental approach* by Natalie C. Barraga. Copyright © 1976 by Wadsworth Publishing Company, Inc., Belmont, California 94002. Reprinted by permission of the publisher.

clearly objects twenty feet or more away. When the eye looks at an object closer than twenty feet, the ciliary muscles increase the convex curvature of the lens so that the closer object will still be focused on the retina. This changing of the shape of the lens is called *accommodation.*

There are also *external ocular* muscles that control the movement of the eyeball in its socket. Those changes made by the external eye muscles are known as *convergence.* Defective functioning of those muscles creates such problems as strabismus (cross-eyedness) and less obvious imbalance of the muscles. Table 5.2 gives a summary of common disorders and anomalies of the eye.

CAUSES OF VISUAL IMPAIRMENTS

The major causes of blindness and other visual impairments have been listed in broad categories to include infectious diseases, accidents and injuries, poisonings, tumors, general diseases, and prenatal influences, including heredity. Other causes of blindness, predominantly hereditary in nature, such as cataracts, optic nerve atrophy, and albinism, remain fairly constant in their appearance across age groups. Hereditary factors remain a much more frequent cause of blindness than do disease and accidents, both of which seem to be declining due to improved control measures and education.

Many diseases and conditions other than those already mentioned can attack the eyeball, cornea, lens, vitreous humor, retina, and optic nerve and cause marked visual deficiencies or total blindness. Common among these diseases are diabetes, syphilis, glaucoma, and keratitis.

Occasionally environmental conditions may result in an unusual prevalence of children with visual handicaps. A condition called *retrolental fibroplasia* reached epidemic proportions in the 1950s. Its cause was the administration of too much oxygen in the incubators of premature babies and it accounted for over half of the visually impaired babies at that time. Since the cause was discovered and less oxygen was used in the incubators, the prevalence has dropped sharply, but not entirely. Sometimes a physician may be faced with the difficult decision of increasing the oxygen supply in order to save a premature baby's life while placing the baby at risk for *retrolental fibroplasia* (Hatfield, 1975).

Another condition, *rubella* or German measles, seems to occur in epidemics every seven to ten years. When mothers are affected in the early stages of pregnancy, the child may be born with a combination of visual defects, auditory defects, mental retardation, and other disabilities.

TABLE 5.2
Common Visual
Disorders and Anomalies

Type of Disorder	Description
REFRACTIVE ERRORS	
Hyperopia	Farsightedness; a condition in which rays of light focus behind the retina, forming a blurred and unclear image; a convex lens before the eye increases bending of light rays and brings them to focus
Myopia	Nearsightedness; a condition in which rays of light focus in front of the retina when the eye is at rest and is viewing an object twenty or more feet distant; a concave lens can refocus the image on the retina
Astigmatism	A refractive error resulting from an irregularity in the curvature of the cornea or lens of the eye and causing light rays to be refracted unevenly at different planes so that horizontal and vertical rays are focused at two different points on the retina; usually correctable with proper lenses
DEFECTS OF MUSCLE FUNCTION	
Strabismus	Crossed eyes caused by a lack of coordination of the external eye muscles; the two eyes do not simultaneously focus on the same object; can be constant or intermittent
Heterophoria	Insufficient action of one or more muscles of the eye marked by a tendency for the eyes to deviate from the normal position for binocular fixation; it creates difficulty in fusing the two images from the two eyes into one image; it is not as apparent as strabismus and can sometimes be overcome by extra muscular effort
Nystagmus	Quick, jerky movements of the eyeballs, resulting in marked visual inefficiency
OTHER ANOMALIES	
Albinism	A hereditary, congenital condition characterized by a relative absence of pigment from the skin, hair, choroid coat, and iris; it is often correlated with refractive errors and loss of visual acuity; the lack of color in the iris allows too much light to reach the retina
Cataract	A condition of the eye in which the crystalline lens or its capsule become opaque with loss of visual acuity; treatment by surgery or other medical processes is usually possible; if the lens is surgically removed, artificial lenses are necessary, and peripheral vision is affected

DEVELOPMENTAL PROFILES

Each individual blessed with normal sight has wondered from time to time what it might be like to be blind or partially sighted. It is obvious that adaptation to sensory loss has implications that are profoundly personal and social as well as educational. A comprehensive special education program must involve all areas of development and adjustment. The developmental profiles of two visually

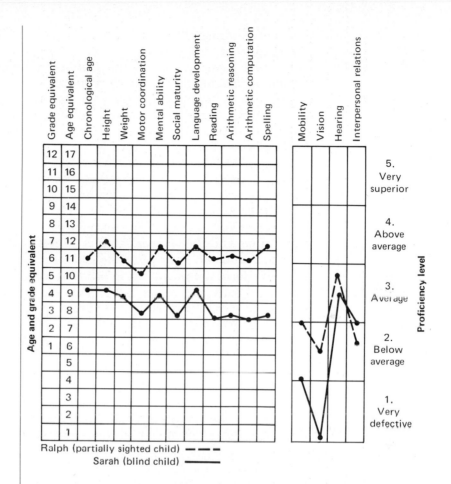

FIGURE 5.4
Profiles of Two Children with Differing Degrees of Visual Impairment

Ralph (partially sighted child) ━ ━ ━
Sarah (blind child) ━━━━

impaired youngsters will be introduced here to highlight some of the adaptation problems of children with visual problems. Figure 5.4 shows the patterns of development of Ralph and Sarah. Ralph, who is partially sighted, and Sarah, who is legally blind, are both educated in the public school setting because special provisions, personnel, and equipment have been made available for them.

Ralph   Ralph is a tall, slim 11-year-old, who has a serious visual impairment for which maximum correction has been obtained with the aid of thick glasses. Ralph can read print material and, in the early grades, he has been able to make a reasonable academic adaptation.

As can be seen by his profile in Figure 5.4, Ralph scored slightly above average in intelligence as measured by an adaptation of the Stanford-Binet Test and is currently doing average work in the school as measured by achievement tests that were administered with no time limits. Yet this profile, while favorable, tends to disguise some current and future academic problems that Ralph is likely to encounter. He will be required to use higher thought processes as he progresses through the educational system and is already beginning to experience the shift from concrete arithmetic to the much more difficult, for him, abstractions of algebra and the spatial concepts of geometry.

Ralph spends most of his time in school with the regular fifth-grade class, but he does leave that program for about an hour a day to work with a specially trained resource teacher who uses a small room and special equipment to provide help for Ralph. Only three or four other youngsters are in the resource room with Ralph at a time, and the teacher can give him a good deal of tutoring in the academic areas in which he needs help.

Perhaps of more concern in school adaptation is how Ralph feels about himself. His visual handicap is serious enough so that he is sometimes unsure whether he belongs to the sighted community or to the blind community. He feels deeply about his awkwardness and inability to perform in athletics—a very important dimension in the life of an 11-year-old boy—but he does not discuss this with anyone.

Ralph also has some interpersonal problems. He reacts with a sharp tongue and a quick temper to any slights or negative comments, real or imagined, about his visual handicap. Consequently, many of the other youngsters tend to ignore or avoid him except when class participation requires interaction. Above all, Ralph is beginning to wonder about his future: What is he going to do with his life when he grows up? How can he be independent? How can he establish friendships with the opposite sex? This is a topic of great importance to Jim, his older brother, who is in high school and whose life seems to revolve around girls. Jim's behavior is a source of amusement to Ralph now, but in a few years he will have to face interpersonal problems more seriously.

Sarah   The second child whose profile is shown in Figure 5.4 is Sarah, an average-looking 9-year-old who has been legally blind since birth. Like many blind children, she does have some limited light perception that can help her mobility somewhat, but she cannot read print and has mastered the Grade 2 braille system that uses contractions, letter combinations, and shortened forms of words to save time and space in reading. In some respects Sarah is making a better adjustment than Ralph, despite her more severe visual handicap, because of a number of factors. Sarah has a warm and understanding mother who has given her strong emotional support and a professional father who provides a comfortable income for the family. Her mother has tried to be a companion for Sarah and has read to her extensively from the time Sarah was 3 or 4. She has helped Sarah through some difficult times, particularly when Sarah was having trouble mastering the braille system. Sarah's father is more distant, not seeming to know how to approach her.

In addition to her visual handicap, Sarah shows some signs of mild neurological damage or mild cerebral palsy, which tends to make her physically awkward, but this condition is not serious enough to classify her as multiply handicapped. As the developmental profile shows in Figure 5.4, Sarah's performance on tests of mental ability and her development in speech and language are average, perhaps a testimony to the intensive work with her mother in her early years, but in arithmetic her performance is somewhat below average.

Sarah lives in an urban area with a large population and consequently where there are a number of visually handicapped children. The school system has arranged for the children to be bussed from around the district to attend a school that provides a special program for them. Sarah is well accepted by her classmates and has one or two close sighted friends. She has not yet had to face problems in relationships with the opposite sex or deal with the often cruel behavior of young adolescents.

Sarah has been affected in an important way by the educational trend of placing exceptional children in the least restrictive environment. She does not have to attend a large state school for the blind far from her home and family, as did many blind children of a generation or so ago. Sometime in the next three or four years, her mother and father will have to decide whether they want her to attend a residential school that provides advanced curriculum and educational facilities for the blind, but for now they are happy that she is at home and able to get special help within the public school program.

CHARACTERISTICS OF VISUALLY IMPAIRED CHILDREN

Various groups of exceptional children, including the blind, have been surveyed extensively with respect to their physical, social, mental, and educational development. Research on the visually impaired has concentrated primarily on the legally blind, and surprisingly little material has been collected regarding partially sighted children.

The major question that has arisen from this research is whether visual impairments, especially blindness, affect cognitive, affective, and attitudinal characteristics. Scholl and Schnur (1976) indicated that researchers have found no specific psychological reactions to visual impairments that are different from the usual reactions to stress or disability. They pointed out, however, that the visual loss causes (1) some restriction in the range and depth of certain cognitive experiences, since the object world can be felt only if it is small and near, and (2) some limitation of experience because of restricted mobility. In addition, Scholl and Schnur pointed out that the range of experience depends on whether the child was born blind or became blinded later, or whether blindness was sudden or gradual.

Does a visual handicap influence the growth of intelligence, social and personality development, sensory and motor performance, and educational achievement? Lowenfeld (1973) has argued that blindness limits perception and cognition in three ways: (1) in the range and variety of experiences, (2) in the ability to get about, and (3) in interaction with the environment. These limitations, in turn, affect the self-perception of the blind child.

Sensory Perception and Compensation

Researchers have been interested in the question of how other sense functions are affected by visual deficiency. The doctrine of *sensory compensation* holds that if one sense avenue, such as vision, is deficient, other senses will be automatically strengthened. It was believed for some time that the blind have the capacity to hear better and have better memories than do sighted individuals.

Chess (1974) presented the alternative view that damage in one developmental area might have a negative effect on other areas. This means that a functional defect in one area retards or distorts development in other intact areas.

It remains possible, though, that blind people make better use of their available abilities in other sense fields. A sighted person may tend to disregard sounds in the environment that have, of necessity, become significant to a blind person. It does not follow that the actual hearing abilities of the two individuals differ.

A study on the ability of blind children to use their sense of touch was conducted by Gottesman (1971). Blind children ages 2 through 8 and a comparable group of sighted children were tested on their ability to identify by touch such things as a key, a comb, a pair of scissors, and geometric shapes such as a rectangle and a cross. No differences were found between the responses of the blind and the sighted groups. Those results suggest that visually impaired children can be expected to successfully follow the various stages of development described by Jean Piaget as long as the visual problem is not complicated by other handicaps, such as mental retardation.

Intelligence   Earlier studies on the intellectual performance of the visually impaired suggested that intelligence was unimpaired since groups of blind children performed at an average level on IQ tests (Pintner, Eisenson, and Stanton, 1941; Hayes, 1941). However, later studies that examined specific dimensions of intelligence yielded more reserved or pessimistic results in line with Lowenfeld's judgment.

Tillman and Osborne (1969) found that although blind children were superior to sighted children on repetitions of series of numbers—a task used to test short-term memory (and attention)—blind students performed significantly worse than sighted students on items that required them to tell how two things are alike (for example, a rose and a potato). The inability to grasp associations indicated that lack of experience was limiting the blind child's ability to link ideas and objects. Other studies seem to confirm the negative effects of limited experience. For example, Kephart, Kephart, and Schwartz (1974) asked thirty-seven normally sighted and forty-nine blind children (5 to 7 years of age) to name the parts that should be included in drawings of a child and of a house. The blind children revealed less knowledge of body parts and house components than did the sighted. Even the 7-year-olds did not mention fingers, cars, or eyes in over 50 percent of the cases. At that age level the study suggests that the manner in which blind children are processing personal and environmental information appears to result in fragmented and distorted understandings of simple and straightforward concepts. The correct responses of blind children to standard test items may hide their incomplete conceptualization of the immediate world around them.

The accumulation of research studies on cognitive development suggests that the ability of visually impaired children to hear and to be able to communicate orally with others has allowed them to develop their intellectual abilities sufficiently to perform in the normal range on standard tests.

For a number of years, teachers and psychologists have pointed to the effective verbalization of visually handicapped children, together with their average performance on achievement tests, to suggest that the handicap itself has had a limited effect on educational attainment. However, recent research has cast doubt on that optimistic assessment, suggesting instead that the verbalization of blind children may often mask substantial cognitive deficits that are a result of the handicapping condition. These deficits show up most clearly in the preschool age range and come mainly from the inability of blind children to link object and verbal labels (the object comb and the word *comb*). Consequently, they are not able to develop necessary classification of objects, a task relatively simple for the sighted child who has visual orientation.

Sighted individuals are often startled to hear a blind person using terminology that seems unusual, such as "look here" and "now I see the problem." In addition, he or she will use various kinds of terms requiring visual imagery, such as "pure as snow." There is doubt that use of such terms represents a full understanding. Demott (1972) tested sighted and visually impaired children on their ability to meaningfully associate words and on their understanding of various words. He found that there were no differences between groups in their understanding of ideas and concepts, and concluded that the blind youngster, just like the sighted one, learns many words and their meanings through their use in the language, rather than through direct experience.

Reynell (1978) studied 109 blind children who were free from other serious handicapping conditions such as cerebral palsy and mental retardation and compared their performance on a number of different dimensions of social adaptation, sensory motor understanding, environmental orientation, verbal comprehension, and language expression. Reynell found that the partially sighted child and the blind child were significantly behind in all these dimensions—they were more socially immature, lacked essential understandings, and experienced special environmental orientation problems. Reynell has suggested that since vision dominates nearly all the early stages of learning that lay the foundations for many of the higher intellectual processes, it becomes important to provide some systematic programming of experiences for young blind children. Blind children need to know as much as they can about common objects and to touch and use the objects while simultaneously hearing their labels so that they have a fuller understanding of the objects and concepts involved. Then, when the school program becomes more verbally oriented in the second and third grades and beyond, the blind child will have the necessary conceptual understanding that links objects with their verbal labels.

Language Development   Bateman (1963) used the Illinois Test of Psycholinguistic Abilities to examine the developmental performance of 131 children enrolled in classes for the partially sighted in Illinois public schools. The results of the children's performance in abilities measured through the auditory channel were average, but they performed below average in visual perception, visual association, and visual memory. If there are problems, they seem to involve the child's ability to associate ideas, rather than the child's basic perception of concepts.

For blind children without additional handicaps, there is little evidence of atypical language development. . . . The area where the question is still quite wide open is that of meaning (including "verbalism"), and the work on meaning has not been adequate. . . . There is some evidence for differences in "richness of meaning," but it is by no means clear whether any such differences have implications for the adequacy of thought or other functional uses of language. (Warren, 1977, p. 244)

Educational Achievement The professional literature before World War II reported that the educational achievement of visually handicapped children did not differ significantly from sighted children of the same age. However, later studies were not as optimistic and indicated slight retardations for both blind and partially sighted children.

Birch et al. (1966) surveyed 903 partially sighted children in the fifth and sixth grades to determine their level of educational achievement. They found these students to be more than two grades below their expected level of achievement. The size of the print used did not seem to make any difference.

It is plausible to believe that the academic problems for visually handicapped children are not apparent in the early years of school, but as the academic content becomes increasingly abstract and interrelated, the special problems of the blind child become more of an educational handicap. There is a lack of reliable evidence on educational achievement, however.

Lowenfeld, Abel, and Hatlin (1967) studied blind students' mastery of braille in the fourth and eighth grades and found them equal to sighted students in reading comprehension, allowing for the fact that blind students require two to three times the reading time allotted for sighted children when measuring comprehension.

Motor Skills It is highly probable that a group of blind children who had had opportunities to climb trees, roller skate, and wrestle along with their sighted peers from preschool days would not be found seriously deficient in motor coordination. Similarly, it would be expected that a group of sighted children who had been sedentary and had not taken part in such activities would be somewhat deficient motorically.

Cratty (1971) has studied aspects of the motor response of blind children and has found that *laterality*, or the preferential use of one side of the body, is not as well established in the congenitally blind as in the adventitiously blind (those who had sight before becoming blind). He has suggested that planned stimulation is necessary for the proper development of motor skills in blind children.

Music   It has often been asserted that music is one area in which the blind have exceptional ability and interest. Although music education is often emphasized with the blind, and history provides testimony of some blind individuals who became noted musicians, there is no evidence to support a claim that the blind in general have superior musical ability. As Napier (1973) said: "These children are exposed to music instruction and related experiences from kindergarten on. . . . If normally seeing children were equally saturated with music, more seeing children might demonstrate musical ability, too"(p. 254).

Personal and Social Adjustment   There are no inevitable personal or social problems that follow from being visually handicapped, nor do their handicaps confer an automatic nobility on visually impaired people. However, the restricted mobility and consequent limited experiences of the visually handicapped child do appear to cause in many a state of passivity and dependency, a learned helplessness.

Fraiberg (1968) speculated that blind children do not initiate activities because they cannot see the consequences of their own acts. Myerson (1971), in discussing the problems of the partially sighted, pointed out that their adjustment difficulties are due to their marginal status (not blind, not sighted). He presented information showing that partially sighted children tend to be less well adjusted than either the blind or the sighted.

The following list contains the thoughts of some visually impaired students about how they are treated in school (Martin and Hoben, 1977).

Teachers should learn what "legally blind" really means. Lots of legally blind kids can do all sorts of things.

Teachers should study handicapped people and learn about them—especially their feelings.

If a teacher treats me different, the other kids think I'm a teacher's pet.

I don't want to see an A on my report card when I know I earned a C.

The worst thing for a handicapped person is for the teacher to pamper him.

It's more fun, more challenge when you have to compete. You don't feel like you're an outsider.

I appreciate the opportunity to get a better position in the classroom, but when the teacher asks me about it in front of the class it makes me feel like an idiot. I would tell teachers: if you want to tell me something that will help, don't make me feel like an idiot doing it.

Just because I'm blind doesn't mean I'm handicapped in other areas. (Martin and Hoben, 1977, p. 19)

Loosely translated, the feelings that are being communicated here are, "Don't treat me like I was helpless. Don't do me any special favors. Let me do it on my own." The reaction of many persons who have not had experience with the handicapped is to lessen their demands and expectations and these students don't want those kinds of "favors."

The importance of emphasizing the social and behavioral side of the visually handicapped adolescent is underscored in a study carried out by Meighan (1971). He gave the Tennessee Self-Concept Scale to 203 blind adolescents who were enrolled in three schools for the blind in the eastern part of the United States. The negative tone of the results was surprising. As Meighan pointed out, this visually handicapped sample "formed a very deviant and homogeneous group whose scores on the basic dimensions on self-concept were all found to be in an extremely negative dimension" (p. 35). In addition, there seemed to be no relationship between good achievement and positive self-concept. Also, no differences within the population were found on variables such as sex, race, or degree of disability, an unusual finding. The author believed that the visual handicap was a dominant factor, overriding other influences and causing the students to develop an uncertain self-identity.

It seems clear that adolescence with its social pressures may be a particularly sensitive period in the maturation of visually handicapped children that merits special attention from parents and educators.

EDUCATIONAL ADAPTATIONS FOR THE VISUALLY HANDICAPPED

Formal efforts to educate children with visual handicaps in the United States began with the establishment in 1829 of a residential school in Boston, now known as the Perkins School for the Blind. It was not until 1900 that the first public school class for the blind was organized in Chicago. The first class for the partially sighted was established in 1908 in England and in 1913 in the United States.

FIGURE 5.5
Number and Percentage of School Children Registered with the American Printing House for the Blind, by Type of School and Year, United States (1949–1981)

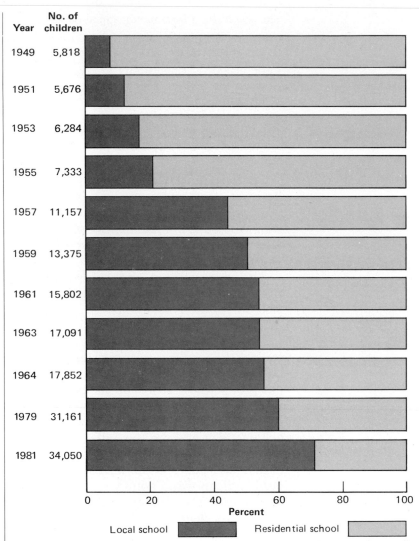

Source: Data for 1949–1964 from J. Jones and A. Collins, *Educational programs for visually handicapped children.* Bulletin No. 6, U.S. Office of Education. Washington, D.C.: U.S. Government Printing Office, 1966, p. 2. Data for 1970–1981 from American Printing House for the Blind.

Since that time there has been a consistent trend toward serving larger numbers of visually handicapped children, and more and more of these children are taught in a day school or public school setting (see Figure 5.5).

Now, about 80 percent of children with visual handicaps receive their education while living at home. A number of obvious adaptations in materials and equipment are needed to fully utilize the visually handicapped person's senses of hearing, touch, smell, residual vision, and even taste. Lowenfeld (1973) has stated some general principles that are also important and not so apparent for adapting instruction to the educational needs of visually handicapped children.

1. **Concreteness.** The educationally blind child's knowledge is gained primarily through hearing and touch. But if the child is really to understand the surrounding world, it is necessary that he or she be presented with concrete objects that can be touched and manipulated. Through tactile observation of models of objects, the child can learn about their shape, size, weight, hardness, surface qualities, pliability, and temperature.

2. **Unifying experiences.** Visual experience tends to unify knowledge in its totality. A child entering a grocery store will see the relationships of shelves and objects in space. A visually impaired child cannot obtain this unification unless teachers present him or her with experiences, such as "units of experience" of a farm, post office, and grocery store. It is necessary for the teacher to bring these "wholes" into perspective through actual concrete experience and to attempt to unify them through explanation and sequencing.

Left on their own, educationally blind children live a relatively restricted life. To expand their horizons, to develop imagery, and to orient them to a wider environment, it is necessary to develop those experiences by systematic stimulation.

3. **Learning by doing.** For a blind child to learn about the environment, it is necessary to initiate self-activity. A blind infant does not reach out for an object because it does not attract him or her. The infant must know of its existence by touch, smell, or hearing. Reaching and contact must be stimulated by deliberately introducing motivating situations like rattles for infants to reach for and games of finding hidden objects with smell or sound.

The visually handicapped child's ability to listen, relate, and remember must be developed to the fullest. He or she needs to learn efficiency and conservation of time because the techniques used to acquire the same information or accomplish the same task are sometimes cumbersome and time consuming. Therefore, the teacher must organize the material better, must be specific in making explanations, and must utilize sound principles of learning.

Getting an Early Start   The importance of experiences during the period from birth to age 5 to subsequent development makes it especially critical for systematic education of visually handicapped children to begin as early as possible. Normal children absorb a tremendous amount of information and experience from their environment in the ordinary course of family events. Specially designed experiences that parallel those of the normal child must be provided for the visually handicapped child. Table 5.3 shows four specific adaptations that can be made to accomplish key preschool milestones, such as feelings of human attachment, the discovery of objects, prehension (the use of the hands in reaching and exploring), and locomotion. The adaptations suggested in Table 5.3 are most likely to be carried out by the visually impaired child's parent, who will need careful instruction in the procedures to be followed.

At the preschool level much emphasis is placed on including the parent as a partner, and the special educator's work often consists of training the parent to interact more effectively with the handicapped child. As special educators extend their efforts toward earlier and earlier developmental levels, they find themselves working with the developmental building blocks on which later knowledge and skills are based.

**TABLE 5.3
Special Programming
for Preschool Blind
Children**

Developmental Areas	Normal Child Expectation	Special Adaptation for Blind
I. Human attachment	Vision plays a crucial role in the establishment of human bonds.	We stressed the importance of "learning to know" through tactile and auditory experience. We encouraged holding and talking to the baby during feeding and also creating "social" times of holding, singing, and playing lap games as the baby's awake times increased.
II. Discovery of objects	Eye-hand coordination in the sighted child forms a nucleus from which many patterns of infant learning and development evolve.	We encourage parents to introduce some form of cradle gym or hanging apparatus over the crib of the baby. Such a toy may be lowered over the baby so that random small movements will bring about touch and sound sensations.
III. Prehension	Prehension—the activity of the baby's hands, their organization, and progressive development—is intimately related to each of the other areas discussed.	We suggest patty-cake games and other informal, improvised lap games that bring the hands together at midline repeatedly and thus encourage their engagement. The hands exploring the face of the mother unite other sense impressions of the mother with manual tactile experience.
IV. Locomotion	It is the reach for the out-of-range object that initiates the pattern for creeping.	When a baby can demonstrate postural readiness for creeping and reach on a sound cue alone, one can initiate the pattern for creeping by providing a favorite sound toy just beyond reach.

Source: S. Fraiberg, M. Smith, and E. Adelson, An educational program for blind infants. *Journal of Special Education,* 1969, 3, 121–153.

Siblings as well as parents can be an important factor in the early emotional life of a blind child. (Photo: © Betty Medsger 1980.)

More educators have become increasingly sensitive to the importance of the early emotional life of the blind child. Barraga (1976) has provided a representative point of view: "With the visually handicapped infant, body play must replace eye play to communicate maternal concerns and love—the facilitators of developing a self-concept. More than the usual amount of time should be spent cuddling, holding, touching, stroking and moving the baby" (p. 20).

Parent involvement with the education of the child is most intimate at the preschool age. Parents of handicapped children need the most help during this time. The school or other agencies that are knowledgeable in the education of the visually impaired can be instrumental in providing helpful and adequate services to the family.

Learning Environment

As in the other areas of exceptionality, there is a push to bring the visually handicapped child into the least restrictive environment, but for many this will not be a mainstreamed regular classroom. The recognition of the variability of needs for children who are visually handicapped has led to a call for a continuum of services. Spungin (1981) has provided the following suggestions as a minimum.

Preschool Program

Children aged 0–5 who have been identified as having a visual impairment will be provided with a qualified teacher and any necessary ancillary services designed to divert the educational and emotional ramifications resulting from such an impairment.

Such intervention will include strategies designed to provide sensory stimulation, body image, gross and fine motor skills, sensory-perceptual motor activities, and experientially based cognitive and language development for the child as well as parent education in the increasing awareness of expected growth and development of their child. (pp. 14–15)

Teacher Consultant

Visually handicapped pupils are enrolled in a regular classroom in the school building which they would attend if they were not visually handicapped and ordinarily require minimal support services. Such services are provided by a teacher consultant for the visually handicapped who spends less than 50% of his/her time in direct instruction to students. More than 50% of the teacher's time is in indirect services such as consultation to parents, regular classroom teachers, and other appropriate school personnel; procurement of materials; assessment; coordination of related services; and other coordinating and supportive administrative activities. (p. 15)

Itinerant Teacher

Visually handicapped students are enrolled in a regular classroom in the school they would attend if they were not visually handicapped and require instruction in the development of special skills associated with the visual handicap. Such instruction is provided by an itinerant teacher of the visually handicapped who spends more than 50% of his/her time in direct instruction to students. (p. 15)

Resource Room

Students are enrolled in a regular class in a school which includes a special classroom for use by visually handicapped students who, ordinarily, require daily support services and specialized instruction. Such support services and direct instruction are provided and/or arranged by a teacher of the visually handicapped students according to the individual student's need. (p. 16)

Special Class

Students are enrolled in a special classroom and, ordinarily, require concentrated instruction for all or most of the school day. Instruction which emphasizes both subject matter skills and development of special skills is provided by a teacher of visually handicapped students in concert with other appropriate specialists. Such students may profit by participating in the regular school classes in special selected subject areas and/or other academic areas as appropriate to the changing needs of the student. (p. 16)

Special School Program

Students are enrolled in a special school which exclusively serves visually handicapped students and/or visually handicapped multiply-impaired students who require specialized instruction and support services beyond that which can reasonably be provided in the regular school programs. Such special school programs may be offered on a day or residential basis.

Students enrolled in special school programs should have access to the education programs in the local school district near the special school, either on a part-time or full-time basis. (p. 16)

Mainstreaming the Visually Handicapped Child

Mainstreaming in one form or another has been a part of the educational program for some visually handicapped children since the early part of the twentieth century.

The greater the number of exceptional children who are placed in regular classrooms, the greater the need for support personnel who have practical experience in the area of exceptionality to be helpers and consultants. The following discussion is between Sarah, a classroom teacher, and Ellen, a specialist in visual impairment. Their conversation about Bruce, a visually impaired student, illustrates the variety of adaptation problems that Bruce and his teacher must face in order to make mainstreaming work.

Sarah: Come on in and sit down. Since things have slowed down a little bit this week, I thought we could take time for a cup of coffee.

Ellen: Thanks. These first few weeks really have been hectic. But I know we're both glad to have finished Bruce's IEP at the conference with his parents last week. How have things been going in class? Is the arrangement we designed working out?

Sarah: It's great except for one thing. Bruce still can't see the chalkboard from where he's sitting and he doesn't really like having a friend make a carbon copy of the board work for him, so he keeps jumping up and down to read what's on the chalkboard.

Ellen: Well, at least I'm glad he doesn't feel self-conscious about not being able to see the board. However, there are a couple of things we can do to alleviate the problem. First, you can be sure to read aloud whatever you write on the chalkboard. That way, Bruce can write important things down from the oral input and go up to the board later to copy longer lists. Most teachers find that oral input helps the other kids too. The other thing we can do is see if the janitor could help put wheels on Bruce's chair. He'd be able to get to the board without jumping up and down then. I'll check with Mr. Payne on my way out tonight.

Sarah: Those are both good ideas. Thanks, Ellen. But now let me tell you what's really got me concerned. It's the other kids. They were really excited about having Bruce in the class at first. Everybody wanted to take him around the school. I'll bet they showed him where the water fountain was at least fifty times! But lately the novelty seems to be wearing off. Today at recess Bruce just sat by the wall and listened to his portable radio while most of the others played softball.

Ellen: Lots of visually impaired youngsters do have a rough time being accepted. In fact, children with low vision, like Bruce, often find it harder to get along with sighted classmates than do children who are totally blind. I guess it's partly because the kids don't always know what Bruce can and can't see, what things he needs help with, and how they should act with him. But there are lots of other factors too, like how well Bruce does in his school work and how he handles group situations. It's hard to put your finger on a single cause.

Sarah: I know what you mean. The other day, Billy Turner—one of the real active tigers in my class—noticed that Bruce's handwriting was . . . well . . . kind of messy, and called the other kids over to look at it.

Ellen: Low vision students often write imperfectly because they see imperfectly. (Looking at Bruce's paper.) Hmm . . . it's certainly not beautiful handwriting, but this special boldline paper we ordered does seem to be helping. I'll plan to work with him on writing during the next few weeks. Another thing—Bruce is about ready to learn to type. Although he can't type class notes because of the noise, he can type assignments and that should help. (Orlansky, 1980, pp. 9–10)

Discussions like the preceding are especially important to help prepare regular classroom teachers, who may have very limited experience in the special needs of the visually handicapped and who may approach the problem with a number of misconceptions. The itinerant or resource teacher who is familiar with the visually handicapped can help the classroom teacher understand the true nature of the problems that these children face. For example, the classroom teacher of a partially sighted boy got upset because he wanted to sit very close to the closed circuit television monitor and also because he tended to hold books very close to his eyes. The teacher's fears that these practices would harm the boy's vision could be dispelled by the expert advice of a special teacher. Another common misconception is that very bright light should always be available to the visually handicapped. Teachers may not realize that dim light will not harm the eyes, and with some eye conditions, such as cataracts or albinism, a child may require dim lighting in order to feel more comfortable.

A number of publications have been developed to help teachers with limited experience become more knowledgeable about the educational world of the visually handicapped. Corn and Martinez

Kevin's a Typical Child . . . and Blind

Kevin Minor attends a regular sixth grade in a central Colorado public school. Blind from birth, Kevin has been in a regular classroom since kindergarten.

"Kevin has succeeded," says his homeroom teacher, "because of his insistence on doing what other kids do, and because of his parents' support in his efforts to do so."

At first, Kevin's mother walked the few blocks with him to school. He wanted to go alone. After much practice, he convinced his parents that he could walk alone, although for several weeks he called home to announce his safe arrival.

Kevin was determined to learn to read in first grade, and he did. His itinerant Braille teacher explains, "Kevin learned Braille with the help of a Perkins Braillewriter and an Optacon, which is a machine that transfers regular printing into Braille. He loves to read and does it well."

One of Kevin's biggest problems in kindergarten came from adults and peers at school trying to protect him. When he was not allowed to use the playground equipment, he made a special appeal, and with his parents' support the ban was lifted. "Now you could not tell him from any other child on the playground," reports his homeroom teacher.

Kevin has adjusted to the fact that his school has no special ramps or guideways. Some blind youngsters use a guide dog or cane, but Kevin does not. "If I've been someplace before," he says, "I usually remember. A few special things help, though, like the spot I have for my coat. A label with my name in Braille tells me where to put it and where to find it."

"Kevin usually remembers very well where things are located," agrees Kevin's reading teacher, who directed a recent play in which Kevin starred. "I only had to tell him once what direction to face for the audience."

Kevin explains, "Scenes in the play with other people were not too hard because I had their voices to guide me. What was hard was my grand entry when I had to jump onto the stage."

In the regular classroom, if information is put on the chalkboard, one of Kevin's classmates sitting nearby usually reads it for him. When Kevin's sixth-grade class began studying map skills, Kevin's teachers provided him with raised maps. They even created a map of his school to show where the rooms were, with Braille symbols and codes.

One unexpected problem arose for Kevin in fifth grade, when several new classmates expressed resentment at his excellent grades. They felt they should be doing better than someone who couldn't see and began to isolate Kevin from their activities. The teacher helped the class to realize how much time and effort goes into Kevin's achievements. With time and Kevin's positive attitude, the resentment disappeared.

Kevin's Braille teacher works with him on other social skills, too, such as looking at the person who's talking. "I can tell if you're tall or short by where your voice comes from," says Kevin.

"My Braille teacher helped me to write my name. She says there will be lots of times and places to use my signature. And, I've found one place already. I can check out my own Braille books." The school library maintains a rotating supply of Braille books for Kevin.

This leads to one of Kevin's favorite activities. "Something not many people do," Kevin claims. "I can read in bed in the dark. 'Lights out' time for me is when Mom takes the book away."

School personnel were taken aback when Kevin showed up for touch football tryouts. But they were surprised and proud when he made the team and completed a successful season as the team's offensive center. "It's his attitude," says the coach. "He really believes he can do things, and he's helped us learn that he's right."

Kevin's ability to develop successful routines at school began at home. He makes his own bed (a job he says he dislikes but which he is very proud he can do), takes out the trash, and has recently begun cooking and preparing weekend lunches for friends.

"At first I was sure the cooking was impossible," said Kevin's mother, "but we worked out ways of making it more safe, such as using a porcelain-topped stove, and wearing short-sleeved shirts while cooking. We cook together and we're quite a team!"

When asked to identify techniques that have contributed to Kevin's success in a mainstream situation, his parents and teachers pointed to these five factors.

Kevin's personality causes him to try new things. Children who are afraid to try should be shown how to break big tasks into small ones and should be encouraged to attempt one of these small challenges each day.

Parents and teachers "spot" for Kevin. They let him try new things, and stay close enough to him so they can help if needed. Kevin did not know, for example, that his mother followed him to school at a distance the first few times he tried it alone.

Parents and teachers realize there are alternative ways to accomplish any given goal and help Kevin find them. Whereas many people think it impossible for a blind child to play football, Kevin's coach discovered that a child could play center by relying only on hearing and touch.

In Kevin's school it's all right to be different. The staff works hard to stress the beauty of diversity and the importance of individual differences. Events are planned to emphasize this, such as the hall poster which read, "It's nice to be the same; it's nice to be different."

Everyone realizes that Kevin is more like other kids than unlike them, and they treat him that way. Kevin himself does much to engender this feeling of normality. But since birth his parents have also reinforced Kevin's confidence in himself and his determination to be like everyone else.

Kevin's positive outlook works miracles. He constantly thinks about what he can do, what he wants to accomplish, instead of what he can't do. He has an active sense of humor that puts people at ease and makes them concentrate on his strengths. Kevin's teacher declares, "This is the most important factor of all. Any teacher or parent who can give a child this sense of optimism has performed an invaluable service."

SOURCE: Marsha Perlman and Vivian Dubrovin, "Kevin's a Typical Child . . . and Blind." *Instructor*, 1979, *88* (February), 175–177. Reprinted from *Instructor*, February 1979. Copyright © 1979 by The Instructor Publications, Inc. Used by permission.

(1978) have produced a manual to provide information for the teacher on the use of special devices, ways in which the visually handicapped can work with printed material, and suggestions on helping the visually handicapped child manage other activities. Following are some examples:

Lamps and rheostats. With variable intensities and positioning, lamps can provide the additional or dimmed illumination that a visually handicapped child may require.

Large-type books. For comfort or for those children who cannot read regular print at close distance even with an optical aid, large-type is helpful. Its quality or typeface is as important to legibility as its size. Spacing between letters and lines is also important.

Raised line paper (writing paper, graph paper, etc.). Raised line paper allows a student to write script "on the line" or to maneuver a graph either by placing markers onto the graph paper or by punching holes to indicate specific points.

Cassette tape recorders. Children use the recorder to take notes, listen to recorded texts, or formulate compositions or writing assignments.

Talking calculator. This hand-held calculator speaks each entry and result. It is capable of performing all the computations of a non-adapted electronic calculator. (Earphones are available.)

More time. Extra time will frequently be needed to complete assignments and exams. Allowing time and a half is usually considered acceptable. The child may complete his work in the resource room or school library. When you are certain that the child understands the work, it may be a good idea to shorten his assignments: for example, you may request that a student do only the odd-numbered problems in the math homework. (Corn and Martinez, 1978, pp. 9–15)

Developing Special Skills

Using Braille

Blind and partially sighted children need to develop a series of special skills to compensate for their communication and spatial problems. For the blind child, learning to use braille is one of the key skills that open the doors of communication with the sighted world.

Braille reading is a system of touch reading developed in 1829 by Louis Braille, a blind Frenchman. Embossed characters are used in different combinations of six dots arranged in a cell two dots wide and three dots high. The symbols are embossed on heavy manila paper in a left-to-right order, and the reader usually

FIGURE 5.6
Braille Alphabet and Numerals

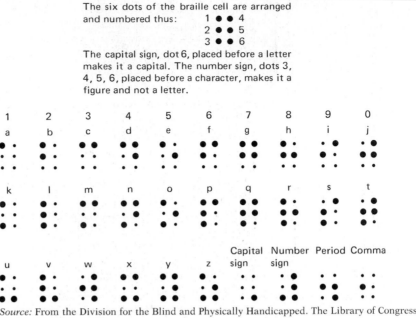

The six dots of the braille cell are arranged and numbered thus:

```
1 ● ● 4
2 ● ● 5
3 ● ● 6
```

The capital sign, dot 6, placed before a letter makes it a capital. The number sign, dots 3, 4, 5, 6, placed before a character, makes it a figure and not a letter.

Source: From the Division for the Blind and Physically Handicapped. The Library of Congress, Washington, D.C. 20542.

"reads" with both hands, one leading and the other following. An advanced reader may use the second hand to orient himself or herself to the next line while reading the line above and may read as much as a third of the line with the second hand. Music, punctuation, and mathematical and scientific notations are based on the same system. Figure 5.6 gives the braille alphabet and numbers.

Although many other systems have been tried, Standard English braille was accepted in 1932 as the system for general use. Standard English braille has been developed on several levels of difficulty. Grade 1 braille is comprised of the letters of the alphabet, marks of punctuation, and numerals. Grade 2 braille, which incorporates 190 contractions and short forms to speed up the reading process, is used in American schools as soon as the students master the basic system.

Even the most efficient blind reader of braille shows an average rate of reading about two to three times slower than that of a print reader. In that area alone, one can understand how blind students can fall progressively further and further behind in total knowledge when compared with the average reader. Attempts have been made to improve the efficiency of braille reading.

Umsted (1972) provided a training program for adolescent blind children to increase their identification and skill in reading the braille code. He found that once the young blind child had learned the braille system, few attempts had been made to improve the efficiency of the youngster's braille reading when he or she attended a secondary program. The assumption was that the code had been effectively mastered and would remain so. However, Umsted found that almost 10 percent of the braille code was not correctly identified by blind students and that an intensive, short-term training program designed specifically to help them become more effective with the code increased their reading level from 90 words per minute to 120 words per minute for a medium reading group, and to an average gain of 25 words per minute for the high reading group. That finding has suggested that continuing attention to the special skills that the blind have to learn can improve their efficiency in learning. Skills, once learned, can atrophy unless given specific practice and review.

Braille writing is another addition to the curriculum of blind children. It is taught later than braille reading. There are various devices for writing the symbols, the easiest and fastest of which is the braille typewriter, or braille-writer machine. It has six keys corresponding to the six dots of the cell. A good braille typist can type forty to sixty words per minute. Braille can also be written by hand, using a special slate and stylus which allows the child to make the indentations in a standrad braille cell.

Typing and Handwriting

Typing, which is seldom included in the elementary curriculum for sighted children, is very important for blind children if they are to communicate with the sighted world, since a very small number of sighted people can read braille. Blind children are taught to use a standard print typewriter as soon as possible, usually in the third or fourth grade. Handwriting is usually very difficult and is no longer emphasized to a great extent, except that an effort is made to teach the child to write his or her own signature. The inability to write one's own name is often a source of embarrassment, which is why the signature is stressed. The typewriter has all but replaced such devices as wire guidelines, which were needed to help teach handwriting.

Mastery of the Environment

Teaching command of the environment is of special importance to blind children in that both their physical and social independence

Blind children are taught to use a standard print typewriter to communicate in written form with the sighted world. (Photo: © Betty Medsger 1981.)

are involved. The ease with which they can move about, find objects and places, and orient themselves to new or strange physical and social situations will be crucial in determining the role they can assume in peer relations, the types of vocations and avocations that will be open to them as adults, and their own estimation of themselves as individuals.

What can be done to aid the blind child in gaining as much mastery of the environment and of himself or herself in the environment as is possible? From a very early age the child can be helped to avoid unnecessary fear, both of new experiences and of injury. Sighted children skin their knees, bump their shins, fall from trees, and step in holes. Blind children ought to have the same "privilege" if they are to experience freedom for the control of themselves and their environment.

Blind children must be taught to feel the difference in the weight of their forks when they have successfully cornered a few peas and when the fork is still empty. A system of marking clothing and organizing it is essential for both efficiency and good grooming.

The use of models, whether of a room, the World Trade Center, or the child's neighborhood, is generally felt to be helpful in showing the relationship of one place, or size, to another. But this is not to say that models are approved as a substitute for the experience. Rather, they are an extension of experiences and can also help give a perceptual or cognitive map of relations and areas too large to be simultaneously included in direct experience.

Orientation and Mobility

The importance of training blind children and adults to move about in their environment cannot be overestimated. One of the greatest limitations imposed by blindness is mobility. The situations that force dependence and may cause the greatest personality and social problems are very likely to involve mobility. The use of the long cane, the seeing-eye dog, and a sighted guide have been tried with adults. Currently there is an effort to introduce mobility training in the curriculum, not only for secondary school students but also for young blind children.

Developing orientation and mobility skills is crucial to a blind person's independence. (Photo: © Betty Medsger 1981.)

One of the most important practical questions in helping the blind to move about their environment independently is how to teach the avoidance of obstacles. That is a good example of how research can help the teacher by identifying the relevant area to be emphasized. It has long been observed that many blind persons can avoid obstacles very well. They make turns in hallways, they stop before they run into a door, and so on. But how do they do it? Is it through sensing the change of air pressure on their faces? Is it their use of some residual light and dark vision? Is it through the sense of hearing?

Cotzin and Dallenbach (1950) carried out a series of classic experiments designed to find the answer. They asked blind persons to walk down a path and stop when they sensed an obstacle placed there by experimenters. Then systematically the researchers eliminated the various possibilities. They put a velvet hood over the face to eliminate the cues from air pressure, then plugged the ears to eliminate hearing, and blindfolded them to rule out residual vision, each in turn. Out of those experiments came a clear and definitive result. The blind were bothered in their judgment only when their ears were plugged! They were clearly using hearing in a way similar to that of bats, which use sound to avoid the walls in a cave. Changes in both pitch and loudness seemed to be used as clues. That information allowed the educational program to focus on enhancing, in natural and artificial ways, the use of hearing for the purpose of effective travel.

An example of the development of an artificial device was reported by Juurmaa (1970). He described a research study using an *ultrasonic torch*, a battery-powered device, which is held by the blind person. The torch emits ultrasonic sounds, which then rebound from obstacles and return so that the difference between outgoing and returning sound waves falls within the audio range. In that way the blind person can discern when he or she is approaching targets. Juurmaa reported that in the research study the blind comparison group that did not use the ultrasonic torch also performed surprisingly well. The remaining question is whether the ingeniousness of the device adds that much to the natural skill of the blind to make up for the disadvantages of carrying such a device around. One of the clear alternatives to mechanical intervention is the training of the blind to use more effectively the hearing capabilities they already have.

The area of personal mobility and independence has a particular significance in adolescence when the child is ready to break away from family restraints and overprotection. In peer relationships, security and comfort in controlling one's self and the environment

Security and comfort in controlling one's self and the environment are particularly important for the blind adolescent. (Photo: © Betty Medsger 1981.)

are most essential to developing poise and independence and to gaining the respect of others.

In relation to orientation and mobility training, physical education, formerly thought dangerous for the visually impaired, is being stressed as part of the curriculum. In residential schools classes for physical education are now a routine part of the curriculum. In local day schools the visually impaired are encouraged to participate in physical education activities with sighted children whenever possible.

Map and Chart Reading

One favorite curriculum adaptation for children with visual handicaps are models or tactual maps representing spatial relationships that children can master through their sense of touch. Berla (1981) discovered that visually handicapped students can improve their ability to read maps if they are specifically taught systematic techniques for searching around a map. Younger children, in particular, seem to profit from such instruction. Teachers should not expect students to discover complex search techniques for themselves. Just as the sighted child needs help in learning the techniques for using a soldering iron or hand drill, the visually handicapped child needs instruction in specific search skills, even when the search is across a map instead of a town.

However, special maps alone are not enough because students must first have some understanding of what the maps represent. Napier (1973) has presented the type of careful and comprehensive activities that must be planned.

Just as there must be readiness activities to prepare for the teaching of reading, there must be readiness activities prior to the teaching of map reading. Before the most rudimentary map can be read, children must experience a given area with all its details and cues. Therefore . . . the classroom is the logical place to begin. In this setting, children learn that coats are hung in the closet left of the main door, that the teacher's desk is straight ahead from the door, that the wastebasket is immediately inside the door on the right, etc. (p. 239)

Listening Skills

It is very important for visually handicapped children to be more proficient than sighted children in listening skills. Much of their education depends on listening to talking books, tapes, and verbal intercourse. Special teachers have developed techniques for developing listening skills, and the research on compressed speech and its utilization has shown a potential for decreasing the time that was once considered necessary for auditory comprehension of talking books. In high school and college blind persons rely on readers to obtain information and must learn to listen to details.

Life Skills

Sarah and Ralph, the youngsters whose developmental profiles appear earlier in this chapter, will soon reach adolescence and they will begin to think about where they are going to live and what they will do as adults. They both value and look forward to an independent, or at least semi-independent, living setting. They will be thinking about going away to school or finding a job and an apartment in which to live. In middle and late adolescence, visually handicapped children need to further develop a whole series of orientation and mobility skills. Think of the numerous things with which you must become familiar when moving into a new apartment or dormitory, including the position of the furniture and the locations of the bathroom, phone, and cafeteria. Sighted people can depend on their effective vision in becoming familiar with their surroundings rather quickly. However, determining the location of objects and places in a new setting represents a major adventure for visually handicapped youngsters who must, through tactual and other senses, make a cognitive map of their environment.

Hatlen, LeDuc, and Canter (1975) have described a systematic attempt to provide effective independent living skills for the visually handicapped. The Blind Adolescent Life Skills Center, located in an urban area, comprised ten apartments in a seventy-five-unit apartment complex with twenty blind young adults living in the center's apartments. The center provided services, including instruction on mobility as well as on orientation to the apartment, on an "on-call" or as needed basis. The instruction included such survival skills as shopping for groceries, preparing simple meals, managing finances, using the telephone for emergencies, and dealing with roommates. In addition, instruction at the center involved communication skills, recreational social skills, and prevocational training, and attempts were made to integrate these skills into daily living tasks. For example, in order to get to a recreational activity, mobility skills must be used. One example of a relatively simple task for a sighted person, but a challenge for one who is visually handicapped, is noted in the following teaching notes:

Pete asked me to help him make a grilled cheese sandwich. He felt he could do everything but turn the sandwiches in the skillet. I've helped him three or four times with this task. Painstaking, but steady improvement. By the time he had turned all six sandwiches he needed no help at all. However, getting the right amount of butter in the skillet, tipping the skillet to spread the butter evenly is not so easy. I'll bring in my pastry brush and help him paint some melted butter on the bread. Pete is eager for concentrated help on living skills and is getting better about asking for help. (p. 112)

Another item of special concern for visually handicapped people is their personal appearance. Since they have no way of seeing how others react to them, they are unable to pick up on visual cues to fix unruly hair, a crooked tie, or unbuttoned clothing. Sighted people know immediately if something is wrong with their appearance by the odd looks they receive from others. Blind people must use their tactual sense to double check their appearance before venturing out into the seeing world.

Content   Most of the content presented to the visually handicapped child is similar or identical to material presented to the sighted child. This is particularly true when visually handicapped children spend the majority of their time in the regular classroom. However, some modifications can be made to address specific areas of adaptive difficulty.

The work of Malone, DeLucchi, and Thier (1981) represents a major attempt to bring special content in science to visually handicapped students. Their program, Science Activities for the Visually Impaired (SAVI), was designed for upper elementary school-age blind and visually impaired students. The project stresses "hands-on" activities that allow students to manipulate objects and conduct experiments. The student is presented with tasks that can be challenging and enjoyable for sighted and visually handicapped children who are working together and is thus appropriate for use in a mainstreamed educational setting.

Figure 5.7 shows an example of an activity, part of a complete instructional module on "Kitchen Interactions," that allows the students to measure the action of acids using common everyday objects plus a special plastic syringe with tactile notches to help visually handicapped students determine the amount of liquid in the syringe. Special braille recording sheets are also available to enable the students to quantify data. Through such experiences the students learn the key scientific procedures of observing, measuring, comparing, calculating, and drawing conclusions.

Other instructional modules in the program cover topics such as "Scientific Reasoning," "Communications," "Magnetism and Electricity," and "Structures of Life." Each module has sets of activities, equipment, and detailed instructions for the teacher, including special vocabulary terms and follow-up activities that the students might wish to do at home or away from the classroom. Programs such as SAVI provide concrete experiences in a systematic way allowing visually impaired students to make full use of intellectual abilities that otherwise might be devoted to verbal interchange which could not be linked to physical environment.

Relationships in the Physical World

Most of the educational methods and techniques for exceptional children have emerged from master teachers and their reports of practical interactions with special children. Expert practitioners have passed their wisdom and teaching methods on to younger teachers and in this way a body of acceptable practice has developed.

An educational theory or developmental theory based on normal children is rarely used to provide guidance on curriculum planning for the exceptional child. An interesting exception to that rule is the use of Piagetian theory in programming for visually handicapped children. Piaget's theory of cognitive development, as the reader may recall from educational psychology courses, takes the child from the earliest sensorimotor stage to the formal operations

OVERVIEW

In *The Acid Test*, the students use baking soda to test for the presence of acid in common foods. They establish that when vinegar (an acid) is mixed with baking soda, a reaction occurs and a gas (carbon dioxide) is given off. When this reaction takes place in a bottle with a syringe stuck into the top, the carbon dioxide pushes the plunger out of the syringe barrel. The amount of acid in a measured sample of vinegar is the *standard* against which the amount of acid in other foods (orange juice, grapefruit juice, lemon juice) is compared.

Finally, the youngsters investigate the variables in the acid/soda reaction to help them "pop the top" (i.e. launch the plunger out of the syringe barrel).

BACKGROUND

How about a glass of acid with your peanut butter and jelly sandwich? Or how about tossing a little acid in the next batch of biscuits you bake? That sounds unappetizing to say the least, but acids are common in many of our favorite foods. The lemon juice that we use to make a tangy glass of lemonade, the buttermilk we use in biscuit dough, and the vinegar bath used to preserve pickles are all examples of acid ingredients in the foods we eat.

A simple technique for testing the acid content of foods involves using baking soda as an *indicator*. When an acid reacts with baking soda, two things happen. First, the acid is neutralized or converted into new substances that are not acidic; and second, a gas called carbon dioxide is liberated in the form of bubbles. The amount of gas produced by this *reaction* can be used to compare the strengths of

Source: L. Malone, L. DeLucchi, and H. Thier, *Science activities for the visually impaired.* SAVI Leadership Trainer's Manual. Berkeley, Calif.: Center for Multisensory Learning, University of California, 1981.

stage through a series of assumptions about progressive interactions that will take place between the child and his or her environment as the child matures. Between the ages of 2 and 7 the child's thinking is supposed to be at the *preoperational* stage because the child's perceptions of objects usually override the thinking operations of the child. For example, the child assumes that a tall, thin glass of water holds more liquid than a short, fat glass even though the child has seen prior evidence that the glasses hold an equal amount of liquid. Between the ages of 7 and 12 the average child is in the *concrete operational* stage. The child can use reasoning ability to solve a problem as long as the problem deals with observable concrete phenomena. The child is able to solve increasingly complex problems by using the capability for logical reasoning. Beyond the ages of 12 and 13 children are presumed to mature into the *formal operational* stage when they can manipulate and reason with abstract mathematical symbols and other symbolic information without referring back to tangible objects.

The questions posed by educators of the visually handicapped include, "What effect does the child's handicap have on the normal progression of cognitive development?" "Does the cognitive development of visually handicapped children follow the same sequence and progress at the same rate as that of normal children?" If substantial interaction with the environment is deemed necessary to give the child the experience to move from one stage to the next, then can inability to see and lack of experience in handling the physical world cause special development delays in visually handicapped children?

Stephens and Simpkins (1974) set out to trace the development of logical reasoning by comparing seventy-five congenitally blind and seventy-five sighted children who were the same age and had equivalent IQ scores. The children were provided a battery of Piagetian reasoning tasks that involved a variety of experiences with the physical environment. The results of this study have suggested that the level of conceptual development attained by sighted subjects was significantly greater than that obtained by the blind children of similar age and aptitude. Stephens and Simpkins were inclined to attribute these results to the lack of early sensory experiences on the part of the blind children. They tried to follow through with a curriculum that attacked this problem by presenting a series of experiences illustrating fundamental constructs in the Piagetian model. The following example of an exercise in that curriculum—"Is It Size or Is It Weight?" (Stephens et al., 1981)—focuses on the relationship of weight and volume as two fundamental constructs that are basic to understanding the physical world around us.

Introduction

The activities in this module illustrate differences between volume and weight. They demonstrate that volume not weight determines the amount of water an object will displace. Situations are provided which demonstrate that what appears to be true may not be. The student discovers that a large object can float while smaller objects sink and that a small heavy object displaces less water than a larger lighter object. The activities, designed for students who are in transition between the concrete and the formal level of thought, provide formal-level conservation of volume tasks as well as tasks related to dissociation of notions of weight and volume.

Piagetian Concept

Conservation of Volume

Procedures

I. Objects that float and objects that sink.

Present the student with the various materials and a container of fresh water. Have the student separate those objects which he/she believes will float from those which he/she believes will sink and list the objects in each group. Then have the student place each object in fresh water and determine whether it sinks or floats. Have him/her record the results and compare them with his/her estimates.

Ask: *Do heavy objects sink and light objects float?*
How do we decide what "heavy" and "light" mean? Even the lightest object on the table is heavy when compared to a strand of hair for example.
Does the material of an object determine whether the object sinks or floats?
In what ways might you group the objects to test whether they sink or float (e.g., volume, shape, weight, texture, hardness, etc.)?

Conclusion: Consideration of the composition of the object in determining which objects sink and which ones float indicates realization that a factor other than weight or volume is involved.

II. Getting floating objects to sink and sinking objects to float.

Ask: *Can you get that aluminum ball to float?*
Some shapes are made of metal. Can they float?
Can you make that wooden cylinder sink?
Can you sink the wooden boats?
What would happen if we put a hole in a wooden boat?
Would the boat still float?

Ask: *Boats float, can you make a clay boat float?*
If you rolled the clay boat into a ball, would it still float?
Can you get the clay boat to sink without just pushing it under?
Why does it sink when you push it under?
Can you put anything on the clay boat and still have it float?
How much does it take to sink it?

Do equivalent amounts of any two different materials cause the clay boat to sink?
Are these amounts equivalent in size, weight, or volume?

Have him/her test his/her answers.

Place a sheet of aluminum foil in a bowl of fresh water.

Ask: *Why does the sheet of aluminum foil float?*
The cylinder and the foil are made from the same material. Why do you think one will float and the other one sink?

Note: If the student says that the foil floats because it is light, remind him/her that aluminum motor boats are heavier than the foil and yet they float. (Stephens et al., 1981, pp. 133, 135–136)

Students' understanding of the concepts tested is indicated by their ability to give correct answers consistently.

Mathematics Adaptation

Another example of how specific content has to be designed to help blind children master concepts is provided by Huff and Franks (1973) on the mathematical issue of fractional parts. It is easy enough to provide an intuitive understanding of halves and quarters by visual demonstration, but for blind students such understanding must be acquired through the sense of touch. Huff and Franks demonstrated that blind children at the primary grade levels (K–3) can master those concepts if they are given three-dimensional circles of wood and asked to place them in a form board nest. After placing a whole circle, the child can learn to assemble blocks representing one-third of a circle and put them together in the nest to form the whole. Given such a tactile experience, blind children can master the idea of fractional parts and make discriminations between the relative sizes of various fractional parts (halves versus quarters) as well as sighted children of similar age can.

In the middle grades (fourth through eighth or ninth grades), visually impaired children are furnished with supplementary materials to help them absorb the same information that sighted children learn. This is accomplished through talking books, recorded audio lessons, and remedial work if the child needs it.

Sex Education

One of the extremely important areas of special instruction necessary for visually limited children is the topic of sexual information and identity. As Barraga (1976) has stated:

By the time visually impaired youth reach high school and begin to think about relationships (and marriage) with those of the opposite sex, they may have many erroneous ideas or be totally ignorant of the basic facts relating to body parts and sexual functioning. . . . Courses in sex education and preparation for marriage and family life are absolutely necessary for visually impaired children and youth. (p. 70)

A great deal of information has become available to help teachers of visually handicapped children approach the topic of family life and interpersonal relations, a curriculum area that was often ignored in the past. Although the facts of sexual reproduction are not overlooked, attention is focused on how people live and work together, as indicated in the following excerpt:

Concept: A man and a woman who love each other marry and become husband and wife to each other and form a new family.

Learning Activities
1. Have children tell about weddings they have attended. Introduce terms such as bride, groom, wife, husband.
2. Note that when husband and wife have children they become father and mother also.
3. Invite children to tell about sister's, aunt's, neighbor's boy friends or girl friends.
4. Ask children "who can marry each other?" And who should not, i.e. sisters and brothers, and other close relatives.

Concept: A family is a group of people who live together and take care of each other.

Learning Activities
1. Discuss the different kinds of family groupings. Help the children to recognize that changes brought about by death, divorce, and separation do affect the composition of a family, but they are still families.
2. Ask children to identify members of their families and encourage them to bring in pictures.
3. Have children relate how their families have changed in size and discuss the effect on the family.
4. Ask children to name the "big people" within families and their relationships (grandmother, grandfather, aunt, uncle, cousin). (Dickman, 1975, p. 36)

The Uses of Technology Advances in the fields of electronics and computers have had important implications for the visually handicapped individual. Only a few of the many devices designed to improve mobility or reading skills can be noted here.

Developed at Stanford University, the *Optacon* scans print and converts print into 144 tactile pins. These pins, when activated by the print, produce a vibratory image of the letter on the finger of a blind person. As a college student, the blind daughter of Dr. John

Linville, one of the inventors, was able to read at sixty to seventy words a minute with the use of Optacon. The device is still being improved, and a blind person may be able to read regular books and notes not available in braille. Bliss and Moore (1974) have indicated that to learn to read with the Optacon, a child must have high intelligence, must spend long periods in training, and must be highly motivated. Barraga (1976) stated that the Optacon is a worthwhile invention because print material can be read without modification. At present, the high cost of the Optacon limits its widespread use by blind children.

At the Massachusetts Institute of Technology a *computer automaton* is being developed that will translate ink print into Grade 2 braille. The procedure is being used extensively at the American Printing House for the Blind. An expansion of the computer braille translator, the *MIT Braille Emboss,* is used with a telewriter. A teacher of the blind desiring a braille output for new materials can request it by phone from a computer center, and it is returned in braille by means of a teletypewriter.

One way of obtaining more rapid information through records and tapes is to increase their speed. This generally produces a distortion. Another system that has been developed is *compressed speech*, which allows the elimination of one one-hundredth of each second, or one-fiftieth or one-tenth, without causing distortion of voice. This compressor, which is now used at the American Foundation for the Blind, can double the word rate while preserving vocal pitch and quality. A blind person can comprehend recorded voices at 275 words per minute, which is comparable to reading print.

An alternative to compressed speech is available in the *Kurzweil Reading Machine,* which converts printed material into spoken English at normal speech rates. The user places the material to be read face down on the surface of the scanner, which the user activates by means of a separate control unit. The scanning mechanism locates the first line of text and begins scanning the page. Within seconds an electronic voice is heard reading the material. Despite its dramatic qualities, the equipment has limited application because it is expensive and not movable.

The *Sonicguide,* which is a device that aids mobility, resembles a pair of glasses that emits high-frequency sounds beyond the range of human hearing. The ultrasound reflects back from objects in or near the travel path of a blind person, and it is fed back into the equipment and transformed into audible signals. Distance is determined by the pitch of the sound, which the user must learn to interpret (Newcomer, 1977).

The Kurzweil Reading Machine converts printed material into spoken English at normal speech rates. (Photo: The Kurzweil Reading Machine, a Product of Kurzweil Computer Products, Inc., a Xerox Company.)

All of these technological advances have several elements in common. First, they require careful and extensive instruction before they can be used effectively. Second, they break down from time to time and provisions must be made for repair and alternative adaptations. Third, they are expensive and often awkward to use in a normal life setting.

Given the continuing advances in the electronics industry, we can expect more of these wonders in the future to aid the adaptation of visually handicapped children to their physical and educational environment.

SUMMARY OF MAJOR IDEAS

1. Visually impaired children are classified for educational purposes as (a) the *blind* who have only light perception and must learn braille and related media without the use of vision and (b) the *partially sighted* or those with low vision who have major limitations in distance vision but who can learn to read print and can be educated by using their eyes.
2. An estimated one or two children out of one thousand require special education because of a visual handicap. Approximately 35,000 children attend local and residential schools for the visually impaired.
3. Approximately one-third of the visually handicapped children who are enrolled in special programs have multiple handicaps.
4. Intelligence and achievement tests reveal only slight retardation for partially sighted and blind children, but there is evidence of subtle intellectual problems in mastering abstract concepts that appear later in childhood and adolescence.
5. The majority of visually impaired children are now educated in local day school classes rather than in residential schools.
6. Parent education is an important element in aiding the early development of skills and attitudes crucial to later adaptation of visually impaired children.
7. Recent attention has been placed on the socioemotional development of children with visual handicaps because some adolescent children experience major adaptive problems.
8. Visually impaired children are placed in regular classes whenever possible, using the services of resource rooms and itinerant special teachers.
9. The organizational pattern of a continuum of special services for the visually impaired in the community is: (a) teacher/consultants, (b) itinerant teachers, (c) resource rooms, (d) cooperative special classes, and (e) full-time special classes.
10. The curriculum content for visually impaired students is similar to that for sighted children, with special emphasis on concrete learning, unified instruction, and self-activity.
11. Children with little or no residual vision acquire knowledge through reading braille, listening to talking books, and using some of the newer technological aids developed to assist in their education.
12. Orientation and mobility training, once confined to adults, have become an important part of the curriculum for visually handicapped children in elementary schools.
13. Technological advances promise further assistance in communication and mobility if costs can be made more affordable.

UNRESOLVED ISSUES

1. The Multiply Handicapped. The increasing number of children who have a variety of complications presents a serious and as yet unresolved issue in the field of the visually handicapped. There are fewer "pure" cases of blindness and more cases of mental retardation combined with blindness or deafness combined with blindness. We need to adapt our educational programs to accommodate children with multiple handicaps as well as those who have a single handicap. The addition of multiply handicapped children complicates an already serious educational challenge to teachers of exceptional children.

2. Words into Speech. As ingenious as the braille system of communication has been, and as well as it has served the visually handicapped for many years, we now would hope that advanced technology could help translate words into speech. Braille books are cumbersome, four to five times the bulk of an ordinary book, and many publications are not always available in braille form. The Kurzweil reading machine offers hope that advanced technology may help reach the goal of improving communication for the visually handicapped. Further development of some easy-to-transport equipment is needed so that the visually handicapped can expand their communications horizons.

3. Technology and the Blind. Although advanced technology has greatly assisted the blind, in some respects it threatens to outrun their needs. Two tools, the computer and the word processor, have transformed office and academic life, but visually handicapped individuals currently have limited access to them. We need to find some way to translate the virtues of these new tools into some practical form that enables the visually handicapped student to use them.

REFERENCES OF SPECIAL INTEREST

Barraga, N. *Visual handicaps and learning.* Belmont, Calif.: Wadsworth Publishing Co., 1976.

A comprehensive and readable introduction to the problems of school children who have visual handicaps. Good discussions of the affective impact of a visual handicap on the child, ways to conduct comprehensive assessments of individual children, and the nature of differential programming.

Dickman, I. *Sex education and family life for visually handicapped children and youth: A resource guide.* New York: Sex Information and Education Council of the United States, American Foundation for the Blind, 1975.

A readable and much needed discussion and teacher guide on one of the key social adjustment problems of visually handicapped children and adolescents. Provides teachers with practical guides to discussions on interpersonal relations, decision making, self-identity, and other pertinent topics. Provides teachers and students with a detailed listing of books, films, and professional associations that deal with the topic of sex education.

Good Start: A multimedia approach to meeting the needs of visually handicapped students. New York: American Foundation for the Blind, 1981.

This package is designed for public school teachers and administrators. The material introduces educators to the needs of visually handicapped children and the ways in which these children can be integrated most effectively into the regular program. Included in the package are six film strips and a variety of publications that have been produced by consultants with many years of experience in working with visually handicapped youngsters in local education programs.

Efron, M. *Project MAVIS (Materials adaptations for visually impaired students in the social studies).* Boulder, Colo.: Social Science Education Consortium, Inc., 1980.

A series of six small sourcebooks directed at regular classroom teachers and educational administrators looking for information on the special educational needs of the visually handicapped student and ways in which they can adapt the learning environment and lessons to help children with visual problems to profit more from the integrated classroom setting.

Malone, L., DeLucchi, L., & Thier, H. *Science activities for the visually impaired.* Berkeley, Calif.: Center for Multisensory Learning, Lawrence Hall of Science, University of California at Berkeley, 1981.

A science program for visually impaired students encouraging the students to manipulate objects and design experiments that help them develop an understanding of their environment. Leaders in science education collaborated with educators of the visually handicapped to create this series. The experiments and activities are designed for all learners, disabled and nondisabled, to enjoy together in an atmosphere of genuine integration.

CHAPTER

6

Children with Hearing Handicaps

Children with hearing impairments present some of the most difficult and challenging problems in special education. Hearing loss interferes with both the reception of language and the production of language. Because language influences practically every dimension of development, inability to hear and to speak is a critical deficit that may have an unfavorable social and academic adjustment.

DEFINITIONS

Hearing is usually measured and reported in *decibels* (dB), a relative measure of the intensity of sound. Zero (dB) represents normal hearing and a hearing loss of up to 25 dB is not considered a significant deficit. The greater the number of decibels needed for a person to respond to sound, the greater the hearing loss. The definitions of hearing loss and degrees of loss are still given in decibels, although there is a trend in this field, as in others, to stress the educational or social implications of the handicap. The hard-of-hearing child is one who, with a hearing aid, can still understand speech, whereas the deaf child cannot. The accepted definitions that follow contain both the physical and educational dimensions of hearing impairment.

A deaf person is one whose hearing is disabled to an extent (usually 70 dB or greater) that precludes the understanding of speech through the ear alone, without or with the use of a hearing aid.
   A hard-of-hearing person is one whose hearing is disabled to an extent (usually 35 to 69 dB) that makes difficult, but does not preclude the understanding of speech through the ear alone, without or with a hearing aid. (Frisina, 1974, p. 3)

Deafness is further distinguished in terms of the time the condition occurred: (1) *prelingual deafness* refers to those who were born deaf or who lost their hearing before speech and language had developed and (2) *postlingual deafness* refers to those who lost their hearing after spontaneous speech and language had developed. As we shall see, prelingual deafness is a much more serious problem educationally.

IDENTIFICATION

The identification of deaf children or children who are very hard of hearing is usually made before they enter school. Children with mild or moderate hearing impairments are more likely to be overlooked. Accurate identification of children with hearing losses is often complicated because in the classroom the symptoms of the condition resemble other disorders such as mental retardation or behavior problems. Children who stare blankly at the teacher may have hearing impairments, or may simply not understand what is being said, or may be so captured by their own anxieties that they block out communication.

Many different lists have been compiled to help the classroom teacher identify a child with a possible hearing loss so that he or she can be referred for more comprehensive examination. The following list has been provided by Stephens, Blackhurst, and Magliocca (1982):

Does there appear to be a physical problem associated with the ears? The student may complain of earaches, discomfort in the ear, or strange ringing or buzzing noises. You should note these complaints and so be alert for signs of discharge from the ears or excessively heavy waxy buildup in the ear canal. Frequent colds and sore throats are occasional indicators of infections that could impair the hearing.

Is there poor articulation of sounds, particularly omission of consonant sounds? Students who articulate poorly may have a hearing problem that is preventing them from getting feedback about their vocal productions. Omission of consonant sounds from speech is often indicative of a high-frequency hearing loss.

When listening to radio, TV, or records, does the student turn the volume up so high that others complain? While it is much in vogue among young people today to turn up the amplification of rock music almost "to the threshold of pain," this determination will sometimes be difficult to make. Teachers can often get clues, however, by observing students listening to audio media that are not producing music, such as instructional records and sound-filmstrips.

Does the student cock the head or turn toward the speaker in an apparent effort to hear better? Sometimes such movements are quite obvious and may even be accompanied by the "cupping" of the ear with the hand in an effort to direct the sound into the ear. In other cases, actions are much more subtle. Teachers often overlook such signs, interpreting them as symbols of increased inquisitiveness and interest.

Are there frequent requests to repeat what has just been said? Although some students pick up the habit of saying, "Huh?" as a form of defense mechanism when they are unable to provide what they perceive as an acceptable response, such verbalizations may also indicate a hearing loss. When a particular student requests repeated instructions frequently, teachers should further investigate the possibility of hearing loss.

Is the student unresponsive or inattentive when spoken to in a normal voice? Some students who do not follow directions or do not pay attention in class are frequently labeled as "trouble makers," which results in negative or punitive treatment. Often, however, these inappropriate school behaviors are actually caused by the inability of the student to hear. They can also be caused if the sounds that are heard appear to be "garbled."

Is the student reluctant to participate in oral activities? Although reluctance to participate orally may be symptomatic of problems such as shyness, insecurity with respect to knowledge of subject matter, or fear of failure, it may also be due to a hearing loss. The child might not be able to hear the verbal interactions that occur in such activities. (pp. 43–44)

MEASUREMENT

Two dimensions—frequency and intensity—are necessary in evaluating a hearing loss. *Frequency* refers to the number of vibrations (or cycles) per second of a given sound wave: the greater the frequency, the higher the pitch. An individual may have difficulty hearing sounds of certain frequencies, whereas those of other frequencies are quite audible. *Intensity*, on the other hand, refers to the relative loudness of a sound.

To determine an individual's level of hearing, it is necessary to know what intensity of sound is needed to be heard by the listener. The *pure-tone audiometer*, a key instrument for measuring hearing acuity, is used to present the individual with sounds of known intensity and frequency. The individual is asked to respond when he or she hears the tone presented through the audiometer. The hearing in each ear is plotted separately, and the level of hearing is recorded on an audiogram that shows decibel loss at each relevant frequency. A hearing level of 30 decibels would indicate a slight hearing loss; a level of 95 decibels indicates a profound hearing loss.

Measurement of the extent of hearing loss and identification of the type of hearing impairment that a child has are complex professional problems. Although comprehensive audiological examinations are rarely done within the school system, the schools will often conduct screening examinations to find youngsters who are suspected of having hearing problems and then refer them for comprehensive medical and audiological testing by professionals in the community.

Screening procedures in schools may involve either individual or group testing of children in kindergarten through third grade and periodic examinations in the higher grades. Those children suspected of having a hearing loss receive a more complete audiometric test.

The degree of hearing loss has major educational significance because it determines the type and amount of special training needed, whether hearing aids and amplifiers may be appropriate,

TABLE 6.1
Degree of Hearing Loss and Educational Significance

Level of Loss	Sound Intensity for Perception	Educational Implications
Mild	27–40 dB	May have difficulty with distant sounds. May need preferential seating and speech therapy.
Moderate	41–55 dB	Understands conversational speech. May miss class discussion. May require hearing aids and speech therapy.
Moderately severe	56–70 dB	Will require hearing aids, auditory training, speech and language training of an intensive nature.
Severe	71–90 dB	Can only hear loud sounds close up. Sometimes considered deaf. Needs intensive special education, hearing aids, speech and language training.
Profound	91 dB +	May be aware of loud sounds and vibrations. Relies on vision rather than hearing for information processing. Considered deaf.

HARD OF HEARING (brace spanning Mild, Moderate, Moderately severe)

DEAF (brace spanning Severe, Profound)

Source: H. Davis, Abnormal hearing and deafness. In H. Davis and R. Silverman (Eds.), *Hearing and deafness.* New York: Holt, Rinehart & Winston, 1970.

and whether alternative means of communication should be taught. In addition to the pure-tone tests, other tests using carefully designed word lists may be used to estimate the ability of the child to hear spoken words (Brackett, 1981). Table 6.1 shows the commonly accepted categories for level of hearing loss. The first three categories are part of the hard-of-hearing group and the last two are in the deaf group. As the degree of hearing loss increases so does the need for intensive professional assistance.

TYPES OF HEARING LOSS

Because of the complicated structure and functioning of the ear (see Figure 6.1), defects in hearing may occur in many different forms. Basically the defects are of two main types: (1) conductive losses and (2) sensorineural or perceptive losses.

A *conductive hearing loss* is one that reduces the intensity of sound reaching the inner ear, where the auditory nerve begins. To reach the inner ear, sound waves in the air must pass through the external canal of the outer ear to the eardrum, where the vibrations are picked up by a series of bonelike structures in the middle ear and passed on to the inner ear. The sequence of vibrations may

FIGURE 6.1
The Human Ear

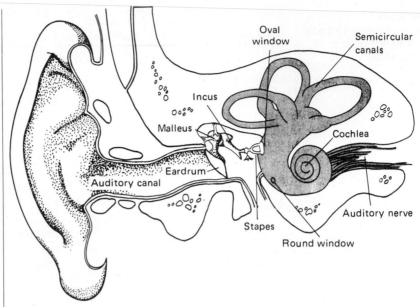

Note: The outer ear consists of the auditory canal. The middle ear consists of the eardrum, malleus (hammer), incus (anvil), and stapes (stirrup). The inner ear consists of the round window, the oval window, the semicircular canals, and the cochlea.

Source: From P. Lindsay and D. Norman, *Human information processing.* New York: Academic Press, 1972, p. 221.

be blocked anywhere along the line. Wax or malformations may block the external canal; the eardrum may be broken or unable to vibrate; the movement of the bones in the middle ear may be obstructed. Any condition hindering the sequence of vibrations or preventing them from reaching the auditory nerve may cause a conduction loss.

That type of conductive defect seldom causes a hearing loss of more than 60 or 70 decibels since the vibrations carried by the bone to the inner ear will still be available to carry sound that cannot be conducted through the outer and middle ear. The audiometer has a bone-conduction receiver as well as an air-conduction receiver and can therefore measure the ability of the individual to pick up sound through bone conduction. Conductive losses lead to conditions of hard of hearing, but not deafness. The auditory nerve itself must be damaged to produce the condition of deafness.

Figure 6.2 shows the audiogram of a child with a conductive hearing loss. On the audiometer this hard-of-hearing child heard airborne sounds at the 40 to 50 decibel level at all frequencies in the better ear (the left). When using a bone-conduction receiver,

**FIGURE 6.2
Audiogram of a Child
with a Conductive
Hearing Loss**

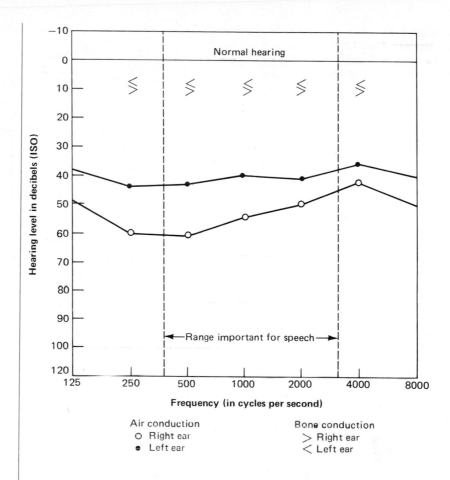

however, the child responded within the normal range. The difficulty was a defect or obstruction in the outer or middle ear rather than a defect in the sensory nerve of the inner ear. As might be expected, an audiogram of this type of hearing loss is fairly even at all frequencies.

A *sensorineural* or *perceptive hearing loss* is caused by defects of the inner ear or of the auditory nerve transmitting the impulse to the brain. Sensorineural hearing loss may be complete or partial and may affect some frequencies (especially the high ones) more than others. Thus in Figure 6.3 the audiogram for a deaf child shows profound loss at the high frequencies and severe loss at frequencies below 1,000 cycles. High-frequency loss is often associated with sensorineural deafness. The bone-conduction receiver in this case gave no better reception since the defect was in the nerve, not in the mechanism that carried vibrations to the nerve.

FIGURE 6.3
Audiogram of a Child with a Sensorineural or Perceptive Hearing Loss

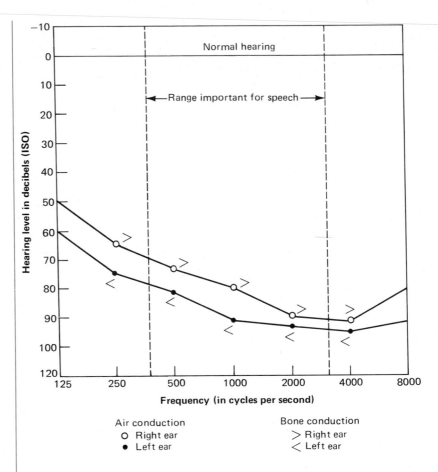

CAUSES OF HEARING LOSS

Most of the available information on the causes of hearing impairment is concerned with deafness as opposed to mild hearing losses. Moores (1982) has presented evidence that documents five major identified causes of childhood deafness in the United States today: heredity, maternal rubella, prematurity, meningitis, and mother-child blood incompatibility. Less severe hearing impairments are frequently caused by otitis media, a common childhood infection of the middle ear. It may be something of a surprise to learn that, with all our sophisticated diagnostic tools, the highest percentage of cases (30 percent) is reported in the category of *cause unknown*.

The Office of Demographic Studies at Gallaudet College, a federally supported college for deaf students in Washington, D.C., has solicited information from the records of 555 educational programs for the deaf (Ries, 1973). It includes statements on the etiology for

41,109 students, approximately 85 percent of the hearing impaired students enrolled in special educational programs. Table 6.2 presents the prenatal and the postnatal causes of hearing losses. The table shows (1) that maternal rubella (German measles), heredity, prematurity, and Rh incompatibility are the most commonly reported prenatal causes and (2) that the most commonly reported postnatal cause is meningitis.

Heredity Many different genetic conditions can lead to deafness. Transmissions have been attributed to dominant genes, recessive genes, and sex-linked genes. Although there is general agreement that heredity plays an important role, it is hard to fix an exact percentage for children whose deafness is due to heredity. Estimates range from 30 to 60 percent (Moores, 1982).

The determination of hereditary influence is not merely a matter of intellectual interest. Because deaf adults tend to intermarry (Al-

**TABLE 6.2
Reported Causes of
Deafness for Students
Enrolled in Educational
Programs in the United
States, 1970–1971**

	Number of Students						
	All Ages	Under 5 Years	5–7 Years	8–10 Years	11–13 Years	14–16 Years	17+ Years
	41,109	2,527	10,216	7,529	9,509	6,759	4,569
Causes[1]	**Number per 1,000 Students**[2]						
PRENATAL							
Maternal rubella	147.8	212.1	361.9	57.9	106.2	28.7	44.6
Heredity	74.8	79.1	53.5	81.8	74.6	92.6	82.1
Prematurity	53.7	52.2	45.4	54.7	58.1	66.4	43.3
Rh incompatibility	34.1	34.4	22.6	35.1	34.3	44.1	42.9
Other[1]	79.8	85.0	64.6	89.2	81.2	90.3	76.1
Unknown	188.3	230.3	149.7	196.7	189.5	193.4	227.6
Not reported	112.5	92.2	83.6	121.5	126.4	127.2	122.6
POSTNATAL							
Meningitis	49.1	72.4	40.8	59.1	44.1	45.6	53.6
Other[1]	132.3	83.9	81.5	147.7	141.7	176.2	162.6
Unknown	49.7	37.6	36.9	56.4	53.2	55.9	57.3
Not reported	134.0	79.9	115.0	156.3	144.5	142.5	134.8

[1]Only etiologies with an incidence of more than 30 per 1,000 (3%) are included. Remaining etiologies are classified in the *other* category.

[2]Each column sums to more than 1,000 because, for about 5% of the students, more than one cause of hearing-impaired loss was reported.

Source: Adapted from P. Ries, *Reported causes of hearing loss for hearing impaired students, 1970–1971,* Annual survey of hearing impaired children and youth, Ser. D, No. 11. Washington, D.C.: Gallaudet College Office of Demographic Studies, 1973, pp. 3–4.

tshuler, 1963), they need to have information on the likelihood that one of their children will be born deaf. If one partner is deaf, what are the genetic odds for producing a child with a hearing problem? The new field of genetic counseling, which seeks to inform couples of the odds of transmitting a special problem to their children, can be an important resource for those who are deaf.

Maternal Rubella   When rubella (also known as German measles) afflicts a woman during the first three months of pregnancy, its effects on the child are often quite serious. Hardy (1968) reported on 199 children who were diagnosed as having been subjected to rubella virus prenatally during the 1964–1965 rubella epidemic. The distribution of defects was found to be 50 percent auditory, 20 percent visual, and 35 percent cardiac. The National Communicable Disease Center reported that the epidemic caused deafness in eight thousand children (Hicks, 1970). Northern and Downs (1978, p. 6) stated that ten to twenty thousand children were affected in the two epidemics of rubella in 1958 and 1964. Rubella has been identified as the most common identifiable cause of deafness from external sources (see Table 6.2).

Prematurity   Children born with birth weights of 5 pounds, 8 ounces or less are usually considered premature. Prematurity has been listed as a cause of deafness in 53.7 out of 1,000 children enrolled in schools for the deaf (Ries, 1973). It has also been listed as a cause of mental retardation and blindness.

There is considerable doubt that the mere fact of prematurity is a cause of deafness. The true cause—rubella, for example—may also stimulate an early birth. In addition, a loss of oxygen or a brain injury incurred during the premature birth process may be the true cause of impaired hearing. At any rate, premature children face a greater than average risk for hearing impairments and many other disorders.

Mother-Child Blood Incompatibility   Rh-positive and Rh-negative blood are incompatible. When a woman whose blood is Rh negative carries a child who is Rh positive, the mother's system develops antibodies that may pass into the fetus and destroy the Rh-positive cells. This condition may be fatal. Those children who survive may have a variety of disorders, including deafness. If Rh incompatibility is diagnosed during pregnancy, the condition can be treated to prevent harm to the child.

8.1% **Meningitis**   According to Vernon (1968) 8.1 percent of deaf children lose their hearing after birth as a result of meningitis, which involves a bacterial invasion that often occurs through the middle ear. Ries (1973) reported 4.9 percent for this etiology. Of the post-natal or exogenous causes of deafness, meningitis has headed the list. The incidence of deafness due to meningitis has been decreasing over the years, possibly due to increased use of antibiotics and chemotherapy.

Otitis Media   This condition refers to infections that cause fluid to accumulate in the middle ear. If the condition is chronic or untreated, it can create mild to moderate hearing losses because the conduction of sound through the middle ear is disturbed. Since this is one of the most common childhood diseases and one in eight children is estimated to have six or more episodes of otitis media before age 6, prompt treatment and careful preschool auditory assessment for suspected hearing loss is called for in such cases.

conductive hearing loss

PREVALENCE

The number of children with seriously impaired hearing or deafness is much smaller than the number of children with many of the other exceptionalities discussed in this text. The smaller numbers in this category create special planning problems for educators. Only about one in one thousand children is deaf and another three or four children out of a thousand are severely hard of hearing (Office of Special Education, 1979). Children whose hearing loss is slight or may be corrected through hearing aids and language therapy may not be considered a serious educational problem and may not even be counted.

1/1000 deaf

3/4/1000 h.of h.

It is likely that the relative prevalence of hearing loss due to the conditions previously described will not change much. If anything, there may be a slight increase because of the medical profession's ability to save many children who once would have died but now may survive with a variety of handicapping conditions.

DEVELOPMENTAL PROFILES

To illustrate the differences in development among children with different degrees of hearing loss, three brief case studies will be presented. Figure 6.4 shows profiles of three children—Sally, John, and Bill. All three children are 10 years old and the profiles are similar in shape, but the intraindividual differences increase with the severity of hearing loss and with the age at onset of deafness. Sally is a hard-of-hearing child, John is a postlingual or deafened child (that is, he became deaf after language had developed to some extent), and Bill is a prelingual or deaf child.

Although the three profiles all represent auditorily impaired children, they differ considerably. They show that the progress such children make depends on the age at onset of deafness, the degree of hearing loss, and the amount of intensive instruction that has been received during the growing stages.

Sally   The upper profile in Figure 6.4 represents Sally, a child with a moderate hearing loss of 45 decibels. This hard-of-hearing child is 10 years of age and is physically average (in terms of height, weight, and motor coordination). In mental ability and in social maturity, there appears to be no difference between her and the average child. In speech development Sally is slightly retarded in that she has some difficulty in articulation and requires speech remediation. Her language development and reading are slightly retarded, while her achievement in arithmetic, spelling, and general information is approximately average. The only difference between Sally and an average child is a slight difficulty in speech development, language development, and reading.

Fortunately, Sally has been fitted with a hearing aid and has received speech remediation. The only special education she has needed is some help in using her hearing aid, in speech remediation, and in speech reading. Otherwise, she is much like the average child and functions adequately in the regular classroom. An itinerant speech-language pathologist gives her speech remediation, auditory training, and speech-reading lessons once a week.

John   The middle profile in Figure 6.4 presents the developmental pattern of John, who has a severe hearing loss. He was born with normal hearing but at the age of four suffered a serious hearing loss in both ears. He is classified as postlingually deaf. Although John is approximately normal in intelligence, social maturity, and physical ability, his speech and language have not developed normally. On the audiometric test he had a hearing loss of 75 decibels even after being fitted with a hearing aid. Fortunately, however, he had learned to talk quite normally *before* his loss of hearing and had developed considerable language ability, so that now he can still learn through the auditory channel with the help of a hearing aid. His retardation in language results from his not

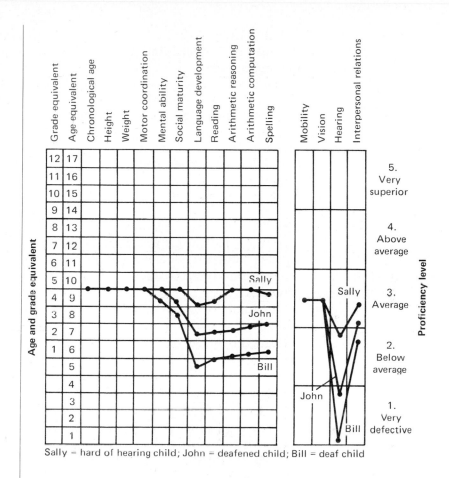

Sally – hard of hearing child; John = deafened child; Bill = deaf child

having developed normally in that area since the age of 4. At present his language is below the 7-year (second-grade) level, and his reading and other academic abilities are also around the second-grade level. The hearing loss has interfered considerably with his educational progress, but with the use of hearing aids, speech habilitation, and other specialized techniques, John is progressing, although at an understandably slower rate than Sally.

Bill   The bottom profile in Figure 6.4 is of a child with a profound hearing loss, which existed at birth. Bill has never heard the spoken word. A hearing aid might alert his attention to environmental sounds but will not help sufficiently in the development of speech and language. Because of the severity of Bill's hearing loss, tested at over 90 decibels, it is necessary to place him in a class for the deaf, or to offer him intensive tutorial service if he is integrated in a regular class.

Bill is still quite defective in speech development. He does not talk as well as a child of 2 1/2 years, even though he has had instruction. His language development is at about the 5-year level. In reading and other academic subjects he is at the beginning first-grade level even though he is now 10 years of age. Bill is considered to be about four years retarded educationally.

CHARACTERISTICS OF HEARING IMPAIRED CHILDREN

The characteristics of a child with a mild hearing loss will in many ways be more similar to a hearing child than to a deaf child, whose condition will cause a number of other serious problems that are linked to the inability to receive or express messages and thoughts.

The fundamental problem of communication for deaf children is comprised of two significant parts: the limitations of a mode of communication with others and the progressive limitations on normal language development. Each of these limitations severely affects the child's developmental processes as well as the areas of academic achievement, social and personal adjustment, and occupational adjustment.

Developmental Characteristics

Cognition

The severe and obvious delays in language development in the child who is deaf pose a question of importance to psychologists and educators alike, and have implications for many hearing children as well. *Can thought operate separately from language?* Is it possible for a child to demonstrate his or her ability to think without having to proceed through the medium of spoken or written language?

Two clearly different and opposing views have emerged. Furth (1966) has suggested that intelligent thinking does not need a linguistic symbol system. Rather, he maintains that language is dependent on intelligence. Whorf (1956) has held that the child's intellectual development is determined by his or her experience with language and that it is language that accounts for the acquisition of concepts. How to prove the opposing points? Furth conducted a series of studies on deaf and normal children's ability to perform tasks related to *classification* ("Put together all the things that go together."), *seriation* ("Arrange the shapes according to size."), and *conservation* of weight or volume ("Which container holds the most liquid?"). Furth found that deaf children were able to perform acceptably on these thinking tasks, especially during the early ages, and contended that logical thinking was possible without strong language input.

On the other hand, other investigators (Schlesinger and Meadow, 1972; Silverman, 1967) found that deaf children who had acquired *some* language consistently outperformed those with less language facility. Deaf children with limited language seemed to be substantially delayed in mastering some of the more abstract concepts. The answer accepted now by many educators and researchers is that deaf children *can* think logically without a linguistic system but that the mastery of such a system is a great help to the child in solving problems or performing academically.

Language

The normal 4-year-old child has mastered most of the syntactic properties of language but the deaf child has serious problems with syntax. The deaf child is taught to impose a subject-verb-object (S-V-O) pattern on sentences when writing or speaking (for example, "The boy threw the ball."), but not all sentences start that way and the deaf child can get confused, as Quigley et al. (1978) have demonstrated:

	Sentences	Deaf Interpretation
Passive:	The boy was helped by the girl.	The boy helped the girl.
Relative:	The boy also kissed the girl who ran away.	The girl ran away.
Complement:	The boy learned the ball broke the window.	The boy learned the ball.
Nominal:	The opening of the door surprised the cat.	The door surprised the cat.

As these children get older, they continue to have serious problems. Following are examples of writing by typical deaf children, ages 10 and 14:

The boy see a dog. The woman more a basket. The will go to picnic. The family went to cat in the picnic. The boy see inside dog. The dog is sad. The boy is Love get dog. The family and see about a dog. The boy play a ball with dog. The woman work stove for meat. The girl help woman to picnic. The man is run. The man see airplane. The woman is drink. The boy go car. The girl give bread a dog. [10-year-old female, Performance IQ of 106, born deaf, Better Ear Average 100 + dB (ASA)]

We will go to pinic. the woman package. A boy give to the dog eat the bread. The dog barked. the boy look at dog. the boy told a woman stop at car. He carried to the picnic dog sa. the mother told her sister put on the table. She park a car. He was fun. Her brothers played baskeball. the dog played with the boy. after whith. He will go home at 6:45. his mother drive a car. [14-year-old male, Performance IQ of 104, born deaf, Better Ear Average of 90 dB (ASA)]. (Quigley and Kretschmer, 1982, p. 83)

Academic Achievement   With such serious problems in language expression, it is not surprising that deaf children experience serious problems in academic achievement. The Office of Demographic Studies at Gallaudet College annually administers the Stanford Achievement Test to hearing impaired children. Gentile (1973) reported the test results for thousands of these children enrolled in residential and day schools throughout the country. The results showed that at age 8 the hearing impaired children scored at about second-grade level in both reading and arithmetic computation. At age 17 the children scored at about fourth-grade level in reading and sixth-grade level in arithmetic computation.

Using the Stanford Achievement Test, Jensema (1975) analyzed the achievement test scores of 6,873 children, ages 6 to 19, who had hearing handicaps severe enough to place them in special education programs. He found that "in a ten-year period from age 8 to age 18 the average hearing impaired student increases his vocabulary score only as much as the average normal hearing student does between the beginning of kindergarten and the latter part of the second grade" (p. 3). In reading comprehension, 14-year-old children read at the third-grade level. In arithmetic computation, a subject not entirely dependent on language, 10-year-old deaf children tested at the third-grade level.

Jensema also found that the age at which the hearing loss occurred and its seriousness played an important role in school achievement: (1) reading achievement was higher for those children who lost their hearing after age 3 than it was for those whose hearing loss occurred earlier; and (2) using the five classifications of relative hearing loss (see Table 6.1), it was found that the less severe the hearing loss, the greater the achievement. As we can see by the profiles in Figure 6.4, Sally's academic performance is hardly affected, whereas John and Bill, who have more serious hearing impairments, are in serious academic trouble.

Trybus and Karchmer (1977) reported the progress in reading and arithmetic of 1,543 hearing impaired students over a three-year period. They found: (1) in reading comprehension at age 9 the students tested at the second-grade level, and at age 20 they tested at about the fifth-grade level; and (2) they progressed at approximately one-third of a year on the average for each age group in reading comprehension.

Table 6.3 shows the relationship of six selected variables to the reading achievement of deaf students. The seriousness of the reading problems increased in relation to the degree of hearing loss and when other handicapping conditions were present. Members of minority groups and males do less well academically, but hearing impaired children whose parents are deaf appear to do better than those whose parents can hear. This puzzling finding is discussed in more detail later in this chapter.

In general, studies on the academic achievement of hearing impaired children have not reported much improvement over the years. The majority of deaf children are seriously educationally retarded. The reading skills of most deaf adults do not exceed fourth- or fifth-grade level. Approximately 10 percent, however, have been able to achieve in academic subjects, including reading at the level of the average child.

4th/5th grade

*10%
achievement*

**TABLE 6.3
Relationships of Six
Selected Variables to
Reading Achievement of
Deaf Students**

Variable	Relationship with Reading Comprehension Level
Sex	Females score slightly higher than males.
Ethnic group	Whites score higher than Spanish-Americans or blacks.
Degree of hearing loss	Achievement level is inversely related to hearing loss.
Presence of additional handicapping conditions	Students with no additional handicaps score higher than those with one or more.
Age child began school	Children entering at age 5 score higher than those entering either earlier or later.
Parental deafness	Students with two deaf parents score higher than those with either one deaf parent or two normal-hearing parents.

Source: R. J. Trybus and M. A. Karchmer, School achievement scores of hearing impaired children: National data on achievement status and growth-patterns. *American Annals of the Deaf*, 1977, *122*, p. 65.

Social and Personal Adjustment   Does the condition of hearing loss with its accompanying communication problems bring forth social and behavioral problems? Although a hearing loss does not inevitably lead to social and personality difficulties, it can create an environment in which such difficulties easily emerge (Meadow, 1980). An example of this kind of environmental influence may be illustrated by a hard-of-hearing child on a playground who wants to get a turn on the swings, slides, or other equipment. Lacking the ability to say "I want my turn" or "It's my turn now," the child with hearing problems may simply pull another youngster out of the way, thus earning the label of "aggressive" and causing some difficulties in interpersonal relationships. Such events repeated over and over again can create social adaptation problems of a serious nature.

Even more problems seem to await the child with hearing difficulties in adolescence. Davis (1981) reported that children with hearing losses who were mainstreamed in a local school program expressed feelings of loneliness and rejection. Friendships are often limited to one or two best friends and hearing impaired youngsters are rarely elected class officers or homecoming queens or cheerleaders. In adolescence, a difficult time at best for many young people, the hearing loss creates a problem of its own because of communication difficulties plus the fact of "difference." During adolescence, more than any other period in the development of an individual, it is important not to deviate from the social norm. As Davis (1981) pointed out:

Hearing impairment, except in rare cases, affects the ease with which communication occurs, and communications form the basis for social interaction. The hearing impaired person's self-concept and confidence influence how rejection by others is perceived and handled. It is a rare hearing impaired child who does not perceive his social relations as inadequate and does not long for full acceptance by peers. If being different is the worst thing that can happen, then the next worst thing is associating with someone who is different. One cannot always control the former, but one can control the latter. It is from this fact that the social problems encountered by hearing impaired adolescents often stem. (p. 73)

Is it any wonder that many of these children yearn for the association of children with similar characteristics with whom they can feel socially accepted and comfortable? Such tendencies to be with other deaf individuals extend into adulthood where one can observe in many large cities a subculture of deaf individuals who have formed a social subgroup among themselves, who intermarry and generally stay apart from the hearing society. Meadow (1980) summarized the personality evidence as follows:

Personality inventories have consistently shown that deaf children have more adjustment problems than hearing children. When deaf children without overt or serious problems have been studied, they have been found to exhibit characteristics of rigidity, egocentricity, absence of inner controls, impulsivity, and suggestibility.

In spite of consistencies in findings of personality studies, it would be a mistake to conclude that there is a single "deaf personality type." There is much diversity among deaf people, and it is related to education, communication, and experience. (p. 97)

Occupational Adjustment Deaf adults can be found in almost any profession but not in the same proportions as hearing adults. To be a member of a minority group and to be deaf results in an unemployment rate far above that of white males and females (about three to five times greater). However, the distribution of the types of occupations most often available to hearing impaired individuals strongly reflects the problems of communication and education that severely limit their potential performance in professional and managerial positions. Schein and Delk (1974) reported that 60 percent of all deaf persons were employed in skilled or semiskilled trades.

60% semiskilled

In addition to the problems that deaf individuals encounter because of their special linguistic and communication difficulties, they must face the prejudice of employers who have concerns about hiring handicapped individuals, despite massive public service campaigns on television to accept the handicapped worker as reliable and efficient.

There has been a strong trend toward broadening vocational training programs for hearing impaired youngsters from specific skill training to providing more general information and work skills. This shift is based on studies suggesting that 60 to 80 percent of deaf persons in the work force were not following the trade for which they were originally trained (Lerman and Guilfoyle, 1970).

In general, there is a common observation that deaf adults can make acceptable occupational adjustments resulting in economic self-sufficiency despite their handicap, even though some occupations are difficult for them to enter or to perform effectively.

MULTIPLY HANDICAPPED CHILDREN

A significant number of children with hearing losses have additional handicaps as well. There is substantial disagreement, however, about the number of hearing impaired children who have other handicaps. One estimate suggests that about 20 percent of deaf students may be categorized as multiply handicapped, whereas others suggest the figure may be as high as 30 to 50 percent (Craig and Craig, 1980). This variation in estimates is due to a number of reasons. The diagnosis of a second handicap is often informal and uncertain. For example, if one considers educational retardation a handicap, then most deaf children would be multiply handicapped. The dividing point on how serious a behavior problem has to be before constituting a handicapping condition also causes variation of reporting from one setting to another. Craig and Craig (1980) reported that the largest number of youngsters who have other handicaps are labeled deaf/mentally retarded or deaf/learning disabled. The combinations of variables that create a severely handicapped individual are dealt with more extensively in the chapter on the severely handicapped.

Rh factor 70%

Vernon (1969) pointed out that several of the major causes of hearing loss were more inclined to produce multiply handicapped children than others. Significant among these was blood incompatibility between mother and child, where an estimated 70 percent of such children had a major disability in addition to deafness. Children of mothers who had rubella during the early stages of pregnancy often had cerebral palsy, mental retardation, blindness, or heart murmurs in addition to a hearing loss. Over half of these children had one major handicap in addition to deafness, frequently diagnosed as an emotional disturbance or aphasia. About one-third of the children who lost their hearing because of meningitis, which attacks the central nervous system, had an additional major handicap. In contrast, those identified as deaf due to genetic transmission had few other handicapping conditions accompanying the hearing loss.

Any of these multiple-handicapping conditions severely complicates the educational program for these children. As noted in Table 6.3, Trybus and Karchmer (1977) found a significantly lower educational achievement among those youngsters with hearing losses who are identified as multiply handicapped. Failure to fully recognize a multiple-handicapping condition may lead to misunderstanding of the true nature of a child's problem. Many of the characteristics assigned to a child because of deafness (for example, hyperactivity) may really arise from a dual problem of a neurological injury that complicates the condition of deafness.

Most observers predict a rise in the prevalence of multiply

handicapped deaf children because the diseases that cause hearing loss are not under complete control and because the medical profession is now able to save seriously damaged children from death but not from the consequences of the handicaps with which they are born. Chapter 10 discusses the problems of children with multiple handicaps in greater detail.

EDUCATIONAL ADAPTATIONS FOR CHILDREN WITH HEARING IMPAIRMENTS

The Use of Hearing Aids

Perhaps the single most important development in this century for helping hearing impaired individuals is the invention of the electronic hearing aid. With it, the severity of hearing loss in some people has been decreased so that people who are "apparently" deaf have become hard of hearing and those who are hard of hearing have become only slightly impaired.

Wier (1980) has offered the following explanation of the way in which a hearing aid works:

All modern hearing aids have three basic components: a microphone, an amplifier, and a receiver. The microphone and receiver transduce energy from one point to another. Thus the tiny microphone on the hearing aid converts acoustic energy into electrical energy (like a telephone mouthpiece does), while the receiver performs the reverse conversion, transforming the electrical energy back into acoustical energy (like a telephone earpiece does).

Between these two components is the amplifier, a device that increases the signal level between the input and the output.

Figure 6.5 shows a variety of hearing aids currently in use. Contemporary hearing aids have been designed to be placed directly into the ear canal, worn in a shirt pocket, built into eyeglass frames, or placed on the bone directly behind the ear. In determining the type of aid most suited to an individual's needs, an audiological analysis is necessary. Consideration is also given to the wearer's concern about appearance.

The development of the transistor has transformed the hearing aid from a heavy, cumbersome unit with large battery requirements to a much more portable unit. Also, instead of uniformly amplifying sounds to the irritation of the listener, microphones can now be directional, increasing only those sounds emitted immediately in front of the listener and reducing sounds coming from the sides or the back of the listener (Northern and Downs, 1978).

Nevertheless, with all their advantages, hearing aids do have

**FIGURE 6.5
Contemporary
Hearing Aids**

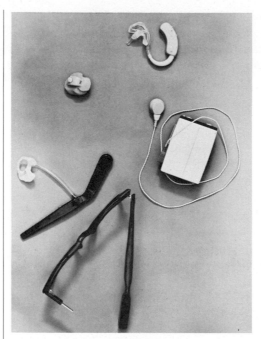

Source: Courtesy of Dr. W. Wilson, University of Washington Child Development and Mental Retardation Center.

some clear limitations. They are most effective for individuals who have conductive hearing losses as opposed to nerve losses, although hearing aids are receiving greater use to compensate in whatever way possible to the degree that the wearer is able to tolerate the device. It is often tiring to use a hearing aid, and the amplificaton of all sounds in addition to those the listener wishes to focus on can produce an irritating background of noise.

Like all mechanical instruments, hearing aids have a tendency to break down or malfunction. Just because a child is wearing a hearing aid does not mean that it is working or functioning at its maximum potential. Various reviews of hearing aids in the school setting have revealed that more than half of them are often operating poorly or not at all (Kemker et al., 1979). The most predominant fault is a weak battery, but a variety of other factors contribute to less than maximal use of hearing aids. Consequently, careful monitoring of these devices within the school setting is needed to make sure that the child is making the most of this valuable tool.

Finally, the hearing aid can be most effective when used in conjunction with a systematic and intense educational program presented by teachers of the deaf. A team of audiologists, speech-language pathologists, and teachers of the deaf may be needed to combine their professional knowledge to design a coherent educational program for the deaf child (Martin, 1981).

Communication Methods

Development and Types of Communication Methods

Throughout the last two centuries there have been heated controversies on the best practices in educating the deaf. Everyone agrees that the major emphasis in education of the deaf is placed on two key objectives—development of *language* and evolution of *communication skills*—because these are the most important vehicles through which the child processes information and expresses himself or herself.

English-speaking educators of the deaf agree that the deaf child must learn to read and to write the English language. People concerned with education of the deaf, however, have held sharply differing views on the modes of communication to be emphasized in teaching language to deaf children. One method stresses the goal of communicating with the larger hearing society and, consequently, the need for speech training and speech reading (lip reading). This method is called the *oral* approach because of its extensive use of auditory training to use the residual hearing available to the child.

The second method emphasizes the use of manual or hand communication with the goal of early mastery of language and a usable communication system with other deaf individuals. The *manual* method includes (1) the language of signs—a language system consisting of formalized movements of the hands or arms to express thoughts—and (2) finger spelling, which is a kind of spelling in the air using the manual alphabet and for which there is a fixed position of the five fingers for each letter of the alphabet (see Figure 6.6). In communicating manually, deaf persons generally use the two modes together, finger spelling some words and expressing others through the language of signs.

This conflict between methods and objectives is more than two centuries old. Although it is generally agreed that the first systematic attempt to teach the deaf occurred in Spain in the sixteenth century by Pedro Ponce de Leon, during the early nineteenth century two major and conflicting centers and schools of thought in educating deaf children emerged in Europe, one in the British Isles

With the manual method, deaf people communicate by using sign language and finger spelling. (Photo: © Betty Medsger 1977.)

and the other in France. The school established in Scotland by Thomas Braidwood stressed the oral method while the school in France established by the Abbe de l'Epee stressed the manual method. In addition, Samuel Heinicke established a school in Germany at about the same time that also followed the oral method.

Thomas Gallaudet wished to begin a program in the United States and visited the Braidwood school to find out more about the oral method. The Braidwood family, however, was most secretive about their methods and Gallaudet, in disappointment and anger, went across the English channel to visit Abbe Sicard, the successor to de l'Epee, and came home to establish a school in Hartford, Connecticut, stressing manual communication. It is interesting to speculate on how education of the deaf in the United States would be different today if Gallaudet had received a warmer welcome from the Braidwoods (Moores, 1982).

The early development of the oral method in the United States was fostered by a man generally known for his invention of the telephone but who actually spent most of his life working with deaf individuals. Alexander Graham Bell opened up new channels for teaching speech to the deaf. His method of *visible speech* helped the child understand the placement of the speech organs in pro-

A.G.B. "visible speech"

FIGURE 6.6
American Manual Alphabet (as seen by the finger speller)

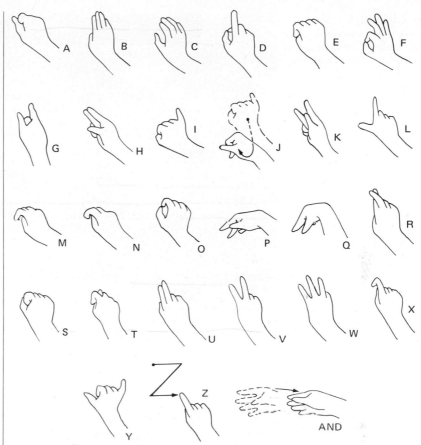

Source: From L. J. Fant, Jr., *Say it with hands.* Washington, D.C.: Gallaudet College Centennial Fund Commission, 1964, p. 1. Reproduced with permission.

ducing speech. His invention of the telephone led to the development and use of hearing aids and to greater emphasis on the use of amplification of sound in teaching speech to children with severely defective hearing. Those inventions advanced oral methods of teaching the deaf and made it possible for many children to understand speech and language who previously could not have done so.

Bell and Gallaudet became implacable rivals, each representing their diverse methods brilliantly. Their differences still reverberate today. Some of the identified methods currently in use are described in the following paragraphs.

ORAL-AURAL METHOD The oral-aural approach is the instructional procedure that uses residual hearing through amplification

These deaf high school students use the oral-aural method, which develops communication skills by means of residual hearing, lip reading, and speech. (Photo: Sheila and Dick Fish, courtesy of The Clarke School for the Deaf, Northampton, Mass.)

residual hearing through amplification

of sound, speech reading, and speech for developing communication skills. School programs that adhere to this approach do not use or encourage the use of the language of signs or finger spelling on the assumption that manual communication will inhibit the child's learning of language and oral skills and impede adjustment to the hearing world.

ROCHESTER METHOD The Rochester method was established in the Rochester, New York, School in 1878. It is a combination of the oral method plus finger spelling. It processes information through speech reading, amplification, and finger spelling. The response is through finger spelling and speech. The manual alphabet presented in Figure 6.5 is used by the teacher who spells every letter of every word as it is spoken. This method is similar to neo-oralism, which is practiced in the Soviet Union with very young children. Reading and writing of the alphabet and words are encouraged.

AUDITORY METHOD The auditory method emphasizes the development of listening skills, especially for children who can profit from auditory training. The procedure is used extensively with children with moderate hearing losses and sometimes with those with severe hearing losses. The auditory method is probably most effective when it is initiated in the early years. Calvert and Silverman (1975) have referred to the approach as the *auditory global* method.

TOTAL COMMUNICATION METHOD The total communication method, sometimes called the simultaneous or combined method, presents finger spelling, signs, speech reading, speech, and auditory amplification at the same time. The Conference of Executives of American Schools for the Deaf (1976) has defined *total communication* as "a philosophy requiring the incorporation of appropriate aural, manual, and oral modes of communication in order to insure effective communication with and among hearing impaired persons" (p. 358).

Jordan, Gustason, and Rosen (1979) investigated the number of classes that use the different modes of communication. In their study they combined the oral and aural (auditory) methods and included a system called cued speech (a system of hand cues used with speech and speech reading). They found that (1) total communication is used most frequently and is used almost exclusively at the high school level and (2) the oral-aural method is the next most frequently used. The two procedures together were used by over 90 percent of the schools surveyed.

Research on Communication Approaches

Those educators supporting the oral approach claim that if a child is permitted to communicate with signs, the child will not make the necessary effort to learn speech. Those educators supporting the manual method claim that language is retarded in children who are not allowed to sign or finger spell and that the process of learning language through speech delays language development. Each school of thought is able to present individual examples of successful performance, but the larger question is, "How do the majority of hearing handicapped children fare under these various systems?" Only in the past two decades has systematic research been conducted to address this question.

The research has taken a number of different approaches. One was devoted to documenting the effects of early oral training. In the 1950s and 1960s, the predominant model of teaching young deaf children (below the age of 6) was to place a heavy emphasis on oral training and speech reading to the extent that manual finger spelling or signing was forbidden. The reason for the prohibition was that signing was so easy for children and the learning of speech so difficult that they would lapse into the use of signs if they had such an alternative available. Evaluations of the effects of such training led to a change in philosophy on the part of many educators. Goldin-Meadow and Feldman (1975) investigated the language development of five deaf children from the age of 1 1/2 who had been exposed to oral training with other deaf children.

By the end of the study, when the children ranged from thirty-two to fifty-four months, two produced no intelligible spoken words and one child produced fewer than five words. The other two children could speak and lip read single words in constrained settings such as pointing to correct items or naming items on flash cards. There was no transfer observed in speech and lip reading to general activities of daily living. (Moores and Moores, 1980, p. 54)

A related discovery that deaf children born of deaf parents were developing in a superior fashion in achievement and socialization to deaf children born of hearing parents caused many observers to conclude that the superiority came from the early and intensive use of manual communication that occurred in the homes of deaf parents (Brasel and Quigley, 1975; Meadow, 1968; Vernon and Koh, 1971). Quigley (1969) conducted a five-year experiment on the Rochester method (the combination of speech and finger spelling) and reported the following conclusions:

1. Finger spelling plus good oral techniques improves achievement in meaningful language.
2. Learning finger spelling is not detrimental to the acquisition of oral skills.
3. Finger spelling produces greater benefits with younger rather than with older children.
4. Finger spelling is one of a number of useful tools for instructing deaf children.

Moores, Weiss, and Goodwin (1978) reported on a longitudinal evaluation of seven public and residential school programs. They found that deaf children, using the combined methods, functioned in the normal range intellectually, possessed prereading skills equivalent to hearing children, and were able to communicate effectively with the total communication method—simultaneous use of speech and manual communication. The speech of these children was still very difficult to understand and they had difficulty comprehending grammatical structure. The data definitely contradicted the belief that manual communication impeded the development of speech in language or that human communication must be limited to one channel.

Moores and Moores (1980) summed up the situation as follows:

Both in the classroom and in less formal settings, the trend seems to be toward the multisensory model; auditory training, manual communication, and speech training are being introduced at early ages and are used in co-ordination with one another. . . . The child is conceived of as a social being with complex patterns of active interactions relative to individuals and his environment. (pp. 59–60)

There is no question that outstanding oral schools such as St. Joseph's and the Central Institute for the Deaf, both in St. Louis, still produce excellent graduates of the oral method. These schools can create a total oral environment that is hard to duplicate in most educational settings. Today the trend is strongly in the direction of total communication, the simultaneous use of all avenues of reception and expression (Jordan, Gustason, and Rosen, 1979).

Additional Skills

In addition to the major communication systems, various other skills are needed by the hearing handicapped child and many of these are taught by different professionals with different skills.

The variety of problems faced by the child with significant hearing loss is such that no single professional is likely to be able to provide total service. These needs require instead a team of professionals each practicing his or her own special function to produce a comprehensive program of education and therapy to help the child adapt as best as possible. Thus a clinical audiologist is necessary to make a careful assessment of the hearing loss in all of its physical and functional dimensions, a speech therapist is required to help the child reach maximum potential in speech reading and speech production, and a special education teacher who is trained to work with the hearing handicapped is needed to provide an individual education plan and a sequence of lessons and to help regular educators understand the special needs of children with hearing losses.

Speech Reading

One of the skills important to deaf or hard-of-hearing children is *speech reading* or lip reading. Speech reading is the visual interpretation of spoken communication. It is the means by which deaf people receive communication from those who can hear. Because few hearing people will take the trouble to learn a complex system of manual communication, the deaf individual who aspires to keep in meaningful contact with the hearing world must learn to speech-read. There are special problems in learning this unusual skill. Many sounds in the English language have a particular visual pattern on the face—for example, the *n* sound looks very different from the *k* sound. However, there are other sounds that are *homophones,* which means that they are articulated in a similar way and look the same on the lips and face. Fifty percent of the words in the English language are estimated to have some other word or words homophonous to them, thus indicating the difficulty of speech reading.

As in the case of manual communication, a number of specific systems and approaches are used to teach youngsters speech reading. When the child is young, the teacher or the parent talks to him or her in whole sentences. At first the child may not obtain any clues, but as the parent or teacher repeats the same expression over and over again in the same relationship to something that the child is experiencing—an object or an act or a feeling—the child begins to get an idea of what is being said. At a later stage those vague whole impressions are converted into lessons that emphasize details, and exercises are given to help the child discriminate between different words and between sounds. Eventually, the teacher uses speech reading as a method to present lessons in school.

There is very little data to suggest how best to carry out the sequence of instruction on speech reading or to explain why some youngsters are especially good at it while others are not. Measured intelligence and other factors often relevant to successful instruction do not seem related to success in speech reading. Careful research and evaluation are called for to systematically improve the instruction in this skill that provides one necessary bridge to the hearing world (Farwell, 1976).

Auditory Training

Teaching the child to listen to sound clues that are available and to discriminate between different sounds is called *auditory training.* The transistor hearing aid is extensively used in auditory training with either individual or group hearing aids. The major aim of auditory training is to help the child at as early an age as possible to learn to discriminate between sounds. That kind of instruction is given to hearing impaired children by the hearing specialist in school in accordance with the needs of the child. Of great importance for this type of training is home instruction, particularly during the preschool period. Parents can help a great deal in auditory training, and one of the goals of the hearing specialist is to instruct the parents and to obtain their cooperation.

Auditory training is used by speech therapists in the schools for children with mild and moderate hearing impairments, but the procedure may be used with the severely impaired at a young age. The method has been called the acoustic method, the acoupedic method, the auditory method, the unisensory method, and the aural method. Calvert and Silverman (1975), who termed the procedure the auditory global method, described it as including the maximum use of hearing and recommended that it be employed with amplification as early as possible. The emphasis on auditory decoding and corrected speech characterizes the auditory training method by whatever name it is called.

Learning Environment

Most children with mild hearing losses are found in the regular public schools, but statistics on the nature of their placement on a continuum of services are not available. More precise figures are available on those children with severe and profound hearing losses.

Table 6.4 indicates the current enrollment in schools and classes for deaf students in the United States as of 1979. The number of students in public day classes and those attending residential schools for the deaf are almost equal, but there are another seven thousand youngsters attending public day schools. Almost five thousand of the students in the public residential schools are day students who attend the residential school essentially as a day school. Therefore, the majority of deaf students in the United States today are attending programs that allow them to live in their own homes and to be educated in special learning environments. It can also be noted that private schools and classes play a very small part in the total picture of education of the deaf.

Early Education

Although there is great diversity in terms of style and approach among educators of the deaf, there is universal agreement among them on the importance of beginning early. Even the child in the crib obtains clues from the mother through her manner of touching (tactile and kinesthetic) and through her facial expressions (visual). As the mother says no, she shakes her head; when she says yes, she

TABLE 6.4
Enrollments in Schools and Classes for the Deaf in the United States, 1979

Schools and Classes	Number of Programs	Student Enrollment	Percentage of Total Enrollment
Public residential schools	62	16,499	37.9%
Private residential schools	6	579	1.3
Public day schools	53	6,908	15.9
Private day schools	16	534	1.2
Public day classes	337	17,481	40.2
Private day classes	19	294	0.7
Multihandicapped only	22	401	0.9
Specified handicapped facilities	26	797	1.8
Total	541	43,493	100.0%

Source: Adapted from W. Craig and H. Craig (Eds.), Directory of services for the deaf. *American Annals of the Deaf*, 1980, *125*, 179. Reprinted by permission of the American Annals of the Deaf.

has a different facial expression and nods. The child soon learns to respond to the lip movements and the facial expression or head movement. Through the tactile sense the child obtains communication clues by feeling the vibrations of the mother's voice as she sings or by feeling her face and throat as she talks.

Parents are asked to talk to the child, even though at first, like hearing babies, he or she does not understand. The child will note in time that lip movements, head movements, facial expressions, vibrations, and signs have some communicative meaning. This sense of meaning develops very slowly at first, but if the parent continues to communicate in a natural way, the child will begin to grasp meaning more quickly.

Most educators of the deaf and hard of hearing recommend a regular, professionally directed training program as early in the child's life as possible. Although these services need not be provided in a school building, many states have relaxed their age requirements for school enrollment so that deaf children can be provided services through special education programs beginning at birth. Youngsters in the preschool-age range may be given tutorial assistance, may attend a special program for hard-of-hearing and deaf children in a nursery school or day care setting, or may be integrated within a larger program for nonhandicapped children.

In any of the settings, a major emphasis is placed on the development of communication skills and social activities, so that the child begins to understand and interact with other children. The major purposes of such early childhood programs for young deaf children are (1) to develop language and communication skills; (2) to give the child experiences with other children in sharing, playing, taking turns; (3) to help the child take advantage of residual

Early childhood programs for the deaf help preschool youngsters to take advantage of residual hearing and to become accustomed to using hearing aids. (Photo: Freda Leinwand/Monkmeyer Press Photo Service.)

hearing through the use of auditory training and developing the use of hearing aids to amplify sound; and (4) to develop readiness for basic reading and arithmetic.

A major part of most early childhood programs is parent education, and many of the programs spend a great deal of time working with the parents of the hearing handicapped child to help them understand the nature and consequences of the hearing loss to the child, and, in some instances, to help the parents become supplementary teachers, carrying out some of the developmental tasks in the home that are a part of the overall special education program so as to reinforce the learning of the child. How thoroughly the parents become a part of the training program is both a function of the parents' readiness for acceptance of that role and of the philosophy of the educators who are responsible for the program. Intensive preschool training is considered by all concerned as a fundamental step in the direction of preparing the youngster for the more difficult school-age period.

Elementary School

If a child with a severe hearing loss has completed an effective preschool program, then he or she may be ready for some type of spe-

Hearing impaired youngsters often spend time in resource rooms receiving instruction in auditory training, language construction, and speech training. (Photo: Irene Bayer/ Monkmeyer Press Photo Service.)

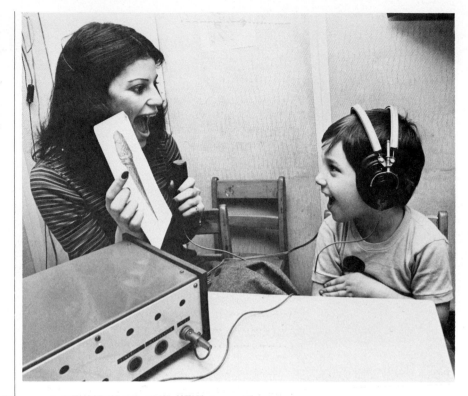

cial program in the elementary school. The increasing popularity of mainstreaming, placing the handicapped child with nonhandicapped peers if at all possible, has sparked vigorous discussions as to how that concept fits with children who are deaf. The wide variety of specialists needed to deal with various facets of the child's development suggests that any school program attempting to mainstream children with hearing losses must include supplementary professional personnel and such personnel should be accessible to the parents. The child's major responsibilities during the elementary years are to learn the basic skills of reading, arithmetic, and language. In most programs, despite the best efforts, the deaf child seems to progressively fall behind the average child in achievement. It becomes difficult to totally mainstream severely handicapped deaf children because they are rarely able to compete at the same academic level as their peers. Many hearing handicapped youngsters spend supplementary time in resource rooms with individual or small group work in auditory training, language construction, and speech training.

Secondary School

During the secondary school period, many youngsters with severe and profound hearing handicaps find their way into special programs focusing on vocational education or, in some cases, enroll in technical schools for the deaf. These schools provide a curriculum designed to generate broad work skills for the deaf individual and focus on the skilled and semiskilled trades, a major occupational outlet for many students. If these students remain in the regular public high school, in a type of mainstream, they have a substantial need for remedial work. Many of them will be performing at a third- to fifth-grade level in academics, and would thus be far behind their classmates in junior and senior high school. In addition, as noted earlier in the chapter, their understanding of language concepts and structure creates substantial academic limitations.

Postsecondary Programs

During the last two decades, postsecondary school programs for the auditorially handicapped have increased significantly. This increase was the result of surveys of the vocational status of deaf adults, such as those conducted in New England (Moores, 1969), that revealed an unemployment rate among the deaf that was four times greater than that for hearing adults and a level of employment primarily fixed at semiskilled and unskilled positions.

A further study designed to locate all hearing handicapped individuals in the United States who had enrolled in or graduated from regular colleges and universities between 1910 and 1965 yielded only 653 persons who had attended an institution of higher learning and only 133 prelingually deaf (deaf before the age of 4, prior to full development of language) who had graduated from college during that time (Quigley, Jenne, and Phillips, 1968). Clearly college for postsecondary mainstreamed hearing handicapped individuals was not providing opportunities for many who wished to enter occupations that require college degrees.

A number of alternative postsecondary school opportunities are available to deaf students. One of the most unique in the world is Gallaudet College, which was established by Congress in 1864 and is the only college in the world devoted exclusively to the education of deaf individuals. It is now an accredited four-year liberal arts college and has added a graduate school, which includes both hearing and deaf students. Gallaudet College also operates the Kendall Demonstration Elementary School and the Model Secondary School for the Deaf.

Another development in higher education was the establishment of the National Technical Institute for the Deaf in Rochester, New York, also supported by the federal government. The institute was founded in 1967 for the purpose of providing opportunities to deaf adolescents and adults for training in technical and vocational pursuits. In addition to that development and because of the expansion of community colleges, a federally supported project was initiated in 1968–1969 to establish three postsecondary programs for deaf students in community colleges at Delgado Vocational Technical Junior College, New Orleans, Louisiana; Seattle Community College, Seattle, Washington; and St. Paul Technical Vocational Institute, St. Paul, Minnesota. Career objectives in those community colleges most frequently selected by deaf students were reported by Craig, Craig, and Barrows (1970) to include graphic arts, sheet-metal working, welding and body repair, food services, machine-tool processing, production arts, prosthetics, and electronics.

Moores, Fisher, and Harlow (1974) evaluated the programs at Delgado Vocational Technical Junior College, Seattle Community College, and St. Paul Technical Vocational Institute. These schools enrolled many hearing individuals but accepted a small group (sixty-five to one hundred) of hearing impaired young adults. The authors found that the development of postsecondary vocational programs had positive results. For example, one of their findings was that 75 percent of the graduates of the programs obtained positions in technical, trade, and commercial enterprises as compared with one-third of nontrained individuals who obtained such employment. This study did not reveal any major shifts or breakthroughs to new types of occupations. There was a tendency to cluster in certain occupations, such as general office practice for females and printing for males.

In reviewing the impact of postsecondary schools, Moores (1982) reminded us of the interdependence of education at the various levels:

It is doubtful that any postsecondary program, no matter how exemplary, can overcome the inadequate education most deaf individuals receive in the early intervention, elementary, and secondary years, despite improvements. Until education of the deaf, in general, begins to provide students with basic skills and helps them to develop to the limits of their potential, the economic position of deaf adults will continue to be below that which they are capable of obtaining. (p. 315)

Curriculum Content   The serious problems that children with severe hearing problems have had in academic achievement are well known. Much of the education has focused on special methods and procedures for teaching communication skills and language in the hope that these skills, once in place, would allow hearing handicapped students to master the regular curriculum. For children with mild hearing handicaps, such an expectation seems reasonable. When these children receive speech and language therapy from a team of specialists, they are able to stay with their classmates through the regular curriculum.

During the past few years, however, it has become increasingly obvious that the more serious the hearing loss, the more likely that specific changes will have to be made in the academic content itself. Quigley and Kretschmer (1982) have pointed out that the hearing child learns to read by breaking the code of the word symbol system through the process of linking the symbols to already-learned language concepts that the child has mastered through speech. The deaf child has no such language base from which to operate and has serious trouble with the syntactic structure of language as well as the concepts. Therefore, one of the major content adaptations involves the teaching of linguistic structure directly to the youngsters, a task that does not have to be done with those who have functional hearing because they learn the structure as they absorb the sea of language in which they are immersed.

The content of educational programs for children with severe and profound hearing losses inevitably includes some effort to teach the structure of the English language. As indicated in the samples of writing of deaf students given earlier (see p. 245), the way in which language is structured is difficult for the deaf child to master. An example of a generative-transformational grammar analytic system was developed at the Rhode Island School for the Deaf (Blackwell et al., 1978). This system presents five basic sentence patterns:

1. noun phrase + verb (e.g., The baby cries.)
2. noun phrase + verb + noun phrase (e.g., The baby drinks milk.)
3. noun phrase + linking verb + adjective (e.g., The baby is cute.)
4. noun phrase + linking verb + noun phrase (e.g., The baby is a boy.)
5. noun phrase + linking verb + adverbial phrase (e.g., The baby is in the crib.)

All other patterns are then taught as transformations of the five basic patterns. Because they start with the noun phrase, it is easy to see how deaf students can be baffled by sentences such as, "Before the boy could turn around, the dog was upon him." All the individual words can be recognized, but the manner of presentation can make the sentence incomprehensible. Nevertheless, the development of a soundly based linguistic system for the deaf child is a major step forward in educational practice.

Mahoney and Weller (1980) have endorsed an ecological approach to language intervention in which language training is done in as practical and social a situation as possible. Play routines and natural social settings, such as mealtime, bedtime, and bathing, are used as opportunities for effective language interaction and communication. When language is presented in the context of a familiar social environment (for example, during mealtime when all the members of the family are engaged in routine activities—the mother in the kitchen, the father setting the table, and so forth), cues that the youngster learns from the environmental context can contribute greatly to mastery of the language as well as providing rich opportunities for practice. Moreover, specialists in language therapy or speech pathology who use this approach become consultants to those who are the primary language models—parents, teachers, and others who have close and continuing contact with the child—rather than serving as the primary deliverers of the language instruction. In this way, specialists can provide help and sophisticated techniques to those primary models who will be in the best position to interact with the child in the natural setting.

There is a manifest need for more curriculum materials that meet the special needs of deaf students. LaSasso (1978) conducted a survey of programs for hearing impaired children and found that almost half of the respondents placed a high priority on the development of special curriculum materials for the hearing impaired.

Technology   The increasing use of films and television as educational media poses a threat of excluding the hard-of-hearing or deaf student who may not hear the sound track that is critical to the film's message. In order to provide access to these experiences, Congress appropriated funds in 1958 for the development of a program entitled Captioned Films for the Deaf. The program was originally designed to improve and enrich the curriculum for the deaf by providing captioned films for use in educational institutions. The original program of captioned films provided a loan service but it has expanded its service to include providing equipment to be used in homes and schools, contracting for the development of educational media, and training personnel in the use of the educational technology. Recently, support from the U.S. Department of Education has allowed for extensive captioning and signing on selected television programs so that the deaf can keep up with current news, drama, and entertainment through this medium.

One of the major advances in technology in the field of deaf children and adults has been the development of a *teletypewriter and*

Deaf and hard of hearing people are now able to enjoy television viewing through captions that are written by trained professionals who translate the more detailed content of a program into fewer words that convey essential information. (Photos: WGBH TV, Boston.)

printer (TTY), a device developed by a deaf orthodontist in 1964. This device enables deaf individuals to communicate through the use of a typewriter by transforming the typed message to electrical signals and then retranslating them to print at the other end of the phone connector. To make a TTY call the person places an ordinary telephone handset on the coupler modum or interface between the typewriter and the telephone. The acoustic coupler then transforms the electrical signals into two sounds at different frequencies which are then transmitted over the telephone and converted back into printed letters on the receiving end (Levitt, Pickett, and Houde, 1980).

A series of similar instruments and systems have been generatd by other companies involved in technology and the more general term now in use is *telecommunication devices for the deaf* or *TDD*.

There are currently over 50,000 stations that send and receive and print messages that allow the deaf to communicate in this fashion despite some difficulty in terms of funding the machines and the cost of the messages. They have proven to be of substantial use for the deaf in communicating across long distances (Schein and Hamilton, 1980).

Future of Deaf Education

What does the future hold for the deaf student? Will there be more exciting technological breakthroughs that will help bypass the handicap of deafness? Will there be some medical breakthroughs to open blocked communication channels? Prickett and Hunt (1977) asked over fifty experts in the field, both administrators and researchers, to indicate the most likely and desirable future changes that might occur in working with deaf individuals. They asked the experts to respond to a wide variety of possible answers and then fed these responses back to the total group, progressively refining the answers until a strong consensus was reached. The ten items ranked most desirable and most likely to happen are listed in Table 6.5. Two of the ten

**TABLE 6.5
Most Likely and
Desirable Events in
Future of Deaf
Education**

1. Preschool and parent education would be standard in deaf education
2. Improved academic achievement and social adjustment for deaf
3. More attention to career education and career needs
4. Need for more professionals in parent-infant training
5. More family life and sex education in schools
6. Increase in programs for multiply handicapped deaf
7. More programming for deaf by mass media
8. Interpreting services for the deaf will continue to expand
9. Improvement in hearing aid technology
10. Need for more teachers to work with multiply handicapped deaf

Source: H. Prickett and J. Hunt, Education of the deaf—the next ten years. *American Annals of the Deaf*, 1977, *122*, 365–381. Reprinted by permission.

Language in Deaf Children: An Instinct

The acquisition of language has always been one of the more intriguing aspects of childhood development. "The child of English-speaking parents learns English and not Hopi, while the child of Hopi-speaking learns Hopi, not English," note Susan Goldin-Meadow of the University of Chicago and Heidi Feldman of the University of California at San Diego School of Medicine.

"But what if a child is exposed to no conventional language at all?" the researchers ask in the July 22 SCIENCE. "Surely such a child, lacking a specific model to imitate, could not learn the conventional language of his culture," they say. "But might he elaborate a structured, albeit idiosyncratic, language nevertheless? Must a child experience language in order to learn language?"

In attempting to answer that question, Goldin-Meadow and Feldman videotaped six deaf children in their homes for one to two hour sessions at six- to eight-week intervals. The 17- to 49-month-old children—four boys and two girls of "normal intelligence"—had not been exposed to manual sign language because their parents wanted to expose them to oral education. Yet none at that point had acquired significant knowledge from their oral-education program.

The youngsters were observed and taped during informal interactions with a researcher, their mother and a standard set of toys. The researchers found that the deaf children "developed a structured communication system that incorporates properties found in all child languages. They developed a lexicon of signs to refer to objects, people and actions, and they combined signs into phrases that express semantic relations in an ordered way."

Perhaps most importantly, the experimenters found, through a complex coding system, that it was indeed the children, and not their parents, who actually devised the communication system. Though the mothers did use "some gestures" in their interaction with the youngsters, "a comparison of the mothers' and the children's signs suggests that indeed it was the children who first produced the system," report Goldin-Meadow and Feldman. Only 25 percent of the signs produced were common between mother and children, and there was "no evidence" that the children were imitating their mothers, say the researchers.

The deaf youngsters' systems were composed of:

Lexicon. Two types of signs were developed to refer to objects and actions. For example, they would point to significant words such as "this" or "there." Or, a closed fist bobbed in and out near the mouth referred to a banana or the act of eating a banana; hands flapped at shoulder height referred to a bird.

Syntax and semantics. The children linked their lexicon into multisignal phrases that conveyed relations between objects and actions. For instance, one child pointed at a jar and then produced a twisting motion in the air. Another child opened his hand with his palm facing upward and then followed this with a "give" sign with a point toward his chest.

"We have shown that the child can develop a structured communication system in a manual mode without the benefit of an explicit, conventional language model," the researchers conclude. They compare the findings with the "meager linguistic achievements of chimpanzees," where chimps have been shown to develop languagelike communication, but only with training. "Even under difficult circumstances, however, the human child reveals a natural inclination to develop a structured communication system," says Feldman and Goldin-Meadow.

SOURCE: "Language in Deaf Children: An Instinct," *Science News*, 1977, *112* (July 30), 70. Reprinted with permission from *Science News*, the weekly news magazine of science, copyright 1977 by Science Service, Inc.

items deal with the increasing need to provide programs with teachers for the multiply handicapped deaf, and two others deal with improving the role of professionals in helping the family. The experts predict an increased emphasis on both preschool and career education, representing a bridge between school and the world of work. Interestingly enough, aside from some hope for improved hearing aid technology and a greater use of television, technology did not rank high in terms of being both likely and desirable. There is some pessimism about new breakthroughs because of a lack of support for research funds to study new problems or techniques in the field.

conductive vs. sensorineural

SUMMARY OF MAJOR IDEAS

frequency - number of vibrations = pitch

1. Children with hearing losses fall into two major categories: hard of hearing and deaf. The functional distinction between the two categories is that the hard-of-hearing child can, with sound amplification, receive language through the hearing sense whereas the deaf child cannot.
2. The intensity of sound (reported in decibels) that is needed to get a response from the child is a measure of the degree of hearing loss.
3. Five categories of level of hearing loss are commonly recognized—mild, moderate, moderately severe, severe, and profound. The first three categories are part of the hard-of-hearing group and the last two categories fall into the deaf range.
4. The identification and diagnosis of hearing impairment in children include: (a) preliminary screening of children, (b) otological and other medical examinations, (c) audiological evaluation, and (d) psychological and educational assessment.
5. The causes of hearing impairment are many. Among the major causes are hereditary anomalies, maternal rubella, prematur-

ity, mother-child blood incompatibility, otitis media, and meningitis.

6. Approximately one in one thousand children is deaf and three to five children in every thousand are hard of hearing.

7. Children with severe and profound hearing losses are generally found to be two to five years below their chronological age in educational achievement in school.

8. Children with severe and profound hearing losses seem to have more serious behavior and personality problems than does the hearing child.

9. Key factors that influence language development and educational achievement of hearing impaired children are: (a) age at onset of hearing loss, (b) degree of hearing loss, (c) measured intelligence of the child, and (d) amount and quality of instruction.

10. Electronic hearing aids have been a great help to children with hearing impairments despite problems with reliability and care.

11. The education of the deaf has a long history characterized by heated controversies concerning the best methods for educating the deaf. The main controversy involves the oral method versus the manual method of communication.

12. The current communication approaches include four interrelated methods: (a) the oral-aural method, (b) the Rochester finger spelling method, (c) the auditory method, and (d) the total communication philosophy. At the present time, the total communication approach seems to be in the most favor.

13. The special educational procedures for children with impaired hearing require the skill of many different professionals and include: (a) training in one of the approved communication approaches, (b) auditory training, (c) speech reading (lip reading), and (d) reading and other school subjects.

14. Learning environments that have been organized for the hearing impaired consist of: (a) public and private residential schools, (b) public and private day classes, (c) public and private day schools, and (d) mainstreaming with support services.

15. Deaf individuals have a good employment record, but the available occupations still seem to be found largely in clerical, skilled, and semiskilled positions. Postsecondary school programs for young people with hearing losses have expanded in recent years.

16. Increased emphasis in the future may be placed on both preschool and postsecondary programs for children with hearing handicaps.

UNRESOLVED ISSUES

1. Educating the Multiply Handicapped Child with Hearing Handicaps. If one out of every four deaf children has some other serious impairment, then it becomes important to design educational programs with these conditions in mind. At present little progress has been made in this area beyond some pilot programs that attempt to provide a systematic program for emotionally disturbed/deaf or learning disabled/deaf children. Teacher-training programs, even in the field of special education, do not often provide background or experience for the development of special educational adaptations for multiply handicapped youngsters. We are in need of major program adaptations and skills for the multiply handicapped deaf.

2. Stimulating Language Development. The growing popularity of the total communication movement is a reflection of a commitment of educators to the importance of language, both from a conceptual and a structural standpoint. It seems likely that preschool programs should increase emphasis on the development of the structural aspects of language. Such concerns need to be organized in a longitudinal and sequential fashion so that the youngster can move from the preschool to elementary school to secondary school programs that build on the language instruction of the previous stage. Much of the linguistic instruction now presented is of an *ad hoc* nature with little relationship between the various educational levels. Development of an integrated "birth through 21" language instruction program is far from realization at this time.

3. Increasing Occupational Opportunities for the Deaf. Although people with severe hearing losses have developed an admirable record of employment, that employment still consists primarily of positions with a rather narrowly based set of technical skills, and the addition of postsecondary school programs has not substantially changed that circumstance. In a world where communication and language have become increasingly important, how does one broaden the opportunities of deaf children so that they can communicate in a hearing world? Most deaf children and adults still find that interaction with the hearing world is extraordinarily painful and difficult. As a consequence, they segregate themselves as adolescents and adults from the hearing society. If we believe that integration is a valuable goal, then we have not provided the means by which the child with severe hearing problems can successfully reach that integration.

4. Determining Factors That Facilitate Speech Reading. One example of the extent of the need for careful investigation is given in a comprehensive review of the topic of speech reading by Farwell

(1976): "Speech reading, the hallmark of deaf education, remains an enigma. Even those deaf persons who are proficient lip readers are unable to explain how they acquired the ability or what factors enable them to use this method of understanding speech" (p. 27). It is quite difficult to teach such skills efficiently if we don't understand the factors that operate in helping the child master this skill!

REFERENCES OF SPECIAL INTEREST

Birch, J. *Hearing impaired children in the mainstream.* Reston, Va.: Council for Exceptional Children, 1975.

A book designed particularly to aid teachers and administrators in creating a positive environment for the mainstreaming of mildly and moderately hearing impaired children. Includes a statement of general principles for mainstreaming, guidelines for administrators, and descriptions of some exemplary programs using the mainstreaming principles.

Moores, D. *Educating the deaf: Psychology, principles, and practices* (2nd ed.). Boston: Houghton Mifflin, 1982.

The most comprehensive textbook on deaf children yet produced. It provides a rich historical background on the past practices in addition to up-to-date reports on current research and educational trends. New material on preschool and postsecondary programs.

Quigley, S., & Kretschmer, R. *The education of deaf children.* Baltimore: University Park Press, 1982.

A comprehensive and readable status report of the various issues and controversies surrounding the education of deaf and hard-of-hearing children. The book is especially good in reviewing essential research that has been collected over the past decade. The evidence regarding the effectiveness of the various communications systems is presented in an even-handed fashion.

Ross, M., & Nober, L. (Eds.). *Special education in transition: Educating hard-of-hearing children.* Reston, Va.: Council for Exceptional Children, 1981.

A series of chapters dealing with different aspects of coping with the hard-of-hearing child in the public school system from audiological and educational assessment to the development of individual education plans. Focuses on ways to help the hard-of-hearing child become a part of the hearing world.

7

Children with Communication Disorders

I n the increasingly interdependent modern world, the ability to communicate with others can be considered a basic skill. Anything that interferes with communication creates a serious problem for the developing child.

Interference with communication is not the only problem created by a handicap in this area; complex sociopsychological feelings emerge when someone is identified as having a communication problem. The agonizing report of a young woman illustrates this point:

My friends tell me I'm attractive, but at 24 years of age I can count all the dates I've had on the fingers of one hand. Boys don't want to go out with girls who talk through their nose like I do. The doctors fixed my cleft lip so you can't hardly see the scar, but my voice is nasal and they say they can't help with that. In grade school the kids called me "honker" or "nosey" and mocked the way I talked. People don't do that now that I am grown-up, but they look at me funny or shy away. Or they are extra kind to me and that's worse. I don't want pity, I just want to live like everybody else. I wonder how many nights I've cried myself to sleep over these miserable years. (Van Riper, 1978, p. 5)

DEFINITION

During the past fifty years the types of services provided by specialists in the field of communication disorders have undergone major changes and expansions. The evolution of this field shows that at earlier stages emphasis was placed on the speech problems of articulation, voice disorders, and stuttering. Later, following World War II, hard-of-hearing children were added as an area of special concern, and, in the past two decades, treatment of language disorders has been included in the expanding responsibilities of this field.

The titles and training of the professionals in the field have also changed. Earlier, university departments that trained specialists in speech disorders were called departments of speech pathology. When the speech of the hearing handicapped was included, departments changed their names to departments of speech and hearing, and when language habilitation became popular, some departments changed their names to departments of communication disorders.

Likewise, specialists in speech habilitation changed their titles with the shifting emphasis. In school systems, specialists were called speech improvement teachers or speech correctionists. After

World War II, when psychotherapy became dominant, the preferred title became speech therapists. In the 1960s, the preferred term became speech clinician or speech pathologist, especially in clinics and hospitals. To emphasize the profession's role in language habilitation, the American Speech and Hearing Association (ASHA) adopted the title *speech-language pathologist* at its 1976 meeting. Incidentally, the professional association itself changed its name to the American Speech-Language-Hearing Association, though it keeps its old and recognized abbreviation, ASHA.

Speech and language disorders should be a familiar term to the reader by now. Many children with other exceptionalities, such as mental retardation, learning disabilities, and deafness, may have extensive communication problems. The definition of a speech problem includes, as do the other definitions of exceptional children in previous chapters, the perception of the viewer, as well as the objective character of the problem itself. Van Riper (1978) has defined *speech disorders* as follows: "Speech is abnormal when it deviates so far from the speech of other people that it calls attention to itself, interferes with communication, or causes the speaker or his listener to be distressed" (p. 43). The key adjectives that characterize defective speech are *conspicuous, unintelligible,* and *unpleasant.*

When language disorders were included as an area of concern in this field, a definition of language impairment was formulated by a task force of the American Speech-Language-Hearing Association (1977). *Language impairment* is:

a state in which an individual does not display knowledge of the system of linguistic *needs* commensurate with the expected norm. Typically, a child is *called* language impaired when his/her skills in the primary language are deficient relative to expectations for chronological age.

DEVELOPMENTAL PROFILE

Figure 7.1 shows the developmental profile of Betty, a 10-year-old speech impaired child with some language problems. For educational purposes she is within the normal range except that her speech, and to a lesser extent her language development, are below average. No very extensive educational adaptations have to be made for her in the regular grades. Special classes are not usually organized for this level of difficulty. Betty is in the regular grades with other children, but an itinerant speech-language pathologist provides Betty with corrective lessons several times a week and gives the classroom teacher additional suggestions on how to help with Betty's speech. With such help, Betty's articulation difficulties can probably be removed or considerably reduced.

FIGURE 7.1
Profile of a
Speech Impaired
Child

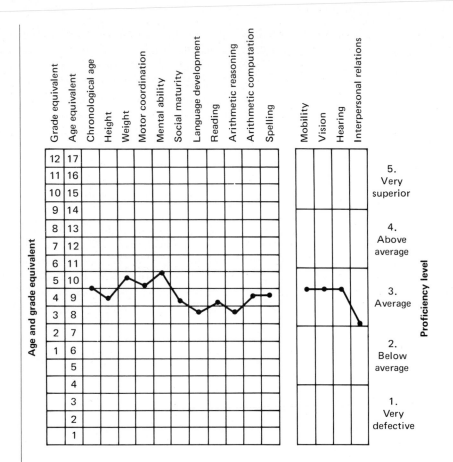

Thus the speech impaired child with an otherwise average developmental pattern does not differ markedly from other children in educational performance or physical development. Betty does not have a special language difficulty except for the minor problem of denying herself practice in communication because she is sensitive about the reactions of others. Such a child does not necessarily have widely varying discrepancies in growth. The educational program provided for her is like that of other children. Special education is provided on a part-time basis by an itinerant speech-language pathologist while Betty is being educated in the regular grades.

As will be discussed in Chapter 10 on multiply handicapping conditions, children with communication problems may, of course, have other handicaps. A cerebral-palsied child may have a motor handicap, a speech handicap, and a visual handicap. With such children a much more intensive special education program will need to be planned.

CLASSIFICA-TION

The American Speech-Language-Hearing Association has defined *communication disorders* as "impairments in articulation, language, voice, or fluency. Hearing impairment may be classified as a communication disorder when it impedes the development, performance, or maintenance of articulation, language, voice, or fluency" (*Comprehensive Assessment and Service (CASE) Information System*, 1976, p. 26). These disorders are distributed quite unevenly in the population.

Articulation About 70 to 80 percent of communication problems found in public schools fall into this category. Children may substitute one phoneme (speech sound) for another, omit phonemes, or distort them.

Voice The human voice varies in pitch, loudness, and quality. The pitch can be too high or low, the loudness can be too weak or strong, and quality problems can range from hoarseness to nasality.

Fluency The speech disorder identified with fluency problems is stuttering. It is a distressing problem to both speaker and listener. It occurs when the forward flow of speech is interrupted abnormally by repetitions or prolongation of a sound or syllable and is marked by avoidance behavior.

Language disorders There are two major language disorders—aphasia and delayed language development. *Aphasia* is an impairment in comprehending or formulating messages probably due to central nervous system damage or dysfunction. *Delayed language development* expresses itself in vocabulary or grammatical deficits that prevent the child from expressing himself or herself as well as age peers.

One of the major difficulties in the classification of communication disorders is the overlapping of categories. Articulation problems in which the formation, blending, and pronunciation of sounds may be impaired are often present without an associated problem. However, articulation problems are also usually present with cleft palate, cerebral palsy, mental retardation, and other associated handicaps. Voice problems may involve quality disorders (such as hoarseness), insufficient loudness, faulty pitch, and resonance disorders. Voice problems usually exist independent of other associated handicaps but may be part of the symptoms of cleft palate, cerebral palsy, and other organic defects.

Aphasia
- messages

DL dev. -
vocab./gramm
deficits

IDENTIFICA-TION AND DIAGNOSIS

In many school systems, the procedure for establishing a communication disorders program follows three stages: (1) screening procedures to identify children who require a full diagnostic assessment, (2) diagnosing those selected through the initial screening and from other referrals, and (3) selecting those children who require and can benefit from special speech and language intervention.

Screening Procedures

Most school systems have established formal screening programs for vision and hearing. Similarly, a speech-language pathologist may conduct screening each year to locate those children who are suspected of having communication disorders. Children who show signs of articulatory, vocal, rhythmic, or linguistic impairment would be selected for further diagnosis. In addition, children who are not detected by this formalized procedure are often referred to the speech-language pathologist by parents or by teachers in classrooms not included in the screening program when there is concern about performance in speech, language, or hearing.

Diagnostic Procedures

Case History

When a child is referred for a speech, hearing, or language examination, the speech-language pathologist obtains a history of the child to determine whether the problem is, or has been, recognized by other persons such as teachers, parents, and physicians. This history furnishes background information on the developmental history of the child in terms of the age at which the child walked, talked, and so forth. It also may include a medical history of illnesses, information about siblings and other family members with similar problems, social history, school achievement, and other examinations previously administered.

Intellectual Assessment

One of the first areas to be assessed in a child with a speech or language defect is his or her intellectual development. In some cases, psychological tests of nonverbal abilities are administered to determine whether a child's delay in speech or language may be due to mental retardation.

A child who is suspected of having a communication disorder may be referred to a speech-language pathologist who conducts a full diagnostic assessment. (Photo: Hugh Rogers/ Monkmeyer Press Photo Service.)

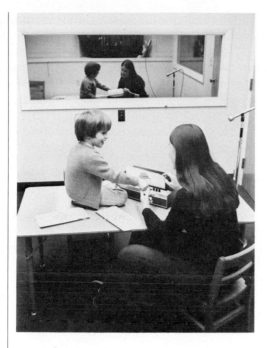

Hearing Assessment

Because hearing loss is one of the likely causes of speech and language problems, a careful audiometric examination is made of the child's ability to receive sound in each ear.

Assessment of Defect

Vocal responses
words
sounds
conversation

A speech-language pathologist attempts to ascertain the defect or defects by (1) obtaining spontaneous vocal responses from the child through response to pictures, (2) asking the child to repeat certain words that will identify an articulation defect, (3) asking the child to repeat sounds in nonsense formation, and (4) obtaining samples of the child's habitual conversation. Each of these procedures— spontaneous speech, imitation, nonsense syllable routine, and habitual conversation—has its place in helping the pathologist to determine the type of speech defect.

Determining Causal and Correlated Factors

If a child has delayed language or a defect in articulation, voice, or rhythm, the next question is "Why?" What factors are responsible for, or associated with, this difficulty? In the examination, the speech-language pathologist evaluates lip movements and structure, dental alignment, palatal structure and function, and pharyngeal adequacy. A judgment will be made about any structural deviation that may contribute to the speech defect. Factors in the home environment will be explored to see if they may influence the speech problem. Some observed symptoms or problems may require the speech-language pathologist to refer the child to other specialists such as an audiologist, an otolaryngologist, a plastic surgeon, a psychologist, or a neurologist.

Ordinarily, the diagnosis suggests the initial remedial procedures. Assessment, however, is an ongoing procedure because many aspects of the child's difficulty will come to light during the process of remediation. The major purpose of the diagnosis is to assess the special defects and so to lead to a program for remediation. The remediation sessions that may follow will depend heavily on ongoing assessment to find out what the child is able or unable to do.

PREVALENCE

The prevalence estimate of various speech and language disorders that occur in the school-age population have been generally accepted for some time (National Institute of Neurological Diseases and Stroke, 1969). If these percentages are basically correct, then a total public school enrollment for the United States of 41,500,000 in 1979 (Dearman and Plisko, 1981) would yield the expected number of children per disorder listed in Table 7.1.

However, the theoretical figures in Table 7.1 do not tell the whole story. In 1978, 856,052 children were reported to have re-

TABLE 7.1
Estimated Prevalence of Speech and Language Disorders

Problem	Expected Prevalence (by Percent)	Expected Number of Children
Functional articulation	3.0%	1,245,000
Stuttering	.7	290,500
Voice disorders	.2	83,000
Cleft palate	.1	41,500
Cerebral palsy	.2	83,000
Retarded speech development	.3	124,500
Impaired hearing	.5	287,500
Language delay	1.0	415,000
Total	6.0%	2,570,000

Source: N. Dearman and V. Plisko, *The condition of education*. Washington, D.C.: National Center for Education Statistics, 1981.

ceived special services for communication disorders, and over 90 percent of these students were seen less than ten hours a week. Where did all the problems go? Or, one might ask, is only one out of three of the estimated number of children with communication problems receiving services?

McDermott (1981) pointed out that one problem in determining the number of children with communication disorders has been that some states counted only those students whose primary problem was speech impairment and did not include those who had other problems, such as mental retardation, in addition to a speech impairment. Unduplicated counts have created the appearance that based on the expected prevalence estimate either there are large numbers of children who are not receiving services or there are fewer children with speech and language disorders than assumed.

A number of factors affect these figures. The vast majority of functional articulation cases reported are found in the earlier grades. Figure 7.2 shows the rapid decrease in prevalence of extreme articulation deviations for males and females from grades one to twelve. According to the study by Hull et al. (1976), males

FIGURE 7.2
Extreme Articulation Deviation

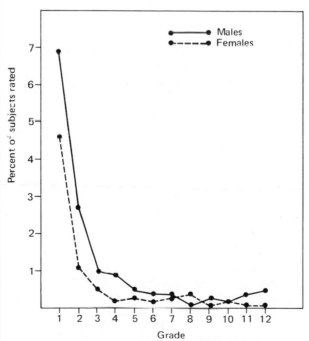

Source: F. Hull, P. Micike, J. Willeford, and R. Timmons, *National speech and hearing survey.* Project No. 50978, Bureau of Education for the Handicapped, U.S. Office of Education, Washington, D.C.: Department of Health, Education, and Welfare, 1976, p. 37.

had a prevalence rate of 7 percent in the first grade while females had a prevalence rate of 4.5 percent. This prevalence dropped to 1 percent for males and to 0.5 percent for females in the third grade, and to 0.5 percent and 0.2 percent in the twelfth grade. No information in the report indicates whether this rapid decrease in rate between the first, second, and third grades is due to remediation, to maturation, or to both remediation and maturation. The problem faced by speech-language pathologists is to predict whether the child will overcome articulatory, voice, and stuttering problems by maturation or will need intervention.

Articulation becomes much less of a problem as children mature and their language and speech improve. In their report of research conducted in a southern city, Gillespie and Cooper (1973) noted that articulation problems accounted for 60 percent of the communication difficulties reported in elementary school but decreased to 38 percent of the communication problems in the secondary schools. Stuttering, however, is reported as frequently as articulation as a problem at the secondary school level. The number and type of communication problems seem highly dependent on the age of the children under consideration.

CHARACTERISTICS OF CHILDREN WITH COMMUNICATION DISORDERS

In the area of communication, just as in mental retardation, behavior problems, and learning disabilities, there appears to be difficulty in drawing a line between mild problems worthy of some school attention and those serious enough to justify expenditures for major professional or special education services. Since each of the major groups of children with communication problems has a distinctive cause and treatment, each will be considered separately.

Producing Effective Speech

Before considering the causes and remediation of communication problems, it is useful to understand various physical requirements for effective speech. (See Figure 7.3 for an illustration of the speech mechanism.) The processes that are needed for sound production are *respiration*, *phonation*, *resonation*, and *articulation*. Freeman (1977) has described these processes:

Respiration, or breathing, provides the source of energy for sound production.
The breathstream activates the vocal cords, causing them to vibrate and produce sound, or to phonate.

FIGURE 7.3
The Speech Mechanism

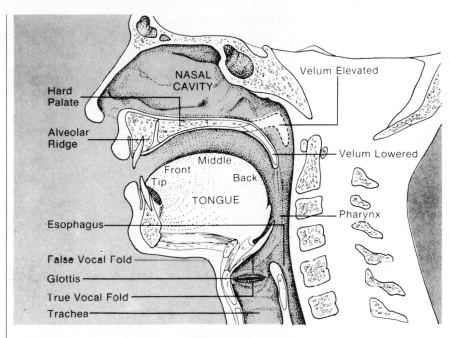

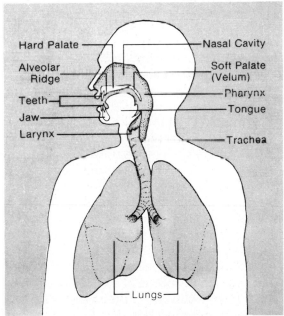

Source: C. Van Riper, *Speech correction: Principles and methods* (6th ed.). Englewood Cliffs, N.J.: Prentice-Hall, 1978, p. 77. Reproduced with permission.

This sound is then transmitted to the cavities and bones of the head and neck where it is resonated—conserved and concentrated—to give a characteristic quality to each voice.

Finally, through movement of the parts of the mouth the sound is shaped into the phonemes of language and articulated with other sounds as speech. (p. 10)

A breakdown in one or more of these systems interferes with speech sound production.

Articulation Disorders   Articulation disorders are those speech deviations that involve substitutions, distortions, omissions, and additions of speech sounds (phonemes). These difficulties may occur at the site of the articulators when the interaction of tongue, lips, teeth, jaws, and palate may be faulty. The oral cavity is modified by the movement of jaw, lips, and tongue producing the various speech sounds. If the movements are faulty, improperly sequenced, or absent, then resulting faulty speech is known as an articulation disorder.

Organic factors, including deviations in the tongue, larynx, pharynx, lips, teeth, hard and soft palate, and the breathing mechanism may cause speech difficulty. More often there are misarticulations with no apparent structural defect. These disorders of functional origin have been attributed to varied influences, including impoverished environment, infantile perseveration, bilingualism, emotional problems, or slow maturation.

Positioning of tongue and teeth, control of air stream, lip rounding, muscle tension—all play a role in proper sound production. Of course, we don't think about all of these motor changes when we speak anymore than we think about all of the separate movements that accompany walking. When speech and language are defective, diagnosticians approach the problem by analyzing the component parts of speech. Try, for example, to say *soup* with your tongue between your teeth. Where is your tongue when you do say it properly? Proper tongue placement is important in helping children properly articulate.

While speech problems obviously involve an incorrect expression of sound, the cause may well lie in a problem of auditory reception. If the child doesn't hear sounds, then he or she won't be able to say them accurately. The following typical interchange between a speech-language pathologist and a young child indicates that the child has trouble listening to his or her own words.

Therapist: Say *sssoup*, not "thoup."
Child: But I did thay *thoup*!

As Winitz (1979) has pointed out:

Whether learning a first or second language, auditory experience is a critical dimension. One must hear a new sound a certain number of times before all of its features are sampled. Equally compelling is the fact that the complex relation between discrimination and production is poorly understood. (p. 469)

Most articulation disorders are remediated by directly modifying the problem and *not* by eliminating its cause. In the case of hearing disorders, however, hearing aids and training in their use do help substantially in improving the child's ability to receive sounds and to hear his or her own sound production.

Nature of Articulatory Defects

The most common speech errors found among articulatory defects have been classified as (1) substitutions, (2) omissions, and (3) distortions.

Typical *substitutions* are as follows: *w* for *r*, as in "wight" for *right;* *w* for *l*, as in "yewo" for *yellow;* and *th* for *s*, as in "yeth" for *yes.* This type of error is commonly found among young children with immature speech. Sometimes a sound like *p* is substituted for almost every plosive sound, as *t* or *k*, or for the fricative *f*, as "I peel punny." The substitution may not always be consistent, for a child sometimes will substitute for a sound that he or she is capable of pronouncing perfectly and sometimes uses easily. Often the position of the letter in the word determines whether the child substitutes, as at the beginning (initial position) of a word, in the middle (medial position), or at the end (final position).

Omissions, when extensive, may make a child's speech nearly unintelligible. The consonants are most likely to be dropped from the endings of words, though they may be dropped from the beginnings or the middles and sometimes from all three positions. Occasionally there is a stoppage of air (a glottal stop) between the vowels of successive syllables that substitutes for a consonant.

Distortions show an attempt to approximate the correct sound. Among older children they are relatively more frequent than omissions or substitutions. Whereas a younger child will omit a sound or substitute another, an older child may try to imitate the proper sound but produce a distortion. A distorted *s* sound can have many near approaches to the correct sound, as the sibilant *s* (whistling), the lateral *s* (air emitted at side of tongue), and the dental *s* (tongue thrust against teeth), all of which can be corrected by the modification of the air stream and shift in oral pressures and positions.

In the broadest sense, articulatory difficulties may permeate every kind of speech deviation. Sometimes they exist alone or are associated with a concomitant dysfunction such as stuttering. Sometimes they occur as one of several speech-handicapping factors, as in cerebral palsy, in which vocal factors such as timing, pitch, and quality merge into the articulatory defects. Table 7.2 provides a summary of research on factors related to articulatory proficiency.

Identification of Articulation Problems

There are several widely used instruments designed to identify articulation problems. Of these, the Templin-Darley, the Laradon, and the Goldman-Fristoe tests are most popular. Each instrument uses pictures of common objects in order to encourage the child to articulate. The particular pictures are chosen to provide a variety of articulation sounds across the range of phonemes so that a total portrait of the child's ability to communicate effectively can be determined. For example, a picture of a boat would allow evaluation of the initial *b* sound and final *t* sound and a shoe will elicit pronunciation of the *sh* sound in the initial position and *oo* vowel sound. The total examination would identify those consonants and vowels that the child is misarticulating and in what fashion, thereby enabling the speech-language pathologist to plan a remedial program focusing on these specific points.

Speech Remediation for Articulation Disorders

Speech-language pathologists assigned to schools for the purpose of correcting various types of communication problems in children find that more than half of the children may display articulatory deviations or defects. Misarticulations are particularly common in young children and often go unnoticed because they are expected. School personnel are therefore not unduly concerned about the kindergarten child who is still unable to make those sounds with which many children after age 5 have no difficulty (for example, *r*, *s*, or *th* sounds). When a child is developing normally, maturation will probably take care of speech development with a little help from a wise teacher or parent.

Since the pathologist does not have the time to help every minor need, he or she must choose the children most in need of help. Unless the young child has an actual disorder and has difficulty com-

TABLE 7.2
Summary of Research on Selected Perceptual-Motor and Psychosocial Factors and Articulatory Proficiency

Causal Factors	Relationship to Articulatory Proficiency
PERCEPTUAL-MOTOR FACTORS	
Developmental and physical health	No relationship between such variables as height, weight, age of crawling or walking, childhood diseases, and articulation.
Intelligence	Within the normal range of intelligence, a slight positive relationship between intelligence and articulation.
Auditory discrimination	Considerable evidence that speech defective children score below nondefective children on tests of speech sound discrimination.
General motor skills	No relationship between such variables as speed or accuracy of eye-hand coordination, balance or rhythm, and articulation.
Oral area Oral structures	No difference between superior and inferior (adult) speakers on size or shape of lips, tongue, and hard palate.
Dentition	No sound-specific relationships between dental irregularities and articulation errors (excepting certain types of lisps).
Oral sensation	Some evidence that poor articulators score lower than normals on oral-form recognition tasks.
Oral motor	Some evidence that children with very poor articulation score lower than normals on tests of rapid speech movements.
PSYCHOSOCIAL FACTORS	
Socioeconomic level	Some evidence that proportionally more children from low socioeconomic homes (as indexed by parent occupation) have poor articulation.
Sex and sibling status	Some evidence that girls, first borns, and children with increased spacing between siblings have better articulation at some ages.
Personality and adjustment	Some evidence that children with severe articulation errors have a greater proportion of adjustment and behavioral problems than nondeviant children.

Source: L. Shriberg, Developmental phonological disorders. In T. Hixon, L. Shriberg, and J. Saxman (Eds.), *Introduction to communication disorders.* Englewood Cliffs, N.J.: Prentice-Hall, 1980, p. 281.

municating with others, the speech-language pathologist will usually give time and nature a chance to work. The pathologist may assist the parent and teacher in working with the child rather than filling his or her schedule with children whose problems do not actually require intensive treatment. The major difficulty involves ability to predict which child with articulation problems will develop appropriate speech without remediation and which one will need assistance at an early age.

The children selected for speech remediation are scheduled either for individual or group lessons. The cooperation of the teacher and the parent is solicited in this matter in order to transfer the practice in individual lessons to the home and school situations. Individual speech remediation may use various approaches.

There are differences of opinion as to whether it is best to have the child practice the sound in isolation (for example, the *s* sound) and then integrate it into normal conversation or to use natural conversation as a basis for remedial work (Winitz, 1979). Both methods appear to have met with success.

Group remediation is utilized successfully by many speech-language pathologists. For example, a developmental speech group may offer the pupil in the primary grades practice in listening to himself or herself and to others, practice in the production of new sounds and words, and practice in social interaction using speech.

In kindergarten and the first and second grades, speech improvement services from the classroom teacher will help every child toward more articulate speech without labeling or calling attention to those who appear to be different. The speech-language pathologist supervises this type of program, providing the teacher with material and routine procedures.

For mild problems, such as articulation cases uncomplicated by organic damage, the mainstreaming approach of keeping exceptional children in the regular classroom and providing supplementary professional services is a pattern that has been followed with children who have had communication problems for many years.

Stuttering　The problems of speech fluency have been reported back at least to Greek and Roman times with accounts of nonfluency in orators such as the Greek Demosthenes and the Roman Emperor Claudius, whose problems have been graphically depicted in a recent television series. Yet we still are baffled by the causes of stuttering and there are many divergent views on which methods can be effective on a long-term basis. Van Riper (1978) has said, "Stuttering occurs when the forward flow of speech is interrupted abnormally by repetitions or prolongation of a sound, syllable or articulatory position, or by avoidance and struggle behaviors" (p. 257).

Many ironies are embedded in this problem, not the least of which is that the natural strategy that people adopt to cope with it turns out to be the wrong thing to do. It is natural for people having difficulty with a task to invest more energy and effort to get it done, whether it is moving a heavy box or trying to loosen a screw that has rusted tight. The extra effort to speak well or fluently, however, tends to make the problem even more severe. As the child who stutters tries harder and harder to force the sound to come out, the block often becomes resistant—the face becomes contorted, muscles tense, the whole body seems to want to push the sound out, but this effort only results in the block that the child is trying to avoid.

Another irony is that in some kinds of speaking activities the child is perfectly fluent. Many children who stutter find to their surprise that they can sing or recite poetry quite fluently. Yet if they try to speak the lyrics of the song that they have just sung, they find themselves back into the speech blockage again.

A number of techniques can be used to create a quick, but temporary, fluency for the child—a type of "false dawn" phenomenon. Children who stutter can often obtain fluency by some type of motor movement while speaking. Thus, swinging one's arms, or pounding one's fist into the thigh, or using other distraction devices works for a time. The youngsters who use such techniques discover to their dismay that once the device (for example, arm swinging) becomes a habit and no longer a distraction, it loses its power to control the block and they are back where they started.

A final irony is that one's fears of stuttering become a trap that catches the child in the middle, with the fears creating the tension, which creates the speech blocks, thereby creating more fears. Webster and Brutten (1974) have described the behavior profile of a stutterer as having several major characteristics such as:

1. failure in fluency of speech by involuntary repetition or prolongation of sounds and syllables
2. a large proportion of the repetitions and prolongations occur in the same words
3. fluency failures are associated with emotional arousal
4. voluntary efforts are used to deal with, or cover up, the involuntary occurrences of stuttering by verbal and nonverbal responses, that is, repetition of words and phrases, changes in speaking rate and intensity, eye blinks, lip purses, arm swings, and so forth.

Webster and Brutten have explained that involuntary anxiety causes the stuttering, thus motivating the stutterer to engage in behavior that helps to avoid the negative reactions of the listeners. Such avoidance can take the form of substituting various sounds so that the child will not say "Get the ball" because the *g* sound develops a block but will say "Hand me the ball." Many children who stutter become experts on synonyms in order to substitute for the sounds that they know cause a block.

Causes of Stuttering

A multitude of theories have been proposed to try to answer the question of why children and adults stutter. Such causal theories range from genetics to home background to neurophysiological imbalances. Each proponent has fiercely defended his or her proposition without considering an obvious answer—all of them may be true in part. Genetics appear to set up a predisposition that influences a neurological set which is triggered if the right type of environmental experiences are present. As Bloodstein (1979) has summarized:

From every source we seem to learn the same lesson. Stuttering is caused by both heredity and environment. . . . Nevertheless, it is true that as long as we remain ignorant of exactly what it is that some people carry in their genes that increases their chances of learning to stutter, and as long as we continue to disagree about precisely what they learn and how, what we do know about the origin of stuttering will seem to be comparatively little. (p. 147)

Treatment for Stuttering

The various treatments for stuttering are as diverse as the theories about its cause. In one popular approach, sometimes referred to as the Iowa therapy, the stutterer learns a rhythmic way to stutter. By using this form of therapy, the pathologist can remove one of the most serious fears of stutterers—blocking on a particular sound and being unable to get out of the block. Instead of worrying about their own reactions, they are given the task of watching how others respond to their speech. They make phone calls, go to stores, ask strangers for directions, anything to force them to face their problem rather than hiding from it. As the stutterers become more comfortable with their stuttering behavior and more able to "stutter" themselves out of their blocks, they begin to improve and remain improved with only minor relapses (Bloodstein, 1979).

The other types of treatments all fit under the general term of *behavior therapies* in which elaborately systematized programs are designed for shaping an approximation of normally fluent speech. This speech is then transferred to daily life and stabilized for permanence. Desensitization is used, for example, in having the student physically relax in the presence of the feared situation (for example, speaking before the class). Such relaxation can reduce the fear behavior and good performance can be acknowledged with positive rewards (Perkins, 1980).

There are special concerns about the young child who seems to reveal a lot of verbal nonfluencies but has not yet shown the tension, eye blinking, contortions, and other characteristics of the confirmed stutterer. Advice to the parents usually consists of urging them to be good speech models and to not call the child's attention to his or her speech by saying, "Slow down" or "Calm down" or "Speak more slowly." Reducing the pressure on the child and seeing that he or she is rested and healthy also helps the child develop normal communications. Further advice consists of calling the parents' attention to their own unwitting reinforcement of their child's stuttering. Consider this example from Perkins (1980):

"Mommy, where does this go?" No reply. "Mommy, I can't make this work." No reply. "It won't fit!" Jerry's frustration mounted and his mother remained preoccupied. "M-m-mommy! Come here!" She came. "M-----ommy, I can't make it fit." She kneeled beside him and gave him her full attention. Intentionally or not, Jerry's mother responded selectively to his stuttering. (p. 472)

The approved procedure would be for the mother to respond to the child when he was using fluent speech by saying, "Let's see how we can put these together," while ignoring the child's nonfluencies.

The erratic pace of treatment and the tendency for relapses make evaluation of competing treatments a difficult matter. All of these techniques seem to work reasonably well in individual cases, but few quick cures last, and permanence—a lasting fluency—is the ultimate goal of the speech-language pathologist.

Cleft Palate   The communication disorder that emerges in children with cleft palate and cleft lip is due not to cerebral dysfunction but to structural deficiencies caused by the failure of the bone and tissue of the palate to fuse.

Most of us do not realize that we all have had a cleft palate at one point in our existence. This takes place at approximately three months after conception. As development of the embryo progresses naturally, these tissues pull together to form the hard palate and the soft palate which then forms a barrier to air rushing through the opening that otherwise would be there. If development is arrested so that fusion does not take place, the child will be born with a cleft in the roof of the mouth and sometimes in the lip. The reason the nasality in speech is noted in many people with cleft palates is that the opening cannot be completely closed off and the air rushes through the vocal cords and through the nose as well as the mouth.

Most of us recall from our childhood a youngster who had a repaired cleft palate and an unusually nasal sounding voice. These youngsters with cleft palates and cleft lips present a clear example of how physical and congenital disorders cast long shadows into the educational and psychological dimensions of the developing child. As Bzoch and Williams (1979) defined it, "Cleft palate is a congenital malformation of the speech and hearing mechanisms which frequently leads to severe and complex forms of communication disorders" (p. 18). Figure 7.4 shows a child whose cleft palate is visible. If the opening continued farther forward, the lip would be split, too, and the child would have both a cleft lip and a cleft palate.

As with other similar conditions, the occurrence of cleft palate seems to be caused by a multifaceted set of conditions with a genetic predisposition combining with some environmental problem while the mother is carrying the child, such as radiation or oxygen deprivation, early in pregnancy.

There are two major strategies by which the cleft or opening can be effectively closed. One is surgery to draw the available tissues together and the other strategy is the use of an *obturator* or a false plate that is fitted into the empty space. The whole purpose of surgical repair or the use of an obturator is to shut off air flow to the nasal passage and produce a more normal voice quality. When surgical procedures are delayed too long, not deemed advisable, or fail to accomplish the desired effect, all is not lost. Skillful fitting of an obturator or prosthetic device becomes, then, the most satisfactory solution to improving speech. Any such procedure for closing the physical opening must be accompanied by a sustained program of speech habilitation if the maximum use is to be made of these correction procedures.

Van Hattum (1974) has described four stages in the remedial program for children who have cleft palates:

1. The parent provides stimulation for prelinguistic speech from birth until 18 months.

FIGURE 7.4
Cleft Palate

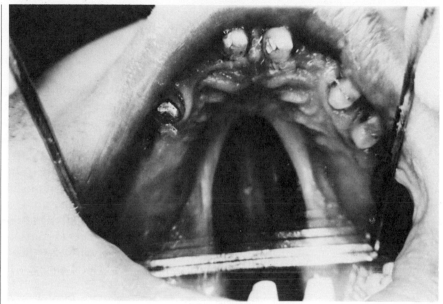

Source: Photograph courtesy of Ralph Blocksma, M.D.

2. From 18 months to 3 years the mother assists a speech clinician in speech and language development and remediation.
3. From 3 to 5 years the emphasis in remediation is placed on correcting or minimizing aberrant speech.
4. From 5 years on, correction and follow-up continue.

Generally the child with a cleft palate will continue to have speech therapy that focuses on velar and pharyngeal contraction, respiratory rhythms of speech, and articulation exercises for as long as needed to help the child gain comprehensible, nonirritating speech.

Voice Disorders   The child who talks in a voice that is too high, with a harshness that grates on the listener, or so low that the listener must strain to hear has both social and communication problems. Although relatively infrequent as a serious problem (about two in a thousand children), voice disorders create major adjustment problems when present and the speech-language pathologist is called to help. Hull et al. (1976) found that 3 percent of the school-age population demonstrated disorders of phonation, or production of sound. In this analysis, many milder cases were probably included to reach the high figure of 3 percent. One of the first steps in understanding voice disorders is to analyze the three basic components of voice.

Voice disorders are concerned with problems of (1) quality, (2) pitch, and (3) loudness. Voice is the production of sound in the larynx and the selective transmission of that sound including its resonance and loudness. The voice is produced by the outgoing air stream passing between the vocal folds in the larynx. From the larynx the sound travels upward through various cavities of the vocal tract, such as the throat, mouth, and nose (see Figure 7.3). The normal voice should produce a clear tone (phonation) emitting from the vibrating vocal folds, and this tone should be appropriate in pitch (not too high or too low). The voice should be heard easily, and a person should be able to increase the loudness of it without undue strain. An inflectional speech pattern—rather than a monotone—is important to give meaning to what is said. The three concerns of quality, pitch, and loudness will be discussed separately.

Vocal Quality

The more common defects in vocal quality are found in (1) *phonation,* or the production of sounds, and (2) *resonance,* or the direction of the sound in voice placement. The phonation, which originates in the larynx, sometimes exhibits a breathiness, hoarseness, or huskiness. It may be caused by structural aberrations that result in failure of the vocal cords to approximate properly in order to produce the correct vibrations in the air flow. When vocalization is impeded by paralysis of the vocal cords, then the cords cannot meet to allow the proper build-up of air pressure below them. The result is breathiness or huskiness.

In every school after an exciting basketball or football game, with its accompanying yelling and tension, many students will speak with hoarse and husky voices, sometimes with a whisper (aspirate quality), and sometimes with no voice at all, owing to inflammation of the laryngeal tissue and the vocal cords. If the student continues to abuse his or her voice on the playground or to reflect tensions in the muscles controlling the vocal folds, abnormal changes in voice quality may be evident. Abuse of the voice may lead to vocal nodules or growths on the vocal folds. Although small nodules will disappear completely with voice therapy, large nodes that have been there awhile may require surgical removal followed by voice therapy to prevent their recurrence.

Resonance depends on the balance of amplification in the various cavities used for this purpose—the oral cavity, the nasal cavity, the pharyngeal cavity (back of the throat), and the laryngeal cavity (the phonation area). This balance of resonance is affected by the size of the cavities and one's ability to direct the air-sound stream as one chooses.

Two types of difficulty are common: (1) hypernasal speech and (2) denasal speech. In hypernasal speech, sounds that should be emitted through the mouth are emitted instead through the nasal cavity, with the result that the consonants (other than /m/, /n/, and /ng/) and the vowels may have a nasal twang. This often occurs in partial or complete paralysis of the soft palate. The same condition sometimes accompanies cerebral palsy when there is a weakness in muscular coordination and control. An unrepaired cleft palate provides an open passageway into the nasal cavity, which can produce an almost unintelligible hypernasality. Often in children with repaired clefts, tissue insuffuciency or muscular incompetence may still create an abnormal misdirection of the air stream.

Denasality is an absence or inadequacy of nasal resonance. Some children sound as if they have chronic head colds or enlarged adenoids or as if they were pinching their noses. Insufficient air flows through the nasal cavities and is evident not only on the nasal consonants but also on sounds that are normally emitted through the oral cavity.

Vocal Pitch

One of the most common problems of pitch occurs at the time of adolescence and affects boys in particular. Some teen-age boys manifest a falsetto voice instead of the change to a lower pitch that usually accompanies the rapid growth of the larynx during puberty. During the transition in adolescence, the voice may break a number of times, to the embarrassment of the boy who is not aware that such breaks are a normal manifestation of a physical change. For boys who continue to speak in a high pitch, there are inevitable social problems.

Generally, pitch disturbances can be corrected when the child is older. Usually one expects a natural voice change, but there are instances of voice disorders that extend beyond the usual falsetto voice or breaks that generally disappear by the time a boy enters high school. Unusual or deviant adolescent voice characteristics can foster withdrawal behavior and embarrassment and may be symptoms of more serious physical problems. For those reasons, a medical examination should be a routine part of the voice examination.

Girls who manifest a pitch that is too low can have similar

adaptation problems and attention should be provided to bring the pitch back into the normal or acceptable range.

Loudness of Voice

Persistent loud talking can be a manifestation of a hearing loss or a personality problem, so careful diagnosis of the problem is required. More frequently, there are children who have the problem of not speaking loudly enough, seen in its most serious form in *aphonia*, a complete loss of voice. The failure to produce adequate breath pressure to generate speech is usually considered to be a psychological problem rather than a physical one (Bloodstein, 1979).

Remediation of Voice Disorders

Since the cause of a voice disorder can be anything from a serious health problem to major psychological difficulties to temporary abuse, the importance of a differential diagnosis before speech therapy begins can hardly be overestimated. Such a diagnosis also requires a diverse set of professional skills rarely, if ever, found in one person. This is why many speech clinics have been organized. In such clinics one can assemble the variety of professionals needed to conduct adequate diagnosis and treatment. It is also why many school systems depend on such clinics as outside sources of help because they cannot afford the range of professionals required to give comprehensive service.

For adequate treatment of voice disorders, the child involved must be aware of and convinced that his or her voice needs to be changed. Once that is done, a more general awareness of the problem can be aided by tape recordings so that the child can hear for himself or herself what the problem is. Some speech-language pathologists use *negative practice* as a technique for awareness. That is, just as in stuttering, children with voice disorders are taught how to produce the abnormality and so become aware of what they are trying to move away from. Then, they can be rewarded for proper production that they can now sense, as moving away from the maladaptive production (Eisenson and Ogilvie, 1977).

With many problems caused by abuse of the voice, the child can be kept away from the environments or settings that cause the abuse until the vocal apparatus has healed. The awareness of the child of the problem and its causes is the major ally of the therapist.

Impairments Associated with Cerebral Palsy

Cerebral palsy is a disorder of motor functioning due to brain dysfunction that, in most cases, is present at or near the time of birth. Since speech is a motor function, children with cerebral palsy very often require sustained attention from the speech-language pathologist. The child with cerebral palsy often has a variety of other problems in hearing and intellectual functioning, and consequently, social adaptation difficulties.

Speech Characteristics of Cerebral-Palsied Children

There are three different types of cerebral palsy and each has its own distinctive communication problems. The most common form of cerebral palsy is *spasticity,* a condition marked by excessive tension of muscles, slow jerky movements, and a "scissors" gait. Whether walking or trying to speak, there is a sense of enormous effort being put forth by the child or adult to do simple motor actions that most of us do automatically.

The speech of the spastic child will often show greater articulatory deviations than the speech of the other types of cerebral palsy. Speech will be labored and indistinct, and sounds will be omitted, slurred, or distorted, especially consonant blends like /sk/ or /sh/. Pitch changes will be uncontrolled and abrupt rather than gradual and continuous. Vocal quality may be husky, guttural, and tense and may show hypernasality of vowels.

The *athetoid* form of cerebral palsy is marked by consistent tremors, involuntary movements that are slow writhing and vermiform or wormlike in nature. The speech of the athetoid child usually is slurring in rhythm and constantly changing in pitch, inflection, effort, and emphasis, not unlike the postural balance characteristic of the athetoid type. Sounds are distorted inconsistently because of the continuous involuntary movements. The voice may lack force owing to respiratory disturbances and excessive movement. It may be unintelligible because of the irregular movements to which the speech musculature is subjected. If there is an effort at voluntary control of these muscle movements, the resulting coordination is much like that of the spastic—hence the term *tension athetoid.*

The *ataxic* child is characterized by a lack of balance in the coordination of muscles. It is usually due to a lesion in the cerebellum. Errors in judgment seem to be common in the force or direction of their movements. As Bloodstein (1979) has summarized, "Ataxic speech is marked by a general inaccuracy of articulation in which errors tend to be inconsistent and unpredictable. Rather than specific distortions or substitution of sounds, there is an extreme lack of precision'' (p. 269).

The causes of cerebral palsy are many, including the mother's contracting rubella early in the prenatal period, injuries, anoxia or lack of oxygen during the birth process, or infections such as meningitis or encephalitis in early childhood. The range of possible involvement of the nervous system is great in individual cases, and it is quite wrong to assume that children with cerebral palsy are inevitably mentally retarded. Often their true ability may be masked by their communication problems.

Speech Remediation for Cerebral-Palsied Children

Often the communication problems of the child with cerebral palsy are accompanied by other problems needing simultaneous attention. It is not unusual to find one child receiving occupational therapy, physiotherapy, speech training, and remedial reading instruction from a team of specialists. The remediation of speech impairments in the cerebral-palsied child does not differ greatly from that for other children. Six major areas require attention.

1. Because of the cerebral-palsied child's physical difficulties in walking, chewing, and swallowing, parents tend to overprotect or do too much for their child. Sometimes speech is delayed or inadequate, partly because the parents do not give the child the opportunity to try to exercise vocal musculature. When that situation prevails, it is necessary to solicit the cooperation of the parents and to motivate speech through experience and exercise.

2. Sometimes the speech-language pathologist must help alleviate the stigmata generally associated with cerebral palsy, including drooling and the tongue protruding or hanging from an open mouth. Efforts should be made to teach the child to swallow acceptably and to close the mouth and enclose the tongue. Again the cooperation of the parents is required since they are in daily contact with the child. Conscientious parents will remind the child to swallow before accumulating saliva in order to prevent drooling.

3. The use of mirrors should depend on the speech-language pathologist's clinical judgment. It is sometimes thought that greater muscular tension may be created when the child sees his or her own reactions. However, others consider this an acceptable technique. With some children, becoming familiar with what they see in the mirror will help them learn to live with their handicap and to profit from the use of a mirror, which can prepare them to control speech and to make adjustments for social interactions.

4. Language is aided by exploration, experience, and the need for verbal expression. The severely cerebral-palsied child is restricted in movement and does not have normal opportunities to move about and explore the environment. He or she needs experiences in motor activities. Since speech is a motor activity, it is necessary to use what speech-language pathologists call a multiple-sense modality approach: the use of auditory, visual, and kinesthetic senses in the production of speech.

5. Children do not speak unless they are motivated to speak. One of the problems with cerebral-palsied children is creating a need for them to improve their speech. Their own efforts to correct inappropriate tongue and jaw movements and to breathe properly require concentrated attention. Supplying the necessary motivation is one of the major concerns of the professional.

6. Finally, it will be necessary for a speech-language pathologist to help the child manage his or her tongue movements, control the synergetic movements of swallowing, control facial movements (grimaces, tics), and control breathing inflection, and intonations of voice.

Remediation for the cerebral-palsied child, as with all children who have neurological injuries, is painfully slow but very rewarding when it occurs. The tendency to overprotect and oversympathize with the struggles of these children is very great and needs to be guarded against.

Language Disorders   A child who develops without language is deprived of one of the most fundamental tools necessary to achieve full maturation as a human being. This is why any serious discrepancy between normal expectations and performance stirs many different professionals into action. Bloom and Leahy (1978), in their volume *Language Development and Language Disorders*, have contended that language involves the interaction of content, form, and use. *Content* refers to ideas about objects and events in the environment. *Form* refers to the conventional system of rules for combining sounds and words to form phrases and sentences. *Use* refers to the way in which language is used and the function for which it is intended. They have described normal language development as successful interaction among content, form, and use. According to Bloom and Leahy, disordered language is identified as any disruption within any of those components or in the interaction among these components.

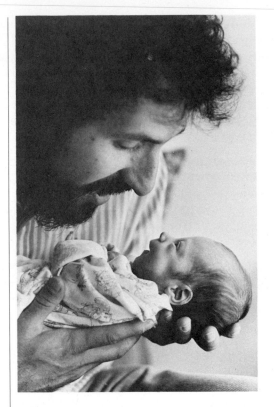

During the early stages of development, a child gradually learns to attach meaning to many sounds in the environment. (Photo: Mark Antman/The Image Works.)

We know that the formation of concepts in the child through experience precedes the use of verbal symbols to represent those concepts. Such cognition of things in the environment is common to animals other than humans, but the use of symbols to represent those concepts is very limited in other species. Certainly the use of the vocal cords, the recognition of the small phonemic differences in speech, and the complexities of grammar and vocabulary mark the greatest differences between humans and animals.

Understanding language precedes meaningful speech. The child learns to associate certain sounds or sequences of sounds with specific objects or situations. The child learns to decode those sound symbols, that is, to understand sounds in the environment that consistently occur in conjunction with other things that he or she knows or is aware of. The child of 8 or 10 months has already learned to attach meaning to many sounds in the environment—both natural sounds and the spoken word. A knock on the door means someone is there; jangling the car keys is a reminder of riding in the car; a sharp "no-no" means cease and desist.

Deviations in the language process have been roughly classified into two related categories: (1) delayed language development and (2) developmental or congenital aphasia.

Delayed Language Development

Children who have trouble understanding or speaking the language code of their peers at a normal age may have difficulty in any one or more of a variety of functions. Bangs (1968) has defined delayed language development as orderly development that progresses at a *slower rate* than normal and is significantly below the appropriate language performance for the child's chronological age. When a child has a language disorder, however, he or she shows a departure from the usual orderly pattern in learning the language code.

Some of the causes of delayed speech and language include hearing loss, mental retardation, behavior problems, and environmental deprivation. Pinning down the cause of delayed speech and language sometimes requires diagnostic services from a number of professions in addition to a speech-language pathologist. The neurologist, for example, looks for evidence of cerebral dysfunction, while the school psychologist attempts to rule out mental retardation. The audiologist is responsible for determining hearing abnormalities and level of acuity, and the social worker, psychiatrist, or psychologist explores factors in the home or environment to throw light on possible emotional factors that might have a bearing on the speech or language problems.

Delayed language development tends to hide other problems in some children. For example, the mentally retarded child shows a retarded mastery of symbols. It is the inability to think and remember that is fundamental in such children. The deaf child, on the other hand, often does not develop language because of the inability to hear, but he or she may have nonverbal symbolic language. The emotionally disturbed child may not respond to language or use it, but may in fact have mastered it even though there is little desire to share that mastery with adults or other peers.

Developmental or Congenital Aphasia

The term *aphasia* has been used to describe the loss of speech and language in adults and older children as a result of a brain injury or trauma. It has been used also to describe children who fail to learn language possibly because of a congenital condition—hence the term *developmental* or *congenital aphasia,* sometimes referred to as *childhood aphasia.*

Eisenson (1971, 1972) has emphasized the difference between congenital aphasia and language retardation or delayed speech and language. He has defined a child with delayed speech as "one whose competence (comprehension and/or performance production) is significantly below what we expect on the basis of age, sex, and intelligence" (1972, p. 194). According to Eisenson, congenital or developmental aphasia is "an identifiable syndrome that must be separately considered among the organic causes of language retardation" (1972, p. 197). He has insisted on definite evidence for "atypical cerebral development" on a congenital basis before a diagnosis of aphasia is made.

The terms *congenital* or *developmental aphasia* and *delayed speech* are often misapplied to children who show deviant language and speech behavior. The terms *delayed speech* and *aphasia* are difficult to differentiate in actual practice. Such differentiation may not be necessary. Instead, the evaluation of the child can deal with a learning disability as related to *auditory-vocal disorders*. This method of attacking the problem of perception, speech, and language can lead to specific programs of remediation. The methods of remediation of language disorders in children are discussed in Chapter 9 on learning disabilities.

Researchers and clinicians have been concerned with a differential diagnosis of delayed speech and developmental aphasia because remediation and prognosis in these areas are believed by some to be slightly different. Delayed speech due to mental retardation leads to efforts to improve the child's vocabulary or semantics. However, if delayed speech is due to a severe hearing loss, the remedial or instructional emphasis is different. Following an initial emphasis on concept formation or cognition, more time may be given to proper syntactic and speech development. The language disorder of a child whose delay is due to environmental factors may differ from that of a child with a brain injury or developmental aphasia.

Remediation of Language Disorders

A wide variety of exercises are available that allow children to strengthen special language deficiencies. When the diagnosis or review of the child's strengths and weaknesses reveal special difficulties in a particular area, the speech-language pathologist can provide specific lessons designed to improve performance in the area of weaknesses or developmental delay. Eisenson and Ogilvie (1977) have provided some examples that are focused on the young child, but the level of difficulty can be adjusted as needed.

Factors Influencing
Language Development

Discussions about the way language develops in children generally are apt to obscure somewhat, by their nature, the differences among children in the way they learn to talk. These differences are apparently very wide, and are nowhere so apparent as in the ages at which children reach various levels of linguistic development such as use of the first words and first sentences. Some say their first words at 9 months or even earlier. Other normal children, including some who grew up to be among the world's outstanding thinkers, are said to have begun to talk as late as age 4 years. There are evidently reasons for these large differences, and knowing what they are would be valuable. As yet these reasons are understood rather imperfectly, but we can summarize some factors about which we can be reasonably sure.

There is little question that intelligence, however we define it, is highly related to language ability and speed of language acquisition. Such a statement must not be misinterpreted. It applies to children as a group. We would be making the most serious error if we judged an individual child's intelligence to be low simply because the child's language was deficient. As we will see, many other conditions besides low intelligence can retard language. Still, for children as a group, the relationship is high. Some children destined to become geniuses are reported to have said their first words at 7 months; mentally deficient children are not likely to do so until they are a few years old.

Another factor in language development is sex. The most recent research findings tend to show that early sex differences in language ability may not be as great as was once thought. Nevertheless, it appears to be true that girls are at least somewhat ahead of boys in the onset of speech and in their level of language development for several years. Why this is so, no one knows. It is easy enough to imagine that some genetic maturational influence is at work. Another speculation offered is that the difference is at least in part environmental. The reasoning is that children tend to identify psychologically with the parent of the same sex. As a result, the little girl models herself on her mother, follows her from place to place, imitates her activities, and in the process receives a good deal of language stimulation from her. The boy tends to develop the same kind of relationship with his father, but in most cases the father is not home as much of the time as the mother is while the children are young.

Still another important influence is the age of the child's associates. Parents of a child who has been slow at learning to speak often blame it on the fact that the child does not have playmates of the same age. The age of a child's associates does seem to have some importance, but in just the opposite way. In general, the older the associates, other things being equal, the faster the development of language. It is difficult to interpret in any other way the repeated observation that only children appear to be linguistically ahead of comparable children with siblings. Stimulation by parents or older siblings seems to have more effect than stimulation by children of the same age. Additional evidence of this is the tendency of children who have been brought up in orphanages—where there are, in a sense, many siblings and relatively few parents—to be somewhat slower than average in language development. . . .

Finally, we cannot ignore the role of heredity. In examining children with retarded language, we sometimes find family histories of similar problems. In one case the mother reported that the boy's father, paternal uncle, and several male paternal cousins had all been late talkers, though they had all in time developed normal speech. We have very little factual information about the relation of heredity to variations among children in the rate of language development, but it is not a far-fetched speculation that biology plays some part.

We have noted a few of the factors that may influence language development. There are certainly many more. Knowledge of the subject is still rudimentary.

SOURCE: O. Bloodstein, *Speech Pathology: An Introduction.* Boston: Houghton Mifflin, 1979, pp. 21–23. Reprinted by permission.

Linking Symbols to Reality
Do these make sense?
   The hot soup is in the refrigerator.
   The porch is inside the house.
   The rug is on the floor.

Language Rules
Here is one pencil, here are two _____ .

Today for lunch, I am eating a hot dog.
Yesterday for lunch I _____ spaghetti.
Tomorrow I _____ hamburgers.

Auditory Perception
Which word does *goat* rhyme with? cat   seek   coat

Visual Memory
Using flannel board patterns, the children arrange a series of pictures depicting a snowstorm in the right order—the snow falling, the men shoveling the snow, the snow melting.

Auditory Memory
A child is sick. After the doctor arrives, the mother must go to the store for aspirin, cold medicine, juices and ice cream. Make sure you remember all of them. (pp. 179–181)

EDUCATIONAL ADAPTATIONS FOR CHILDREN WITH COMMUNICATION DISORDERS

Language, speech, and hearing services are offered by speech-language pathologists often in hospitals and clinics but also in public and private schools, in university speech clinics, and through private practice. This section will describe briefly the options for delivery of services to the schools.

In many respects, the communication disorders treatment program exists outside or apart from the formal school program.

Professionals who cope with children with communication disorders can form a clinical team that provides many different services but does not impinge on the regular school program. The mainstream emphasis noted in Chapter 1 fits well into the existing speech-language programs for the child with communication problems. These children will typically respond to the general educational program with some additional outside assistance for their special communication problems.

Treatment Priorities   The school system has to provide services of an appropriate nature to all students participating, but decisions can be made on who gets the limited services and where the services will be offered. A number of professionals have concerned themselves with the priorities that should be observed in providing speech and language services within the educational program. Zemmol (1977) has suggested the following priorities:

1. **Communication disorders** Severe articulation, voice, fluency, or language problems require intensive intervention. These disorders often interfere with academic achievement and social adjustment and a variety of professionals may be needed to plan a treatment program. Severe stuttering, cerebral palsy, and cleft palate are examples of communication disorders.
2. **Communication deviations** These children have mild to moderate articulation or voice problems that may be causing additional school adaptation difficulties.
3. **Communication development** This refers to efforts on the part of speech language pathologists to facilitate the improvement of all children's primary linguistic skills. The goal is to prevent the development of many mild speech problems.

In the past and the present, most of the attention of professionals has been focused on communication deviations, mild to moderate functional articulation cases. One of the reasons for this choice is that many states or communities establish case loads for the speech-language pathologist that may involve 75 to 100 children. It would be impossible to cope with that many severe cases, which is why the practitioners often ignore the urging of others who are not directly in the service delivery situation that they provide more service to the severe cases.

During the last decade, emphasis has shifted to the broader field of communication disorders in general, rather than remaining concentrated in the area of articulatory disorders. Many articulatory defects have the tendency to disappear without speech remediation as the child matures. Also, it has been found that, in order to be more effective, a speech-language pathologist must not only work with the child but must integrate the work with the regular teacher and the parents. They also have to broaden their operation from placing emphasis on speech problems to including language development and language disorders. Consequently, the training of speech-language pathologists has been broadened to include the study of language, linguistics, language disorders, and learning disabilities, in addition to the traditional areas of articulation, voice, and stuttering.

Van Hattum (1976) has suggested that the remediation of children with articulatory disorders should continue but that visual aids and taped programs could be used for a majority of the children under the supervision of a speech clinician. That move would free the speech clinician to become a supervisor, an administrator, a master clinician, a consultant, or a counselor. Van Hattum has recommended that the duties of speech clinicians should emphasize the supervision of aides, "early case selection, . . . language (studies), more services to special groups, extension of services to new areas, . . . prevention, and improved methods of accountability" (p.61).

The effectiveness of the various treatments for communication disorders over time is a much discussed, but little researched, topic. One study at the Kent State University Speech and Hearing Clinic that did pursue this question of treatment effectiveness was a fifteen-year follow-up of fifty children initially diagnosed as communicatively impaired (King, Jones, and Lasky, 1982). The investigators wished to determine the educational level achieved by these children and whether their communication problems continued into adolescence and adulthood. The children had been seen at the clinic when they were between 3 and 6 years of age. There were thirty-six males and fourteen females in the final group, not an especially unusual sex ratio for communication problems.

In terms of educational functioning, eleven of the fifty children had been held back a grade at one time or another in their school career, and over half reported difficulty in one or more academic subjects. Nevertheless, most seemed to be proceeding in an acceptable if not outstanding manner in school subjects.

The research team found that the more serious the problems were in the early diagnosis, the more likely such problems would extend into adulthood. Of those who had been originally diagnosed as having no speech, 80 percent still were reporting communication difficulties. Of those who had been diagnosed as having a language disorder or delayed speech, 67 percent were reported to have a continuing problem. However, of those who had been diagnosed as having only articulation problems, only 16 percent were reported as still having difficulty.

On the positive side, several of the children took part, later in their school careers, in "activities which demand sophisticated levels of communication such as forensics, thespian activities, student council, and serving as officers of organizations. One subject won first prize in a national debate contest" (King, Jones, and Lasky, 1982, p. 31).

Implications for Classroom Teachers

Speech-language pathologists use many techniques to promote carryover of newly learned speech patterns into the classroom. These techniques include: (1) workbooks that are kept in the children's desks or cubby holes for regular review by teachers, (2) weekly conferences with teachers regarding specific speech objectives, and (3) devices and props that are used to remind the children to use their corrected speech pattern. One of the major tasks of the specialist is to help the classroom teacher use these tools effectively.

One of the major shifts in emphasis in the communication disorders field is the increasing attention paid by speech-language pathologists to language difficulties. There appears to be a much greater increase in cases that are identified primarily as language problems and a corresponding decrease in the proportion of cases of children with articulation disorders. This underscores the degree to which the professionals have expanded their earlier responsibilities as speech correctionists to include broader communication problems, both expressive and receptive (Taylor, 1980).

There would also seem to be a major difference between the type of program provided by the speech-language pathologist at the secondary school level as opposed to that provided at the elementary school level. A great deal of attention is placed on individualized work at the secondary level, and the emotional status of the student is taken into account to a greater extent. There are fewer standardized materials at the secondary level and speech-language pathologists must design and develop their own materials both for children with speech impairment and those with language problems (Neal, 1976).

Recent trends in language development and language instruction that increase the responsibilities of the speech-language pathologist have been noted by Schiefelbusch (1980). Following is a list of some of the more visible concepts:

1. **Developmental language** The tracing of language from the birth cry to the development of adult roles. More attention has been paid to how earlier experiences result in later behavior.
2. **Functional language** The emphasis on training children language that can be put to direct use for social and affective communication, as opposed to learning to say . . . sounds in isolation from words or sentences.
3. **Infant intervention** An emphasis on prelinguistic language (that is, gestures) and special training for children in danger of being derailed from the normal tract of acquiring skill in language use.
4. **Alternative modes of language** The development of special nonspeech strategies for seriously impaired children who are taught to use sign language, communication boards, and electronically presented symbol systems (see Chapter 10 on multiply handicapped children).
5. **Ecology of language** The child is trained to use language in a variety of environmental contexts. Language learned in a special training lesson may not be carried over to other settings so the focus is on seeing to it that the child transfers skill in different settings. (pp. 9–10)

Service Delivery Options

The organization of programs for language, speech, and hearing disorders in the schools varies depending on the size of a district and other local factors. The following sections present some of the more common delivery services.

Itinerant Service

In the past, the most common delivery system has been the itinerant model in which a speech-language pathologist travels from school to school to give direct service to children enrolled in the regular classrooms. This model is most applicable to areas with small schools or to rural areas. In small schools and in sparsely settled areas, there may not be a sufficient number of children in one school to maintain the services of one speech-language pathologist on a full-time basis.

Resource Room

The resource room stations a speech-language pathologist in a room that accepts, individually or in small groups, children with language, speech, or hearing problems. In this model, the child is enrolled in a regular classroom, as in the itinerant model, but receives direct service in the resource room at scheduled periods. The model is applicable generally to large schools that have a sufficient number of children to warrant the full-time services of a speech-language pathologist. A modification of this model is to have one pathologist spend only a half day in one school and either serve as a resource teacher in another school for a half day or serve as an itinerant teacher in several schools.

Consultative Services

This model provides a school system with a speech-language pathologist who serves as a consultant to regular classroom teachers, special class teachers, aides, administrators, parents, and curriculum specialists in organizing a speech and language development program. The pathologist in this capacity provides specialized materials and procedures, inservice education, demonstration sessions, and other activities designed to improve the communication skills of children in natural settings—the classroom and the home.

Self-Contained Special Classroom

This type of delivery system is used for children with severe disabilities that cannot be managed in the regular classroom with supportive help. Such classes are organized for children with delayed speech and serious language disorders. Children can be grouped for instruction in a small special class in which individualized, as well as group, instruction is practiced.

Special School

This model is sometimes common in private schools where the whole school is devoted to children with communication disorders. In such schools the classes are small and the children are grouped according to developmental level or type of disorder.

Residential School

For children who require residential care as well as educational services, there are residential schools that handle children with severe disorders. In such schools are found cerebral-palsied children with speech and language defects, severe cases of developmental aphasia, and similar problems.

Preschool Services

For young children who are actually or potentially language and speech handicapped, consultant help from a speech-language

Parents of young children who may be potentially speech and language handicapped are encouraged to improve the communication skills of the child at home. (Photo: Alan Carey/The Image Works.)

pathologist is given to parents and preschool teachers who are in a position to help the child. Although not common in the past, this model is becoming more popular as early childhood education for the handicapped increases. The growth of early childhood education has necessitated the recruitment of specialists for this work.

Diagnostic Centers

This model provides an interdisciplinary team for the diagnosis and temporary remediation of children assigned to these centers. The procedure provides a more thorough diagnosis of the problem and initial experimentation with effective procedures for remediation. Such centers are sometimes found in hospitals and in university departments of speech and hearing sciences.

Role of the Speech-Language Pathologist

From the variety of settings and options for delivery of services to language, speech, and hearing handicapped children, it is obvious that a speech-language pathologist must be able to serve in more than one capacity. An itinerant or resource speech-language pathologist must be prepared to deal with a large variety of speech, language, and hearing handicapped children. He or she must deal with all the types of handicaps discussed earlier—articulation problems, voice problems, stuttering, language disorders—as well as with problems found among children with hearing handicaps, cleft palate, and mental retardation.

It is necessary for speech-language pathologists to be competent in a number of areas. For that reason, their training has been extended in those three hundred or so universities and colleges that prepare these specialists. Departments of education in most states have these same requirements for certification, based on the recommendations of the American Speech-Language-Hearing Association, the professional organization representing this field.

The general duties that can be performed by speech-language pathologists in the schools have been suggested in a publication entitled Project Upgrade (1973). Their duties include the following:

1. **Supervision and administration of programs for children with communication disorders** For every ten to twenty-nine speech-language pathologists in the school system, a supervisor is required to organize and supervise the program and personnel. Such an individual should not only be certified but should have broad experience with all communication disorders.
2. **Identification and diagnosis** In other areas of special education, the diagnostician may be a psychologist or a physician who refers the child to a teacher for education. In speech pathology, the diagnostician assesses the child and also provides the necessary remediation. This procedure may be the preferred one, since diagnosis by others sometimes leads to classification but not to remediation when the two functions of diagnosis and remediation are accomplished by two or more individuals.
3. **Consultation** Speech-language pathologists can devote all their time to professional consultation such as: (a) demonstrating procedures, (b) providing inservice training of regular and special teachers to serve children with minor problems, (c) training and supervising communication aides, (d) disseminating information to teachers and administrators, and (e) serving as a consultant to parents and preschool teachers.
4. **Direct services** The large majority of speech-language pathologists devote their full time to identifying children with communication disorders and to directing remedial services for the children selected. In this capacity they serve children who stutter, children who have voice problems, hearing handicaps, articulation defects, and language disabilities, and children with communication disorders associated with cerebral palsy, mental

retardation, emotional disturbance, and developmental aphasia. Services are also provided to preschool children and infants.

5. **Recording and reporting** Speech-language pathologists are required to keep records and reports on all children with communication handicaps. The report is part of the school record and is treated by the school as such. The case record includes a statement of the problem, the assessment, the remediation and assignment, and the termination.

Speech-language pathologists regard themselves, and are regarded by the teachers of the regular school program, as bona fide members of the staffs of their schools. They attend faculty meetings and, in some instances, maintain a regular place on the inservice agenda. They confer regularly with each classroom teacher in the building one or more times per week. It is a policy of the district for teachers to hold parent conferences following the first grading period of the year. The speech-language pathologists attend these conferences so that both the teachers and parents become aware of the children's speech and language goals and their relation to academic achievement.

One conclusion appears certain. This dynamic field that has changed so much over the past few decades is unlikely to remain at a standstill now. Continuing changes are likely as speech-language pathologists try to find their proper role in the array of professionals serving exceptional children.

SUMMARY OF MAJOR IDEAS

1. Speech and language habilitation has been a part of public school programs since the beginning of the twentieth century. In the past two or three decades, services have been greatly expanded.

2. An expressive communication disorder is defined as speech that (a) draws unfavorable attention to itself, (b) interferes with communication, or (c) affects adversely the speaker or listener.

3. A child is called *language impaired* when his or her skills in the primary language are deficient relative to expectations for the chronological age.

4. Communication disorders are classified as disorders of articulation, voice, fluency (stuttering), and language.

5. The prevalence of articulation, voice, fluency, and language disorders appears to be at a rate of 4 to 6 percent for moderate and severe disorders.

6. Most articulation disorders in school children are found in the

first and second grades. The number of cases drops markedly by fourth grade as a result of maturation or treatment or both.

7. The physical processes needed for proper sound production are respiration, phonation, resonation, and articulation. If any of these processes breaks down, speech production will be impaired.

8. Special education of children with communication handicaps includes (a) screening to identify children who require full diagnostic assessment, (b) diagnosing those selected through the initial screening and from other referrals, and (c) aiding those who require special speech and language remediation.

9. Articulation disorders seem most strongly related to limited early experience in listening to speech and auditory discrimination. It is the easiest of the major categories to remediate when it is uncomplicated by organic disorders.

10. Fluency disorders or stuttering remains difficult to treat for permanent results. It is treated by behavior therapy—methods that help the child facing his or her fears—and by negative practice—learning to become more comfortable with stuttering.

11. Voice disorders are the result of significant deviations in quality, pitch, and loudness. Treatment involves careful diagnosis, removal of the cause, if possible, and helping the child become aware of how he or she sounds in order to progress to more acceptable sounds.

12. Language disorders fall into two major groups—delayed language development and oral language disorders (aphasia). Remediation focuses on attempts to help the child exercise those areas of special weakness such as visual memory, linguistic rules, auditory perception, and so forth.

13. Moderate to severe communication disorders appear to be long lasting, despite treatment and require continued help into adulthood.

14. The most common school models for the delivery of language, speech, and hearing services are itinerant teachers, resource rooms, and consultative services, which fit well into existing mainstream philosophy.

15. Children with more severe communication handicaps may be found in self-contained classes, special schools, residential schools, home and hospital services, as well as public and private clinics.

16. The major change in the operation of the modern speech-language pathologist has been an increase in attention to children with language disorders.

17. A typical speech-language pathologist serves in many capacities including (a) supervision, (b) identification and diagnosis, (c) teacher and parent consultation, and (d) direct services to children.

UNRESOLVED ISSUES

1. **Caseload Quotas.** Over the past thirty to forty years, speech-language pathologists in the schools have traditionally spent 75 to 80 percent of their time on children with articulation problems, dividing the rest of their time among the more serious problems of voice disorders, fluency problems, and language difficulties. There is a question as to whether this has been the best division of time and a suspicion that the reason such a practice continues is to show a large caseload in order to justify financial support for the professional within the school program. Meanwhile, children with more serious problems receive less remedial attention than they should. What can be done to ease the caseload quota without jeopardizing program funding so that professionals can devote more time to children with serious communication problems?

2. **Whom Do Language Problems Belong To?** There appears to be a growing professional dispute over who has responsibilities for helping learning disabled children. There are psychologists, learning disability teachers, remedial reading specialists, and speech-language pathologists, all of whom have a legitimate professional claim to skills that can provide help and assistance to these children. The general public, however, will be predictably unenthusiastic about nonproductive struggles among professionals as to who has the right to give help. In the end, the group that appears to be doing the most good for the youngster will win. That is, no doubt, where the focus of attention should be.

3. **Origins of Communication Problems.** Despite a long history of clinical work with a variety of communication problems, the causes of some of the major disorders—stuttering and language disorders, for example—are still mysteries. This does not mean that help cannot be provided just because the cause is unknown. Clinical practice and experience have led the way to a number of successful therapeutic approaches. Nevertheless, if one wishes to discuss prevention of a condition rather than remediation, then knowing its cause becomes a central issue. Major research projects are needed if we are to have more insight into the sources of these various problems and to develop ways to stop their incidence in the next generation.

REFERENCES OF SPECIAL INTEREST

Bloodstein, O. *Speech pathology: An introduction.* Boston: Houghton Mifflin, 1979.

A general textbook particularly noteworthy for its section on stuttering, which gives a comprehensive review of past and current theories of stuttering and the most accepted forms of treatment. Chapters on aphasia and cerebral-palsied speech also merit attention for their overall coverage of these often neglected topics.

Hixon, T., Shriberg, L., & Saxman, J. (Eds.). *Introduction to communication disorders.* Englewood Cliffs, N.J.: Prentice-Hall, 1980.

A compilation of chapters, each written by recognized and well-known specialists in this field. In addition to coverage of the typical speech disorder areas, it also includes several chapters on language problems and two chapters on hearing problems. One of the most current of the available books on this topic.

Van Riper, C. *Speech correction: Principles and methods* (6th ed.). Englewood Cliffs, N.J.: Prentice-Hall, 1978.

Perhaps the most widely used text by one of the most respected professionals in the field. A comprehensive view of all speech disorders and their treatment is given with a lesser emphasis on language problems than later textbooks.

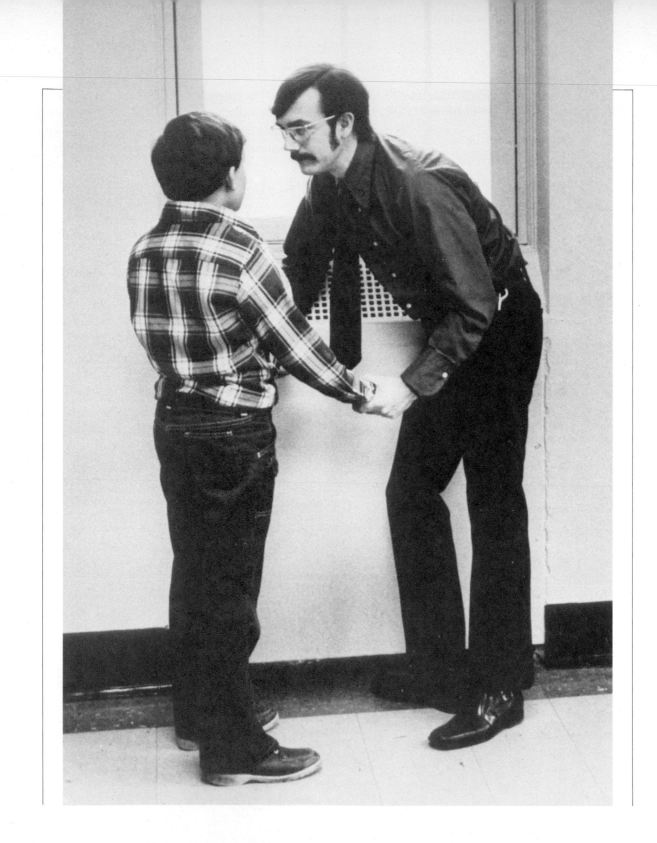

Children with Behavior Problems

F ew experiences are quite so disturbing to sensitive and alert teachers as encountering children who seem chronically unhappy or distressed or who seem to be driven to aggressive and antisocial behavior that can only lead to increasingly serious social difficulties. Teachers may sometimes feel that they are viewing such problems as if from a far mountain watching a car about to crash on a distant highway, knowing there will be great damage but unable to do anything about it. One teacher's report will help give the flavor.

I can't stop worrying about one little girl in my first grade. She behaves so peculiarly. She doesn't talk most of the time, though she can talk. She answers the other children and me with animal sounds. She hides under chairs like a dog and barks at people. . . . She has been on a clinic waiting list for six months, and I've had the child up for special service to test her for three months. In the meantime, the class all laugh at her, and she just gets worse, and I don't know what to do. (Long, Morse, and Newman, 1980, p. 212)

DEFINITION

Defining behavior problems in children is characterized by special difficulties. Most definitions are based on the criteria that children with behavior problems will reveal consistent age-inappropriate behavior resulting in social conflict, personal unhappiness, and school failure. Because practically all children reveal age-inappropriate behavior at one time or another, the definition of this category depends on the dimensions of *intensity* and *duration* to distinguish between normal and exceptional behavior. Professionals in this field disagree on the extent to which the degree and persistence of certain behaviors necessitates classification of a child in this category. Such disagreements result in widely varying estimates of prevalence.

Moreover, the child's behavior is not the only variable that determines classification in this category. The person who perceives the child's behavior as inappropriate also plays a key role in the decision. Clearly, some kinds of behavior would be unacceptable regardless of setting. Children who physically attack others when frustrated, who constantly weep and are manifestly unhappy, or who are hyperactive to the extent that they never seem to be able to respond to adult direction all have characteristics that are troublesome, to one degree or another, regardless of the social setting. However, the acceptability of a wide range of other behaviors depends on the attitude of the perceiver:

Your child is a sexual delinquent.
My child is exploring new relationships.

Because practically all children exhibit inappropriate behavior from time to time, criteria for identifying problem behavior depend largely on the intensity and the duration of specific behaviors. (Photo: © Elizabeth Crews.)

Your child has a sick mind.
My child has an unusual sense of humor.

Your child is unhappy.
My child is sensitive.

It is easy to see that each interpretive statement refers to the same behavior and that is why later definitions tend to incorporate the perceiver in the portrait: "Behavioral disabilities are defined as . . . a variety of excessive, chronic, deviant behaviors ranging from impulsive and aggressive to depressive and withdrawal acts which violate the perceiver's expectations of appropriateness and which the perceiver wishes to see stopped" (Graubard, 1973).

Wood (1982) has suggested that a definition of problem behavior or a set of actions that follow from the definition should include four elements:

1. The *disturber* element: What or who is perceived to be the focus of the problem?
2. The *problem behavior* element: How is the problem behavior described?
3. The *setting* element: In what setting does the problem behavior occur?
4. The *disturbed* element: Who regards the behavior as a problem? (pp. 7–8)

FIGURE 8.1
Profiles of Two
Children with
Behavior Problems

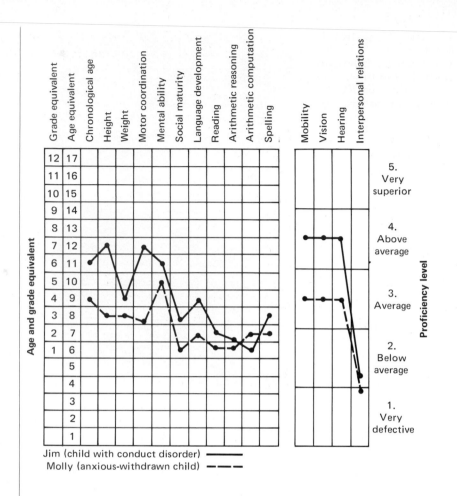

Jim (child with conduct disorder) ————
Molly (anxious-withdrawn child) - - - - -

It is possible, however, to overdo the apparent confusion and disagreement about the definition. Many children with behavior problems would receive a unanimous vote on the question of whether they show problem behavior, and these are the children we are interested in studying and helping in special education.

DEVELOP-MENTAL PROFILES

Figure 8.1 shows the profiles of two youngsters—both have behavior problems and are experiencing academic difficulties in school. However, each child expresses these problems in very different ways.

Jim   Jim is an 11-year-old who appears to be sullen and angry most of the time. He rarely has been seen to smile and has a history of terrifying temper outbursts. Under conditions of frustration, he sometimes will blow up and attack the nearest person around in such a frenzy that other children give him a wide berth and often hesitate to interact with him.

Stories in the neighborhood recount Jim's cruelty to animals and he has been said to torture and kill cats and dogs. His language borders on profanity and he has been known, even at this young age, to challenge teachers with the phrase, "What are you going to do about it?" Jim is a threat, not only to his peers, but also to the teacher's image of his or her own competence. His physical skills are advanced, even though his interpersonal skills are not, and this tends to complicate the situation. As he grows older, he will become less physically manageable. One can view temper outbursts of a 5-year-old with some tolerance; the same outburst from a 15-year-old can be scary indeed.

The school personnel are actively seeking alternative placements for Jim on the grounds that they may not be capable, either physically or psychologically, of coping with Jim's problems. Jim comes from a father-absent home, and his mother is somewhat disorganized and seems to have given up long ago trying to control Jim. His social contacts seem limited to a few other youngsters who have similar angry and acting-out propensities, and those who are close to Jim worry about his future.

His performance in school, as seen in Figure 8.1, is two to three grades below his grade level, and his unwillingness and hostility in accepting correction or help cause his teachers to despair.

Molly   The second profile in Figure 8.1 shows Molly, a 9-year-old girl in the fourth grade, who is having a difficult time at school. In contrast to Jim, who tends to externalize his problems, Molly tends to internalize hers. She dissolves in tears and seems to be in the midst of a depression much of the time. She is not able to make friends with the preadolescent girls who have formed the major social group in the classroom, and Molly seems to be lonely and alone. Molly is so quiet that if it wasn't for the manifest unhappiness that shows in her face and physical demeanor, she would go unnoticed in school. She, like Jim, is seriously behind in her academic work.

Molly's middle class parents are concerned about her and have tried many different routes, including therapy, to help her, but so far few gains have been noticed or identified. She is a source of great frustration to her parents who cannot understand why she cannot be like her older sister, Christine, who seems to be effortlessly successful in her academic and social spheres. Molly is not the personal threat to the teacher that Jim is to his because she does not challenge the teacher's ability to control the classroom. But she does challenge those teachers who wish to have the children in their classes pleased and happy in school and who are bound to be upset by their inability to modify the sadness and low self-concept that is portrayed in Molly's behavior.

CLASSIFI-CATION OF BEHAVIOR PROBLEMS

Jim and Molly represent different subcategories of the larger group of behavior problems. How many such subcategories are there? The educational treatment given to Jim and Molly and children like them can be quite different, and it is important to know how many and what kinds of problems to plan for in education.

In the past it was left up to clinicians who treated disturbed children on a day-to-day basis to note certain patterns and regularities and to try to group their cases in some meaningful fashion. The accumulation of these clinical decisions was then organized into psychiatric categories.

Two of the major classification systems developed from clinical experience are the third edition of the *Diagnostic and Statistical Manual of Mental Disorders* (DSM III) and the Classification System of Psychopathological Disorders in Childhood.

The DSM III, which was developed by the American Psychiatric Association, has five axes or dimensions that include both personal and environmental factors. These five dimensions are Clinical Syndromes, Personality Disorders and Specific Developmental Disorders, Physical Disorders and Conditions, Severity of Psychosocial Stressors, and Highest Level of Adaptive Functioning for the Past Year. There are many subcategories in each of the major categories that cover disorders other than behavior disorders. For example, included under the heading "Developmental Disorders" are Specific Reading Disorders, Developmental Language Disorders, and Motor Coordination Disorders—all of which might fit under learning disabilities rather than behavior disorders (American Psychiatric Association, 1977).

The Classification System of Psychopathological Disorders in Childhood, proposed by the Group for the Advancement of Psychiatry (GAP), recognizes eight major categories of disorders of presumed psychosocial origin and over forty subcategories within the major headings. It relies on psychoanalytic concepts and processes and includes among its major categories Healthy Responses, Reactive Disorders, Developmental Deviations, Psychoneurotic Disorders, Personality Disorders, and Psychotic Disorders (see Paul and Epanchin, 1982).

Both systems have their supporters. However, because they seem more interested in classification from a medical-psychiatric viewpoint than from an educational perspective, we will follow another approach to classification of behavior problems in this chapter.

A somewhat different approach, made possible by the availability of computer facilities, involves the use of statistical techniques that isolate clusters or patterns of behavior that are interrelated. By using check lists, rating scales, and similar measuring devices to evaluate large numbers of children, it is possible to sort out clusters of responses that separate one group of children from another. This approach has yielded four patterns of deviant behavior in children: conduct disorder, anxiety-withdrawal, immaturity, and socialized aggression (Quay, 1979).

The child who has a *conduct disorder* is one who defies authority; is hostile toward authority figures (police officers, teachers, and so forth); is cruel, malicious, and assaultive, and has few guilt feelings. This category includes children who are described as hyperactive, restless, and hyperkinetic. Jim (Figure 8.1) clearly fits into this category.

The *anxious-withdrawn* child is shy, timid, withdrawn, seclusive, sensitive, and submissive. He or she is overdependent and easily depressed. According to Quay's study, such children come mostly from overprotective families in the higher socioeconomic levels. Molly (Figure 8.1) tends to fit into this category.

The *immaturity* dimension refers to children who are inattentive, sluggish, lacking interest in school, lazy, preoccupied, daydreamers, drowsy, and reticent. They resemble children sometimes labeled autistic or prepsychotic. They appear to be less able to function in the regular classroom than do children who are labeled neurotic or children with conduct disorders.

The *socialized-aggressive* child has some of the same characteristics or behavior problems as the child with a conduct disorder but is socialized within his or her peer group, usually a gang or companions, in misdemeanor and crime. Stealing, truancy, and gang behavior are noted. Although such behavior may not be considered maladaptive within the specific environment in which it is manifested, it does present a clear danger to the larger society.

PREVALENCE

Any line drawn between "normal" children and children with behavior problems is obviously going to be difficult to define. All children show aggressive and antisocial behavior at one time or another, and all children show fearful behavior. The difference between children identified as special problems will be in *how often*, *how strong or intense*, and *how appropriate to the situation*.

The studies on prevalence show a great disparity in the frequency of behavior problems in school children. Estimates vary from around 2 percent (Froomkin, 1972) to 8 percent (Ullmann, 1952) to 10.5 percent (Bower, 1960) to 20 to 24 percent (Kelly, Bullock, and Dykes, 1977; Salvia, Schultz, and Chapin, 1974). While some of these differences may be due to different judges using different levels of problem intensity as yardsticks or criteria, Wood and Zabel (1978) have offered another explanation: most of the identification procedures require teachers to rate children in their classrooms *at that point in time* as having behavior problems. Apparently many children will manifest behavior problems at one time or another in the school program, and a one-time screening will identify them. Wood and Zabel believed that the low incidence figures of 2 to 3 percent generally refer to those students who have such serious, recurrent, or persistent problems in adjusting to school as to need special programming over an extended period of time.

The large number of children who show sufficiently maladaptive behavior problems to justify their being identified by teachers on a one-time basis also makes apparent the need to provide teachers with assistance in helping children to cope with these stressful situations and in promoting healthy social development.

What is the prevalence of behavior problems from the teacher's viewpoint? Rubin and Balow (1978) reported teacher ratings on a large group of children (1,586) from kindergarten through sixth grade in which the teachers were asked to identify whether these children had behavior problems. More than half (59 percent) of all the children who received three or more teacher ratings were classified as having a behavior problem at least once in the period between kindergarten and sixth grade. Among the subjects who received six teacher ratings (and were in the school for six years), 60 percent of the youngsters were considered to have behavior problems by at least one teacher. Male students were identified three times as often as females as having a consistently identified problem, and those who were identified by their teachers in three different years as requiring special help amounted to 7 percent of the school population. Since this sample was conducted on a random basis and the students themselves showed average intelligence scores, there is no reason to believe that the sample is biased. The results would suggest that the number of children with behavior problems who are dealt with in the schools is significantly greater than the 2 to 3 percent figure officially designated by the U.S. Department of Education.

What is one to say about the indication that 60 percent of the children in elementary school are identified by their teachers as needing some special attention? The reason for these high figures may be that teachers were asked to identify those children who are problems, rather than those who are "extremely difficult" problems. Also, of course, different teachers define *problem* differently. The definition of *problem* was the responsibility of the individual teacher and was not dictated by any set of outside criteria.

There is general agreement that the percentage of children who need intensive and consistent special education programming as a result of their behavior problems is rather small (2 to 3 percent of the general population). However, the same behavioral and emotional symptoms at a lesser level of intensity are obviously present in much larger numbers of youngsters. No matter how stringently we raise the standards for identifying children with behavior problems (and no one has suggested that the prevalence is less than 2 to 3 percent), at least one million school-age children have serious behavior difficulties requiring specific help.

IDENTIFICATION

A wide variety of evaluation tools are available to the schools for identifying children with behavior problems. Each has its strengths and weaknesses, and most school programs tend to use a combination of instruments instead of trying to pick out the best one. Table 8.1 describes briefly some of the more common methods and the more traditional instruments that include *tests*, *ratings*, *observations*, and *interviews*. Perhaps the most common approach used to identify children with problems is the behavior check list, or teacher rating scale, primarily because it is inexpensive to use in terms of both money and personnel. The psychological tests, such as the self-concept scales and the projective tests, may have more evidence of validity but require a considerable degree of sophistication in test administration and clinical experience in order to interpret the results of the tests effectively. Many schools do not have the psychologically trained personnel to use these sophisticated measures.

The items that appear on the check list represent various kinds of behaviors that the teacher would be expected to observe. The Walker Problem Behavior Identification Check List, for example, presents items such as the following:

1. has temper tantrums
2. has no friends
3. refers to self as dumb, stupid, or incapable
4. must have approval for tasks attempted or completed

TABLE 8.1
Methods of Identifying
Behavior Problems

Method	Example of Instruments	Strengths and Weaknesses
Projective tests	Rorschach Ink Blot Thematic Apperception Test (TAT)	Gives testee opportunity to use ambiguous stimuli to reveal personal needs and perceptions. Often difficult to interpret. Needs highly qualified clinician.
Objective tests	Minnesota Multiphasic Personality Inventory Piers-Harris Children's Self-Concept Scale	Establishes patterns of answers of testee compared to answers of identified disturbed children or adults. Requires reading skills. Depends on honest answers.
Behavior check lists	Quay-Peterson Behavior Problem Check List Walker Problem Behavior Identification Check List	Teachers or parents are asked to identify the presence of certain key behaviors. Depends on accuracy of observer. Hard to measure intensity or frequency.
Behavior observation	McKinney SCAN	Child is observed in the classroom. No predetermined answers to which the child's responses are compared. Need large samples of behaviors for adequate diagnosis.
Interview schedules	Vineland Social Maturity Scale	Information is collected from parent with predetermined set of questions. Usefulness depends on skill of the interviewer.

The teacher is asked to check if he or she believes that a youngster exhibits any of these particular characteristics. Most children will show these behaviors or traits at some time or other; therefore the criteria used to measure disturbance are *how often, how intense,* and *how inappropriate* is the child's behavior.

Occasionally, a child's behavior is measured with observation scales which allow a minimally trained observer to give a record of a student's performance in various school settings. Following are some of the categories currently in use with the McKinney SCAN observation scale used by a classroom observer:

1. **Constructive self-directed activity.** The child is performing an appropriate classroom task on his or her own without direct teacher supervision or teacher participation in his or her group.

2. **Off-task behavior.** The child's eyes are off the task and he or she is inappropriately manipulating the task materials, or the child is physically wandering in the classroom, or the child is engaging in other inappropriate gross motor activity.
3. **Dependency/aggression.** The child is engaged in excessive attention-seeking behavior directed toward peers or teacher, or the child is physically or verbally abusive to a peer or teacher.

Feagans and McKinney (1981) have been able to use the scale to differentiate various exceptionality groups in the primary and elementary grades.

Despite the more liberal definition of children with behavior problems, which now includes the perceiver as well as the child, most instruments now in use still focus exclusively on the characteristics of the child and do not take into consideration the nature of the environment. Judgment on the role of the environment is still left to the discretion of the individual observer or clinician.

CHARACTERISTICS OF CHILDREN WITH BEHAVIOR PROBLEMS

Conduct Disorders

The families in which children with conduct disorders are found follow some predominant patterns. Frequently, the father is aggressive and hostile and does not hesitate to use physical force for discipline. In Jim's case, his father treated what he thought was Jim's misbehavior with spankings that verged on beatings. Apparently, hostility breeds hostility, and Jim became even more of a problem when his father walked out on the family, leaving Jim's mother to cope with him. As is common in such families, the mother was inconsistent with discipline and preoccupied with financial survival. Hetherington and Martin (1979) have summarized the rationale for the family system that produces a child with a conduct disorder:

It has been proposed that extremely restrictive, power assertive discipline, particularly in a hostile family environment, leads to a frustration of dependency needs and a heightened predisposition to respond aggressively. If the opportunity to express this aggression occurs through inconsistent discipline, laxity in one parent, or active reinforcement for aggressive behavior outside the home, this may increase the probability of antisocial aggressive responses by the child. (p. 263)

Whatever the basic cause of the problem, there is little question that children with conduct disorders are a serious problem in a school setting. They show a marked inability to persist in a task, often disrupt the class, are distractible, and present a constant irritation to the teacher because of their inability to follow directions and maintain a learning set. As education has become more directly involved with these children, increasing concern has been expressed about their academic status.

The developmental history of hyperactive behavior, often associated with conduct disorder, reveals that the more manifest elements of that syndrome disappear over time. Douglas (1972) reported that hyperactivity decreased over the preadolescent age range, *but* impulsiveness and the inability to attend remained a serious problem. These youngsters are apparently unable to control their impulses in order to cope with the situations in which care, concentrated attention, and organized planning are required. They tend to react to the first idea that occurs to them or to those aspects of the situation that are the most obvious or compelling. Douglas stated that they have a marked inability to "stop, look, and listen."

As might be expected, such children do not make ideal students! A child with a conduct disorder has more problems than just the disturbance itself. In most cases a serious academic problem accompanies the emotional or behavioral discrepancy. Glavin and Annesley (1971) compared a group of 130 behavior problem boys, identified by means of a behavior check list, with 90 normal boys of the same age and IQ level. Among the behavior problem boys, 81 percent were identified as underachieving in reading and 72 percent in math. Feldhusen, Thurston, and Benning (1966) indicated that, by the third grade, children nominated by teachers as manifesting socially disapproved behavior had already fallen far behind in their reading and arithmetic achievement. Similar achievement results have been reported by Werry (1968) and by Graubard (1964) who found extreme underachievement in disturbed youngsters in residential treatment centers.

The inability to delay gratification and poor control of impulses undoubtedly play a major role in these youngsters' problems with school adaptation.

Keogh (1971) has summarized the literature on the relationship between hyperactivity and learning disorders and has concluded that a wide variety of studies have substantiated that some hyperactive children have learning problems and are poor achievers in school. Both clinical and educational observers have noted that hyperactive children are variable in learning performance, sometimes doing excellent work and sometimes failing miserably. Keogh has discussed three possible reasons for the cause of learning problems in hyperactive children:

1. Excessive extraneous movement, especially in the head and eyes, appears with learning difficulties, and heightened motor

activity may disrupt learning by interfering with the accurate intake of information, particularly through the visual channels.

2. Hyperactive children may have a different approach to problems. They tend to make decisions impulsively. Impulsive children have difficulty solving problems because they react to the first reasonable inference and fail to evaluate the quality of the choice or to consider other possibilities.

3. Hyperactivity may be merely one symptom of neural impairment.

In a later publication, Keogh (1977) has discussed the importance of attention in learning and behavior disorders. Special attention is paid to hyperactivity and impulsive characteristics because these characteristics seem linked to later delinquency. Two of the characteristic responses identified with delinquent children are their impulsiveness and their inability to delay gratification.

One of the fundamental questions pertaining to children with conduct disorders is whether they do not understand correct behavior or whether they know how to behave correctly but choose not to. Do these traits go away over time? Do children like Jim mature and become good citizens growing out of their youthful problems? Some do, of course, but an important follow-up study by Robins (1966) suggests that many do not. She analyzed the performance of over five hundred adults who, as children, had received treatment in a child guidance clinic. A structured interview was given to 524 individuals who had been seen for various problems thirty years previously in a child guidance clinic of a major metropolitan area. The elements used to diagnose adult sociopathic personality were work history, marital history, drug use, alcohol use, arrest, belligerence, unusual sexual behavior, suicide attempts, impulsiveness, truancy combined with other school problems, financial dependence, performance in the armed forces, vagrancy, somatic complaints, pathological lying, maintenance of social relationships, lack of guilt, and wild behavior in late adolescence. A control sample of 100 adults who had spent their childhood in the same neighborhood and school district was identified, and they were given the same structured interview as the former clients of the child guidance clinic.

Only 4 percent of the control subjects had shown five or more antisocial symptoms as adults, while 45 percent of the clinic group exhibited five or more antisocial characteristics. The problems experienced by the clinic groups as adults were not attributed to the stigma of being a "problem child," rather they were linked to the nature and severity of the childhood behavior that occasioned referral in the first place. The individuals who as children had been referred to the clinic because of antisocial behavior showed the most difficult adult adjustment. Those who as children had been referred for the miscellaneous problems of temper tantrums, learning problems, speech difficulties, and so forth, did not show major antisocial tendencies in adulthood.

One hundred adults from Robins's total group who had been diagnosed by psychiatrists as having sociopathic personalities on the basis of written materials and structured interviews had had chaotic and disturbed childhoods. Their histories showed juvenile theft, incorrigibility, running away from home, truancy, associating with bad companions, sexual activities, staying out late, and so forth. Most of them were discipline problems in school and had been held back at least one grade by the time they appeared in the clinic. Most of them never even graduated from elementary school. Impulsive, antisocial behavior, rather than fearful and shy behavior, appears to be the symptom with the most ominous prediction for adult problems.

One of the most distressing elements in the development of behaviorally disturbed children is that their problems seem to carry over from one generation to another. In their own families, 78 percent of Robins's clinic group have already been divorced with a record of high rates of desertion and unfaithfulness in comparison with control samples. Perhaps more significant are the figures on the level of behavior problems in spouses of individuals from the clinic group. Spouses in the partnerships showed a high incidence of neglect, alcoholism, and desertion relative to the comparison sample, suggesting that unstable and asocial persons tend to marry similar persons. It is also no surprise to see that the problems of the children born into such families are much greater than those found in the comparable control group.

The problems of asocial and antisocial behavior, unless dealt with vigorously in a child, may well lead to antisocial behavior in adulthood, which in turn may create a family atmosphere resulting in a new generation of antisocial children, and so the cycle will continue.

Anxiety-Withdrawal and Immaturity

Anxious or withdrawn children are often a bigger threat to themselves than they are to others around them. Since they are usually not disruptive, they do not cause classroom management problems. However, sensitive teachers will often worry about a child who is visibly unhappy and wonder what can be done to bring a smile to the sad and troubled faces that frequently appear in their classrooms.

Children who fit into the category of anxiety-withdrawal tend to have parents who have similar problems. Maladjusted parents tend to have maladjusted children. In contrast to children with conduct disorders who might be said to show "too much behavior," the anxiety-withdrawal children show "too little" (Quay, 1979). They would have too much *ego control,* referring to the degree to which a child maintains control over impulses, wishes, and desires. Defects in ego control can occur in terms of too much control (the child who is rigid and unable to be spontaneous) and too little *ego resiliency,* which describes the flexibility of control depending on the setting. The resilient child can delay gratification when the situation calls for it, but is also able to respond spontaneously and enthusiastically when appropriate (Block and Block, 1980).

One of the concepts that helps us understand children such as Molly is *learned helplessness,* or an understanding on the part of the person that nothing he or she does can prevent unhappy or negative things from happening. Learned helplessness results in severe deterioration in performance after failure, as though the child has said, "It is all happening again." These children have low self-concepts anyway, so failure in a school task or a social setting can only confirm for them their worthlessness and their helplessness in the face of an unfriendly environment. Molly's poor performance on tasks in the classroom may be much worse than she is capable of doing simply because she has been so pessimistic about herself and her own ability. Low self-esteem seems to be at the heart of much of the underachievement of anxiety-withdrawal children.

Where does the fearful child come from? Although a number of theoretical models explain withdrawn and fearful behavior, most

Failure in a school task can only confirm for anxious-withdrawn children their worthlessness and helplessness in the face of an unfriendly environment. (Photo: Jean-Claude Lejeune/ Stock, Boston.)

professionals would agree that chronic anxiety in children comes from being in a stressful situation, not being able to get out of the situation, and not being able to do anything to improve it. Inability to modify the situation adds to the feeling of helplessness and low self-image of the child. To a college student, a situation creating chronic anxiety might be a crucial examination looming on the horizon. To a younger child, anxiety can stem from being forced to live in a family where he or she feels unwanted or living in a home with an abusive parent. Nothing that the child does seems to be right or leads to praise or love and affection from the parent. The child is often too young to understand that a parent may be working out his or her own problems and that the parental reaction has little to do with the child.

One of the most extreme instances of low self-image is manifested in suicide attempts. The phenomenon of suicide in young children is receiving increased attention. Although instances of suicide are very infrequent, particularly below the age of 15, some cases of young suicidal children have been studied. Cohen-Sandler, Berman, and King (1982) have studied seventy-six children who had been admitted to an inpatient psychiatric unit of a children's hospital for being suicidal, being depressed, or having a variety of psychiatric conditions not related to suicide. In seeking to understand what separated suicidal youngsters from the other two groups, the authors concluded, "In a context of intensely stressful chaotic and unpredictable family events, children who otherwise were incapable of making an impact on these circumstances seem to use suicide as a means of interpersonal coercion or retaliation" (p. 184).

In short, suicide often represents an intense rage against more powerful adults and is seen by the child as the only action that will have some impact on those at whom he or she is angry. The incidence of suicide seems to increase tenfold in the group of children between the ages of 15 and 19 when compared to suicides of younger children, because the older children have the physical ability and easier access to weapons and other devices to carry out their self-destructive desires.

In less intense situations, the withdrawn child is often observed as having limited or ineffectual social relationships. This is due in part because others are not comfortable with individuals who are continually self-destructive and unhappy and also because withdrawn children have less practice in socializing. Whenever past social relationships have been unpleasant, there is a tendency to avoid the potential for similar relationships if at all possible. If a girl's early experiences with her father have been unfavorable, she may transfer her bad feelings to all men ("All men are alike!") and never be able to differentiate one from another. Since her tendency is to withdraw in social settings, she is not likely to try out new relationships that will help her discover that there may be important differences.

The views discussed in the preceding paragraphs rest heavily on positive and negative reinforcement as controlling forces in anxious-withdrawn behavior. Other points of view, however, try to project a long-range pattern in personality development.

Freudian theory assumes that the child passes through a variety of stages of development on the way to maturity. If there are breakdowns in the essential family relationships necessary to progress through these stages, then conditions are generated for the creation of neurotic symptoms that can prevent the child from maturing into a healthy adult. For example, the male child is supposed to go through a stage during which he wishes to replace his father (the *Oedipus complex*) to a stage of identification with, and acquisition of, the characteristics of the feared and respected adult of the same sex. If there is an especially brutal or cruel relationship between father and son, the boy can never really adopt the characteristics of the father but must live in fear that the father will take revenge on him for his unacceptable impulses to replace the father in relationship to the mother.

Non-Freudian psychiatrists and psychoanalysts place less emphasis on psychosexual development and more on general interactions with the social environment as the basis for emotional problems. The emphasis on progression through stages remains, however, as does the language of psychoanalysis. For example, *regression* is the retreat to an earlier stage of development; *fixation* is remaining at a given stage beyond the time expected. Both those terms suggest that there have been psychic or emotional barriers that have arrested the normal progress of the child.

Extreme dependency is another manifestation of the withdrawn child. Maccoby and Masters (1970) have reviewed a vast amount of literature on the relationship of parental behavior to child behavior and have concluded, "There is evidence that dependency is associated not with warmth but with its polar opposite, rejection or hostility" (p. 140). The parent who withdraws love and affection creates panic in the child; the child reacts in the way that has elicited affection in the past; the child becomes more babylike or dependent. Thus, the strategy of being cold and distant, which a parent might adopt in an attempt to "cure" the child of dependency by forcing the child to grow up, may actually increase the likelihood that the dependency behavior will continue to occur.

Not much is known about the special nature of immature children, but there is likely to be much similarity between these children and those who are anxious-withdrawn. The most serious of these disturbances, schizophrenia and autism, are discussed in Chapter 10, "Children with Multiple, Severe, and Physical Handicaps."

Socialized Aggressive   The other patterns of behavior previously noted can be described as maladaptive, whereas the socialized aggressive represents a pattern that, although disturbing to teachers, may be quite appropriate given the subculture from which many of these children come. Further, these children may manifest few indications of personal anxiety or maladjustment. The question is whether the culture or society that the child belongs to is maladaptive.

Bronfenbrenner (1979) focused on the family as a child-rearing system and called for careful appraisal of the environmental stresses and supports experienced by families in our society and the subsequent effect on the child. He maintained that the alienation of children and youth reflect a breakdown of the interconnections among the various segments of the child's life—family, school, peer group, neighborhood, and the world of work. Therefore, the question previously asked regarding what's wrong with that child becomes "What's wrong with the social system?"

The socialized delinquent often has conflict in values that he or she must cope with in the school situation. For example, our culture values both loyalty and honesty. Children from a particular subculture, especially one that is not sympathetic with the value systems of the public schools, may cheat on a regular and systematic basis. The individual child must then face the problem of whether to be honest and report the cheating of friends, or whether to be loyal to the subgroup. Such value conflicts are not uncommon and probably result in some tension for those students who are trying to keep one foot in their cultural peer group and one foot in the larger society.

FACTORS RELATED TO BEHAVIOR PROBLEMS

Environmental Factors

Social Environment

A poor social environment may create a predisposition toward an individual nonadaptive response. Even within highly destructive social situations, however, many youngsters are performing in a socially acceptable fashion. They demonstrate that individual patterns of development and response can sometimes overcome an unfavorable social situation.

One of the dimensions that seems to be influential in shaping the behavioral patterns of children is the phenomenon of *modeling* or imitating the behavior of others. Bandura (1969) and his associates have conducted a decade of research on the issue of what factors cause children to imitate behavior that they observe, either in person or on television or in movies. Some of the most relevant conclusions from a series of research studies are:

1. Children who watch aggressive models who are rewarded for their aggressiveness tend to be more aggressive themselves.
2. Children tend to identify with the successful aggressor and find reasons why those who are aggressed against deserve their fate.
3. Children who see models who set high standards and reward themselves sparingly behave in like manner. The behavior of the models is influential in the development of self-control.
4. There is no evidence that viewing violence dissipates aggressive drives and makes a person more healthy (the catharsis hypothesis). Instead a frustrated TV viewer watching violence is more likely to act out violent impulses.

Those findings seem to confirm the work of Whiting (1963) who studied the behavior of children in many different cultures around the world. He concluded that *status envy* is a prime force in the development of personality. A child most envies the person who can

Children who watch aggressive models who are rewarded for their aggressiveness tend to be more aggressive themselves. (Photo: © Jack Prelutsky/Stock, Boston.)

withhold the resources he or she values most highly, and the child tries to identify with that person.

The implications of those results for a social environment that is chaotic, has few positive models, and tends to reward the aggressor would be the production of many aggressive and antisocial children who have little tolerance for the "delayed gratification" required by the school program. Also, when one is a member of a social minority group and feels that that group is an outcast in the more general society, then predictable feelings of alienation develop.

Seeman (1967) described the elements of alienation, or seeing oneself as apart from the general society. Such feelings predominate in minority groups who feel little loyalty or attachment to the general culture that they perceive as exploiting them.

1. **Powerlessness.** The person who experiences a sense of powerlessness expects outside forces to control personal and social rewards. Such a person has little expectancy that his or her own behavior can be useful in gaining those rewards.
2. **Meaninglessness.** The individual regards social affairs as incomprehensible and has little hope of ever being able to predict the outcome of social events.
3. **Normlessness.** The individual believes that he or she is not bound by conventional standards of conduct in the pursuit of goals. Normlessness implies a high expectancy that socially unapproved means must be used to achieve those goals.
4. **Value isolation.** The individual rejects the values of society and assigns low value to the goals and behavior highly valued by most other members of society.
5. **Self-estrangement.** The individual is continuously engaged in activities that he or she does not value highly (that is, school or a boring job).

Any child or adolescent growing up with that cluster of feelings is a fine candidate for "delinquency" as that term is defined by the majority culture.

Newman (1976) has pointed out that alienation of youth in the 1970s served a larger purpose in reminding the adult community of the problems within the social structure of our society.

1. They have taught us about the rigidity and sterility of our sexual patterns, based upon outmoded needs of societies when many children, not few, were needed; when homosexuality was societally wasteful; when the penalty of sexual contact between the sexes was often unwanted babies and disgrace.
2. They have pointed out the real failures in our society: inhumaneness,

phony values, lack of ability to listen, loneliness, and waste of spiritual values.

3. They have revealed that in our great efforts to gain "the good life" we have lost much of the good in life. The goals of achievement and success have become so important that we have forgotten just what it is that we are trying to achieve. (p. 85)

Family Environment

Children cannot be immune from societal problems and the current family instability. Hetherington (1979) has estimated that 40 percent of the current marriages of young adults will end in divorce, and that 40 to 50 percent of the children born in this decade will spend some time living in a single-parent family. The problems and stresses caused as a result of the divorce situation have been rather carefully analyzed. Hetherington has pointed out: "Boys from divorced families, in contrast with girls and children from nuclear families, show a higher rate of behavior disorders and problems in interpersonal relationships in the home and in the school with teachers" (p. 853).

A number of reasons have been given to explain why boys are more influenced by divorce. Perhaps boys receive less positive support and nurturance and are viewed more negatively by mothers and teachers in the period following divorce than are girls. Boys may then be exposed to more stress, frustration, and aggression and have fewer available supports immediately following divorce.

Hetherington has also concluded that a conflict-ridden intact family may be more harmful to the family members than a stable home in which parents are divorced. Divorce can often be a positive solution for a family that is functioning in a destructive manner. However, most children experience divorce as a difficult transition, and life in a single-parent family can be viewed as a high-risk situation for parents and children.

Biophysical Factors

During the past few decades there has been a strong tendency to believe that behavior which is manifested in social problems is due to the interactions of the child with his or her family, and then the peer group, neighborhood, and subculture. The inappropriateness of these interactions has been viewed as the cause of consistent behavior problems. However, Schwarz (1979) has pointed out that there is creditable evidence indicating the significant role of heredity in helping to shape behavior and personality. Major sex differences occur in conditions such as infantile autism, hyperactivity, stuttering, alcoholism, antisocial personality, various depressive illnesses, and schizophrenia. Infantile autism, hyperactivity, and conduct disorders occur in males four to eight times more often than in females. Depression and social phobias appear in females beyond puberty two to three times more frequently than in males. Such dramatic sex differences can be interpreted as due to the different treatment of males and females in our society, but they can also suggest a sex-linked genetic factor, or a combination of both. More investigation will be needed to sort out this complex issue.

EDUCATIONAL ADAPTATIONS FOR CHILDREN WITH BEHAVIOR PROBLEMS

Two decades ago the preferred treatment for children with behavior problems was psychiatric in nature. Since that time emphasis and responsibility have shifted from mental health professionals to educational personnel. Several factors have influenced this change. In the first place, only a small proportion of the children needing help could be treated by the limited number of psychiatrists, psychologists, or social workers available. Second, the traditional mode of mental health treatment in which the child might receive one or two hours a week of counseling or therapy generally has not proven successful in changing behavior. As a result, the bulk of responsibility has shifted from a pattern in which teachers were seen as supplementary personnel while the mental health professionals were regarded as the responsible treatment agents to the current practice in which teachers are seen as the responsible agents for treatment and receive supplementary help from psychiatrists, psychologists, and social workers.

Educational and Psychological Strategies

A wide variety of educational and psychological strategies are used in working with children with behavior problems, and these are briefly summarized in the following paragraphs.

Psychoeducational Strategy

The focus of the psychoeducational approach is on assessing the child's needs and developing an individual plan and educational prescriptions. The bulk of the program modifications are made within the school setting, unlike psychotherapy which removes the child from the school setting. The teacher is expected to be the key figure in implementing this strategy.

Psychodynamic Strategy

The prime objective of this strategy is to help children become aware of their own needs, desires, and fears. Proponents of the psychodynamic model place emphasis on psychiatric procedures such as diagnosis, treatment, decision making, and evaluation. Maladaptive behavior is viewed as symptomatic of intrapsychic conflict, and treatment focuses on removing the underlying cause of the conflict. It is believed that removal of a symptom (for example, aggressive behavior might be seen as a symptom) without elimination of the cause would only result in the substitution of another symptom.

psychiatric procedures

Behavior Modification Strategy

The proponents of behavior modification view all behavior, maladaptive as well as adaptive, as learned. The behaviorist views the manifested behavior as the problem that must be dealt with, unlike followers of the psychodynamic strategy who see behavior as a symptom of a deeper problem. Behavior modification is accomplished by specifying those behaviors that are to be changed and providing differential reinforcement to strengthen the behaviors that are desired.

Ecological Strategy *interactional*

Supporters of the ecological model (Rhodes, 1967) maintain that human problems result from improper interactions between the child and the environment (family, siblings, teachers, children, cultural subgroups, and so forth). Treatment consists of modifying elements in the ecology, including the child, so that more constructive interactions between the child and environment take place.

Skills A variety of techniques and procedures for coping with children with problem behavior have been introduced into the schools since those institutions became the focal point of treatment. These procedures attempt either to teach the child how to gain control over impulsive or other unwanted behaviors or to strengthen the child's use of prosocial behaviors that are already in his or her repertoire but not used as often as school personnel believe they could be.

Teaching Self-Control

One of the relatively new techniques used in special education to help children with behavior problems is to instruct them in self-control. For Jim, this means that the teacher works with him to improve a series of self-awareness skills whereby he can increase his own control over his hyperactivity or distractibility. Camp and Bash (1981) described a "Think Aloud" program that has been designed to help teach self-control to impulsive and aggressive boys during the early elementary years. Because problem behavior of this type appears most often in boys, they are often used as the focal point of such programs. In this case, there are four specific questions that the child is asked to consider: (1) What is my problem? (2) How can I control it? (3) Am I following my plan? (4) How did I do? In essence, the children are asked to stand outside themselves and begin to view their own performance. By observing their own behavior, they are then able to gain some control over it. If boys like Jim can understand the signals that trigger their aggressive behavior or hyperactivity, then they are in a better position to control behavior that previously had been outside their own management.

Camp and Bash reported that after thirty training sessions members of the experimental group in the study not only increased their scores in intelligence tests and reading tests but also received more favorable teacher ratings of interpersonal behavior. Even more important, the study showed a generalized effect of the training program on such dimensions as reading and classroom social behavior. Apparently youngsters can be helped to see the signals in their environment that trigger their unacceptable behavior, to inhibit impulses to respond immediately, and to develop a plan of action to meet situations. In many respects, the goal of learning such skills is as important to the education of these youngsters as are the more academic goals of reading and arithmetic. Furthermore, until these children achieve such social goals as maintaining self-control, they will be unlikely to learn much of the more traditional academic skills.

Overcoming Learned Helplessness

While children like Jim are taught skills to control impulsive behavior, there are also techniques to help depressed children like Molly cope with their environment. Dweck (1975) reported an attempt to improve the status of elementary school children who evidenced extreme learned helplessness. One group of children received success-only treatments in which the tasks were arranged so that the students succeeded in the vast majority of situtations. Members of another group, when they failed, were given instructions to see what role they had played in the failure. The youngsters in the latter group improved their performance when they were shown how to avoid failure, whereas those who had a heavy dose of success failed miserably when failure finally did come. Dweck concluded, "An instructional program for children who have difficulty dealing with failure would do well not to skirt the issue by trying to ensure success, or by glossing over failure" (p. 684).

Much of the work with fearful or withdrawn children is still done by mental health professionals outside the public school program. The limited budgets of school systems do not allow them to employ a battery of psychiatrists, psychologists, and social workers. The release of pent-up feelings and unspoken fears in a protected environment is one of the major goals of most child therapists. Classroom teachers can often notice changes in a child when he or she has someone to talk to and relax with.

Making Value Decisions

There have been attempts to design curriculum materials to help youngsters make good decisions in conflict situations. Kohlberg's (1969, 1976) model of moral development has been used as a basis for such instruction. Galbraith and Jones (1976) employed this approach in presenting the following hypothetical situation.

The security guard at the factory had just finished his lunch and was walking around the loading dock on Emerson Street. As he turned the corner to climb the stairs, he nearly tripped over the twisted body of a man. The man was moving around on the pavement of the parking lot and appeared to be in great pain. The guard turned the man slowly and found a very severe wound on the man's chest. The man was losing a lot of blood from the injury.

The guard knew that the man needed medical attention fast. The guard ran one block down Emerson Street to Community Hospital to seek help for the badly injured man. He raced into the emergency entrance and ran from room to room looking for help. At first he only found a mother with her hysterical child who had just fallen from a tree and broken an arm. As he went out of the treatment room, he met the nurse who was on duty in the emergency room. He quickly told her the story and urged her to follow him up the street to help the man. The nurse told him that the interns were all out on other calls and she could not leave the hospital. The guard insisted that the man would die without her help and told her to follow him to the parking lot. As the guard turned to rush out the door and return to the injured man, the nurse pointed to a large sign on the wall of the emergency room:

HOSPITAL EMPLOYEES
MAY NOT LEAVE THE BUILDING
WHEN ON DUTY

The nurse turned and the guard was gone. She wanted to help, but she knew that the hospital rule was strictly enforced.

Should she follow the guard to help the injured man or stay at her duty station in the emergency room?

The students are guided through a discussion of the developmental principles and moral issues that are involved in the dilemma of the nurse in the hospital. Children at both the preadolescent and adolescent levels who have been provided with special training in this area have been found to respond with more mature decisions, and this superiority of response continued even after a year had passed (Blatt and Kohlberg, 1975).

Modifying Behavior

One of the most widely used techniques to encourage prosocial behavior and discourage antisocial behavior is behavior modification, using the principles of *operant conditioning* and *task analysis*.

Operant conditioning functions through controlling the stimuli that *follow* the responses. For example, a child sucks his or her thumb when watching television. The mother arranges to press a button that will turn off the television when the thumb is in the mouth and turn on the television when it is not. Soon the child learns not to indulge in thumb sucking in order to keep the television on. In that situation, the operant (thumb sucking) is controlled by the stimulus (television off) that follows. Operant conditioning is based on the principle that behavior is a function of its consequence. The application of a positive stimulus (television on) immediately following a response is called positive reinforcement; the withdrawal of a positive stimulus (television off) constitutes punishment.

The principles of operant conditioning have been applied extensively to controlling the behavior of children with acting-out behavior problems. This is accomplished by first specifying the behaviors that are to be changed, such as a child's constant jumping up, bothering others, and running around the room for one excuse or another. To shape the behavior in a classroom would require the teacher to provide step-by-step lessons that the child can do while seated and then to reinforce that acceptable behavior. Ordinarily teachers pay attention to children when they are out of their seats disrupting others and ignore them when they are working quietly.

Such teacher behavior may actually reinforce disruptive student behavior. To change such a situation, the teacher must positively reinforce the child for doing lessons and staying seated.

The use of behavior modification techniques with special behavior problems is often objected to because the techniques "treat the child like a slot machine" (insert the token, get good behavior) and, as a result, would have little impact on the child's basic personality. Such criticisms are more than a little unfair. The educational objective is to create a positive response in the child that can be expanded and used for better overall social adjustment.

The usual procedure in behavior shaping in the classroom is to establish goals and organize the tasks in small steps so that the child can experience continuous success. This procedure is referred to as *task analysis.* The child can then receive positive reinforcement for each step or part of the total task as it is completed (arithmetic, reading, or spelling, for example). School assignments are presented to the child programmed in easy steps. As the child completes a task that can be accomplished successfully in a specified period of time, the teacher checks the work, praises the child (social reinforcement), and gives him or her a mark, a grade, a token, or some other tangible reinforcement. In that way the child is able to work at assignments for longer and longer periods and to accept increasingly more difficult ones.

Figure 8.2 shows the type of record keeping that is an essential part of the behavior modification technique (Kroth, Whelan, and Stables, 1972). The child's program is divided into *before, during,* and *after* intervention phases. The teacher first establishes a *baseline,* the performance of the child before treatment begins. In this case the child completed only about four of twenty problems assigned over a ten-day period. The teacher, having previously noticed that the child liked to play with a puppet in free time, made a contract with the child providing that if the problems were completed during the allotted time, the child would have twenty minutes of free time to play with the puppet. Figure 8.2 shows the dramatic change in constructive behavior that followed the establishment of the contract. On day 23 the teacher decided to test the stability of the new pattern of behavior and collected seven days of data on what happened after the reward of the puppet play was no longer used. The results shown in the figure are fairly typical. The rate of performance decreased somewhat but did not fall back to the previous baseline performance. In other words, the treatment maintained much of its effect, probably strengthened by the increased self-concept of the child for the demonstrably improved performance. This technique can clearly be utilized by regular or special classroom teachers with a little additional effort and planning and can provide the tangible record of improvement so important to both the student and teacher.

Axelrod (1971) has reported on a variety of studies using token reinforcement, the use of marks or poker chips to be exchanged later for more tangible rewards (for example, more recreation time). The studies were almost unanimous in suggesting that token reinforcement does produce clearly favorable changes in the behavior of children within the classroom.

**FIGURE 8.2
Record of a
Child-Teacher
Contract**

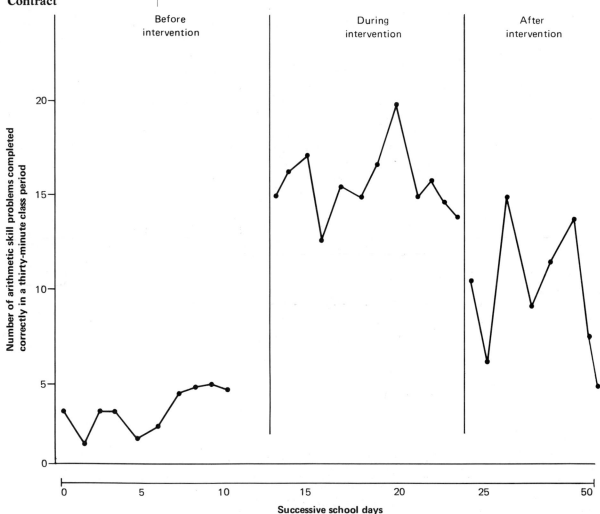

Note: Contract specified that child could earn time to play with a puppet if arithmetic problems were completed within thirty minutes.
Source: R. L. Kroth, R. J. Whelan, and J. M. Stables, Teacher applications of behavior principles in home and classroom environments. In E. L. Meyen, G. A. Vergason, and R. J. Whelan (Eds.), *Strategies for teaching exceptional children.* Denver: Love, 1972.

Learning Environment   Learning environment modifications for treating children with behavior problems are generally designed to improve the interchanges of the child with the environment. They may involve major changes in the social envelope in which the child operates. Proponents of this ecological strategy believe that a total redefinition of the nature of social pathology is required. Rhodes (1967) has stated:

> In this alternative view of disturbance it is suggested that the nucleus of the problem lies in the content of behavioral prohibitions and sanctions in the culture. Any behavior which departs significantly from this lore upsets those who have carefully patterned their behavior according to cultural specifications. (p. 449)

It has become popular to state that the cultural background of the child with behavior problems must be taken into account. But what is culture? According to sociologists, culture is a combination of all those beliefs, values, and perceptions that a given group of people hold in common. Every culture has its customs or behavioral regularities that combine both meaning and value. Customs define those behaviors that are considered normal, right, or correct (Montgomery, 1982).

The functions of the culture are continuity, passing customs and rituals along to the next generation; communication, using common symbols that have a shared meaning such as the handshake or the frown; prescription, those internalized roles that are self-evident standards of behavior passed along to us from infancy; and proscription, identifying those not of the culture and punishing those who violate cultural rules. It is clear from these characteristics that the school is a subculture of its own using all of these functions to maintain itself.

The treatment of the child with behavior problems can be either *procultural* or *countercultural* in nature. The *procultural* interventions are designed to cure the emotionally disturbed child by changing him or her to fit into the culture as it exists. Montgomery (1982) has pointed out that procultural intervenors convey the following messages:

1. The world is the way we, the helpers, say it is.
2. The emotionally disturbed individual has a distorted, incomplete, and more alien view of reality.
3. Everyone would be a lot happier if the child would or could adopt the reality as communicated by the school.
4. We are the road to salvation.

Thus, the devices of providing special classes, resource rooms, token economies, drug therapy, and so forth, are designed to modify

MODIFY

the child and to bring him or her into line with the established culture of the school.

Those types of intervention that are *countercultural* in nature are designed to bring about changes in the existing culture, reducing the need to change individual children. Illich (1970) has maintained that schools as they now exist are harmful to children and need to be eliminated! The development of preschools by groups of parents who reject many of the values associated with traditional schooling reflects a countercultural attitude. The highest priority in such preschools is to free the individual child from the pressures of conformity, obedience, and competition—fundamental values of the public school. Other countercultural interventions involve the use of litigation to ensure the civil rights of students, legislation requiring the schools to provide certain kinds of services, and books presenting a view of education that is sharply different from the traditional philosophy.

The Re-Ed Program

Hobbs (1966, 1970, 1979) and his colleagues have implemented the ecological strategy with programs for emotionally disturbed children called Re-Ed (a project for the re-education of emotionally disturbed children). As indicated earlier, the ecological approach rejects reliance on psychotherapy and assumes that "the child is an inseparable part of a small social system, of an ecological unit made up of the child, his family, his school, his neighborhood and community."

Two residential schools in the Re-Ed program were organized to house approximately forty children each, ages 6 to 12. The plan was to re-educate these children for a short period of time (four to six months) and at the same time, through a liaison teacher, to modify the attitudes of the home, the school, and the community. The entire program was oriented toward re-establishing the child as quickly as possible in his or her own home, school, and community.

The general program of re-education practices a number of principles, some of which follow:

1. **Life is to be lived now.** This is accomplished by occupying children every hour of the day in purposeful activities and in activities in which they can succeed.
2. **Time is an ally.** Some children improve with the passage of time. But a child should not remain in a residential setting for long periods since this length of time may estrange the child from his or her family. Six months in the residential center is the stated goal of Re-Ed.

Helping Children Cope with Stress

Stressful home, school, and community experiences can influence a pupil's ability to learn and behave appropriately in the classroom. Teachers can use stress, however, to teach coping skills and concepts, such as:

1. Stress is a natural and acceptable part of life.
2. Stress is not necessarily good or bad; the effect of it depends on the frequency, intensity, and duration.
3. Some pupils experience multiple stresses —developmental, economic, psychological, and reality stresses.
4. During stress some pupils become flooded by their feelings and behave inappropriately.
5. During stress, some pupils are unable to help themselves and will respond negatively to adult help and support.
6. During stress, pupils can create their own feelings in teachers and, if the teachers are not well trained, also their behaviors.
7. If the stress cycle follows its normal pattern, the stressful incident will end up as an intense power struggle between teacher and pupil.
8. When a power struggle develops, neither pupil nor teacher is a winner.

9. To change this stress cycle to a coping cycle, teachers must have the ability to:
   a. be in touch with their feelings;
   b. recognize that these feelings originally came from the pupil;
   c. verbalize their own feelings;
   d. decode the pupil's feelings;
   e. support the pupil's feelings but not the pupil's inappropriate behavior;
   f. show how coping with a difficult situation leads to feelings of competence, success, and pride;
   g. demonstrate a feeling of hope and not helplessness about life;
   h. reduce stress by lowering school standards;
   i. reduce stress by redirecting the pupil's feelings into acceptable behavior;
   j. reduce stress by helping the pupil to accept disappointment and failure;
   k. reduce stress by helping the pupil to complete one task at a time;
   l. reduce stress by having the pupil help less fortunate students;
   m. reduce stress by separating the pupil from the setting; and
   n. reduce stress by having the pupil seek professional help.

SOURCE: N. Long and B. Duffner, "The Stress Cycle or the Coping Cycle? The Impact of Home and School Stresses on Pupils' Classroom Behavior." In N. Long, W. Morse, and R. Newman (Eds.), *Conflict in the Classroom* (4th ed.). Belmont, Calif.: Wadsworth, 1980, pp. 227–228. Reprinted by permission of Wadsworth Publishing.

3. **Trust is essential.** Trust, according to Hobbs, is not learned in college courses, but some of those working with emotionally disturbed children "know, without knowing they know, the way to inspire trust in children."

4. **Competence makes a difference.** The arrangement of the environment and learning tasks must be so structured that the child is able to obtain confidence and self-respect from his or her successes.

5. **Symptoms can and should be controlled.** The treatment of symptoms instead of causes is emphasized.

The *teacher-counselor* is the key staff person in re-education programs and is not only trained to operate as a special teacher but is also well grounded in counseling methods designed for disturbed children. A *liaison teacher-counselor* works in the program to form effective alliances between home, school, and child. When the child is removed from the regular school and placed in a Re-Ed school, the liaison teacher-counselor keeps the school aware of his or her progress in the program and prepares the child and the school for

Some children who may not be able to cope with stressful situations may benefit from professional help. (Photo: © Meri Houtchens-Kitchens, 1982.)

his or her re-entry into the public school when such time approaches.

A comprehensive follow-up evaluation was conducted on Project Re-Ed by Weinstein (1974). The progress of the children was compared with the progress of children who had comparable emotional problems but were not in the Re-Ed program as well as with a group of "normal" children of similar age and background.

Comparisons of the three groups of children were made six months and eighteen months after the Re-Ed group had completed treatment. The results showed that the treated children had more positive self-concepts and greater confidence in their ability to control their own situations than did the untreated disturbed children. The Re-Ed children were judged by their teachers to be better adjusted than the untreated disturbed children both academically and socially. Although the Re-Ed students were doing better than the disturbed children who were not treated, the Re-Ed graduates continued to show more maladjustment on all measures than the group of children designated as normal. In other words, the re-education program did not change the disturbed children into "normal" children, but it did reduce the level of their disturbance by a significant degree. It is always worthwhile to be cautious about the effects of treatment and not to give the impression that treatment, even when clearly superior, will completely transform the exceptional child into a child indistinguishable from other children.

Hewett (1980) has contrasted the ecological and psychodynamic approaches by drawing an analogy between the psychodynamic model and a baseball game. You can imagine that someone from another culture who is trying to understand the nature of the game might adopt a strategy of paying exclusive attention to the behavior of the first baseman. This observer would follow in great detail and report at length on the first baseman as he fields, throws, bats, runs, and so forth. It is unlikely that, even with the most intense examination of this one player, the observer would be able to understand either the nature of the game of baseball itself or guess at the true reasons for the particular behavior of that one player.

Hewett goes on to suggest that the traditional clinical or psychodynamic approach has been to study one particular deviant member of a social system. To study a child in great detail, similar to the study of the first baseman, without examining the social systems in which the child is embedded, is likely to inhibit full understanding of the child and his or her behavior. We can observe the behavior of a child but not be able to interpret it effectively without also studying the total social context in which the child exists. It is the virtue of projects such as Re-Ed that they try to touch on all pertinent elements in the social system.

Open Education Program

Knoblock (1973) has advocated an open education therapeutic setting for emotionally disturbed children. The open education program, with its freedom and flexibility, provides a setting in which the child can act out feelings and the trained teacher can immediately react to them. Children who have conflicts with authority and who have a continuing battle with a structured program can work out their feelings with an adult who is nonauthoritarian in an environment that does not create a constant excuse for battles with authority.

Knoblock has pointed out that the open education program requires decisions on the part of the child and also allows the child to exert a degree of control over his or her own environment. Both features, in turn, provide a more constructive ego development since disturbed children often have negative self-concepts and feelings of inadequacy. Knoblock appears to be primarily addressing the problems of the withdrawn child rather than the disruptive child in recommending this particular setting.

One general rule that might stand the test of application is that withdrawn and inhibited children need the opportunity to expand and express themselves and to try out new behavior styles. Behaviorally disruptive children need to have environmental controls so that their own impulsive behavior does not carry them away and create a large variety of secondary problems.

Using Psychoeducational Strategies

Children with behavior problems have been affected by the legislative climate and its effect on education just as other exceptional children have. The Education for All Handicapped Children Act (PL 94–142) exerted pressure on the educational system to place these children in the least restrictive environment. The task of educational planning is to arrange the lessons and setting to accommodate the children in a learning environment that is as close to normal as possible.

Figure 8.3 presents six stages in the development of an individualized education plan (IEP). In the initial stages, the child is referred by teacher, parent, or professional, and action is taken to plan an appropriate education.

During the stages in which the IEP is developed, a comprehensive evaluation is conducted that includes measures of achievement, self-concept, family data, and the like. After the data have been collected, the child study team meeting is held, attended by the teacher, psychologist, principal, and other personnel. They will

**FIGURE 8.3
Stages in the
Individualized
Education Plan**

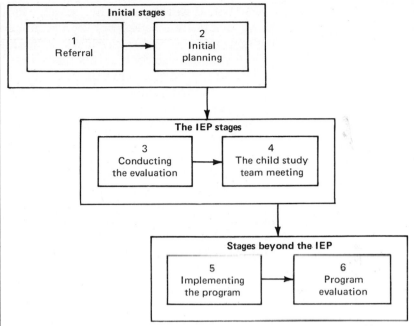

Source: J. Lerner, D. Dawson, and L. Horvath, *Cases in learning and behavior problems.* Boston: Houghton Mifflin, 1980, p. 3.

review the accumulated evidence and develop a set of educational objectives.

The fifth and sixth stages, as seen in Figure 8.3, cover the implementation and follow-up evaluation of the program. The plan will have action steps that the teacher will have to take. Figure 8.4 shows the action plan for a student. After the plan is implemented, information is collected to demonstrate the degree to which the program has been carried out.

By now, it is fairly well established that mainstreaming of exceptional children, that is, bringing the exceptional child into physical proximity with the nonhandicapped child, will not automatically result in a healthy social interaction between the two. Can the teacher take specific kinds of actions in arranging the learning environment or in changing his or her own style to bring about healthy relationships? Johnson and Johnson (1981) tried to address this question in a study with forty third-grade students, eight of whom were identified as having severe learning and behavior problems. Some of the exceptional students were provided cooperative learning experiences with the nonhandicapped children in which group performance was important, and some were provided individualized learning activities. The experiences that the students had working together to achieve mutual goals did promote social relationships between handicapped and nonhandicapped students, and those relationships carried over into other situations in the class. It seems likely that by carefully arranging tasks and the learning environment, the teacher can take an active role in facilitating the social integration of exceptional children in the regular program.

One of the questions of great interest to the school is whether the lack of social skills in delinquent youngsters is due to an unwillingness to perform appropriately or their inability to recognize appropriate behavior. McFall (1976) has suggested that some individuals behave maladaptively simply because they do not know the proper social skills. He compared the responses of sixty adolescent boys—twenty in an institution for delinquents, twenty who were labeled good citizens and who came from the same basic socioeconomic background, and twenty youngsters identified as student leaders—to items on the Adolescent Personality Inventory. This inventory presents a series of social problem situations that have to be solved. Some examples of the problems follow:

1. The school principal threatens to suspend you for hassling a substitute teacher.
2. You want to ask the manager of McDonald's for a job.

FIGURE 8.4
Sample IEP
Action Plan

Name of Student	Rita Sunday	Subject Area Vocational Awareness

Level of Performance Can write paragraphs using correct grammar, can read 6th grade material with adequate comprehension, just beginning

Annual Goals To learn the skills in obtaining and retaining a job, to receive a broader picture of jobs   to explore careers

available, to learn the skills for living independently

Objectives	Evaluation	Date Achieved
1. To be able to write a neat, effective business letter with 95% accuracy	Write letter to business agency requesting job-related information	
2. To be able to successfully fill out application forms for jobs and/or further training with 100% accuracy	Quiz using three different application forms	

3. To develop an interest in at least one particular career field by completing all of the following tasks:
  a. reading literature on the job
  b. developing a written description of it
  c. visiting locations in the community related to the job
  d. compiling a reference book with at least 15 different items of information about the job
	Student will keep a log related to each task; teacher observation	

4. To verbally explain (including eight items of information) each of the following:
  a. rental contracts
  b. insurance needs
  c. banking needs
  d. transportation costs and alternatives
	Teacher observation of oral reports using a structured checklist of items covered by a student	

Source: A. Turnbull, B. Strickland, and J. Brantley, *Developing and implementing individualized education programs.* Columbus, Ohio: Charles E. Merrill, 1978. © 1978 Bell & Howell Co. Permission granted for noncommercial reproduction.

3. Your father tells you to stay home on Saturday night.
4. Your friend is angry because you dated a girl he likes.

In answers to forty-four set situations, a clear difference in responses separated the delinquent boys from the other two groups, with the delinquent boys showing significantly fewer social skills and more instances of inappropriate social behavior.

In a follow-up study, even when the items were provided to the students in a multiple-choice arrangement so that socially appropriate behaviors were listed, the delinquent youngsters still chose less socially acceptable behaviors. The lack of understanding of appropriate social skills may represent one base for a specific curriculum or training program for youngsters identified as either socialized delinquents or children with conduct disorders.

One of the techniques that has emerged from the field of mental health and that has been used successfully by teachers is the *life space interview*, designed by Redl (1959). Redl has stressed the importance of a careful interview with the student directly following a particular crisis situation or event so that the child is faced with the consequences of his or her own behavior immediately instead of waiting a day or more for a regular counseling session, by which time the child has forgotten or has built sufficient defenses around the event for self-protection.

A particular incident with Jim is useful to describe the life space interview. Jim had been on the playground unmercifully razzing and teasing another youngster, Paul, who had done something to irritate Jim in the classroom. Paul, finally out of desperation, struck out at Jim, giving Jim an excuse to then strike back. A life space interview would entail sitting down quietly in a private setting with Jim and discussing the incident in all its details. The teacher can then ask Jim to express his views on the incident and discuss with Jim the role that he played in creating the event. Jim should have full opportunity to verbalize his own attitudes about the situation and to allow his feelings about Paul to be expressed. Ideally the life space interview ends with a plan for resolving the problem or for preventing similar problems in the future through some specific steps that can be taken. Some evidence supports life space intervention as a means for reducing the amount of maladapted behavior not only by inhibiting undesirable behavior but also by generating alternative solutions (DeMagistris and Imber, 1980).

The Helping Teacher

One of the more innovative suggestions for providing help to the beleaguered classroom teacher is the concept of the *helping teacher*.

Although there are certain periods during which very disturbed children cannot function in a large group setting, generally they can benefit from and fit into the regular class. (Photo: Hiroji Kubota/Magnum.)

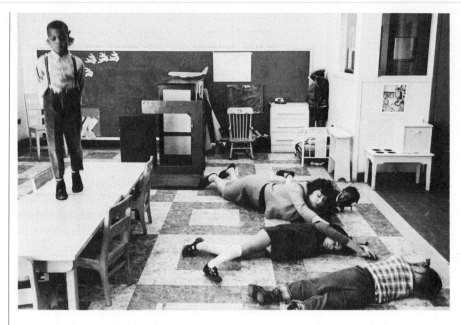

This concept came from the understanding that the classroom teacher with twenty-five to thirty children cannot cope with all aspects of the classroom environment without some degree of assistance. Who should provide that help? Morse (1976) proposed the *helping teacher* based on his work with disturbed or disturbing children. Some of the propositions advanced by Morse in support of the helping teacher follow:

1. Even the very disturbed child is not "disturbed all the time," meaning that there are only certain periods when the disturbed pupil cannot function in the larger group setting. These periods may be at certain regular times or in the press of a crisis. But most of the time, the disturbed child could benefit and fit into the regular class.
2. What is needed is direct assistance. Consultation is one thing, but real help is another. Psychologists and the like might offer advice, but they do not know what it is like to try to administer a classroom with these kids in the room.
3. The direct service helping teacher should be omnipresent, not itinerant, and be trained as a teacher, but as a special teacher. The helping person should be able to respond to the disturbed child in crisis, but be able to help with both academic and emotional problems for all children. Many of the disturbed youngsters needed direct counseling help with their self-concept, but just as many could find growth through therapeutic tutoring.
4. There were times when the helping teacher could assist best by coming in and taking over the classroom while the regular teacher worked through a phase of a problem with a youngster.

5. Help should be based upon the reality of how the child was able to cope with the classroom and not on categories, labels, or diagnostic criteria. It was pointed out that many normal children need help during a crisis in the classroom or in their lives just as the chronically and severely variant youngster does. (pp. 1–2)

The helping teacher generally uses techniques that are an extension of the regular education procedures with an emphasis on support and encouragement. In addition, the helping teacher is able to provide important liaison services, not within the capabilities of the heavily burdened classroom teacher. Children with behavior problems often need the help of a wide variety of professionals, pediatricians, psychologists, and paraprofessionals, and the helping teacher can coordinate that type of assistance. Morse has summed up the nature of the relationship as follows: "The plan envisions co-team teaching of the special and regular teacher. There is no intent to replace, only to supplement. The best staff education will come as a result of offering direct help; through service comes change. The job is overwhelming, all agree, but the direction has stood the test of time" (p. 8).

Drug Therapy   Most of the program interventions discussed herein are educational or psychological in nature. Another form of assistance from the biomedical field is worth noting. In the past decade, a wide variety of psychoactive drugs have been used separately or in conjunction with educational treatments in an attempt to deal with the behavior problems of some children.

Connors and Werry (1979) have reviewed the literature regarding the relative effectiveness of differing types of drugs with children who have learning and behavior problems and reached the conclusion that *stimulants*, in particular, have shown a positive effect when used with careful dosage and in conjunction with educational programs. There seems to be evidence that for some children the introduction of a proper dosage of stimulants improves both their behavior and mental functioning. The observed improvement in mental functioning is widely regarded as not due to a direct stimulation of mental processes but rather to the removal of barriers (that is, hyperactivity, limited attention, and so forth) that have inhibited the full use of mental processes in the child in the past.

A special problem is noted by Sprague and Sleator (1976). In studying the effect of drug management on older learning disabled children, they found that the optimum dosage for the influence of

DRUGS reducing inhibitory mental processes

social behavior differed from that required for optimum cognitive behavior! As a result, a difficult educational, or even ethical, decision must be made as to which dosage is appropriate and which outcome is more desired, since it seems likely that one cannot optimize both of these educational objectives at the same time. On the basis of a recent study on the use of drugs with hyperactive children, Charles, Schain, and Zelnicker (1981) have advocated individual dosages relative to specific child responses as the recommended practice.

Finally, Barkley (1979) and others have made a strong recommendation for cooperation of parents and a variety of professionals in drug therapy. Barkley has pointed out that the value of medication is to facilitate changes in the child such that certain responses become more likely (for example, attentiveness) or less likely (for example, aggressive outbursts). However, whether such responses actually occur depends on additional educational program dimensions.

SUMMARY OF MAJOR IDEAS

1. Children with behavior problems exhibit impulsive, aggressive, anxious, or depressed behavior of such duration, intensity, and inappropriateness that the school feels compelled to take special action.
2. Four major patterns of school problem behavior can be categorized as conduct disorders, anxiety-withdrawal, immaturity, and socialized aggression.
3. There are major disagreements on the prevalence of behavior disorders, ranging from 2 to 24 percent, based on the ambiguity of separating normal from abnormal behavior. There is general agreement that at least 2 to 3 percent of children have behavior problems that require intensive and prolonged treatment.
4. Identification methods include tests, rating scales, behavior observations, and interviews. A combination of these methods is often used in school settings.
5. There has been a shift in the responsibility for treatment of children with behavior problems from mental health professionals to school personnel.
6. Strategies to modify the educational program for children with behavior problems include different approaches labeled as psychodynamic, psychoeducational, behavior modification, and ecological.
7. There appear to be genetic influences that interact with well-recognized psychological and sociological factors in some children with behavior problems.

system of differential reinforcement

8. Behavior modification techniques have shown special consistency in achieving the specific objectives stated for them.
9. A variety of techniques that teach the child to observe his or her own behavior seem to be successful in helping children manage acting-out behavior problems more effectively.
10. Drug therapy carefully applied under competent supervision also appears to modify hyperactive behavior when it is combined with educationally designed experiences.
11. Even when treatment is effective, children with behavior problems are not expected to move completely into the normal range. Even after specific successful treatment, it is likely that observers will still be able to differentiate the behaviorally disturbed child from the normal child.
12. Treatment of withdrawn or depressed children generally focuses on strategies that enable the child to express hidden fears and to improve, through developing competence, their low self-concepts.
13. There is a major movement to allow educational and paraeducational personnel, including parents, to play a larger and larger role in the implementation of treatment programs, with a correspondingly lower emphasis on highly trained but scarce psychiatric specialists.
14. One strategy for helping children with behavior problems has been to focus on the ecological setting—the interaction of the child with his or her environment. Treatment consists of direct counseling with the child as well as attempts to change the surrounding environment so that it will be more receptive to the child.

UNRESOLVED ISSUES

1. **Increasing Use of Paraprofessionals.** One of the serious limiting conditions in delivering quality educational services to children with behavior problems is the current need for highly trained personnel to carry out the programs that have been discussed. Unless a way can be found to use paraprofessional personnel, as has been done in behavior modification programs, it will not be possible to provide the assistance needed for the large number of youngsters who are identified as having behavior problems.

2. **Determining the Mental Health of Society.** How can one judge the mental health or maturity of a society or a subculture as opposed to the mental health of an individual? We have a wide variety of instruments designed to place the individual on a scale of mental illness or mental health but nothing comparable for the larger culture. If we believe that part of the problem faced by some

problems of some
children involves inappropriate demands by the society, then how can we judge the level or kind of inappropriateness?

3. Understanding the Causes of Behavior Problems. Since World War II the predominant thinking about causes of problem behavior has focused on psychological or sociological dimensions. Either the child was mentally ill because of unusual or bizarre psychic processes or was showing abnormal behavior as a result of some negative sociological or ecological conditions. Now, with increasing sophistication of analysis, the role of genetics in causing or influencing emotional behavior problems has been reintroduced. We need to sort out the relative role played by these various forces in creating undesirable and unproductive behavior.

REFERENCES OF SPECIAL INTEREST

Lerner, J., Dawson, D., and Horvath, L. *Cases in learning and behavior problems: A guide to individualized education programs.* Boston: Houghton Mifflin, 1980.

A detailed set of case studies designed to take the practicing educator through the process of developing an education plan from referral, to evaluation, to the child study team meeting and the eventual implementation of the program. A useful tool for those who will be a part of such planning teams.

Long, N., Morse, W., and Newman, R. (Eds.). *Conflict in the classroom: The education of emotionally disturbed children* (4th ed.). Belmont, Calif.: Wadsworth, 1980.

A mix of short stories, sociological treatises, and a variety of educational and mental health articles, all dealing with disturbed or disturbing children. Most of the articles have appeared in journals elsewhere, but it is a great convenience to have them bound together. The editors have shown excellent judgment in their selections.

Paul, J., and Epanchin, B. (Eds.). *Emotional disturbance in children.* Columbus, Ohio: Charles E. Merrill, 1982.

A collection of chapters on various aspects of educating disturbed children. The emphasis is on education and a wide variety of the newer methods and procedures are included. This text probably reflects the best in current trends, even if these trends are still not widely practiced at this time. Evenhanded and eclectic.

Quay, H. C., and Werry, J. S. (Eds.). *Psychopathological disorders of childhood* (2nd ed.). New York: John Wiley, 1979.

A comprehensive collection of chapters each dealing with a major topic relating to childhood psychopathology. Chapters address topics such as childhood psychoses, behavior therapy, pharmacotherapy, and educational programming. Particularly excellent in reviewing research on various topics.

Rhodes, W., and Head, S. *A study of child variance. Volume I—Theories and conceptual models; Volume II—Intervention techniques; Volume III—Service delivery systems.* Ann Arbor, Mich.: University of Michigan, 1974.

This three-volume set provides the most comprehensive review to date of the child at variance with the society. It portrays the importance of social factors as they impinge on the child in trouble with authorities, and the role, positive and negative, played by the various social institutions that try to modify the child's behavior or ecology.

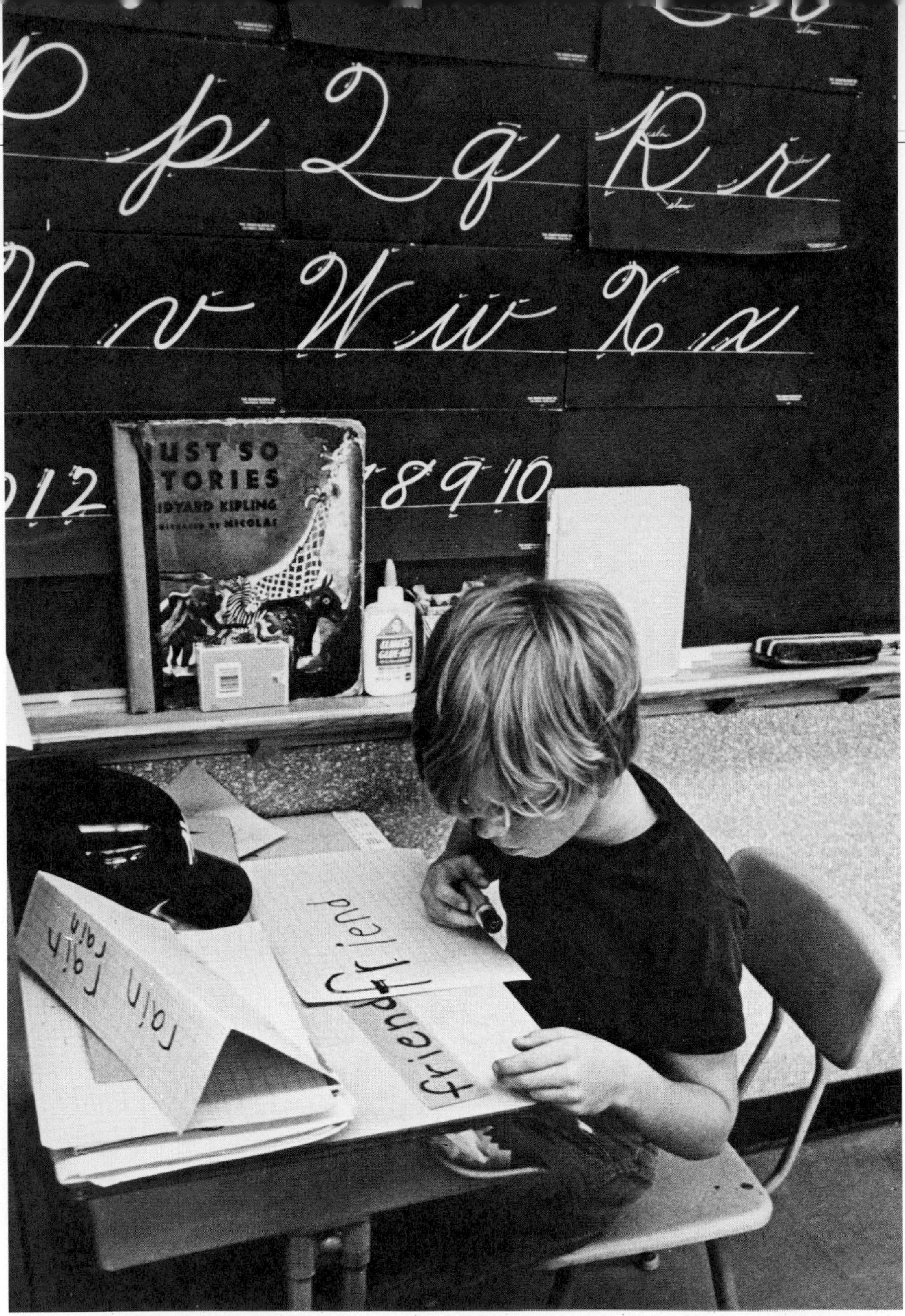
friend
friend
rain
rain
rain

Children with Learning Disabilities

T he label *learning disability* includes the heterogeneous group of children who do not fit neatly into the traditional categories of handicapped children. A substantial number of children show retardation in learning to talk, do not acquire other communication skills, do not develop normal visual or auditory perception, or have great difficulty in learning to read, to spell, to write, or to calculate. Some children are not receptive to language but are not deaf, some are not able to perceive visually but are not blind, and some cannot learn by ordinary methods of instruction but are not mentally retarded. Although such children form a heterogeneous group and fail to learn for diverse reasons, they have one thing in common: discrepancies (intraindividual differences) in abilities and achievements.

IDENTIFYING AND DEFINING LEARNING DISABILITIES

Because of the heterogeneous nature of this group of children, the concept of learning disabilities has been hard to describe in a few sentences or by a numerical designation, such as an IQ score or a decibel loss. Furthermore, because the field has been of interest to educators, psychologists, psychiatrists, neurophysiologists, pediatricians, ophthalmologists, optometrists, speech pathologists, and others, the problems have been viewed from the different perspectives of each of those disciplines. In general, however, there are two broad concerns in defining or identifying these children: (1) etiology (cause) and (2) behavior.

Medical terminology tends to label learning disorders in terms of etiologies and relates them to abnormalities in the brain. Thus terms such as *brain injury, minimal brain damage, minimal cerebral dysfunction,* and *central nervous system disorders* are used to describe deviations in development. Behavioral terminology attempts to label the disorders according to their behavioral or psychological aspects. From the behavioral perspective, then, such terms as *perceptual handicaps, conceptual disorders, reading disabilities, language disorders,* and *arithmetic disabilities* are used.

Learning Disability Criteria

There appear to be three criteria or factors that must exist before we can say that a child has a learning disability. They are (1) a discrepancy between abilities or between potential and achievement, (2) an exclusion factor, and (3) a special education criterion.

The Discrepancy Criterion

Children with learning disabilities are those who have (1) significant developmental discrepancies among various aspects of their psychological behavior (perception, seeing relationships, visual-motor ability, attention, memory, and so forth) or (2) unexplained disparity between some areas of their academic achievement and their other abilities or achievements. Developmental imbalances among such functions as linguistic, social, or visual-motor abilities are generally noted at the preschool level, while discrepancies among general or specialized aspects of intellectual development and academic achievement are observable at the school-age level. A preschool child who does not talk at the age of 4, for example, but who has other perceptual, cognitive, and motor abilities that appear normal would be suspected of having a learning disability. A school-age child who has relatively average mental ability, has made normal progress in arithmetic computation and other achievement areas, but has not learned to read after three years of adequate schooling, may have a learning disability in reading.

The Exclusion Criterion

Most definitions exclude from the learning disability designation those difficulties in learning that can be explained by general mental retardation, auditory or visual impairment, emotional disturbance, or lack of opportunity to learn. The exclusion factor does not mean that children with hearing and vision impairments or children who are diagnosed as mentally retarded cannot *also* have learning disabilities. Those children require multiple services.

The Special Education Criterion

Children with learning disabilities are those children who require special education for their development. A child who has not had an opportunity to learn and is retarded educationally will learn by ordinary methods of instruction at his or her level of achievement. For example, if a child has not been in school up to the age of 9 or 10 and is found to have normal cognitive and perceptual abilities but has not learned to read or achieve in arithmetic, that child could not be considered learning disabled even though there is a discrepancy between ability and achievement. Such a child will learn by developmental methods of instruction and does not need special education, which has been defined earlier as extraordinary or atypical education involving special techniques not ordinarily used with regular students. In other words, the criterion of need for a special method because of some developmental disorder that has inhibited the child's ability to achieve is an important one— one that sometimes is not included in the criteria for identification. That criterion is necessary, however; it requires that, following a diagnosis of discrepancy and exclusions, the diagnostician must specify the special remedial program needed by the child. Without that criterion, a child will just have a label.

Using these three identifying criteria, we can describe learning disabilities as follows: *A learning disability is a psychological or neurological impediment to spoken or written language or perceptual, cognitive, or motor behavior. The impediment (1) is manifested by discrepancies among specific behaviors and achievements or between evidenced ability and academic achievement; (2) is of such nature and extent that the child does not learn by the instructional methods and materials appropriate for the majority of children and requires specialized procedures for development; and (3) is not primarily due to severe mental retardation, sensory handicaps, emotional problems, or lack of opportunity to learn.*

Definitions   In 1968 the National Advisory Committee on the Handicapped of the U.S. Office of Education defined *specific learning disabilities*. Its definition was used by Congress in the Learning Disability Act of 1969. With only a few changed words, it was included in the 1975 Education for All Handicapped Children Act as follows:

The term "children with specific learning disabilities" means those children who have a disorder in one or more of the basic psychological processes involved in understanding or in using language, spoken or written, which disorder may manifest itself in imperfect ability to listen, think, speak, read, write, spell, or to do mathematical calculations. Such disorders include such conditions as perceptual handicaps, brain injury, minimal brain dysfunction, dyslexia, and developmental aphasia. Such term does not include children who have learning problems which are primarily the result of visual, hearing, or motor handicaps, of mental retardation, of emotional disturbance, or of environmental, cultural, or economic disadvantage.

The federal definition, although acceptable with slight modifications by many state agencies, was not completely satisfactory to all associations. A joint committee of the American Speech-Language-Hearing Association, the Association for Children with Learning Disabilities, the Council for Learning Disabilities, the Division for Children with Communication Disorders, the International Reading Association, and the Orton Dyslexia Society have formulated the following definition (reported by Hammill, Leigh, McNutt, and Larsen, 1981).

Learning disabilities is a generic term that refers to a heterogeneous group of disorders manifested by significant difficulties in the acquisition and use of listening, speaking, reading, writing, reasoning or mathematical abilities. These disorders are intrinsic to the individual and presumed to be due to central nervous system dysfunction. Even though a learning disability may occur concomitantly with other handicapping conditions (e.g., sensory impairment, mental retardation, social and emotional disturbance) or environmental influences (e.g., cultural differences, insufficient/inappropriate instruction, psychogenic factors), it is not the direct result of those conditions or influences. (p. 336)

All the definitions quoted above have in common the implication that there is an intrinsic psychological or neurological factor that has inhibited or interfered with the normal development of the child in mental operations, language, and academic school programs. All the definitions tend to exclude children with mental retardation, sensory handicaps, and lack of opportunity to learn.

It should be pointed out that not all children who have a discrepancy between their potential and academic achievement are learning disabled. There are a large number of factors contributing to underachievement. Figure 9.1 illustrates the major factors, mentioned in all of the definitions, that can account for underachievement in school children. It should be noted that the identifiable intrinsic conditions (within the child) that can lead to underachievement in school are mental retardation, sensory handicaps of blindness and deafness, and serious emotional disturbance. Underachieving school children who are diagnosed as having these intrinsic conditions are not considered learning disabled.

The right section of Figure 9.1 refers to extrinsic environmental conditions (outside of the child) that can lead to underachievement. These include lack of opportunity to learn, failure to attend

FIGURE 9.1
Conditions Leading to Academic Underachievement

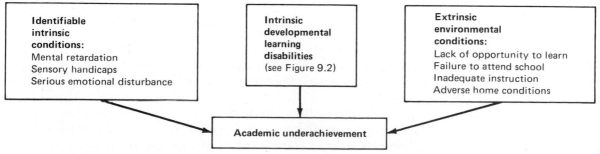

school, inadequate instruction, adverse home conditions, and so forth. These underachieving children are not considered learning disabled according to the definitions because the conditions are extrinsic to the child. A change in the environment can counteract the adverse influences.

The center column entitled *intrinsic developmental learning disabilities* includes disorders affecting memory, attention perception, thinking, and language. These can lead to underachievement in school subjects. This, however, is implying that the disabilities in academic progress are the result of an intrinsic "psychological or neurological process" or "a group of disorders manifested by significant difficulties in the acquisition" of reading, arithmetic, spelling, and handwriting. The developmental and academic learning disabilities will be discussed further in the section on classification.

CLASSIFICATIONS AND CHARACTERISTICS

Learning disabilities are of such varied kinds that it is difficult to classify them or even to draw up a specific list of the different types. After a year of study and discussion, the Bureau of Education for the Handicapped of the U.S. Office of Education formulated guidelines for the identification of learning disabilities in the following areas (*Federal Register*, December 29, 1977):

1. oral expression
2. listening comprehension
3. written expression
4. basic reading skills
5. reading comprehension
6. mathematics calculation
7. mathematics reasoning

Thus, the federal delineation of the characteristics of learning disabilities in children confined learning disabilities to three areas: (1) receptive and expressive language, (2) reading and writing, and (3) mathematics.

Few if any authorities, however, restrict learning disabilities to the areas named in the federal formulation. Myers and Hammill (1976); Brutten, Richardson, and Mangel (1973); Lerner (1981); and Reid and Hresko (1981) have referred to disabilities in motor development, attention, perception, memory, listening, speaking, reading, writing, written expression, arithmetic, as well as self-concept and social skills.

Learning disabilities can be considered under two broad categories: (1) developmental learning disabilities and (2) academic learning disabilities. Figure 9.2 illustrates these two types or classifications of learning disabilities. The major components of developmental learning disabilities include attention, memory, perception, and perceptual-motor deficits. These disabilities appear to contribute to many other difficulties in learning and have therefore been labeled *primary disabilities*. *Secondary disabilities* (thinking disorders and language disorders) often develop in conjunction with difficulties of attending, remembering, and being aware of concepts, objects, and spatial relations. There are, of course, many and varied interrelationships among and between both developmental and academic disabilities. The right side of Figure 9.2 represents the academic disabilities of reading, arithmetic, spelling, and writing. These are the first problems to be noted by teachers and require more careful diagnosis to unearth deeper relationships. Since these are the problems most familiar to school personnel, they will be discussed first.

Academic Learning Disabilities

The term *academic learning disability* refers to a significant inhibition or blockage in learning to read, to write, to spell, or to compute arithmetically. These disabilities are noted at the school-age level. Generally, a child is considered learning disabled when there is a wide discrepancy between the child's potential and his or her academic achievement. Figure 9.3 shows a profile of a child with a significant disparity between his potential as measured by mental age, language age, and arithmetic computation age, and his performance on oral and silent reading tests. Note that this child, now placed in the fifth grade, has a mental age of 11 years on an intelligence test, is able to understand fifth- and sixth-grade books when they are read to him (language age of 10 years), and scores at the fourth-grade level on arithmetic computation tests that do not require

**FIGURE 9.2
Types of
Learning
Disabilities**

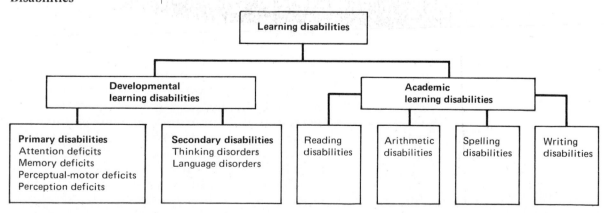

FIGURE 9.3
Profile of a
Child with a
Significant Reading
Disability

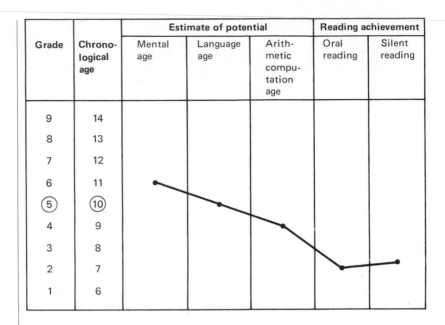

Grade	Chrono-logical age	Estimate of potential			Reading achievement	
		Mental age	Language age	Arith-metic compu-tation age	Oral reading	Silent reading
9	14					
8	13					
7	12					
6	11					
⑤	⑩					
4	9					
3	8					
2	7					
1	6					

reading. His reading performance after five years in school is still at the beginning second-grade level. The disparity between his potential for reading and his actual reading grade is between two and three years. He is considered learning disabled in reading.

Similar discrepancies can be found in children who have learning disabilities in writing, or in spelling, or in arithmetic.

Developmental Learning Disabilities   *Developmental learning disabilities* refer to deviations in the development of a number of psychological and linguistic functions that normally unfold as the child grows up. These disabilities are often, but not always, associated with deficiencies in school achievement. The link between the two is not always clear. Some reading failures have been associated with perceptual-motor deficits, but other children with the same perceptual-motor difficulties have learned to read. In some instances the association between developmental and academic difficulties may be described as *a lack of prerequisite skills*. For example, before children learn to write they must develop certain prerequisite skills such as eye-hand coordination, memory, and sequencing abilities. In learning to read, children need visual and auditory discrimination ability and memory, the ability to see relationships and to learn from the redundancies of experience, and the ability to concentrate their attention.

Some of these developmental learning disabilities are discussed in the following paragraphs.

Language Disorders

Language disorders are the most common learning disability noted at the preschool level. Generally, the child does not talk, does not talk like older brothers or sisters did at a similar age, or does not respond adequately to directions or verbal statements. The diagnosis and remediation of language disorders are discussed later.

Thinking Disabilities

Thinking disabilities are difficulties in the cognitive operations of concept formation, problem solving, and association of ideas. *Problem solving* is one form of cognitive behavior in the learning hierarchy. It requires the analysis and synthesis of information and assists the individual in responding or in adapting to new and different situations. *Concept formation* is represented by the ability to classify objects and events; for example, recognizing that a boat, a car, and a train are all used for transportation.

Thinking disorders are closely related to oral language disorders. In a study of 237 children assigned to classes for oral language disorders in California, Luick et al. (1982) found that these children showed a consistent profile on the Illinois Test of Psycholinguistic Abilities (ITPA), a test of psycholinguistic, memory, and perceptual-motor abilities. Figure 9.4 shows the profile for the 237 children. Note that the children were relatively normal in visual- and motor-expressive abilities but were (1) deficient in auditory-receptive and verbal-expressive abilities and (2) most deficient in auditory association and grammatical closure, tests of inner or central language. Actually, 97 percent of the 237 children had deficiencies on these two inner language tests. In other words, children assigned to these oral language classes in California had as their major disability oral language thinking disabilities, which were determined by tests of auditory association ("Father is a man, mother is a _____ .") and grammatic closure ("This is a bed; these are two _____ .").

Memory Deficits

Memory deficits, either visual or auditory, are the inability to remember or recall what has been heard or seen or experienced. Children with marked visual memory problems may have difficulty learning to read by a reading method that relies on recall of the visual appearance of a word. Likewise, a marked disability in auditory memory may interfere with the child's development of oral language.

FIGURE 9.4
Profile of Scaled Scores on the ITPA of 237 Children Assigned to Classes for Severe Oral Language Disorders

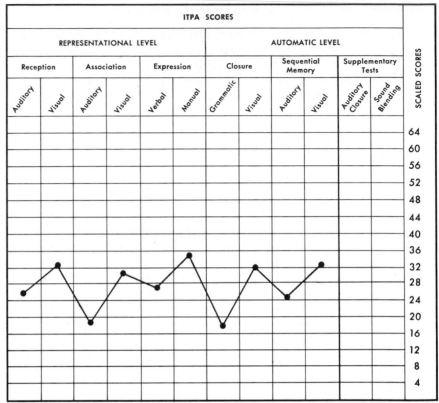

Source: A. Luick, S. Kirk, A. Agranowitz, and R. Busby, Profiles of children with severe oral language disorders. *Journal of Speech and Hearing Disorders*, 1982, *47* (February), 88–92.

Attention Disorders

Attention is a necessary prerequisite for learning a task at hand. It refers to the ability to select from numerous competing stimuli—auditory, tactile, visual, kinesthetic—that impinge on the organism all the time. As described by Ross (1976), selective attention "helps us limit the number of stimuli that we process at any one time" (p. 60). When a child attends and responds to too many stimuli, the child is considered distractible. Ross considers an attentional learning disability to be "the result of delayed development in the capacity to employ and sustain selective attention" (p. 61). Such a child may be always on the move, is distractible, and cannot sustain attention long enough to learn, or cannot direct his or her attention purposefully.

Perceptual-Motor and Other Disabilities

There are *visual* disorders comparable to disabilities in understanding and using *verbal* symbols. Children who are slow to gain meaning from road signs (symbols), danger signals, directional arrows, and printed words like *men* and *women* or their pictorial equivalents may have a specific difficulty in visual decoding. They may be slow in responding to the meaning of pictures or numbers, in understanding absurdities in funny pictures, and in understanding what they see.

An extreme example of this is a boy who had adequate vision but who could not recognize his classmates by sight. He could identify them only when he heard their voices or was told their names. He could not attach meaning to things he saw. Similarly, some individuals cannot express concepts without words, cannot show how a spiral stairway goes up and around, or how a man chops down a tree.

Johnson and Myklebust (1967) have pointed out that there are many factors in the environment with which such a child cannot cope. These need not be sights and sounds that signify deeper meaning, but can include awareness of objects in the environment, and especially the child's own relation to them. Left-right orientation, body image, spatial orientation, motor learning, putting jigsaw puzzles together, and visual closure are important abilities that do not involve the translation of symbols to gain meaning. Gearhart (1976) gave the name *nonverbal disorders* to these difficulties.

PREVALENCE

How many children with learning disabilities are there in a given population? This is a question that has been raised by school officials and by legislators. Because of the difficulty of defining learning disabilities, most statements of prevalence are based on estimates or even "guesstimates" derived from meager empirical information.

Most of the studies that have been made on the prevalence of learning disabled children tend to include educationally retarded children as well as learning disabled children who require special methods of instruction for their development (criterion 3, discussed earlier). Myklebust and Boshes (1969) estimated that 15 percent of their population were slightly underachieving. When a stricter criterion was used, 7 percent were considered learning disabled. Likewise, Meier (1971), who studied the prevalence of educational retardation in 2,400 second-grade children, found that 15 percent were considered learning disabled. He stated that slow learners (IQ scores below 79) and children with learning disabilities were referred and described by the teachers in the same way. By using stricter methods of diagnosis, he concluded that 4.7 percent were learning disabled.

The difficulty in arriving at an adequate prevalence estimate of learning disabilities in a school population is similar to or even greater than that found in mental retardation (see Chapter 4). Some define a learning disabled child educationally as one who is below grade- and age-level achievement. Others consider a child learning disabled only when the child has a developmental learning disability (attention, language, and so forth) that manifests itself in educational retardation. The lack of agreement on who is or is not learning disabled has resulted in the inclusion of children with minor learning difficulties, similar to the inclusion of slow learners in classes for the mentally retarded. As a result, the enrollment in services for learned disabled has increased from year to year.

Table 9.1 presents the number and percentage of children receiving special education and related services in programs for the mentally retarded, speech impaired, and learning disabled from 1978 to 1981. It should be pointed out that the percentages for the speech impaired and mentally retarded populations have remained relatively constant over the years. The percentage for learning disabled children, however, has increased from 2.3 in 1978–1979 to 3.01 in 1980–1981. As indicated in the table, the largest enrollment is in programs for the learning disabled. Previous figures from the U.S. Office of Education concerning the enrollment of learning disabled children were 120,000 in 1969 and 260,000 in 1975. In 1980–1981 the enrollment had reached 1,455,135—a phenomenal increase.

TABLE 9.1
Handicapped Children Receiving Special Education and Related Services under Public Laws 94-142 and 89-313 (1978–1981)

	1978–1979		1979–1980		1980–1981	
	Total	Percent of Population	Total	Percent of Population	Total	Percent of Population
Speech impaired	1,214,994	2.4%	1,188,967	2.4%	1,177,792	2.4%
Mentally retarded	915,635	1.8	882,173	1.8	849,890	1.8
Learning disabled	1,154,430	2.3	1,281,379	2.6	1,455,135	3.0

Source: Adapted from W. Healey, B. Ackerman, C. Chappell, K. Perrin, and J. Stormer, *The prevalence of communicative disorders: A review of the literature* (Final Report). Rockville, Md.: American Speech-Language-Hearing Association, 1981, pp. 77–79.

CAUSES OF AND FACTORS CONTRIBUTING TO LEARNING DISABILITIES

Causes of Learning Disabilities

From an educational point of view, the etiology of a condition rarely has relevance. To know that the etiology of a learning disability is brain injury or cerebral dysfunction does not alter the educational program. Whether or not a teacher knows the etiology, he or she uses a developmental curriculum, starting where the child is in behavior and assisting the child in going up the developmental ladder step by step.

When medical treatment is involved, a knowledge of etiology is often very valuable. One teacher, for example, struggled for several months without success with a child's remedial reading problem. If it had been suspected earlier that the child had a brain tumor, the teacher would have made a medical referral. A medical diagnosis in that case was eventually helpful and led to an operation for a brain tumor. It is important for a teacher of learning disabled children to know something about etiology in order to aid in diagnosis and remediation and to know if and when such knowledge is applicable. Gaddes (1980) thinks that neuropsychological knowledge aids the diagnosis of a learning disability and that this understanding can lead to more effective prescribing of remediation.

Researchers have attempted to identify the factors that inhibit a child's ability to learn. Some of the most common etiological factors will be discussed here briefly. They include (1) brain dysfunctions, (2) genetic factors, (3) nutritional and other environmental factors, and (4) biochemical factors.

Brain Dysfunction

The brain is the control center of the body. When something goes wrong with the brain, something happens to any or all of the physical, emotional, and mental functions of the organism. Scientists have not yet been able to specify or precisely locate the functions of the central nervous system sufficiently to explain all behavior. What we have at present is only partial knowledge of the relationship of the central nervous system to behavior and partial knowledge of the relationship of behavior to special disabilities.

Although the term *learning disabilities* is relatively new, the condition in adults and children is as old as humanity. Injuries to the brain that led to the loss of the ability to understand language, to speak, or to read led neurologists to investigate the relationship between brain function and communication. In the United States Samuel T. Orton (1928) proposed a theory of cerebral dominance, which could account for a child's stuttering or inability to read. Orton postulated that when neither of the two cerebral hemispheres was dominant over the other, the child began twisting symbols and seeing *no* as *on* and *saw* as *was*. He called it the theory of *strephosymbolia* (twisted symbols). Since the time of Orton there has been less emphasis on neurologic factors but greater emphasis on psychoeducational factors and on methods of remediation.

Genetics

Efforts have been made by a large number of people to study the heritability of reading, writing, and language disabilities. Such studies have been made on families that have had many members with reading or language problems. Hallgren (1950) conducted an extensive family study in Sweden. The prevalence of reading, writing, and spelling disabilities among the relatives of those diagnosed as dyslexic provided strong evidence that such conditions run in families and are consequently inherited. Hermann (1959) contrasted identical twins, all of whom were dyslexic, with fraternal twins. Only one-third of the fraternal twins showed both children of the pair to be dyslexic. In the other two-thirds of the fraternal twins, only one child of the pair was dyslexic. Because the identical twins had a greater frequency of reading disabilities (dyslexia) than did the fraternal twins, he accepted that kind of evidence to support the hypothesis that reading, spelling, and writing disabilities are inherited.

DeFries and Decker (1981) conducted the most extensive family study of reading disability at the Institute of Behavioral Genetics at the University of Colorado. They administered a series of psychometric tests to 125 reading disabled children and their parents and siblings, and to 125 control families. The reading disabled children obtained lower scores on some cognitive tests (spatial reasoning and symbol processing speed). The researchers concluded that the data "conclusively demonstrates the familial nature of reading disability . . ."(p. 24).

Environmental Deprivation and Nutrition

In this area the two problems that have been studied most are the lack of early environmental stimulation and the effects of severe malnutrition at an early age. These two etiological factors are not always independent, for, in many circumstances, malnutrition and lack of early psychological stimulation are both operating on the same child. Cruickshank and Hallahan (1973) reviewed and summarized the studies on environmental deprivation and malnutrition. They concluded from the studies conducted on both animals and children that although a definite relationship between malnutrition and learning disabilities cannot be established, the bulk of the evidence suggests that severe malnutrition at an early age can affect the central nervous system and hence the learning and development of the child.

Biochemical Factors

There are many children with learning disabilities who are not known to have neurologic problems or any history of genetic or environmental deprivation. One hypothesis is that they have some unknown biochemical imbalance comparable to phenylketonuria as seen in the mentally retarded.

It should be stated that the use of drugs to ameliorate learning disabilities is still a largely untested area; scientific studies to determine the values and dangers have yet to be done. For example, the use of drugs with hyperactive children with learning disabilities has resulted in considerable controversy. From time to time a report that a certain drug can ameliorate learning disabilities appears, but such reports generally are not substantiated by further research. In an extensive review of research on the use of drugs, Adelman and Comfers (1977) stated that stimulant drugs sometimes have a short-term effect in decreasing hyperactivity.

Factors Contributing to Learning Disabilities

In the past much emphasis was placed on finding the cause of a malady, but with learning disabled children the cause is frequently unclear and often unknown. While the neurological cause may be irremediable, the behavior can be remediated.

For that reason diagnosticians seek out associated or contributing factors that have interfered with learning instead of causes. For example, a sound-blending disability may contribute to poor reading in some children when certain methods of teaching reading (such as a phonic method) are used. It should not be considered a cause of poor reading, rather it is a contributing factor because deaf children learn to read and do not have sound-blending ability.

The search for contributing factors within the child (physical or psychological) or in the environment focuses on those conditions that have been found to occur frequently with the disability under consideration and that need correction or amelioration. These contributing factors may be (1) physical, (2) environmental (including instructional), or (3) psychological.

1. *Physical conditions* that may contribute to a learning disability include visual and hearing defects, confused laterality and spatial orientation, poor body image, hyperkinesis (hyperactivity), undernourishment, and other physical problems that can inhibit the child's ability to learn.

2. *Psychological conditions*, referred to in this text as *developmental learning disabilities*, include attention disorders, poor auditory or visual perception and discrimination, language delay or disorder, inadequate thinking abilities, defective short-term auditory or visual memory, and so on.

3. *Environmental factors* refer to conditions in the home, community, and school that may adversely affect the child's normal development psychologically and academically. These include traumatic experiences, family pressures, instructional inadequacies, or lack of school experience. Although these conditions affect school progress, these children may not be considered learning disabled unless the environmental conditions have contributed to deficits in psychological processes of memory, attention, and so forth.

The Relationship Between Causes and Contributing Factors

The possible relationships between causes and contributing factors may be explained as follows:

1. According to some authorities, the aberrations of behavior are caused by an abnormality of the biological organism due to a brain dysfunction, a biochemical imbalance, genetics, or nutritional or environmental deprivation. The biological scientist hopes that the search for causes will lead to prevention.

2. The physical conditions of defects in vision, hearing, and laterality are not all caused by brain damage or genetics or biological imbalances, but may occur for other reasons. Unlike etiological factors, these difficulties in most cases can be overcome by physicians or educators. Vision can be corrected or improved by vision training. Hearing can be aided by hearing aids, by auditory training, or by both. Physical and occupational therapists can help correct problems of laterality or physical incoordination. If the contributing factor can be trained or ameliorated, the condition should be considered a contributing factor rather than a cause.

3. The deficient psychological or developmental conditions can be improved through proper special instruction. Some physical conditions are associated with psychological deficits. A child who has a significant uncorrected eye muscle imbalance may have a fusion problem that may be contributing to a deficiency in visual memory. Sometimes a delay in one developmental function may delay another developmental ability. A deficit in selective attention and auditory memory may be related to a delay in language development.

4. Deficits in academic achievement may be related to developmental learning disabilities. For example, a language disorder or a significant attention deficit may contribute to a retardation in reading or arithmetic.

5. In some cases social and occupational maladjustment is related to significant educational retardation. It has been known for some time that delinquent children are educationally retarded. This does not imply a cause-and-effect relationship, for we are not certain whether the delinquency influences educational retardation, or whether educational retardation contributes to delinquency, or whether each interacts with the other to produce an unfavorable result.

The differences between causes and contributing factors are fundamental. The purpose of searching for causes is to prevent the condition. The purpose of searching for contributing factors is to remediate the condition. Education, conceived in a broad sense, is designed to ameliorate or remove the physical and developmental contributing factors.

DIAGNOSIS OF CHILDREN WITH LEARNING DISABILITIES

The major problem in identifying and diagnosing children with learning disabilities is to pinpoint the atypical behavior, explain it, differentiate it from similar problems of other handicapped children *(differential diagnosis)*, and determine the remedial program best suited to ameliorating the disability. Identification and diagnosis are somewhat different for preschool than for school-age children. At the school-age level the identification process begins when the child fails in learning to read, to spell, to write, or to calculate. At the preschool level the child is identified through developmental disabilities because he or she has not yet had the opportunity to fail in academic subjects.

For the child of any age, however, there are general criteria for making a differential diagnosis. Is the child's atypical behavior a disability, and if so, what is the nature of the disability that requires remediation? Some of the major determinants are:

1. Does the child have a learning disability or is the lack of achievement in language, reading, or other areas the result of some other handicap, such as impaired hearing, general mental retardation, lack of instruction, or lack of opportunity to learn? The reason for differential diagnosis is that the remediation of a child with a learning disability is different from the instructional program for children with other handicaps, even though the observable problem, such as a language deficit, may be the same. For example, delayed speech and language in a child may be the result of a marked hearing impairment, severe mental retardation, or an emotional problem. A deaf child is taught to compensate for hearing loss by developing communication through sensory avenues other than hearing, whereas a child who does not understand language but who has no hearing loss or general mental retardation is taught primarily to process language through the sense of hearing.

2. If it is decided that the child has a learning disability, the next question is "What abilities and disabilities does the child have?" Inherent in the concepts of learning disabilities is the concept of intraindividual differences, or discrepancies among the child's areas of development. If a child has been in school under ordinary instruction for three years and has failed to learn to read, the diagnostician looks for areas in which he or she *has* learned. Is the child's language average? Does he or she have adequate mental ability to learn to read? Has the child learned other school subjects such as arithmetic? If the deficit is in reading while all other abilities and achievements are average or near average for the child's age and mental ability, then the child can be said to have a learning disability in reading and will be diagnosed as a child with a learning disability.

3. The third question is how can the child's deficit be explained? If mental retardation or sensory deficits are present, the explanation is clear. If emotional or environmental deterrents are present, the factors leading to the disability are also clear. When explanations are not present, the diagnostician asks what contributing or inhibiting factor can be found in the child's information processing system that can account for the task deficit. If the child does not understand oral language, is the disability the result of a marked deficit in auditory discrimination, in vocabulary, in understanding syntax, or in other factors in auditory processing? The determination of the exact nature of the associated deficit is essential to organizing an appropriate remedial program.

Diagnosis of Preschool Children As indicated earlier, the identification of preschool children is not based on failure in academic subjects, but is more directly related to behavior observed by parents and preschool teachers on tasks typical of the child's agemates. Many deficits can be observed in young children. Among them are (1) failure to understand or respond to meaningful expressions such as oral language or visual symbols; (2) failure to be in tune with the environment or the child's own relationship to it, including poor motor control, body image, and visual and auditory discrimination; and (3) lack of attention and related disorders. In diagnosing preschool children an examiner relies on observations of parents and teachers, rating scales, informal clinical diagnoses, and norm- and criterion-referenced testing. The task of a diagnostician is analogous to that of a detective. Both must gather clues and formulate and discard hypotheses until arriving at the solution that best fits the available evidence.

Language Disabilities

The most common learning disability noted at the preschool level is a language disability. To diagnose a child with language disabilities, a psychoeducational examiner does the following:

1. obtains a description of the language behavior as observed by the parent, the preschool teacher, or both
2. peruses the medical record to see whether there are possible explanations from a medical point of view
3. studies the family situation to determine whether there are factors in the home that contribute to the disability
4. examines the child, using formal and informal tests to determine the abilities and disabilities of the child in
   a. understanding language
   b. relating things heard with past experiences
   c. talking (what is the extent of the child's vocabulary and use of syntax?)
5. determines what the child can do and cannot do in a specific area (if, for example, the child functions well in most areas but does not talk, the next step is to find out if he or she understands language: if the child does not understand oral language, the next step is to find out if he or she can discriminate between words, between phonemes, or between common sounds in the environment)
6. organizes a remedial program at the point at which the child can perform, and moves step by step into areas in which the child could not initially perform

Perceptual-Motor Disabilities

In diagnosing perceptual-motor disabilities in preschool children, a psychoeducational examiner asks the usual questions about medical and home background and through ratings, interviews, and formal and informal tests attempts to discover the contributing factors and significant manifest difficulties of the child. Some of the questions an examiner tries to answer through the psychoeducational assessment are:

1. Can the child interpret the environment through the significance of what he or she sees (visual decoding or visual reception)?
2. Can the child recognize the whole when only a part is seen (visual closure)?
3. Can the child recognize visual objects and pictures rapidly (speed of perception)?
4. Can a child recognize a specific object embedded in a picture (figure-ground perception)?
5. Can the child express ideas in motor terms (nonverbal) through gestures, dramatics, and writing (motor expression)?

Attentional and Other Disabilities

The psychoeducational examiner, through observations and formal and informal tests, attempts to answer questions such as the following:

1. Can the child sustain attention to oral or visual stimuli?
2. Is the child highly distractible?
3. Does the child persevere in the face of difficulty or initial failure?
4. Can the child discriminate between two pictures or objects (visual discrimination), between two words or sounds (auditory discrimination), or between two objects touched and felt (haptic discrimination)?
5. Is the child oriented in space? Does he or she have right-left discrimination?
6. Can the child remember immediately what was heard, seen, or felt?
7. Can the child imitate the examiner orally or gesturally? Can the child mimic?
8. Does the child have adequate visual-motor coordination? Is the child clumsy?

This list can be expanded indefinitely, but it illustrates the questions a psychoeducational examiner has to raise in diagnosing disabilities.

Diagnosis of Academic Disabilities At the school-age level, teachers usually refer children for diagnosis because they are failing in basic school subjects (reading, writing, spelling, and arithmetic). After mental retardation, deafness, blindness, lack of opportunity, lack of motivation, and other conditions are excluded as causes, many learning disability authorities assume that associated developmental disorders are inhibiting the learning of those subjects. Consequently, a diagnosis of the academic disability requires an assessment of many variables.

To assess a child's learning disability and to organize an appropriate remedial method for the amelioration of the disability, it is necessary to follow a systematic procedure in diagnosis. The diagnostic process generally proceeds in five stages or steps, namely: (1) determining whether the child's learning problem is specific, general, or spurious; (2) analyzing the behavior descriptive of the specific problem; (3) discovering possible physical, environmental, and psychological contributing factors; (4) evolving a diagnostic inference (hypothesis) on the basis of the behavior and the contributing factors; and (5) organizing a systematic remedial program based on the diagnostic inference. These five steps apply to the diagnosis of a child with any academic disability. The five steps in diagnosing a reading disability, the most common type of learning disability, illustrate the process.

Miss Jones, a third-grade teacher, had an 8-year-old boy in her class who was unable to read beyond the primer level. After working with Carl for four months without success, she decided there was something drastically wrong with the boy because he seemed not to learn readily nor to remember what he had learned from one day to the next. She consequently referred Carl to a child-study clinic.

1. **The first step taken at the clinic was to determine whether the learning problem was specific, general, or spurious.** To that end a general intelligence test was administered to find out if the child had the mental capacity necessary to learn to read. If Carl should be found to have an IQ score of 50, one would not expect him to be able to read. He was found, however, to have an IQ score of 104 on the Stanford-Binet Intelligence Scale. He also scored at a second-grade level on an arithmetic computation test, although, as Miss Jones had predicted, he scored at a first-grade level (6 years, 3 months) on a series of reading tests. The psychologist analyzing the problem now had the following information:

Chronological age	8-4
Mental age	8-10
Language age	8-2

Arithmetic computational age   7-8
Reading age   6-3

There was a discrepancy between the chronological age, mental age, language age, and arithmetic achievement age on the one hand, and the level of reading on the other hand. The child had attended school with fair regularity, had had adequate teaching for over two years, and still had not learned to read. It was clear that a problem did exist and that it was specific, not general. Carl could not read although the apparent capacity was there, as indicated by his other abilities and achievements.

2. **The second step taken at the clinic was to analyze the behavior descriptive of the specific problem.** It was necessary to specify the exact nature of the problem, to delineate in greater detail than before just what the child could and could not do in the reading process. It was necessary to know more than the *level* of reading. It was necessary to know *how* the child read. What faulty habits did he display in reading? How did he attack new words? What kinds of words did he confuse? What kinds of errors did he make? How fast did he try to read? A skilled diagnostician can answer some of those questions by observing the child read, but diagnostic tests are important additional aids to clinical judgment. In the case of Carl diagnostic and other reading tests revealed that the child did not make use of phonics. Although he could tell the sounds of the different letters in isolation, he sounded only the first letter or two of a word. It was also noted that he had had difficulty learning to write his name and found it difficult to reproduce short words from memory. He guessed at most words from context or from interpreting the pictures in the book. He knew a few sight words but often confused similar words such as *that* and *what*, *the* and *ten*, *see* and *she*.

3. **The next step taken was to discover the possible physical, environmental, and psychological factors contributing to the disability.** The clinic staff knew that there are many reasons why children fail to learn to read. Did Carl have poor school attendance? Was there an abnormal home background? Was he culturally deprived? An investigation of those factors proved negative. No such conditions were found that could explain his reading retardation. A medical examination revealed no abnormalities. Visual acuity was normal, and on an audiometric test the boy appeared to have normal hearing. His inability to learn to read was therefore not the result of visual or hearing impairment. Should Carl's condition merely be labeled "dyslexia"? Should it be assumed that he must

be brain injured? The staff knew that those designations would be of little help to the teacher since they would only be substituting the word *dyslexia*, a medical term, for the term *severe reading disability*, an educational term.

There remained one other handicap for the clinic to investigate. Was it possible that the child was so emotionally disturbed that he was unable to concentrate and learn? The teacher reported that he could not concentrate on the reading workbooks she gave him, that his attention to reading materials was very short, and that he resisted pressure to read. A psychiatric examination did not confirm the hypothesis of emotional disturbance, for Carl appeared normal in interpersonal relations and did concentrate on other tasks not involving reading and spelling. His concentration on arithmetic lessons, for example, was adequate. The psychiatrist concluded that the inability to learn to read was not the result of an emotional condition.

The next question was, Are there physical or psychological correlates that have contributed to the reading disability? In the search for correlates that might contribute to the reading difficulty and at the same time be the springboard for remediation, the psychoeducational diagnostician administered tests that might show some developmental contributing factors. The tests did show marked intraindividual differences in the boy's perceptual abilities and in some of his mental operations. Although functioning at or above his chronological age in most of the tests Carl was very deficient in visual sequential memory (the ability to remember a sequence of figures or letters), auditory closure (the ability to recognize a word when only a portion is provided—"rabb" for *rabbit*), and auditory synthesis (sound blending). Those are deficiencies quite commonly associated (together or in isolation) with poor reading.

4. **The next step taken was to find a diagnostic hypothesis (inference) based on the errors in reading and the contributing factors observed in the second and third steps.** The diagnostic inference is one of the most important factors in diagnosis. It involves specifying the relationship among symptoms and the contributing factors that have inhibited a child's learning to talk, read, write, or spell. It requires experienced clinicians who can use the relevant tests, select the relevant facts, and put the pieces together in organized form so as to explain the child's inability to learn. The diagnostic hypothesis must select the relevant variables in the case and pinpoint the specific disabilities on which the remedial program can be organized.

For Carl two working hypotheses evolved from the information at hand. (1) From the observation that the boy did not sound more than the first letter or two of a word although he knew the sounds of all of them in isolation, it was conjectured that he had not learned the skill of sound blending. That conjecture was verified by the child's low score on a sound-blending test. That disability would explain why he had so little success in trying to use phonics in deciphering unknown words. (2) The second inference came from a low score on a visual sequential memory test coupled with the fact that the boy had learned very few sight words and showed confusion and uncertainty on many of the ones he thought he knew. The hypothesis was that Carl's inability to remember a sequence of letters made it difficult for him to identify sight words because he had poor memory of what the complete word was supposed to look like. The hypothesis was corroborated by his difficulty in learning to write his name and to reproduce short words from memory. The two handicaps, inability to use a phonic approach in identifying words and inability to use a sight-word approach, gave this boy no usable technique for decoding the printed page.

5. **The final step now required by Public Law 94–142 (Education for All Handicapped Children Act) in any diagnosis is organizing a systematic remedial program—an individualized education program (IEP)—based on the diagnostic hypothesis.** The crux of a diagnosis is the effectiveness of the remedial program it generates. The program should be based on the inferences made in the fourth step and should attempt to alleviate the symptoms and, if possible, the contributing factors observed. This IEP, which must be reviewed annually by a committee includes (a) a statement of the child's present level of educational performance, (b) a statement of annual goals and short-term objectives, (c) a statement of specific special education and related services to be provided, (d) other needed administrative services. In Carl's case recommendations were given for improving visual memory for words, suggesting particularly the use of a kinesthetic method in learning new words and thereby training the use of visual imagery and visual memory (writing words and phrases from memory) in the process of reading. Likewise, specific suggestions were made for developing sound-blending ability, which in most cases is rather easily acquired once the knack is understood. The remedial program began by teaching the boy words and phrases by the kinesthetic method (to develop visualization ability); later, exercises in sound blending and phonics were introduced. Through this approach Carl learned to read.

EDUCATIONAL ADAPTATIONS FOR CHILDREN WITH LEARNING DISABILITIES

Remediation Strategies As we have seen, children with learning disabilities compose quite a diverse group. It should be no surprise then to find that the strategies and teaching approaches designed to help those children are also quite diverse. It is possible to cluster the various approaches into three broad educational strategies: (1) task training, in which the emphasis is on the sequencing and simplification of the task to be learned; (2) ability or process training, in which the focus is on the remediation of a specific developmental disability; and (3) ability- or process-task training, in which the first two approaches are combined and integrated into one remedial program.

Task or Skill Training

One of the fundamental strategies that teachers have always used with children who are having difficulty in learning in school is to modify the nature of the task to be learned. In most instances the modification is simplifying the task by breaking up the lessons into component subskills—into smaller and simpler units. Task analysis (previously discussed in the chapter on mental retardation) allows the child to master elements of the task and then synthesize the elements or components into the complex level required by the total task.

The remedial approach for failure in the complex psychomotor skill of swimming, for example, may be to teach the child how to kick his or her legs, how to tread water, how to keep from breathing under water, and so forth. The child is then asked to put each of those skills together through supervised practice until the child demonstrates the ability to complete the complex skill by swimming across the pool. Similarly, in academic subjects such as reading and long division, the task analysis strategy would be to simplify complex tasks so that the components can be mastered independently. The teacher can break up the complex task of reading a paragraph into (1) learning syllables or phonetic elements in a word, (2) learning separate words in the sentence, (3) learning a sentence, and (4) building up the skills to the point of eventually reading the paragraph. The task analysis approach does not assume any special learning problem or ability deficit within or intrinsic to the child other than lack of experience and practice with the task.

Ysseldyke and Salvia (1974) have advanced two theoretical models for teaching children with learning disabilities, namely: (1) analyzing the child's abilities and disabilities and (2) analyzing the task and the direct training of the terminal behavior or task. They concluded that the task analysis or behavioral approach is the "most parsimonious." That point of view is supported by the applied behavior analysts who advocate (1) finding out what the child can and cannot do in a particular skill, (2) determining whether or not the child has the behaviors needed to succeed in the task, (3) defining the goals in observable terms, and (4) organizing a systematic remedial program using reinforcement techniques. The applied behavior analysts do not infer processes or abilities that underlie difficulties but rely solely on the child's interactional history and the current behavior and environmental situation. They feel that their approach, which is task oriented and observable, is the most straightforward approach, and to some it is the only approach needed.

BEHAVIOUR ANALYSTS

This is the approach often used by the regular teacher in remediating minor learning problems in children. For such problems aid can be obtained from the resource or consulting teacher in task analysis and direct teaching. Because no developmental learning disability is apparent, the direct teaching of reading, writing, spelling, or arithmetic after a task analysis can be accomplished by the regular teacher.

Not all theorists agree that the training of specific skills is effective. They state that a complex task like reading cannot be subdivided into a series of discrete skills and then reassembled. Reading is greater than the sum of its parts. Furthermore, it is questionable whether children learn the sequence of skills in the order that adults who have task analyzed the reading process have determined. Torgesen (1979) has pointed out that it may be a mistake to ignore psychological process disorders when dealing with children who are learning disabled. The normal child who has no neurological or psychological impediments to learning profits from direct skill-instruction procedures. This approach, however, may not apply to the severely learning disabled child who also exhibits a developmental learning disability.

Ability or Process Training

In the second major remedial strategy the teacher or remedial specialist identifies a particular disability in the development of an individual child that, if not corrected, would continue to inhibit the learning processes regardless of how the teacher reconstructs the task. In such a case the teaching emphasis becomes focused on remedial attempts to overcome the particular disability that seems to be blocking progress.

In the example of the child who could not swim, the problem

might have been the child's extremely weak upper arm and shoulder muscles. The remediation strategy in that instance would be the successive building up of arm and shoulder strength through particular exercises, weight lifting, and so forth until the child had the minimum ability or skill necessary to allow him or her to perform the tasks required. Similarly, in the case of a severe reading retardation, the child may have a disability or intrinsic deficiency in visual memory, in sound blending, or in language that interferes with the ability to remember words or to synthesize sounds the child recognizes into a word.

Process training refers to special training procedures that attempt to develop or ameliorate psychological deficits or developmental learning disabilities in children, such as attention, language, discrimination, thinking, memory, and so forth. These are considered prerequisite skills to future learning. Special exercises in the discrimination of geometric forms, it is expected, will transfer later on to the discrimination of letters and words. Actually, the curriculum of the nursery school and kindergarten is designed to develop these psychological processes. If a child does not pay attention, the teacher attempts to create an environment that will aid the child in selective attention. If the child does not listen or does not understand directions, the teacher attempts to improve auditory reception. If the child has difficulty in problem solving, or in reasoning, or in talking, the teacher attempts to improve these processes.

There has been much controversy concerning process training. Many believe that memory or attention or reasoning or other psychological processes cannot be improved by specific training. One of the difficulties these controversies focus on is that memory or attention cannot be trained in isolation. They have to be trained in something; for example, attention to a task, or memory for words or pictures. The major point is that if a child is trained to remember pictures, will this memory ability transfer or generalize to memory for words?

Research in these areas has been equivocal. Hammill and Larsen (1974) reviewed thirty-eight studies of psycholinguistic training that had been evaluated by the ITPA and concluded that "the idea that psycholinguistic constructs, as measured by the ITPA, can be trained by existing techniques remains nonvalidated" (p. 11). In a re-evaluation of the same studies, Lund, Foster, and McCall-Perez (1978) questioned the conclusions of Hammill and Larsen. The re-evaluation noted that a substantial number of the studies did produce positive results, that many of the studies had been poorly controlled, and that Hammill and Larsen were not justified in their conclusions. In reviewing the criticisms Hammill and Larsen

(1978) attempted to justify their earlier conclusions by stating that "the overwhelming consensus of research evidence concerning the effectiveness of psycholinguistic training is that it remains essentially nonvalidated" (p. 412). Kavale (1981) used meta-analysis, a statistical method used to combine the findings from many different research studies, on the same studies reported by Hammill and Larsen and concluded that "extant research, contrary to previous research reviews which were found to underestimate the positive effects of intervention, has demonstrated the effectiveness of psycholinguistic training"(p. 496).

Process (Ability)-Task Approach

Most specialists believe that for the ordinary child with problems evolving from poor teaching or lack of opportunity, the task training approach is adequate and effective. Children with severe disabilities as in the case of Carl, however, require "child analysis" as well as "task analysis." The resultant remediation will involve ability and task training in the same remedial procedure; that is, teaching the child to use a particular process in accomplishing the desired task. We can label this approach as *process-task training* or as *aptitude-task interaction*. It means that we integrate the process and task in remediation. Instead of teaching visual discrimination of abstract, meaningless symbols, we will train visual discrimination of letters and words. The process-task approach integrates remediation of the process dysfunction with the task development as analyzed. That approach is the one generally used by those who analyze the abilities and disabilities of the child and who make a task analysis of the sequence of skills required by the task itself. Those who practice the process-task or aptitude-task-interaction approach are considered diagnostic-prescriptive teachers because they do both child analysis and task analysis and match the instructional materials with the ability of the child to respond.

The following example in reading illustrates the process-task approach to remediation. Tom, who had attended school regularly up to the age of 9, was referred because he was unable to learn to read in spite of his tested IQ score of 120 on the WISC. Analysis of the child's information-processing abilities showed a deficit in visual memory. He was unable to reproduce in writing and from memory words presented to him visually. He demonstrated the deficit in visual memory both on informal and formal tests. The procedure for process-task remediation in this case called for a program that would develop visual memory with the words and phrases to be taught. This procedure of training the ability of visual memory on the task itself is process-task training. The Fernald Kinesthetic

Method (Fernald, 1943) is a system of training memory for words, not in the abstract—as is done in ability training of memory for digits or objects alone—but directly with the words and phrases needed by the child in learning to read. The Fernald method is a process-task approach since it trains visual memory of words and phrases.

Raschke and Young (1976a; 1976b) have supported the process-task approach. They compared the behavior-analysis model with the process model. They state that neither approach alone has the answer and propose what they call a *dialectic-teaching approach,* which they assert can integrate the two approaches into one system. Essentially the model assesses the abilities and disabilities of the children (intraindividual differences), makes task analyses of the skills to be learned, and prescribes remediation in the functions and skills to be developed. This dialectic system they maintain "permits the teacher to assess, program, instruct, and evaluate the child's psycholinguistic characteristics in the same system as his skill competencies and consequential variables" (1976b, p. 245). Lerner (1981) has discussed the concept of skill training versus process training and agrees that both process training and skill training are "integral parts of the field of learning disabilities" (p. 178) and are both needed for diagnosing and remediating learning disabled children.

It should be noted that in some instances the distinctions among these three remediation strategies are not clear-cut. All three remedial approaches are adequate in different situations and with different children. Each is valuable when used in the appropriate setting. Direct task training is sufficient for minor academic problems and for the majority of corrective academic problems. The process remediation approach is suitable for training the ability for its own sake, especially at the preschool level. The process-task approach may be necessary for the severer cases involving a dual problem of a specific developmental disability and an academic disability. Such a disability requires the specialized help of a learning disability specialist who can organize a remedial program that would include the training of the developmental disability and the academic disability.

The controversy over direct task training versus process-task training may not be warranted. One approach, task training, is suitable for the mild problems that do not need the degree of amelioration that a developmental learning disability does; the other, process-task training, is the preferred remedial method for a child who has an obvious developmental learning disability that has interfered with the development of academic achievement. Each

[margin note: behaviour-analysis model combined with process model.]

teacher needs to apply or match the method best suited to the child and his or her needs at a particular stage in development.

Remediation Programs　As indicated earlier, learning disabled children fall into two broad categories, academically disabled and developmentally disabled. The programs used with learning disabled children will be discussed briefly. These include remedial programs for (1) developmental learning disabilities, including oral language disorders, and (2) academic learning disabilities.

Developmental Learning Disabilities

The developmental learning disabilities are rarely remediated in isolation. Memory, for example, is developed in relation to a task. If spelling is being taught we devise strategies for developing memory for words so that when the child is to reproduce a word he or she will remember how it looked. Similarly, attention is developed in combination with a task since attending behavior must be developed in relation to a task. Thinking, reasoning, problem solving, and categorizing are likewise developed in reading, language, and arithmetic, and not in isolation. The process-task strategy discussed in the preceding section is necessary to remediation of developmental learning disabilities.

The curriculum of the preschool is a curriculum for enhancing developmental abilities, usually referred to as *cognitive* abilities. This is clearly described by Lerner, Mardel-Czudnowski, and Goldenberg in *Special Education for the Early Childhood Years* (1981). In addition to programs for developing motor control, sensory motor integration, and perceptual-motor development, the authors deal with teaching cognitive skills. They define cognitive skills as a series of mental activities that involve knowing and recognizing, organizing ideas, developing concepts, problem solving, remembering, understanding relationships, drawing inferences, generalizing, and evaluating. This list is similar to the list of developmental learning abilities described in Figure 9.2. (Those interested in programs and activities at the preschool level for ameliorating deficits in concept formation, spatial relations, number concepts, classification skills, sequencing, and so forth, should consult the sources listed in "References of Special Interest" at the end of this chapter for detailed suggestions.)

PERCEPTUAL-MOTOR DISABILITIES　Initially, the perceptual-motor approach to learning disabilities arose from concentrated study of brain-injured children. In the United States Strauss and Lehtinen's publication in 1947 of *The Psychopathology of the Brain-Injured Child* generated widespread interest in the problem of specific learning disabilities. Strauss's main thesis was that children with brain injuries incurred before, during, or after birth are subject to major disorders in perception, thinking, and behavior; and that these disorders affect the child's ability to learn to read, write, spell, or calculate. Strauss and Lehtinen's educational methods consisted of instructional procedures and environmental changes that would correct or ameliorate the disturbances in perception, thinking, and behavior. Those techniques were integrated with procedures for teaching reading, writing, spelling, and arithmetic. Strauss and Lehtinen's work stimulated many subsequent developments in the study and remediation of learning disabilities. Among these developments are the perceptual-motor approaches of William Cruickshank, Newell Kephart, and Raymond Barsch.

While Cruickshank et al. (1961) conducted research on the characteristics (dissociation, perseveration, figure-ground confusion, and so on) and treatment of hyperactive brain-injured children, Kephart (1964) stressed the perceptual-motor match. According to Kephart, who minimized brain dysfunction and emphasized developmental psychology, the earliest encounters of a child with the environment are through motor activities, and this muscular movement is a prerequisite for later learning. The normal child acquires normal patterns of movement by stages.

Kephart's approach to motor pattern development and remediation is to fill in the gaps in the sequence of generalizations that enable the child to integrate and manipulate the information received from the environment, such as an understanding of form, space, and rhythm. He therefore recommends various training activities such as: (1) sensory-motor training using walking boards, trampolines, making "angels in the snow," and various games to teach variations in movement, rhythm, and bilateral as well as unilateral abilities; (2) chalkboard activities designed to develop movement patterns and matching visual perceptions; (3) ocular-motor training to help the child match his or her visual control to the motor and kinesthetic patterns that have been learned; and (4) form perception exercises using pegboards, stick figures, and puzzles, for example.

Kephart's approach is applicable to certain children with specific perceptual-motor problems, but its proponents do not claim that the procedures are beneficial for all children with learning disabilities. Children who do not have visual-motor perceptual problems but who have retardation in auditory, vocal, and language disorders may require different kinds of remediation.

Barsch (1965, 1967), who like Kephart also worked with Strauss, developed what he called a *movigenic* curriculum. He alleged that learning difficulties encountered by children are due to deficits in movement efficiency, and so his remedial program is designed to improve movement efficiency or movement coordination. Cratty and Martin (1969), Delacato (1963), and Valett (1967) also stressed motor exercises as an effective procedure for helping learning disabled children.

VISUAL-PERCEPTUAL DISABILITIES Another group of workers has been involved in visual-perceptual training. Among these are Getman (1965), an optometrist, and Frostig and Horne (1964). The latter developed tests for five visual-perceptual skills, and also developed a remedial program for ameliorating difficulties in the five perceptual areas.

Research on the efficiency of the Frostig-Horne remedial program has not provided clear-cut positive evaluations. Myers and Hammill (1976) have reported contradictory results. The use of the materials appears to increase children's scores on the Frostig Developmental Test of Visual Perception, but whether these children show improvement in reading achievement remains a question. Kavale (1982), on the other hand, found a positive relationship between perceptual skills and reading achievement. Contrary to Myers and Hammill's report he found that "visual perception is an important correlate in the complex variables related to reading achievement" (p. 51).

ORAL LANGUAGE DISABILITIES One definition of language could be "any form of oral or written communication." This discussion of remediation of language disorders will be confined, however, to auditory-verbal or auditory-receptive disabilities, which involve (1) receptive language (understanding the spoken word), (2) subvocal thinking (the inner process of manipulating verbal concepts), and (3) expressive language. Further discussion of language and speech development and of language disorders is found in the chapter on communication disorders.

Johnson and Myklebust (1967) evolved methods of remediation for what they called *psychoneurological learning disabilities*. These disabilities included reauditorization, or the inability to recall words the child has learned; auditory motor integration, or the inability to imitate or repeat words; and deficiencies in syntax. Remedial methods included (1) beginning language training early, (2) teaching the child to understand oral language before training oral

reauditorization

auditory motor integration

expression, (3) using simple words and simultaneously presenting an experience, (4) selecting the vocabulary to be taught based on the child's experience, (5) teaching concepts, and (6) beginning with the child's immediate concerns—such as parts of the body—and gradually progressing to more complex oral language. The system begins with training reception, then expression, then syntax, followed by reading and writing.

McGinnis (1963), a teacher of deaf children at the Central Institute for the Deaf in St. Louis, found that some children who lacked oral language did not have a hearing loss but still were unable to understand language or to talk. She recognized two types of language disorders: (1) receptive aphasia and (2) expressive aphasia. McGinnis believed that in both conditions inner language had been developed but auditory reception was deficient. To develop both auditory reception and verbal expression, McGinnis began remediation with an elemental approach using a phonetic method of first teaching sounds, next using the learned sounds to form words, and then matching the word with pictures to derive meaning. She called this strategy the *association method*. Once the child learned to understand some words and to express them, he or she began to add vocabulary from incidental learning.

While the McGinnis method emphasizes auditory receptive training, a remedial method based on behavior modification developed by Gray and Ryan (1973) emphasizes oral expressive behavior. Gray and Ryan's system teaches expressive language to non-language children using the principles of operant conditioning. The system carries the child step by step through a finite core of basic grammatical forms and is founded on the hypothesis that once a mini-language based on the grammatical forms is acquired, the child will continue to learn new forms and new grammatical rules through his or her own experiences. For each grammatical form taught, the child proceeds through a sequence of tasks involving the variables of (1) the response required from the child, (2) the stimulus provided, (3) the kind of reinforcement given, (4) the reinforcement schedule, (5) the criteria for proceeding to each next step, and (6) the model that lets the child know what response is expected. The system, known as the Monterey system because it was developed at Monterey, California, is formalized and highly structured. The method of presentation is standardized, allowing no variations. It is most valuable with children who have not developed speech and who need practice in expressive language.

A number of language development programs have been developed using the information processing model of the Illinois Test of Psycholinguistic Abilities (Kirk, McCarthy, and Kirk, 1968). This model, in simplified form, has been described by Karnes (1975) as follows:

Pretend that a person is a computer. A computer is a machine which receives information (INPUT) which may be stored (MEMORY) for later use or processed in some way (ORGANIZATION). Ultimately, the product of processing is expressed in some way, such as a tape or paper print-out (OUTPUT). People, to continue the analogy, receive information through their senses (RECEPTION). Sometimes this information is merely stored or remembered (MEMORY), but at other times partial information may be in some way completed for better understanding (CLOSURE) or several bits of information may be organized into a new and different whole (ASSOCIATION). Finally, expression is either verbal or gestural or both (VERBAL or MANUAL EXPRESSION). (p. 2)

The series of language training kits prepared by Karnes for parents and teachers include the following: *The Karnes Early Language Activities* (1975) for parents and teachers of children from 18 months to 3 years of age; *Learning Language at Home* (1977) for parents of children from 18 months to 5 years of age; and *Goal: Language Development*—Level I, 1972, for children 3 to 6; Level II, 1977, for children in grades two and above. Those programs are an outcome of Karnes's research with normal and exceptional children of school age and with parents and young children, especially of low-income families. The research with mothers of disadvantaged and handicapped infants led to the preparation of materials for very young children. Karnes, Zehrbach, and Teska (1974) have reported on research showing the efficacy of these programs with disadvantaged children. A follow-up study showed normal development through the third grade.

Using as a base a doctoral dissertation by James Smith (1962) in which it was found that mentally retarded children can profit from language lessons designed from the ITPA model, Dunn and Smith (1967) developed a series of instructional kits to be used for a whole class of children ages 2 to 8. Much emphasis is given to the development of oral language through exercises, games, and lessons. The lessons are arranged in sequence and are designed to develop the psycholinguistic processes of auditory and visual reception, association, and verbal and manual expression. Directions for the teacher are explicit and follow a systematic, well-rounded approach. These kits have been revised and extended by Dunn and others through 1982 by the American Guidance Service.

The MWM program, developed by Minskoff, Wiseman, and Minskoff (1975), is also based on the ITPA model. It is presented on two levels: Level I (1972) for ages 5 to 7 and Level II (1975) for ages 7 to 10. Each level includes three sets of materials: record booklets, a series of manuals for the teacher, and a series of workbooks for the children. An inventory of observable language behavior is contained in a record booklet used by the teacher in estimating each child's ability in the twelve subtests of the ITPA. The teacher answers a series of questions such as "Does the child have difficulty learning abstract words?" and "Does he or she have difficulty in self-care tasks?" Explicit directions for the use of materials and workbooks and for developing each task are presented in the teacher's manuals. Each level contains tasks in auditory and visual reception, auditory and visual association, verbal and manual expression, auditory and visual memory, grammatic and visual closure, and auditory closure and sound blending.

A number of other programs, some of them less formal, exist. Among the books that outline these programs are Bush and Giles's *Aids to Psycholinguistic Teaching* (1969), Lombardi and Lombardi's *ITPA: Clinical Interpretation and Remediation* (1977), and *Psycholinguistic Learning Disabilities: Diagnosis and Remediation* (Kirk and Kirk, 1971).

Academic Learning Disabilities

The most common academic disabilities for which teachers refer children for diagnosis are reading, spelling, arithmetic, and writing. As we have pointed out, many learning disabilities are not detected until the child begins to fail academically in school.

READING DISABILITIES Failure in reading is the most common and frequent indication of learning disabilities in school-age children. Nearly all children are exposed to reading experiences, sometimes beginning at home, sometimes in kindergarten, but most commonly when they are admitted to the first grade. When children fail to learn to read in the first or second grade, they are often referred by their teachers for an assessment to determine why they have not learned and what remedial procedure will ameliorate their problems.

A large number of remedial reading methods have been developed for children with learning disabilities. Included in this section will be brief descriptions of the kinesthetic method and phonic methods. For more extensive treatment, refer to Kirk, Kliebhan, and Lerner (1978).

The *kinesthetic method* was developed by Grace Fernald (1943; Fernald and Keller, 1921), a psychologist who became interested in children who had difficulty in learning to read or spell. The Fernald method of teaching disabled readers has withstood the test of

One of the steps in the first stage of Fernald's kinesthetic method requires the learning disabled child to trace the form of a known word while saying it. (Photo: Alan Carey/The Image Works.)

time and has been used in various forms by many teachers. Fernald (1943) has described in case studies the progress made by severely disabled readers following training by the kinesthetic method. The method involves four developmental stages: (1) In stage one the child traces the form of a known word while saying it, then writes it from memory, comparing each trial with the original model. (2) In stage two he or she just looks at the word or phrase while saying it, then tries to write it from memory, comparing the result with the model until successful. (3) In stage three the child writes the word but does not vocalize it until successful. (4) In stage four he or she begins to generalize and to read new words on the basis of experience with previously learned words.

The Fernald kinesthetic method has been beneficial to some children with certain kinds of reading disabilities, probably because the procedure encompasses important variables in learning. First, integrating the visual input with the motor experience strengthens the learning process because an additional sensory channel is used.

visual input integrated with motor experience

Second, by writing and using a motor movement, attention is focused on the visual task. Although the method has been called "kinesthetic," its more important function may be that of training visual sequential memory, or visualization ability and attention to detail, since the emphasis of the method is to *write* words from memory. Third, the method has a built-in feedback system. The child can write the word, check it with the original word, and, if it is incorrect, try again to write it from memory. It can be self-correctional. *The Fernald method is a good example of the process-task remedial procedure, for it remediates the developmental disability (visual memory) in the task of reading.*

Many *phonic methods* have been developed, but only three of the most commonly used phonic remedial methods will be briefly mentioned here.

The phonic-grapho-vocal method of Hegge, Kirk, and Kirk (1936) was developed while the authors were working with educable mentally retarded children who were also classified as disabled readers. The Hegge, Kirk, and Kirk *Remedial Reading Drills* are a programmed phonic system that emphasizes sound blending and incorporates much kinesthetic experience. The drills follow the same principle found valuable in programmed learning: (a) the principle of minimal change, each lesson incorporating only one new sound; (b) overlearning through many repetitions of each new sound in a variety of settings, plus frequent review drills; (c) promptings and confirmation; (d) only one response taught for each symbol; and (e) providing the child with reinforcement through immediate knowledge of his or her success and by social reinforcement given by the tutor.

The visual-auditory-kinesthetic *(VAK) method* of Gillingham and Stillman (1936; 1965) is a phonic system for the remediation of reading disabilities. Like the Hegge, Kirk, and Kirk *Remedial Reading Drills*, it has been used successfully since its development including during the period in which the use of phonics was severely criticized. In this method children learn both the names of the letters and the sounds of the letters. Sounding is used for reading, but letter names are used for spelling. A systematic procedure is followed in which the child is told the name of a letter and then its sound. The child then says the sound and traces it or writes it from memory. After learning some consonants and vowels, the child is required to sound each letter and blend the sounds into a word. After the child has learned to sound, write, and read three-letter words, those words are made into stories; the child reads them silently and then orally. A variation of the Gillingham method has been designed by Slingerland (1974), who entitles the method the *multisensory approach.*

PHONIC METHODS

phonic - grapho - vocal

visual - auditory - kinesthetic

Other phonic and related systems include *Distar* by Engelmann and Bruner (1969), Spalding and Spalding's *Writing Road to Reading* (1957), *The Peabody Rebus Reading Program* by Woodcock, Clark and Davies (1967), and the *Initial Teaching Alphabet* (ITA) by Pittman (1963).

SPELLING DISABILITIES Spelling disabilities are often associated with reading disabilities. It is true that poor readers are generally poor spellers, but the reverse is not always true, for some good readers are poor spellers.

Hannah, Hodges, and Hannah (1971) have presented an excellent analysis of spelling. They discuss the structure and strategies that can be used in teaching spelling from kindergarten to eighth grade. No mention is made in their comprehensive book, however, of what to do with the child who fails in the spelling program—in other words, with the child who has a learning disability in spelling.

Peters (1975), a British authority on the teaching of spelling, has stated that children who have difficulty learning to spell tend to be low in intelligence, low in visual perception of word forms, careless, and slow in handwriting.

The first task of a teacher is to determine the present level of spelling skill and that of other academic skills for comparative purposes. From the oral and written spelling of a list of words within the child's level of spelling skill, the examiner or teacher can note the kinds of errors that are made. Examples of some of these errors follow:

1. The child uses primarily a phonic approach, spelling words like *walk* as "wok" and *tough* as "tuf." These errors indicate that he or she has learned phonics and is not using other techniques of spelling.

2. The child writes a word as a whole when the word is known but does not start when he or she does not know it. This may mean that the child has learned some words visually but has no method of attack to use when unable to recall the word visually.

3. He or she reverses letters in a word spelled orally or in written form.

4. The child makes errors in some words that indicate an inability to discriminate certain sounds such as in *pin* and *pen*. If the child pronounces words incorrectly, he or she may spell them according to a mispronunciation of them.

WRITING DISABILITIES Writing disabilities are often found in children who can read and spell orally but who have not learned to express their ideas in writing.

motor - perceptual

Writing disabilities may include (1) difficulties in handwriting stemming from poor motor coordination, body image, laterality, visual imagery, ocular control, and problems that may affect the ability to copy and/or form letters and words spontaneously, and (2) difficulties in organizing concepts and putting them down on paper. conceptual

Sometimes basic problems of motor coordination, perceptual-motor difficulties, and left-handedness must be attacked in conjunction with the child's difficulty in handwriting. The left-handed child may need some special help in orienting himself or herself to paper and pencil; the child whose handedness has been changed may need some help in overcoming reversals or misorientation of letters; the child with ocular-motor or perceptual-motor problems may require a sequential program for keeping between the lines on the paper, forming letters, and spacing. Such help should be developmentally programmed, beginning with tracing, then connecting dots, and finishing incomplete letters, words, and finally sentences.

Difficulties in organizing concepts and putting them down on paper involve conceptual problems and are often closely associated with other problems found in reading, spelling, and oral expression. The child who has difficulty in organizing ideas and in seeing relationships, time sequences, and other such mental operations will have difficulty writing a meaningful sequence of sentences. The child with a poor vocabulary or one who lacks an understanding of word relationships or the inflections of plural and past and future, for example, will have difficulty in writing. Poor auditory comprehension may also be related to poor written expression.

ARITHMETIC DISABILITIES Arithmetic disabilities of a severe nature are less frequent than reading disabilities and receive less attention. With the availability of inexpensive electronic calculators, a temporary solution to the learning problem is available, but it does not eliminate the value of knowing the fundamental arithmetic skills.

Arithmetic disabilities may be found in children of normal intelligence who are adequate in reading and spelling. Just as children who are doing fifth- and sixth-grade work in arithmetic computation may be reading at the first-grade level, so children who are reading at the fifth- and sixth-grade level may be unable to add or subtract. Such a condition has been labeled *dyscalculia* in the literature.

As with language and reading disorders, arithmetic disorders were observed originally in adults who had suffered cerebral injuries. Chalfant and Scheffelin (1969) have cited the early works of Henschen on brain-injured adults who, on autopsy, were found to have lesions in one or more different areas of the brain. They also cited the work of Gertsmann and others who found lesions in the parieto-occipital region in the dominant hemisphere. With children it is difficult to determine whether the arithmetic disability is the result of a genetic factor or a cerebral dysfunction acquired before, during, or after birth or whether it is due to poor instruction, to emotional factors, or to lack of early exposure to quantitative thinking.

The diagnosis of arithmetic disabilities is similar to the diagnosis of any learning disability, including (1) determining whether a disability exists by comparing other skills to the level of performance in arithmetic, (2) analyzing types of errors in arithmetic, (3) studying the contributing factors that are present, (4) evolving a diagnostic hypothesis, and (5) organizing a remedial program. The most important part of the analysis is to study the kinds of errors that are made in arithmetic calculation. The usual procedure is to test the child formally or informally on counting; reading and writing numerals; the four basic operations of addition, subtraction, multiplication, and division; using fractions, decimals, and percentages; and a cognitive understanding of space, time, and quantity.

Remediation of errors in arithmetic is generally successful when the instructional procedures are programmed step by step, beginning at the level at which the child is performing and moving upward only at the rate at which the child can learn successfully. For severe arithmetic disabilities a one-to-one tutoring situation can best adapt to the rate of progress and provide adequate reinforcement when needed. If the disability is the result of lack of motivation, poor instruction, or other environmental factors, the remediation of mechanical errors is generally adequate. If, however, the retardation in arithmetic is the result of other factors such as inadequate spatial relations, inadequate visual-motor integration, lack of verbal ability, deficiencies in inductive thinking, and other correlates, it is necessary to use a process-task approach to remediation by organizing the instruction so as to include the use of the disabled process in relation to the task requirement and by developing an understanding of the errors observed during the operation of the task.

Cawley and Vitello (1972) have designed a model for teaching arithmetic to handicapped children. It includes an interaction unit between the child and the teacher, a verbal-processing information unit, and a conceptual unit. These are operative within a learning unit that uses types of learning styles and factors that influence learning. Cawley and Goodstein (1972) have developed materials to implement the teaching of arithmetic to handicapped children. Be-

Children who have a common disability can receive instruction in a self-contained classroom. (Photo: © Meri Houtchens-Kitchens, 1982.)

cause the teaching of arithmetic is quite involved, the reader is referred to the following sources for a description of the various methods of teaching. Bartel (1975) has described the Stern Structural Arithmetic, the Cawley-Goodstein system, the Montessori materials, the Cuisenaire Rods, and other methods and materials.

Learning Environment

Children with learning disabilities are an extremely heterogeneous group and hence cannot be educated by any one method or by one organizational procedure. Consequently, there are a large number of organizational procedures for dealing with the different kinds of learning disabilities. Various settings can provide diagnosis and remediation for these children: public schools, private schools and clinics, college and university diagnostic centers, and other programs.

The most common service is found in the public schools, especially now that laws have been passed making it mandatory that all children be given appropriate education according to their needs. The most common types of organization within both private and public schools are (1) self-contained classes, (2) resource rooms, (3) itinerant teachers, and (4) consulting or helping teachers. These environmental programs are similar in organization to those described for other groups of exceptional children and need not be repeated here.

Teaching Personnel

To the question of which administrative procedure is most effective, only one answer can be given: All can be effective if used with the right children. The consultant teacher system is most effective when used for minor problems of educational retardation, especially for problems in reading, spelling, arithmetic, and related school subjects. It would not be effective for severe cases of specific learning disabilities because such children will require considerable individual tutoring by a knowledgeable specialist. One remedial specialist cannot teach more than six or eight children with severe learning disabilities each day, whereas a consultant teacher may serve many children during the same time. Likewise, self-contained classrooms may be managed with eight to twelve children, some of whom have a common disability. Thus the method of organization must take into consideration the kinds of services to be rendered, the degree of severity of the disability, the adequacy of the specialist, the size of the school, and many other factors.

The major aim of programs for the delivery of services to children with learning disabilities, as to all children, is to provide appropriate education. The programs for children with learning disabilities overlap those for children with speech handicaps, communication disorders, and remedial reading problems. Regardless of the discipline, however, the specialists diagnosing and helping children with learning disabilities are learning disability teachers whether their backgrounds are in remedial reading, communication disabilities, or learning disabilities in general.

Organization for Mild and Severe Learning Disabilities

One of the major organizational problems is determining which children are considered learning disabled for reimbursement purposes. Some school systems select children with minor learning difficulties who require some help, and tend to include 5 to 10 percent of the school population, usually children having difficulty or lacking interest in learning to read up to their grade level. Others restrict the enrollment to the most severe disabilities and include 1 to 2 percent of the school population.

Learning Disabled Adults

The problems created by learning disabilities may not disappear when the individual leaves school. Because of efforts to develop public awareness of learning disabilities through television programs and magazine articles, young adults have recognized that their problems are related to learning disabilities.

What is the life of a learning disabled adult like? There are few descriptions in the literature, although one case report is presented by Schwartz, Gilroy, and Lynn (1976). These adults sometimes have great difficulty finding their niche in the world. They have trouble finding and keeping a job, developing a satisfying social life, and even in coping with individual daily living.

Frank is one example of a learning disabled adult. Frank, a 36-year-old man of average intelligence whose specific difficulty was in reading, sought help at a university learning disabilities clinic. Employed as a journeyman painter and supporting his wife and two children, he had learned to cope with many daily situations that required reading skills. Although he was unable to read the color labels on paint cans, could not decipher street and road signs, and could not find streets or addresses or use a city map to find the locations of his housepainting jobs, he had learned to manage by compensating for his inability to read. He visually memorized the color codes on the paint cans to determine the color; he tried to limit his work to a specific area of the city because he could not read street signs. When he was sent into an unfamiliar area, he would ask a fellow worker who could provide directions to accompany him, or he would request help from residents of the area to help him reach his destination. He watched television to keep abreast of current affairs and his wife read and answered correspondence for him. However, inevitably the day came when advancement was no longer possible if he did not learn to read. Moreover, his children were rapidly acquiring the reading skills that he did not possess. His handicap was a continual threat for him and finally led him to search for help. It is remarkable that after so many years of failure and frustration, Frank recognized his problem as that of a learning disability and had the fortitude and motivation to attempt once again the formidable task of learning to read (Kirk, Kliebhan, and Lerner, 1978).

What is unique about the adult who is learning disabled? Frequently, learning disabled adults are self-identified and self-referred. They must be intimately involved in both the diagnostic and remediation process. They are likely to be highly motivated to learn the skills they know that they need in life. They want to know what test results mean and what the goals and purpose of the remediation program are. It is their commitment to the program that enables them to succeed (Cox, 1977).

Since adults are no longer in school, they must find other agencies from which to seek services. Most clinics are not geared to handling the learning disabled adult. Learning disabilities specialists must enlarge their scope to provide service to the adult—a very neglected individual.

The ACLD organization has formed a committee to deal with this problem. Inquiries about joining the Learning Disabled Adult Committee of ACLD can be sent to ACLD, 4156 Library Road, Pittsburgh, Pennsylvania

15234. Local groups are also being organized to identify and support learning disabled adults. One such organization is "Time Out to Enjoy, Inc.", 113 Garfield Street, Oak Park, Illinois 60304. The Association of Learning Disabled Adults, P.O. Box 9722, Friendship Station, Washington, D.C. is another self-help group.

SOURCE: J. Lerner, *Learning disabilities: Theories, diagnosis, and teaching strategies* (3rd ed.). Boston: Houghton Mifflin, 1981, pp. 474–476. Reprinted by permission.

All will agree that any child with minor or major difficulties needs some help to achieve at his or her maximum level. State legislators and the Congress have objected to the employment of a large cadre of learning disability specialists for children with minor problems. If special reimbursement were to be made for minor problems, the most inadequate schools, they say, would obtain the most money. They claim that this approach would be subsidizing inefficiency.

Possible solutions to those problems have been suggested by Kirk (1978) who has recommended that two groups of special teachers be used. One group would be assigned as consultants to the regular teachers to assist them in organizing instruction for the 5 or 10 percent in each class who have mild problems and are in need of additional help. Such a consultant might be able to serve thirty or more such children each year. Another group would consist of highly trained learning disability specialists who would accept children who need more than consultant help and require individual tutoring for at least an hour a day, five days a week. In that way the children would be differentiated according to the instructional program they need. One group would be the responsibility of the regular teacher with consultant help. The other would be the responsibility of the diagnostic-prescriptive specialist for the learning disabled who would tutor six to eight children a day and assist in their adjustment and participation in the regular class.

SUMMARY OF MAJOR IDEAS

1. Learning disabilities afflict a heterogeneous group of children who are not developing or learning normally but who do not fit into the traditional categories of handicapped children. The label incorporates terms for conditions previously called brain injuries, dyslexia, developmental aphasia, and perceptual handicaps, among others.
2. Many attempts have been made to define learning disabilities. The general areas of agreement are that a learning disabled

child can be identified by three major criteria: (a) a significant discrepancy between developmental areas or between intellectual ability and academic achievement; (b) a disability not explained by sensory handicap, mental retardation, emotional disturbance, or lack of opportunity to learn; and (c) the need for specialized instruction in order to develop maximally.

3. The prevalence of learning disabilities in the general population ranges from 1 to 2 percent for the severely learning disabled to 5 to 15 percent for children with mild difficulties in learning. In 1982 over 3 percent of children were obtaining services for mild and severe learning disabilities.

4. Learning disabilities are of two kinds: (a) disabilities in academic subjects, and (b) developmental learning disabilities.

5. Learning disabilities have been variously believed to be caused by: (a) genetic factors, (b) brain damage, (c) biochemical factors, and (d) environmental deprivation and malnutrition.

6. Factors contributing to an academic disability are those conditions in a child that may inhibit or interfere with a child's academic progress in school. These contributing factors include physical aberrations in vision, hearing, laterality, body image, as well as the developmental learning disabilities of memory, attention, perception, thinking, language, and related mental operations. These conditions are generally amenable to amelioration or remediation, whereas causes are not.

7. The diagnosis of learning disabilities in preschool children requires an assessment of discrepancies in developmental abilities.

8. The diagnosis of school-age children requires an assessment of a significant discrepancy between potential (as measured by mental tests) and achievement in a specific subject; an assessment of symptoms and correlates; a diagnostic hypothesis; and a remedial prescription (IEP).

9. Three strategies for remediation are: (a) task training, in which the emphasis is on simplification and sequencing of the components of the task to be learned; (b) process (ability) training, in which the focus is on the remediation of a specific developmental disability or dysfunction; and (c) process-task training, in which the first two approaches are integrated into one remedial program.

10. Remedial programs for perceptual-motor and visual-perceptive disorders have been developed by numerous authors.

11. Remedial programs for children with language disorders have been developed by various authors and specialized materials and methods have been organized in kits for the development of oral language facility.

12. Remedial programs for severe reading disabilities are variations of a kinesthetic and a phonic method generally administered to an individual child.
13. Remediation for spelling, writing, and arithmetic disorders are also discussed.
14. The organization of special education services for learning disabled children is similar to that for other handicapped children, namely, the self-contained special class, the resource room, the itinerant diagnostic-remedial specialist, the consultant teacher, and adaptation in the regular grades.
15. Services for learning disabled children are found in public schools, private schools, clinics, and colleges and universities.

UNRESOLVED ISSUES

1. Potential and Achievement Discrepancy. Although federal regulations specify that a learning disabled child must have a discrepancy between potential and achievement, the degree of discrepancy has not been specified. As a result, learning disability programs have become quite diverse. One school system may use a two-year discrepancy while another system uses one-half year or one year as the criterion for eligibility for services. In one wealthy suburban area of a city 8 percent of school children were enrolled in services for the learning disabled, while only 1 percent of children in a lower socioeconomic area of the same city were enrolled in such services. What needs to be resolved is a more objective criterion for enrollment in learning disability services and a differentiation between mild, moderate, and severe disabilities similar to practices with other handicapped children.

2. Environmental vs. Constitutional Factors. Another major issue is to differentiate between educational retardation due to instructional, motivational, and other environmental conditions, and educational retardation as a result of an intrinsic (psychological or neurological) impediment which manifests itself in academic retardation. The latter learning disabled child will require special methods of remediation, while the child who is educationally retarded from environmental influences will learn to read by the same methods used with all children with minor adaptations.

3. Differentiating Services. The rapid increase in enrollment in services for the learning disabled has been phenomenal. School boards and superintendents have become concerned with the rapid increases in enrollment, from 0.1 percent in the early 1970s to over 3 percent in the 1980s. It is obvious that many children are now receiving learning disability services who could be better served through other programs or by slight adaptations of the regular school program. This issue has become of concern to state and federal authorities because of the increases in the cost of these services.

REFERENCES OF SPECIAL INTEREST

Alley, G., & Deshler, D. *Teaching the learning disabled adolescent: Strategies and methods.* Denver: Love Publishing, 1979.

This is one of the few comprehensive books that deal with adolescent learning disabilities. The field is covered under three broad areas: (1) remedial education for reading and mathematics, an extension of the elementary educational program; (2) a compensatory program stressing basic skills and using peer tutoring and other strategies; and (3) alternating curriculum including life-adjustment skills.

Kirk, S. A., Kliebhan, J. M. & Lerner, J. W. *Teaching reading to slow and disabled learners.* Boston: Houghton Mifflin, 1978.

Because the procedures are similar for both groups, this book combines the strategies of diagnosis and remediation in reading for both slow and disabled learners. The book describes informal and formal methods of diagnosis, different systems of teaching developmental reading, and various remedial methods, and includes a review of research studies on reading with slow learners and reading disabled children.

Lerner, J. W. *Learning disabilities: Theories, diagnosis, and teaching strategies,* 3rd ed. Boston: Houghton Mifflin, 1981.

This is a comprehensive book covering all aspects of learning disabilities. It includes four chapters of background information, two chapters on diagnosis and clinical teaching, seven chapters on theories and strategies of remediating motor and perceptual handicaps, listening comprehension, reading, writing, spelling, mathematics, and social and emotional development. The last three chapters deal with administrative considerations.

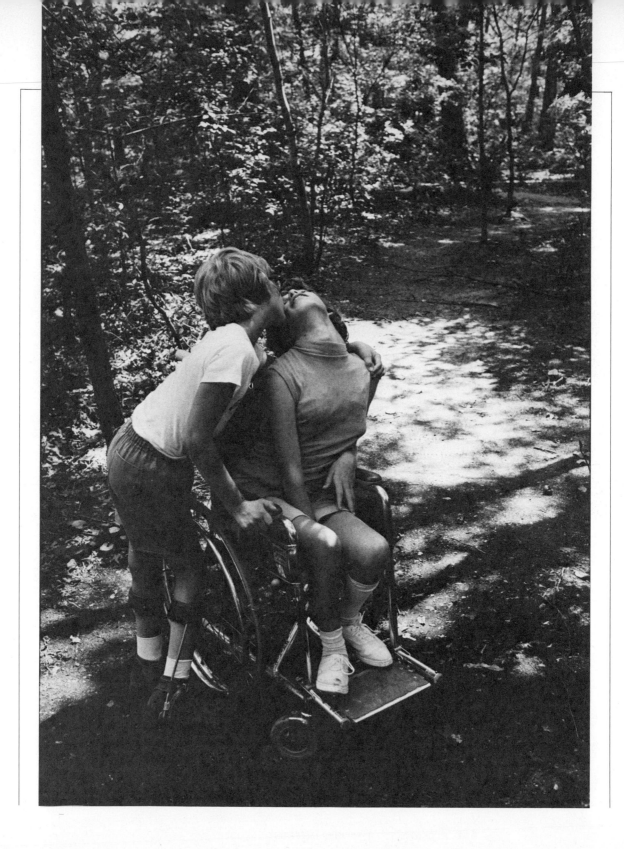

10

Children with Multiple, Severe, and Physical Handicaps

Throughout this text, we have emphasized the point that handicapped children do not always fit into neat, well-defined categories with uniform characteristics. There are not only individual differences among children with hearing, visual, mental, and social impairments, but there are children who have more than one impairment and children who are severely handicapped. The child who has two or more impairments requires very special education. This chapter will describe children with multiple and severe impairments and the provisions that education makes for their maximum development. It will also discuss characteristics of and educational adaptations for children who have nonsensory physical handicaps and other health impairments.

DEFINITION

Snell (1978) defined the *multiply handicapped* population as follows:

1. All moderately, severely, and profoundly mentally retarded individuals.
2. All severely and profoundly emotionally disturbed individuals.
3. All moderately and profoundly retarded individuals who have at least one additional impairment (i.e., deafness, blindness, crippling condition). (p. 6)

To this we would add the group of children who have multiple sensory problems, such as deaf-blind children.

Sontag, Smith, and Sailor (1977) offer a "basic skills" definition, stating essentially that multiply and severely handicapped children are those whose primary educational needs are the establishment and development of basic skills in social, self-help, and communication areas which represent the child's potential for survival in a supervised or protected world.

In the past, many multiply and severely handicapped children were excluded from public schools and, in some instances, assigned to residential schools. Multiply handicapped children tended to be excluded from public schools because they did not fit into programs provided for their handicaps. Often the key criterion for accepting such children in the public schools was that they had been toilet trained. If a child had multiple handicaps, he or she was assigned to the residential institution for the more severe of his or her handicaps. For example, a deaf–mentally retarded child would be placed in a residential institution for the mentally retarded. Frequently in such residential institutions, there were no facilities or

PREVIOUSLY

personnel capable of providing special education for the hearing impaired.

As noted in previous chapters, because of litigation under the Civil Rights Act and the Education for All Handicapped Children Act (PL 94–142), it is now mandatory for public schools to educate *all* children. This means that the schools must now organize for the multiply handicapped and for the most severely handicapped children within the framework of a public school system.

Turnbull (1979) summed up the legislative and judicial actions that provided the basis for the increased educational attention to the multiply and severely handicapped:

No handicapped child may be excluded from a free public education.
Every handicapped child will be nondiscriminately evaluated, so that his strengths and weaknesses may be identified, improved, or remedied.
Every handicapped child is entitled to an appropriate and individualized education.
Every handicapped child will be educated with nonhandicapped children to the extent possible.
Every handicapped child has the right to procedural due process so he can challenge the actions of state and local educational authorities.
The parents, guardians, or surrogates of each handicapped child have the right to share with educators the making of decisions that affect the child's education. (p. 1108)

Ironically, this long-delayed attention to the needs of the more severely handicapped child seems to have resulted in a downturn or significantly reduced attention to the problems of mildly retarded children. Haywood (1979), a past president of the American Association on Mental Deficiency, wrote an article that asked plaintively, "What happened to mild and moderate retardation?" It has become obvious that the availability of research money and special training resources can, intentionally or not, dramatically change the focus in a field of service or study.

Clearly these trends interact with one another significantly. A new area of emphasis emerged as court cases reaffirmed the right of every child, regardless of the level of handicap, to an appropriate education. Legislation, such as the Rehabilitation Act of 1973, placed special emphasis on services to those with the most severe handicaps. Changes are noted in the number of articles written on these topics. As Haywood (1979) pointed out, despite the fact that there are twelve times as many mentally retarded persons in the educable range as in the severely handicapped range, the number of articles in the *American Journal of Mental Deficiency* on severely and profoundly retarded children exceeded those devoted to the

As a result of PL 94-142, schools must now organize for the multiply and severely handicapped within the framework of a public school system. (Photo: © Meri Houtchens-Kitchens, 1982.)

mild and moderate. This was not due to editorial policy, but represented a true portrait of the research and scholarly work conducted.

DEVELOP-MENTAL PROFILE

Figure 10.1 shows the developmental profile for a multiply handicapped child who is profoundly mentally retarded. Although Dan is 10 years of age, his mental development does not extend much beyond the ability to perform on test items at about the 2- to 3-year level. This low performance is repeated in all the areas of social, intellectual, and linguistic development. It is a profile that surely creates deep concern for parents or for a school system. The additional problems of mild cerebral palsy and some suspected hearing problems complicate this developmental portrait of severe handicapping conditions. Developmental portraits such as the one shown in Figure 10.1 are not as useful for planning a program as an inventory of skills that the child has mastered. Dan can feed himself and announce his toilet needs most of the time, and his mother understands many of his gestures. These skills provide a starting point for further training.

FIGURE 10.1
Profile of a Multiply Handicapped Profoundly Retarded Child

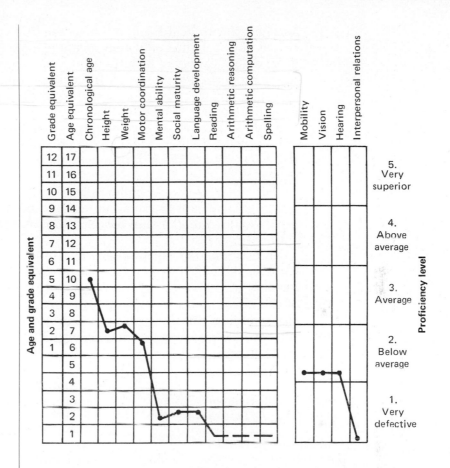

Despite his massive problems, Dan remains an individual with likes and dislikes. He reacts emotionally, but on the developmental level of a preschooler. As his mother says, "When he flashes that big smile at you, it's enough to break your heart." Quite clearly, Dan has been unable to form reasonable relationships with children his own age who see him as an extremely strange child and avoid him if at all possible. The goal of academic performance in the usual sense of reading and arithmetic is beyond reasonable aspirations for Dan. His training focuses on the areas of self-care and some social skills. It is more than likely that Dan will be restricted to a life of partial dependence given the limits of current medical and educational capabilities.

PREVALENCE

Advances in medical science have produced an ironic situation. Inroads have been made on specific problems, and many children survive difficult health and physical conditions from which they would have perished only a few years before. They survive, however, with a variety of handicapping conditions. The result is a lesser proportion of children with a single, uncomplicated disability and a greater proportion of children whose development is complicated by a number of handicaps.

Table 10.1 shows a range of agents that can produce multiply handicapped children. Those listed are only examples of many more conditions, which, fortunately, do not occur with high incidence.

The groups of diverse children clustered under the category of multiple handicaps are small in number, but each child requires a great deal of attention and concern from medical, social, and educational agencies.

Statistics on the exact number of children with multiple handicaps are difficult to obtain because of variations in definition from place to place, but the figures in Table 10.2 give a general portrait of this small group, marked by great diversity, that requires extensive planning. Since youngsters with these serious problems are almost inevitably being seen by one or more professionals, these

TABLE 10.1
Sample Conditions Leading to Multiple Handicaps

Time of Injury	Affecting Agent	Agent Activity	Typical Result
Conception	Translocation of chromosome pairs at birth	Serious changes in embryo and fetus, often fatal	Certain chromosomal regroupings can lead to Down's syndrome and mental retardation
	Inborn errors of metabolism such as phenylketonuria	Inability to carry out normal chemical and metabolic processes; injures fetal development	Results in severe retardation and other complications; can be reversed partially by early diagnosis and special diet
Prenatal	Drugs such as thalidomide	Drug used as a sedative for mother; can arrest normal development of embryo	A markedly deformed child with serious anomalies of heart, eye, ear, limbs, and others
Natal	Anoxia (sustained lack of oxygen to fetus during birth process)	Prolonged lack of oxygen can cause irreversible destruction of brain cells	Cerebral-palsied child who may or may not have mental retardation and other defects affecting vision and hearing
Postnatal	Encephalitis and meningitis	Infectious diseases (measles, whooping cough, and others) can lead to inflammation of brain and destruction of brain cells	Can lead to a variety of problems such as lack of attention and hyperactivity; causes epilepsy, mental retardation, and behavior problems

Category	Children Served	Percent of Group in Special Schools and Institutions
Multiply handicapped	55,089	49%
Severely/profoundly retarded	31,946	100
Seriously emotionally disturbed	167,055	27
Deaf-blind	3,395	38
Orthopedically handicapped	36,973	38
Other health impaired	50,226	10

Source: N. Dearman and V. Plisko, *The condition of education.* Washington, D.C.: National Center for Education Statistics, 1981, p. 270.

seriousness
implies
separateness

numbers arc likely to reflect a realistic approximation of the true prevalence for school-age children.

As the seriousness of the condition increases, there is a tendency to provide a more separate type of educational experience for the exceptional child, as reflected by the percent of children in special schools or institutions. In the case of orthopedic handicaps, the problem more often lies with the child's limited mobility, which requires special facilities to allow easy access. Furthermore, because of the unique nature of each child's disabilities, there is a wide range in age and abilities found in the programs in which they are placed.

CHARACTERISTICS OF CHILDREN WITH MULTIPLE HANDICAPS

Although innumerable combinations of exceptionalities are possible, some combinations appear more often than others or are more difficult to cope with and thus deserve special attention. The following sections focus on multiple handicapping conditions that have as their major dimension mental retardation, emotional disturbance, or impairment of two senses.

Major Dimension: Mental Retardation

Chapter 4 noted that the major problem of mental retardation was the slowness with which such children learn or retain what they learn. When this problem is combined with other problems, such as trouble with information reception and expression, then the special educator must deal with serious difficulties.

Mental Retardation and Cerebral Palsy

As pointed out in Chapter 7, "Children with Communication Disorders," there is a tendency to assume that children with cerebral palsy are mentally retarded. A recognizable relationship exists between the two conditions because whatever genetic or environmental insult damages the central nervous system sufficiently to cause cerebral palsy—an injury to the motor system—may also cause enough damage to the cerebral cortex to create retardation. But, the relationship is hardly universal.

Holman and Freedheim (1958) tested over one thousand cases in a medical clinic and found 59 percent of the cerebral-palsied children testing in the retarded range.

Schonell (1956) found 45 percent of 354 cerebral-palsied children testing in the retarded group.

Hopkins, Bice, and Colton (1954) tested 992 cerebral-palsied children and found 49 percent testing in the retarded range.

A recent review of this literature by Stephen and Hawks (1974) estimated that 40 to 60 percent of children with cerebral palsy were mentally retarded.

With cerebral-palsied children, it is hard to justify making a diagnosis of mental retardation based on an intelligence test that was standardized on children with adequate speech, language, and motor abilities. Since many cerebral-palsied children have expressive problems in both the speech and psychomotor areas, test results are often questionable. All we can conclude from the previous data on the intelligence of cerebral-palsied children is that when they are tested with instruments standardized on other populations, the IQ scores of about one-half of cerebral-palsied children will be under 70. This is almost surely an overestimate when one considers the broader definition of mental retardation now in use.

Often poor speech and the uncontrolled writhing or spastic movements of cerebral-palsied children give the lay person an unwarranted impression of mental retardation. There is actually little direct relation between intelligence and degree of physical impairment in cerebral palsy. A cerebral-palsied individual with severe writhing or uncontrolled spasticity may be intellectually gifted, while one with mild, almost unnoticed physical involvement may be severely mentally retarded. Suffice it to say that the assessment of mental retardation in cerebral-palsied children is extremely difficult. If, after prolonged appropriate instruction, the child does not make relatively average progress in most areas, the assessment of mental retardation may be more valid.

Mental Retardation and Hearing Impairment

The special language development and communication problems of the deaf and the slow learning and retention difficulties of the retarded are brought together in children who are hearing impaired and mentally retarded. In the past, those who were mentally retarded–deaf were usually assigned to residential schools for the mentally retarded. Actually, nine out of ten such persons were confined in public institutions for the mentally retarded (Task Force Report on the Mentally Retarded–Deaf, 1973).

In a review of this problem for the American Speech, Hearing, Language Association, Healey and Karp-Nortman (1975) have reported that hearing impaired–mentally retarded individuals are those "who have hearing impairments, subaverage general intellectual functioning, and deficits in adaptive behavior. The combination of these three factors requires services beyond those traditionally needed by persons with either mental retardation or hearing impairment" (p. 9).

Healey and Karp-Nortman (1975), summarizing other studies on the prevalence of the hearing impaired–mentally retarded, have estimated that 10 to 15 percent of children and adults in residential institutions for the mentally retarded have hearing losses and that a similar number of children in schools for the deaf are mentally retarded. Regardless of the accuracy of those figures, it is still a fact that many of these children require quite unique educational services and that placement in residential schools organized primarily for the mentally retarded or for the deaf is not necessarily meeting their needs.

Mental Retardation and Severe Behavior Problems

One of the most frequent combinations of multiple handicaps in the field of exceptional children is the merging of emotional or behavioral disturbance and mental retardation. The retardation part of the combination affects the ability to learn, while the emotional disturbance interferes with attending behavior and motivation.

Although the extent to which these two conditions occur together is still uncertain, it is thought to be substantial. Balthazar and Stevens (1975) have summarized a variety of research studies indicating that a substantial percentage of youngsters in institutions for the mentally retarded show neurotic or psychotic behavior patterns. Also, many persons hospitalized for emotional disturbance show indications of mental retardation. In addition, other disturbed-retarded youngsters and adults can be found in state prisons, correctional facilities for delinquents, orphanages, and other institutions. Balthazar and Stevens have concluded that "the knowledge is certain that there is a relatively high predisposition for emotional disturbance among the mentally retarded" (p. 9).

A range of emotional and behavior disturbances can be identified with mental retardation; however, these types of disturbance do not often include sophisticated neurotic defenses such as sublimation and reaction formation, behaviors that require a high degree of language development and intellectual sophistication. Robinson and Robinson (1976), after reviewing the studies on personality with the mentally retarded have stated:

We have seen, for example, that as a group the retarded tend to be more anxious than nonretarded children; that both their positive and their negative reaction tendencies toward adults tend to be heightened; that many have come to expect failure as a way of life and have learned to defend themselves against it; . . . their self-concepts may be more negative and certainly are more defensive than those of nonretarded children. (p. 195)

It is possible to identify two major strategies that have been tried in an effort to provide specific help in improving the status of emotionally disturbed and severely and profoundly mentally retarded individuals. These are drug therapy and applied behavior analysis.

The most common drugs used are phenothiazines, tranquilizers or antipsychotic agents, diphenhydramine, which seems effective with highly anxious children, particularly with young children, and amphetamines, which have been useful in reducing hyperkinetic (distractible) behavior. Like all powerful therapies, drugs need to be used with care and with full knowledge of their limitations. The temptation to use drugs as a management device in an overcrowded and understaffed institution is great (Connors and Werry, 1979).

The principles of applied behavior analysis can be used by staff members with limited educational background if they are trained and supervised by a competent behavioral therapist. Some basic principles of behavior analysis focus on (1) observing responses that are already available in the child, (2) reinforcing desirable behavior, (3) ensuring that the reinforcement is immediate and is given whenever the desired response occurs, and (4) task analyzing the target behaviors. All these principles are well within the operational capabilities of day care workers and attendants in institutions. As a result, there has been an increasing tendency to use task analysis and operant-conditioning principles as a standard for both daily management and for dealing with specific behavioral responses.

Roos and Oliver (1969) have compared the progress of three groups of severely and profoundly retarded institutionalized children under conditions of (1) operant conditioning, (2) special attention but not operant conditioning, and (3) no special attention. On the basis of independent ratings by attendants and teachers, Roos and Oliver have concluded that the group trained through operant-conditioning procedures showed significantly greater improvement than did either the control group or the placebo group. Both the formal and informal experiences with these operant procedures have encouraged their extension and application in increasing numbers of settings.

Major Dimension: Behavior Disturbance   Children who respond to attempts at instruction in a bizarre or unusual fashion always cause special problems for educators because the tried-and-true methods that work so well with other children seem to have little effect on these children.

Autism

Autism is a term used to describe a group of children who show bizarre behavior and serious developmental delays in social and communication areas. There is some disagreement about whether such children properly fall under the category of emotional disturbance or communication disorder, but in whatever category they are placed, they present a difficult set of problems for educators. The National Society for Autistic Children (1979) provided this definition:

Autism is a severely incapacitating life-long developmental disability which usually appears during the first three years of life. It occurs in approximately five out of 10,000 births and is four times more common in boys than in girls. It has been found throughout the world in families of all racial, ethnic, and social backgrounds.

Rutter (1978), a British educator of great influence, identified four criteria that distinguish autistic children from other exceptional children.

1. Severe impairment in relating to parents, family members, and other people.
2. Delayed and deviant language development, characterized by inappropriate use of language when it does occur and including peculiar patterns of speech such as echoing words or phrases.
3. Stereotyped behavior ranging from repetitive body movements such as finger flecking or twirling to ritualistic behaviors such as insisting on lining up toys or furniture in a particular order.
4. These behaviors have an early onset and are present from the beginning of life, usually prior to 3 years of age.

The total effect of such differences is to create an image of bizarreness that is extremely upsetting to parents and teachers alike. For example, George, an attractive boy of 8, was difficult to understand because he made up words for his own use. He often dragged around the house a motheaten stuffed animal that he called his "toe bunny." No one was ever able to translate that term into anything, but he would not go to bed without it. George could often be found in the backyard holding a branch in his hand and rocking back and forth in a ritualistic fashion talking in incomprehensible gibberish to the branch. Yet he scored above the retarded range on intelligence tests that did not require him to give a verbal response.

A couple of decades ago George's parents would have had another burden to bear. The professionals might have called his mother a "refrigerator" personality and identified her coolness as a possible cause of her son's condition. Few believe such a proposition today. In reviewing the educational strategies for the autistic child, Gallagher and Wiegerink (1976) summed up the state of knowledge at that time and their conclusions remain appropriate.

1. Autistic children are educable.
2. Their unique learning characteristics are due to basic cognitive deficits in information processing.
3. Such deficits can be compensated for, in part, by carefully structured educational programs with specified developmental learning sequences and enhanced reinforcing stimuli.
4. Structured education programs should begin early in life, with the parent or parent surrogate as the primary teacher.
5. Educational programs for these children are feasible and, in the long run, less costly than institutional care.
6. The provision of appropriate educational programs for these children is not a manifestation of public generosity but rather a reflection that these children, too, have a clear right to an appropriate education.

Schopler and Bristol (1980) have summed up what is known about causation of autism.

1. For individual children, the specific causes are usually unknown.
2. There is probably no single underlying cause to account for autism. Instead there are multiple causes.
3. Most likely the primary causes involve some form of brain abnormality or biochemical imbalance characterized by impairment in perception and understanding.

[handwritten margin note: STRUCTURED LEARNING PROGRAMS]

How Can Sam's Needs Be Met?

How do parents of a severely handicapped child plan constructively and realistically for his future? What are the most pressing problems to be addressed, and what, in anticipation, can parents do about them? The urgency of these questions and the difficulties in finding answers has become a central concern to me, the mother of a nonverbal, 21-year-old autistic child. . . .

Planning for our child's immediate future has been an integral part of our family's ongoing present during all the years of his childhood. Adequate and appropriate remedial services did not exist when he and we needed them. Together with other parents we have worked to find, to support, and to create the necessary educational and social opportunities. Now, despite years of struggle, it is clear that he, who will be socially dependent throughout his life, will further require that provisions be made for a sheltered living and working situation, for adequate financial support, and for a caring person to act as advocate for his needs. The discussion that follows is the fruit of years of thought, the kind that occupies parents in the long nights after their more immediate cares are set aside. This thought expresses itself in questions, not answers. Generally speaking, one does not know the answers. . . .

Sam, our son, is an exceptionally handsome 6-foot-2-inch, 190-pound young man. At first glance he can "pass for normal," and part of learning to enjoy living with such a child is to be able to respond with compassionate humor to the baffled responses that he evokes, as well as to be understanding and helpful when people are frightened of him. Sam is a gentle, loving person who, in spite of his size and physical maturity, evokes affectionate response not only from his family but also from other persons with whom he comes in contact, persons such as his sister's friends, young children who enjoy playing with him, and adolescents who are hired to act as companions to him.

Nonverbal expressively, with comprehension hard to assess, Sam can follow simple verbal directions. As long as the request or suggestion fits into his expectations, he responds appropriately. But his confusion and his attempts to do something when instructions are not the usual ones suggest the degree of distress he must feel in a verbal world that he cannot share. Sam moves easily in those environments that are familiar and structured, his home and his school. His self-help skills are fair to good. He dresses himself completely and with an innate color sense. He is still learning to brush his teeth well enough to suit his dentist; shaving is new and hard to master. Independence in showering and in food preparation is hampered by his apparent inability to distinguish degrees of heat. Most difficult of all for us, his parents, and perhaps for him, is his inability to know what to do with himself in his unstructured free time. Aside from a retreat into stereotyped, world-shutting-out autistic behaviors, Sam is lost when there is "nothing to do." He shows that he wants something to do. He paces, he impatiently hums, and eventually he finds something irritating (to us) to do like dumping liquid soap down the sink—if he is left alone too long.

Sam the man, in spite of his body size, is emotionally like a small child. His jumping up and down with glee or excess spirits shakes the house. Bizarre behavior? Perhaps. But Sam's present childlike unrestrained delight, the eager vividness in his face at the sight of food or persons he likes is a quality we treasure, for it developed slowly from the withdrawal and misery of his earlier years. Today, even in the body of a man, Sam the emotional child is a lovely fey person, one who knows how to enjoy simple pleasures, who has a kind of unselfconsciousness and delight that is infectious and lovable.

His expressions of distress are equally unrestrained. Suddenly, without apparent antecedents he will be found weeping silently, inconsolably, or he may beat his head and bite his hands in what appears to be deep frustration or inturned anger. Although Sam uses self-destructive rather than outwardly aggressive behaviors to express his distress, the spectacle of an almost 200-pound man so unrestrained is frightening to the uninitiated. . . .

Sam's needs are not those of an adult; they are the needs of a growing person whose emotional and cognitive development has not progressed in the usual way. . . . For whatever the reasons, the development [of severely handicapped autistic children] is not only atypical but retarded or arrested at levels of early childhood. In order for development to continue, the environment must be able to meet the individual's needs as they exist at his particular developmental level. For Sam this means looking at his childlike qualities, identifying related needs, and attempting to provide an environment condu-\ cive to progressive growth.

This focus on childlike qualities and on meeting childlike emotional needs may sound like heresy to those who are struggling to help retarded persons become accepted as adult citizens in our society. At first glance my point of view may appear contrary to enlightened efforts to plan working and living environments on the principles of *development* and *normalization*. These principles emphasize making available to retarded persons situations of living and working that are as similar as possible to those of the mainstream of society. But development and normalization are not necessarily the same thing. It is important to distinguish between developmental needs that may be atypical and normalized patterns of living.

The proponents of development and normalization rightly specify that the retarded person as well as the normal one needs provision not only for shelter and for reasonable safety but also for the right to take risks. These as well as opportunities for work and play, for companionship, and for sexual expression are necessary for continued growth and development as a human being. They imply an environment where physical, cognitive, social, and emotional needs are met. Provision of good physical care is relatively easy; to meet cognitive, social, and emotional needs is more complex.

What are the emotional needs of autistic persons such as Sam? In spite of his physical maturity and well-developed genitals, he is not a heterosexual, mature person. He has not developed and is not likely to develop the interpersonal skills that lead to adult sexual expression. Yet Sam needs other human beings who not only care about him but who enjoy sharing with him in reciprocally satisfying human contact. Sam does not need a sexual partner in the adult sense, but he needs someone to hug occasionally as well as someone to comfort him when he is troubled. As mentioned above, Sam can evoke this response from persons beyond his family circle; I believe it is related to his childlike qualities, and I do not want him to lose that asset. He needs the security of an environment simple enough and structured enough so that he knows how to meet its expectations. He also needs stimulation in the form of going places and doing things. He needs the ambience of an atmosphere where other people know how to enjoy themselves and can take pleasure in including him, at least on the periphery. These persons can provide for Sam not only role models but also experiences that he cannot yet provide for himself. Such an environment, shared with other more competent persons, can enable Sam to maintain his zest for life and to expand his options. . . .

Residential and work facilities expressly designed to meet the needs of severely handicapped autistic people are virtually nonexistent. That adequate services do not exist for persons who are mentally handicapped is not news. The thrust to deinstitutionalize retarded persons and the philosophy and techniques designed to help them move into the mainstream of society are geared to the vast numbers of moderately handicapped persons. The principle of *normalization* does not, in my view, consider with any sophistication the *developmental* needs of these handicapped people—certainly not of autistic people. These are yet to be identified, and this must take place before they can be incorporated into programs. In the rhetoric of planning agencies there will always be a small number of persons who "require institutionalization." It is convenient to ignore the evidence that institutions are equally damaging to severely handicapped autistic persons and that given the right environment they too can often continue to develop and become productive human beings.

To prevent long-term institutionalization for these people and the attendant loss of their humanity, social planning should include (1) provision for residential facilities with an interpersonal environment that fosters maturation; these will need to be sheltered situations that are shared with nonhandicapped persons; (2) provision of a network of sheltered situations where there is simple productive work to be done that is comprehensible and therefore satisfying to these people.

In order to enable social planners to effectively provide for autistic people, there will need to be research investigating (1) the developmental and, particularly, the emotional needs of severely handicapped autistic adults; (2) the meeting of these needs as they affect the person's ability to develop emotionally as well as cognitively; (3) identification of the factors that enable handicapped and nonhandicapped persons to share their lives with one another in a way that is growth producing for both groups (there are, apparently, a few residential situations that may meet this criterion. Communes having care of the handicapped person as their "product" is one possibility. Sheltered villages [where retarded and nonretarded persons share each other's lives] suggest that there could be value in an indepth exploration into the relationship between the villagers, both handicapped and nonhandicapped. The essence of the successful sheltered village concept may be not that it is sheltered but that it promotes shared living); (4) the kinds of work situations that are satisfying as well as possible for these people. There needs to be creative problem solving that goes beyond the assembly line and sheltered workshop paradigms. This should include exploration into the kinds of activities that have *meaning* to autistic people and a development of the requisite skills. For example, could these people be productively used on farms where animal functions must be tended and food (which they understand) is produced? What about work teams with a mentally competent person (possibly one with a physical handicap) to structure the task, to supervise the workers, and to negotiate with the employer?

There also needs to be further research into the development and the dissemination of teaching methods appropriate to both children in schools and adults in work and living situations that can develop autistic people's motivation for independent work and play.

As I take our 6-foot-2-inch son out for a walk after supper because he is physically restless (there being no nearby recreation program that *uses* his enormous physical vitality, and if there were, he could not get there without my taking him), as I stay up beyond the hour I would like to go to bed because my adult child is not yet ready to settle down but cannot manage to make the decision to go to bed on his own when he is ready, I wonder how much longer we can continue our efforts to provide for our own needs in relation to him as well as how to continue to smooth the path for other parents who share similar problems.

The educational approach to autistic children leans heavily on behavior analysis and operant conditioning to help these children who often have limited or nonexistent speech for communication purposes. The remediation is slow and erratic, but clear gains have been made using these approaches in an intensive treatment setting (Quay and Werry, 1979).

Behavior Disturbance and Hearing Impairment

As in many areas of handicapping conditions, there is no accurate estimate of the number of emotionally disturbed–hearing impaired children. The number depends on the criteria for emotional disturbance and the degree of hearing loss considered. Altshuler (1975), a psychiatrist who has specialized in the treatment of emotionally disturbed–deaf children, reviewed the literature and concluded that "the 8 percent estimate [of deaf children who are emotionally disturbed] nationwide is a marked underrepresentation." He estimated that one to three out of ten deaf students present significant emotional problems that warrant attention.

Professionals who work with emotionally disturbed–deaf children tend to classify their condition as mild, moderate, or severe. Severely involved children have, in some instances, been removed from schools for the deaf because their teachers were unable to cope with their bizarre behavior. About these children, Ranier (1975) has stated:

It is my strong feeling on the basis of our two decades of experience in the psychiatric care of the deaf, as well as the reports of others, that there is a significant core of deaf children who cannot be educated or managed even in special classes without a total therapeutic milieu under psychiatric direction. Temporary separation of the child from his environment and placement in a <u>controlled therapeutic</u> setting is <u>essential to help the child develop better control, better socialization, and better identification</u>. Drug and behavior therapies as well as recreation, art, and occupational skills need to be furnished. At the same time, special teachers can provide continuing education on an individual basis. (p. 19)

Ranier indicated that, following that type of program, the child could be returned to the special class and to the home.

Mild and moderately emotionally disturbed–deaf children are often enrolled in residential and day schools for the deaf. In such classes teachers tend to emphasize pupil adjustment, success in tasks assigned, and, in general, a more structured program. Emphasis on education and cooperation of parents is a major program element.

As yet, standard programs for emotionally disturbed–hearing impaired children have not been highly developed. The group is so heterogeneous that each child will need an individualized education program to fit his or her specific needs to an extent greater than that required for many other handicapped children.

Major Dimension: Dual Sensory Impairments When one of the two major systems (vision and hearing) that bring information to the child has been impaired, the special education program <u>emphasizes the unimpaired sense</u>. For the child who is visually handicapped, emphasis is placed on listening to records, tapes, and so forth to help compensate for the visual channel problem. For the child who is deaf, the visual channel is used to establish a communication system based on signing, finger spelling, or speech reading (lip reading). But what does one do when both channels are impaired?

How can a child so afflicted learn speech and language when he or she can neither hear nor see? It is testimony to the resilient human spirit of both handicapped individuals and those who work with them that even such seemingly insurmountable handicaps can be partially overcome.

Whenever deaf-blind people are discussed, the first name to

come to mind is that of Helen Keller, who has become a symbol of what devoted teaching can do against great odds. With the help of Anne Sullivan, her tutor and constant companion, and a keen mind, this deaf-blind individual achieved speech and other ways of communication as well as a high level of academic accomplishment. The popular play and movie *The Miracle Worker* is based on Helen Keller's early discovery of the world around her with the help of Anne Sullivan. The challenge for educators is how to make more Helen Kellers out of the three thousand deaf-blind children in the United States.

The *deaf-blind child* has been defined by the Bureau of Education for the Handicapped (1969) as

a child who has both auditory and visual impairments, the combination of which cause such severe communication and other developmental educational problems that he cannot properly be accommodated in special education programs either for the hearing handicapped child or for the visually handicapped child. (p. 1)

In the past the education of the deaf-blind has been largely conducted in private residential schools for children of parents who could afford such education. To deal with the problem nationally, the federal government passed legislation in 1968 to establish ten model centers for deaf-blind children. These centers were each given responsibility for a wide geographic area, thereby enabling families of these multiply handicapped children to receive some degree of help wherever their children resided in the United States. This program, begun in 1969, has provided a wide variety of family counseling services, medical and educational diagnoses, and itinerant home services, as well as teacher-training opportunities and full-time educational programs for deaf-blind children. As Dantona (1976) has stated:

These centers also conduct a program for helping state educational departments and other responsible agencies develop appropriate state plans assuring the provision of meaningful relevant and continuous services throughout the lifetime of the deaf-blind person; and each center collects and disseminates information about practices found effective in working with deaf-blind children and their families. (p. 173)

These programs have brought more comprehensive diagnostic facilities and more trained personnel in contact with the deaf-blind child and encouraged educators to think seriously about how to cope with this rare, but difficult, problem.

The term *deaf-blind* is something of a misnomer because it implies the complete loss of both sensory avenues. In actual practice most of these children have some residual vision or residual hearing that can be used in educating them. Other senses, such as touch, are also used in the almost exclusively tutorial approach that must be used to meet the special and idiosyncratic needs of the deaf-blind child (Wolf and Anderson, 1969).

EDUCATIONAL ADAPTATIONS FOR CHILDREN WITH MULTIPLE HANDICAPS

Educational programs for children who are multiply handicapped or severely retarded are relatively new. According to Sontag, Smith, and Sailor (1977), the emphasis on the education of these groups of children began seriously in about 1970. They felt that the inclusion of this difficult group into public education would lead the way to the goal of the education of all handicapped children.

With the help of federal grants that have supplied more personnel, residential institutions have tried to provide training in self-care and independence for severely handicapped children and adults. While it is important to try to help the residential schools that have been overcrowded and understaffed, there is a parallel goal today to deinstitutionalize children and adults from the residential schools. With proper training and supervision, some of these children and adults have the potential to adapt to community facilities.

To emphasize deinstitutionalization and normalization, Brown, Nietupski, and Hamre-Nietupski (1976) have advocated that "severely handicapped students should be placed in self-contained classes in public schools. . . . They have the right to be visible, functioning citizens integrated into everyday life of complex public communities" (p. 3). The goal of deinstitutionalization has been reached in many communities where severely handicapped children are found in self-contained classrooms and special schools designed to meet their needs.

Components of a Comprehensive System

Haring and Bricker (1976) have described the necessary components for a comprehensive system of education for most types of multiply and severely handicapped children, regardless of the type of handicap. A summary of the six components follows:

1. **A developmental framework** The developmental approach accepts three basic ideas. First, that growth or changes in behavior follow a developmental hierarchy (for example, children vocalize before uttering words); second, behavior acquisition moves from simple to more complex responses (that is, children focus their

Specific curriculum materials must often be provided to meet the special needs of a severely handicapped child. (Photo: © Gregg Mancuso/Stock, Boston.)

eyes before learning to read); and third, more complex behavior is the result of coordinating or modifying simpler component response forms. Most developmental education will follow those basic principles. Since the developmental model assures that the simpler forms of behavior serve as building blocks for complex responses, it is therefore important to start with those simpler building blocks.

2. **Early and continuous intervention** Early intervention reduces the possibility of the child's developing inappropriate responses and brings important support to the primary caregivers—the parents—at a time most needed.

3. **Systematic instructional procedures** Once the teacher determines which behavior should be taught and in what sequence others follow, specific procedures should match the stages of learning a particular skill. These stages can be divided into five distinct phases: (a) acquiring, (b) strengthening, (c) maintaining, (d) generalizing, and (e) applying the new skill.

4. **Appropriate curricula** Specific curriculum materials must often be developed to meet the special needs of the severely handi-

reduces inappropriate responses

a sm g/2f

Physical therapy is one type of adjunctive service provided for severely handicapped children. (Photo: © Charles Kennard/Stock, Boston.)

[handwritten margin notes: CURRICULA CRITERIA]

[handwritten margin notes: materials/ objectives in behaviour terms procedures, criteria.]

capped. The criteria for selecting these materials should be that (a) they are flexible and can be used in a variety of settings since we wish to help children acquire skills that can be adapted to a variety of situations; (b) the training materials must include precise behavioral descriptions of objectives, the procedures for reaching these objectives, and the criteria for determining when the objectives have been met; and (c) there must be a direct link between the curriculum materials and objective measures of progress.

5. **Adjunctive services** Severely multiply handicapped persons have a wide variety of disorders—physical, sensory, and psychological, as well as educational—and therefore require that a diverse group of disciplines be available to provide treatment. Children with chronic health problems need consultative medical supervision. Children with muscular problems must have attention from specially trained individuals who can work directly with teachers and parents. Other children will need the services of physical therapists, speech-language pathologists, and other specialists. One of the increasingly important roles played by all of these adjunctive services is the provision of specific training and instruction to the parents themselves, since the parents are the primary caregivers and the most highly motivated persons to help the child develop on a consistent basis.

6. **Objective evaluation** One of the most difficult jobs facing educators is the development of evaluation systems that will allow for the assessment of programs on a daily, weekly, and yearly basis. This issue can be partially dealt with by developing curricula that have evaluation or assessment built into the programs themselves.

Table 10.3 provides a developmental program across a number of dimensions that shows what might be expected of a profoundly retarded child from preschool age to adulthood. The adult goals seem limited and far from the normal educational goals even for other children with handicaps. Yet the impairment is so severe with these children that the objectives represent reasonable goals. Given these goals, then, a careful set of interactions with the child can be established in attempting to reach a modest level of success in self-care, language, social adaptations, and other areas (Luckey and Addison, 1974).

Content   Using the broad goals noted by Luckey and Addison (1974) we can put together an organized sequence of activities that shows the teacher how to proceed in specific steps. As Sherr (1976) has stated, the most adequate programs will have to be developed in the public schools, since it is in this setting that a full-service program can be offered at reasonable cost to the public. The mandate that public schools are required to educate all children has created a demand for organized curricula for the severely and multiply handicapped child. The essentials of a curricula for this group

TABLE 10.3
Developmental Program Emphasis for Profoundly Retarded

	Preschool Age	School Age	Adult
Sensori-motor development	Enriching environment and encouraging exploration of interesting and attractive surroundings	Identifying sound patterns, locations, tonal qualities, rhythms	Responding to music activities, signals, warnings
Physical development	Rolling, creeping, and crawling	Overcoming obstacles; walking on ramps and stairs, running, skipping, jumping, balancing, climbing	Riding vehicles; participating in gymnasticlike activities and track and field events
Self-care	Passive dressing; accommodating body to dressing; partially removing clothing	Removing garments; dressing and undressing with supervision; buttoning, zipping, and snapping	Dressing with partial assistance or supervision
Language	Increasing attention to sounds	Recognizing name, names of familiar objects, and body parts	Listening to speaker
Social adaptation	Recognizing familiar persons	Playing individually alongside other residents	Sharing, taking turns, waiting for instruction

Source: Adapted from R. E. Luckey and M. R. Addison, The profoundly retarded: A new challenge for public education. *Education and Training of the Mentally Retarded,* 1974, 9, 123–130.

of children include: (1) self-help skills, (2) gross and fine motor skills, (3) communication skills, (4) socialization, (5) prevocational and vocational training, (6) functional academics, and (7) recreation and leisure skills.

An example of the target behaviors that one may wish to introduce into or to eliminate from the child's repertoire can be seen in Table 10.4. Here both the normal behaviors that one expects and a range of inappropriate behaviors that might face the teacher are shown (Watson, 1972).

The curricula that have been developed for the severely and profoundly handicapped and implementation of these programs have been influenced by task analysis and operant conditioning. An example of such a curriculum is *The Teaching Research Curriculum for the Moderately and Severely Handicapped* developed by Fredericks and others at the Teaching Research Infant and Child Center in Oregon (1980). This curriculum was developed over the years by

TABLE 10.4
Self-Help Skills:
Summary of Training
Goals or Target
Behaviors Selected for
Children in Behavior
Modification Program

Skill	Target Behaviors
Eating	Can sit at table and eat neatly with spoon or fork (or equivalent to age level).
	Lack of inappropriate behavior: Does not jump up from table until meal is completed; does not throw food or eat with fingers; does not take food from someone else's plate, scream, or cry; does not chew food with mouth open; does not swallow solid food without chewing it; does not pound eating utensils on the table; does not spin plate, drop it, or throw it.
Drinking	Can drink neatly from an appropriate size cup or glass held in one hand (unless younger than age 3).
	Lack of inappropriate behavior: Does not pound cup on table, drop it, or throw cup or its contents; does not place fingers or hands in cup or blow bubbles; does not put food, napkins, utensils, clothing, or other objects in cup; does not spin cup; does not spit contents or gargle.
Undressing	Can remove pants, shirt, coat, dress, underpants, undershirt, or other undergarments (with or without buttons, zippers, or snaps), socks and shoes (either with buckles or laces) without assistance or supervision (or equivalent to age level).
	Lack of inappropriate behavior: Does not damage garments when removing them; does not throw them on the floor and leave them.
Dressing	Can put on pants, shirt, coat, dress, or underclothing (with or without buttons, zippers, or snaps), socks and shoes (either with buckles or laces) appropriately without assistance or supervision (or equivalent to age level).

Source: J. Watson, *How to use behavior modification with mentally retarded and autistic children.* Tuscaloosa, Alabama: Behavior Modification Technology, 1972.

Gross and fine motor skills of severely handicapped children can be improved through physical activities. (Photo: Anestis Diakopoulos/ Stock, Boston.)

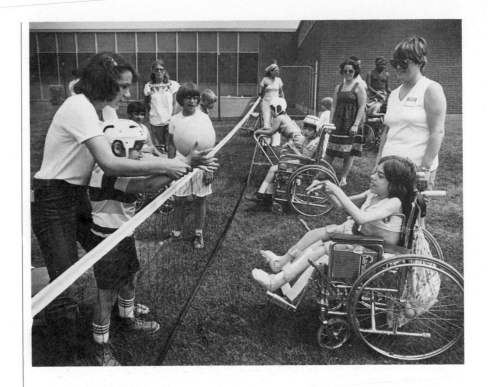

teachers of preschool handicapped children and includes task analysis of the behaviors to be taught with detailed steps in teaching the target behaviors.

According to Fredericks, each of the areas, such as self-help skills, has three possible subcomponents: (1) skills, (2) phases, and (3) steps. A *skill* is a complex behavior requiring the acquisition of a number of subordinate behaviors before it is acquired. A *phase* is a breakdown of the skill into parts or units, and a *step* is a minute breakdown of the phase. An example of a self-help is dressing (a skill). A phase of dressing could be removing pants. The eight phases in teaching a child to develop that aspect of dressing are described as:

Phase I	Student removes final leg of pants from foot.
Phase II	Student removes pants from one foot when both feet are in legs.
Phase III	Student sits down.
Phase IV	Student pushes pants down to ankles from the knees.
Phase V	Student pushes pants down to ankles from the thighs.
Phase VI	Student pushes pants all the way down to ankles.
Phase VII	Student grasps each side of pants at the waist.
Phase VIII	Student positions self in front of chair and completely removes pants. (Fredericks et al., 1980, p. 78)

Recent attempts have been made to produce a functional and chronological age-appropriate curriculum for the severely handicapped. This means that a 16-year-old severely handicapped boy is *not* asked to solve a four-piece puzzle of a dog even if that task corresponds to his "mental" level. Instead, the goal is to focus on those activities that the handicapped child can carry out to some degree like his or her nonhandicapped peers. Eating, communicating, and turning on a television set are but a few.

Brown et al. (1979) have suggested, "Since nonhandicapped adolescent and young adult students frequently make independent purchases at grocery stores, department stores, and drugstores, shopping skills should receive considerable attention in the curriculum for severely handicapped" (p. 86). They believe that the curriculum should focus on functional items as much as possible, rather than substitutes for the real world.

This	Not This
Placing coins in a vending machine	Placing pegs in a pegboard
Walking across bleachers at a sporting event	Walking a balance beam
Teaching students to zip their own jeans	Using a zipper on a zipper board
Learning to identify restrooms and exit signs	Learning the names of the primary colors

One of the goals in working with multiply handicapped children is to engage them in interaction with their environment and with the people around them. One example of a specific approach is given in Table 10.5, a cued commands chart that includes various requests for action on the part of the handicapped child. For most children, of course, responding to a parental request or command is an easy matter, hardly justifying a complex list and record-keeping procedure. For the multiply handicapped child, such responses are made with great difficulty; therefore, description of the situation and the criterion that designates success are useful to a parent or to a child care worker who is helping the child. Once the lists are constructed, it is not hard for a trained nonprofessional to follow through and to give the child extensive practice in responding appropriately.

Strategies   The general strategy by which programs are planned for the multiply and severely handicapped are noted as follows:

1. isolating the necessary behavior components to reach a specified terminal state

TABLE 10.5
Cued Commands Chart

Verbal Cues for Behaviour. (handwritten)

| Uses: | 1. To select functional commands to teach in Following Cued Commands. |
| | 2. To suggest commands for aides and volunteers to use frequently. |

Commands	Materials/Situation	Suggested Criterion
"Sit (down)." (tap/point to place)	S is standing near chair, mat, toilet, swing.	S sits in the indicated place for at least 5 seconds.
"Stand (up)." (raise your arms/hands)	S is sitting on floor, in chair, in swing.	S stands up and remains up for at least 5 seconds.
"Let's go/Come on." (beckon and start walking)	S is sitting or standing next to you.	S walks with you at least 5 feet without stopping.
"Go over there." (point and nod your head toward place)	S is standing by you.	S walks to the indicated place (10 feet) and stops.
"Hold my hand." (stretch out your hand)	S is standing or sitting by you.	S places his hand in/on yours for at least 5 seconds (while walking or balancing).
"Stop/No." (shake index finger)	S is engaging in undesirable behavior.	S stops the behavior for at least 5 seconds.
"Look." (point to place)	S is near a window or some stimulating target.	S turns his head in the indicated direction for at least 5 seconds.
"Give me ———." (hold out your hand and point to object)	S is holding an object.	S releases the indicated object in your hand.
"Take ———." (hold out object)	S's hands are empty, but you are holding something.	S takes the indicated object and holds it for at least 5 seconds.
"Get ———." (point to object)	S is near an object: holding it; it is hanging on a hook or rack.	S goes to and picks up the indicated object.

Source: J. Tawney, D. Knapp, C. O'Reilly, and S. Pratt, *Programmed environments curriculum.* Columbus, Ohio: Charles E. Merrill, 1979.

Strategies (handwritten)

② sequencing for acquisition (handwritten)

2. sequencing those components according to the best information available on normal acquisition patterns   *③ activities to learn steps* (handwritten)
3. generating a variety of activities to train each of the necessary steps in the developmental hierarchy (Bricker and Iacino, 1977, p. 170)

Figure 10.2 indicates a developmental hierarchy map in the area of motor development. Starting from birth, this map indicates the expected sequence of motor development for the first two years. A youngster who has cerebral palsy and is seriously delayed in motor development as a consequence can be placed on this map in terms of his or her present development, and the teacher will know what is the next expected skill on which to begin working.

One outstanding feature of the current training emphases on early development is the extensive detailing of basic skills usually thought too routine or basic to be a part of an instructional program. For example, Greg, a 6-year-old quadriplegic youngster with

FIGURE 10.2
Motor Training
Lattice

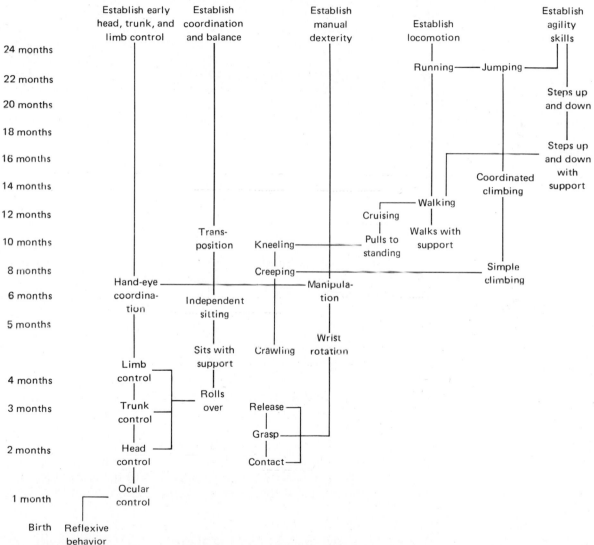

439 EDUCATIONAL ADAPTATIONS FOR CHILDREN WITH MULTIPLE HANDICAPS

very limited motor skills, can still be approached through exercises designed to help him develop his visual attention.

Attending Given the command "Greg, look at me," he will look at the teacher so that eye contact is made for 3 seconds on eighteen of twenty trials conducted on two consecutive days.

Turning head to right With Greg placed supine on a mat, his head positioned by the teacher so that his right cheek is flush against the mat, Greg will hold his head in this position independently for a 2-minute period.

Eye tracking Placed in a prone position on the table with a bolster under the armpits, Greg will track horizontally and vertically for a total of 3 minutes out of a 5-minute block of time, as judged acceptable by the teacher and one independent observer.

Shifting gaze Properly supported in his wheelchair so that his head is free to turn to the left and right when two toys are held 18 inches apart and alternately squeaked or rattled, Greg will shift his gaze from one toy to another within 5 seconds of the sound on 80 percent of the trials on three of four consecutive days (McKenzie et al., 1977, p. 106).

The more handicapped the child, the more detailed and precise the analysis of the skills to be taught must be. Even the simplest task can turn into a marvel of complexity once one breaks down every single component of the task itself. Figure 10.3 gives a framework for tying one's shoes. As one can see, such a task analysis reveals the full range of a complex sequence of simple behaviors necessary for the final act to be successful. It also provides a basis for step-by-step instruction so that one can identify the point at which the child is having trouble and at which specific instructions should be given.

Communication Skills

Regardless of the particular handicap, many children with serious physical and mental handicaps have major communication problems, and new devices have been developed recently to allow children who may never learn to talk to communicate their basic needs.

The earlier the child's training begins, the more likely the training will start with prelinguistic communication, adding verbalization later if possible. Bricker and Carlson (1980) have provided a practical illustration of the consequence of teaching a child to nod her head.

Teaching a toddler to shake her head affirmatively (1) increases her communicative repertoire, (2) enables her to express her emotional state with some sophistication, and (3) equips her with a convenient response mode for learning conceptual material presented to her by her teacher. (p. 35)

Vanderheiden and Harris-Vanderheiden (1976) have described three components needed for an expressive communication system.

1. *A physical mechanism* or means of indicating or transmitting the elements of a message to a receiver,
2. *A symbol system* and vocabulary to provide the child with a set of symbols which he can use to represent things and ideas for communication to a receiver,
3. *Rules and procedures* for combining and presenting the ideosymbols so that they will be most easily interpretable by a receiver.

transmitting
symbolizing

rules for
symbols
transmission

FIGURE 10.3
Lattice for
"Shoes Tied"

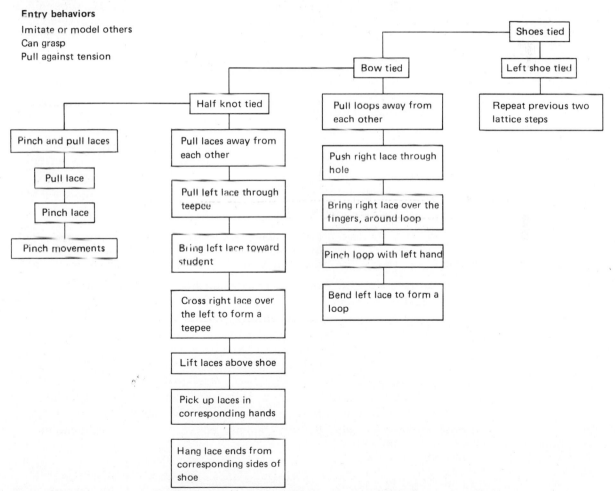

Model for developing instructional materials

Entry behaviors
Imitate or model others
Can grasp
Pull against tension

Source: D. Smith, J. Smith, and E. Edgar, Prototype models for the development of instructional material. In N. Haring and L. Brown (Eds.), *Teaching the severely handicapped* (Vol. 1). New York: Grune & Stratton, 1976, p. 167.

To get a better understanding of these components, let's take a brief look at what they might look like for a normal child and for a nonvocal physically handicapped child.

The physical mechanism which the normal child uses to present or transmit the elements of his message is his oral speech mechanism. With this mechanism he is able to transmit specific sound patterns which represent different ideas or concepts. These sound patterns, or spoken words, form the child's *symbol system*. The child uses these symbols (spoken words) to transmit his ideas to a receiver. In presenting these words to a receiver, however, the child must follow certain *guidelines* concerning their combination and order of presentation if his message is to be easily and correctly interpreted by the receiver.

Fortunately, for the vocal child, the potential to develop these three components is present in infancy. Given normal stimulation, it develops early in the child's life and provides him with an effective means of communication and interaction with others during most of his growth and development. (p. 17)

Table 10.6 gives an illustration of the three components, their function in a normal child and in a child using a special communication board.

For many multiply handicapped children, the inability to communicate becomes one of the most fundamental problems preventing them from interacting successfully with their environment and consequently impeding their ability to learn from these experiences as nonhandicapped children do so readily. A new strategy—augmentative systems for communication (Yoder, 1980)—has been de-

TABLE 10.6
A Simple Model of Expressive Communication Components for Normal and Nonvocal Motor Impaired Children

Component	Function	Component Represented in the Normal Speaking Child	Component Represented in a Child Using a Communication Board
Physical mechanism	To provide the child with a means of specifying or transmitting the elements of his or her message to a receiver	Oral speech mechanism	Pointing board
Symbol system and vocabulary	To provide the child with a set of symbols which he or she can use to represent things or ideas for communication	Spoken words	Pictures, printed words, other symbols
Rules for combining and presenting symbols	To provide the rules and procedures for presenting the ideosymbols so that the message will be most easily understood by the receiver	Syntax, grammar, etc.	Syntax, grammar, etc.

veloped to aid the nonspeech child. These devices allow many multiply handicapped children for whom speech is difficult to communicate their basic needs and even their ideas to others.

The augmentative systems are not designed to replace speech but, as the term suggests, to add to and supplement what speech is available. Yoder (1980) has described three separate types of approaches.

Direct selection In this technique, the child is presented with a board on which a series of pictures or words appear and the child can point to those pictures that symbolize his or her needs. For example, with a communication board, Dan (the child whose developmental profile is shown in Figure 10.1) can point to the picture of a child drinking a glass of water and his mother will know what he wants. This is a fast and efficient system that effectively handles basic needs and routine requests. Even a child with severe cerebral palsy who is not able to point with his or her hands can hold a pointing stick in the teeth or gaze directly at the desired object. However, communication boards (see Figure 10.4) have limitations for more complex messages.

Scanning With this method, the user responds with a prearranged signal to the desired message elements that appear in a prearranged sequence. The child may be able to nod the head or move the wrist to indicate assent. The person interacting with the child presents question choices one at a time ("Do you want something to eat?" "Do you want to go outside?" and so on), and the child signals "yes" when the sender reaches the desired question or message element. A slide tape or other automated devices can work in a similar fashion.

Encoding In this approach, the child may communicate through a pattern of multiple signals—for example, Morse code or finger spelling and signing used by deaf children. This provides the opportunity for a much larger and richer set of communications as long as the recipient of the communications also knows the code.

The multiply handicapped child may use all three approaches in some combinations. Through these techniques, even the most seriously handicapped child can find a way to communicate and become a part of society.

Figure 10.4 shows two different types of communication boards. The board at the bottom graphically depicts the elements that a child with limited reading skill could use with a pointer. The sentence construction board shown at the top of Figure 10.4 enables a more advanced child to construct messages and communicate at a higher level.

FIGURE 10.4
Communication Boards for Alternative Modes of Communication

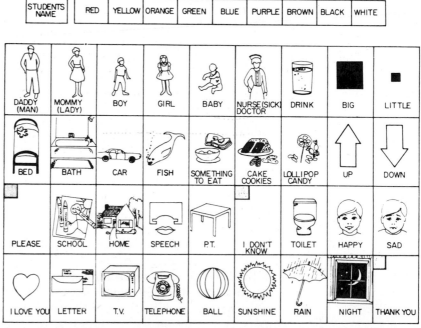

		0 1 2 3 4 5 6 7 8 9 10					
YES.	HI.	HOW ARE YOU?	I DON'T KNOW.	PLEASE.	THANK-YOU.	GOOD-BYE.	NO.
WHO	VERB			WHAT	WHERE	WHEN	

WHO	VERB			WHAT	WHERE	WHEN	
I MOMMY 　DADDY SANDY 　LINDA BOY 　GIRL YOU TEACHER THERAPIST HOUSE- MOTHER	HAVE 　PLAY GO 　AM READ 　SEE MAY LOVE LISTEN 　IS WANT 　ARE WILL 　EAT LIKE 　GET	A NOT IN FOR THE WITH AT TO AND	BIG 　MY LITTLE SICK GOOD 　BAD HAPPY 　SAD	BALL 　COOKIE PRESENT 　FUN CAR 　PUZZLE BED 　WORDS STORY 　LETTER GAME 　CAKE CANDY 　MAT BOOK 　DRINK	HOME PLAYROOM BATHROOM 　UP SCHOOL OUTSIDE ROOM 　P.T. STORE 　INSIDE DOWN SPEECH DINING ROOM	NIGHT YESTERDAY TOMORROW WEEKEND SUMMER EASTER CHRIST- MAS THANKS- GIVING TODAY	RED YELLOW ORANGE GREEN BLUE PINK PURPLE BROWN BLACK WHITE

STUDENTS NAME	RED	YELLOW	ORANGE	GREEN	BLUE	PURPLE	BROWN	BLACK	WHITE

DADDY (MAN)	MOMMY (LADY)	BOY	GIRL	BABY	NURSE (SICK) DOCTOR	DRINK	BIG	LITTLE
BED	BATH	CAR	FISH	SOMETHING TO EAT	CAKE COOKIES	LOLLIPOP CANDY	UP	DOWN
PLEASE	SCHOOL	HOME	SPEECH	P.T.	I DON'T KNOW	TOILET	HAPPY	SAD
I LOVE YOU	LETTER	T.V.	TELEPHONE	BALL	SUNSHINE	RAIN	NIGHT	THANK YOU

Source: E. McDonald and A. Shultz, Communication boards for cerebral-palsied children. *Journal of Speech and Hearing Disorders*, 1973, *38*, 73–88. Used with permission from the American-Speech-Language-Hearing Association.

HCEEP Network   In 1968 Congress passed the <u>Handicapped</u> <u>Children's Early Education Program</u> (HCEEP) which was designed to demonstrate the usefulness of preschool programs for handicapped children. In particular, it was hoped that the demonstrations would encourage states and local communities to consider establishing such services themselves. The program has focused on the problems of moderately to severely handicapped children and their families (DeWeerd, 1979). Over two hundred programs have been supported under HCEEP, which has proven to be an important catalyst for the implementation of new services and program extensions by state and local communities. The following programs and services are included in HCEEP:

Demonstration centers provide services to handicapped children and their families and present an exemplary model of the best of current practices.

Outreach centers have been successful demonstration centers that are designated to provide special services in training staff, demonstrating information, and helping others.

State implementation grants are special grants given to states to help them plan for the development and extension of state services for young handicapped children.

Early childhood institutes conduct long-term studies on the effectiveness of training methods, parent-child relationships, and so on, to find better ways to work with young handicapped children and their families.

Technical assistance is supplied by organizations whose purpose it is to provide continued training and special assistance to the demonstration centers and state departments of education.

Figure 10.5 briefly describes the nature of the program provided by one of the HCEEP demonstration centers.

Evaluation   The programs for the severely handicapped have not been operating long enough to be subjected to an evaluation of their efficacy. Clinical reports indicate that many children thought to be educationally hopeless have responded to stimulation and programming. One such attempt (Fredericks et al., 1975) described a preschool setting where six moderately to severely handicapped children were integrated into a day care program with over thirty normal children. The handicapped children were a year or two older than the nonhandicapped children whose ages were 3 to 6 years.

A well-organized and structured program designed to facilitate social behavior and language development was carried out at the

FIGURE 10.5
Portrait of an HCEEP
Demonstration
Center

Center on Human Development Preschool Program

Fiscal Agency: University of Oregon

Address: Center on Human Development
901 E. 18th Street
Eugene, Oregon 97403

Phone: 503/686-3575

Year of Funding: Second

Project Staff:

Director, 6 Teachers, Physical Therapist, Speech Pathologist (.50), 10 Aides

Characteristics of Target Population:

Sixty-five children ranging in age from seven months to five years: 50 have handicapping conditions that range from mildly to severely disabling; 15 children are functioning within normal limits. Twelve additional children and families are served in a home-based outreach program.

Program for Children:

Upon entering the home and school programs, all children are assessed in each of the curricular areas: conceptual learning, social behaviors, language, motor development, self-help, and academic skills. Following the initial assessment, individualized prescriptive programs are written. The individualized programs are implemented in home settings via the parent-infant program and in six classroom units where handicapped children work and play with their nonhandicapped peers.

Measures of Child Progress:

Three types of instruments are used to measure child progress:
1. Standardized instruments such as the Bayley Scales of Infant Development which are administered at the beginning and termination of the school year.
2. Student Progress Record, which is a state-wide assessment instrument, to monitor child progress from the beginning to the end of the school year.
3. Curriculum-linked assessments which are used to establish specific training objectives and progress toward acquisition.

Program for Parents:

Parents meet regularly with the staff to discuss their child's progress. Parent training is done through observation, classroom participation, parent training manual, and meetings. They are also active advocates for the children within the community, the state and the region.

Staff Development:

Weekly staff meetings are held to discuss problems that arise in the classroom. Consultants are brought in on a regular basis to provide outside evaluation and to keep the staff abreast of new information and intervention strategies.

Source: Handicapped children's early education program. Washington, D.C.: Bureau of Education for the Handicapped, Office of Education, 1979.

① day care center. In social behavior the special educators tried first to draw the handicapped youngsters from unoccupied behavior to independent play with toys and objects. A second stage in socialization was to help the handicapped children play in parallel activ-② ity with the normal children. Finally, the environment was ar-
③ ranged by the adults to facilitate associative play with the normal peers, who were encouraged and rewarded for interacting with the handicapped children. In language behavior there were attempts to reinforce and reward all verbal and nonverbal communication attempted by the handicapped children and to create situations that required verbalization on the part of the handicapped children to other peers and adults.

This carefully designed program reported meaningful gains in drawing the handicapped children from isolation into social interaction with their peers and a small but meaningful improvement in language expression. What this program illustrates is the benefit accruing from a carefully structured program and trained personnel. Merely placing handicapped children in the same physical environment as normal children without such measures is unlikely to produce major results. The Head Start program currently mandates that 10 percent of the youngsters selected for that program be handicapped. Unless that placement is accompanied by appropriate program design and personnel training, it is unlikely that the goals of integration will be met. Fredericks et al. (1975) commented:

> But it is critical to emphasize that, for moderately and severely handicapped children to benefit from placement in day care, Head Start, or any other preschool environment, the type and extent of training that must be provided to the staff is complex and of long duration. Specifically, it has been suggested here that carefully structured procedures are probably necessary to facilitate the child's improvement of social play and language interactions and generate interactive behaviors with nonhandicapped children. (p. 205)

CHARACTERISTICS OF CHILDREN WITH PHYSICAL HANDICAPS

The category of children with physical handicaps and other health impairments refers to a variety of nonsensory conditions that affect the child's well-being and that can create special educational problems centering around mobility, physical vitality, and self-image. Included in this broad category are conditions such as congenital malformations, epilepsy, muscular dystrophy, asthma, rheumatic fever, cerebral palsy (uncomplicated by mental retardation), and diabetes. Such physical handicaps or conditions are sometimes accompanied by other sensory, behavioral, or intellectual deficits as described in the sections on the multiply handicapped earlier in this chapter.

Increasing advances in biomedical science have sharply reduced or eliminated many of these conditions as serious educational problems, though their health implications may continue. The incidence of polio has been substantially reduced by the development and use of polio vaccine. Epilepsy, a condition in which the convulsive seizures of children had impaired their learning opportunities and social development, has been dramatically improved by the development of appropriate medication that controls the majority of seizures.

Table 10.7 shows some of the common conditions that have been grouped under the category of children with physical handicaps and other health impairments. Most of these conditions, as seen in the table, affect either mobility or physical vitality and a number of them require regular medication. On occasion, some disorders, such as cerebral palsy, affect the physical appearance of an individual and thus create an important secondary problem with which to cope. The intensity with which a handicapping condition may affect a child varies widely. For example, severe cases of asthma can result in limited mobility and in a hunched-over and unusual appearance because the child has continual difficulty breathing; however, in most instances, children with asthma, as with children who have epilepsy or diabetes, do not look physically different from the normal child, except under conditions of acute attack.

Because of problems with mobility and physical vitality, some of these young children remain homebound and must receive some special instruction at home, either by telephone or by having visiting teachers bring lessons to them. However, most of these youngsters are able to go to school on a reasonably regular schedule. The problems that the school may have in adapting the program for these children relate to each child's physical vitality, mobility, plus their own feelings about themselves and their perceived deviation from the behavioral and social norms of children their own age. These children are certain to have feelings about the unfairness of life to them, a "Why-did-this-happen-to-me?" reaction. It can be helpful for a parent or a teacher to permit expression of and to empathize with these emotions.

The number of children in this category is quite small in comparison to many of the other areas of special education. A national survey, noted earlier in this chapter, pointed out that there were less than 100,000 children combined in the two groupings of orthopedic handicaps and other health impairments (see page 419), making up less than 3 percent of the total number of children served under special education.

One of the heaviest burdens that many physically handicapped children and adults must carry is the revulsion and withdrawal behavior that many people show when they see an individual who has an obvious physical handicap. Why do so many people flinch and appear uncomfortable when they see a child with cerebral palsy or a deformed or missing limb? Perhaps the condition of the handicapped child reminds us of our own vulnerability. Perhaps there is something in human perception that is disturbed by a deviance from expected symmetry. We are not that far from our primitive heritage. Consequently, the malformed child distresses us and the urge to turn away or to rid ourselves of the offending image is great. It is the mark of maturity in our society that we have in many instances suppressed that urge in favor of a more constructive response.

TABLE 10.7
Common Physical Handicaps and Other Health Impairments

Condition	Description	Special Problems			
		Mobility	Regular Medication	Physical Vitality	Unusual Appearance
Asthma	A disorder marked by spasmodic contraction of bronchi causing shortness of breath		X	X	
Cerebral palsy	An impairment of motor function due to brain injury at or near the time of birth	X			X
Cystic fibrosis	A hereditary disease characterized by general dysfunction of the pancreas resulting in serious pulmonary problems		X	X	
Epilepsy	A group of disorders resulting in periodic seizures or convulsions		X	X	
Diabetes	A disorder of carbohydrate metabolism characterized by insulin deficiency; can lead to coma unless medication is provided		X	X	
Muscular dystrophy	A condition noted by progressive weakness and atrophy of skeletal muscles	X	X	X	X
Rheumatic fever	A condition created by infectious disease that results in damage to and reduced function of the heart	X		X	

The self-concept of a physically handicapped child depends in some measure on the attitude of others toward him. (Photo: © David S. Strickler/The Picture Cube.)

Whatever the cause, the negative reaction of many people can hardly be hidden from physically handicapped children. If our self-concept is built in some measure on the attitudes of others toward us, then can the self-concept of the handicapped child be immune from such negative experiences?

Children who are physically handicapped may have any number of additional problems or may have only the specific physical handicap by itself. Naturally if one or several of the other exceptionalities are involved in a significant way, the child will be referred to as multiply handicapped instead of just physically handicapped.

Although it is difficult to draw any general characteristics of physically handicapped children since they vary so much in cause and condition, there is a tendency to have some of these children influenced unduly by their environment and by the expectations that educators place on them. Fassler (1970) found that children with cerebral palsy performed better on psychological tests if they were allowed to wear a type of ear muff that reduced the distracting auditory sounds around them. Similar auditory muffling for normal children did not result in any change in performance.

The limited vitality and endurance that many physically handicapped children face are indicated in a study by Fair and Birch
(1971) who found that when physically handicapped children were
given a rest period between sections of a standardized achievement
test they performed better on the second section than did handicapped children who were given no rest. Rest periods did not seem
to influence the performance of nonhandicapped children. Thus,
many physically handicapped children seem to have problems of
distractibility and endurance that need to be taken into account in
educational planning.

Although there appears to be no inevitable set of negative characteristics accompanying any of the physical disorders, secondary
problems are likely to emerge. A large sample of children with
asthma, 199 boys and 172 girls between the ages of 6 and 12, were
given a wide range of tests, the results of which were compared
with a nonallergic sample of 419 boys and 400 girls. This comparison found that the allergic children were less well adjusted, had
more behavior problems, and were less intellectually gifted. In
terms of their interpersonal relationships, children with allergic
reactions were less likely to be chosen as leaders, or not likely to
be chosen first for games and other activities. They were, however,
able to get along with others and make new friends.

Stories told in the course of projective tests, such as the The-
matic Apperception Test (TAT), revealed that children with allergic
disorders expressed more than the usual verbalizations and bizarre
themes, more fears, and more fantasies. In conditions such as
asthma, when a child literally has to fight for the next breath, fantasies regarding death and early concern about death are not unusual (Rawls, Rawls, and Harrison, 1971). The limited research
suggests that children with physical handicaps and other health
impairments would be liable to have special personal and social
adaptation problems.

A child with no visible handicap under normal circumstances,
such as one who has asthma, epilepsy, or diabetes, may find that
other children are puzzled or shocked when he or she has a sudden
acute attack. Joe, a nine-year-old with epilepsy, periodically has
grand mal seizures (even though medication has helped to reduce
them) during which he falls to the floor and writhes about uncon-
scious. This can be a startling experience for classmates who are
not prepared. The teacher would be well advised to share with
Joe's classmates that he may have such a seizure from time to time
but that it is not damaging to him or others. The teacher can even
assign responsibilities in advance to some of the children to move
pieces of furniture out of the way so that Joe won't bump into

them during a seizure. Such a matter-of-fact approach, indicating that this is just another of life's problems that has to be coped with, communicates to the other children a more comfortable feeling about the seizure and, of course, about Joe himself.

EDUCATIONAL ADAPTATIONS FOR CHILDREN WITH PHYSICAL HANDICAPS

Modifications   Because of the heterogeneity of physically handicapping conditions, it is difficult to describe facilities for all the children. One child may have a deformed arm, another may have diabetes. One is mobile in the classroom, another is mobile on crutches, and still another is confined to a wheelchair. One has some verbal language facility, another may have emotional problems. With these differences in physical and mental abilities in mind, it becomes obvious that we can consider here only the more general types of modification.

School Adaptations

One of the most notable changes brought about by PL 94–142 and its companion, Section 504 of the Vocational Rehabilitation Act of 1973 (PL 93–112), is that the physical environment in the school has been made more hospitable to the physically handicapped and multiply handicapped child as a part of normal expectations, not as an unusual innovation. We now see ramps for wheelchairs, guardrails in toilets, nonskid surfaces, and other environmental modifications that encourage independence. Section 504 provides the basis for those changes with the following statement: "No otherwise qualified handicapped individual in the United States . . . which solely by reason of handicap (will) be excluded in the participation in, be denied the benefit of, or be subjected to discrimination under any program or activity receiving federal financial assistance" (Abeson and Zettel, 1977, p. 127).

Despite such legislative mandates, evidence suggests that much remains to be done in modifying local environments. Physically handicapped students often have their most difficult problem in getting into the learning environment in the first place. Although strong emphasis has been placed on the removal of physical barriers, a review of the current status of schools on a national basis by the Office of Civil Rights (1980) found that only

60 percent of school buildings were accessible to children with physical handicaps
55 percent of classrooms were accessible

51 percent of science laboratories were accessible

24 percent of toilets were accessible

Transportation

The transportation phase of the program for physically impaired children is expensive. Most will require transportation to and from school. They may be scattered in many areas of the city and will have to be transported for some distance. This means providing facilities for loading some of the children into the bus and arranging their seating for safety and comfort, especially if they have severe handicaps.

Special Equipment

In some schools special rooms for physical and occupational therapy are equipped with the necessary materials used in treating muscle disabilities and in improving motor coordination. Special chairs and cutout tables, which will support a child as he or she sits or stands, are common classroom equipment. Sometimes such equipment has to be made to specifications for a particular child if the physician in charge recommends special supports in a chair or table.

In addition to the modifications necessary in the gross physical environment, the teacher will need numerous aids and devices for instructional use. All of these pieces of equipment have special purposes: book racks for children who cannot hold books, ceiling projectors for children in bed in hospitals or at home, electric typewriters with remote control devices for children in bed, cots for special rest periods, and so on. What is actually needed in a particular class depends on the children in the class. The child who has to have support to stand needs a standing table. The child who cannot use his or her hands to turn pages needs an automatic page turner. The child who cannot follow a line or hold a pencil firmly needs a pencil holder or guides in writing. Special equipment is usually obtained only when there is a specific requirement for it since it is just an aid and has to be selected on an individual rather than a group basis.

Medical Supervision

School authorities are responsible for the total program of the child, which includes not only classroom instruction but also the child's health program. The physician may recommend special care and specifically prescribe that the child is to have rest periods and not become fatigued, that the child's diet is to be controlled according to physical needs, or that a particular postural aid is to be used to correct certain deformities.

Individualized Instruction

Because of the heterogeneous nature of this group of children and because of the wide range of adaptations necessary for varying abilities and achievements, much of the work is individualized. Since many severely and multiply handicapped children have limited firsthand experiences about their community or about the world, secondary experiences are necessary, especially through the use of visual aids, field trips, and particularly appropriate educational films and television.

The attitude of the teacher toward each child's personality and adjustment is of utmost importance. He or she must not only understand the physical problems and their requirements but also help motivate the child who is depressed and withdrawn, dampen the tantrums that sometimes follow frustration, and, in general, promote the personal and emotional adjustment of these children.

Preschool Programs

As with previously discussed areas of exceptionality, there is an emphasis on an early start for the physically handicapped child through systematic instruction in the preschool years. This may be done by bringing the physically handicapped child into a day care setting or through parent training programs. As with other parent programs, one of the first tasks is to deal with the emotional reaction of the parents to the fact that their child is handicapped. As Douglas and Hoffman (1978) have pointed out:

The parents . . . very frequently have a tendency to shield the handicapped child from experiences (in part as a protection of the child from potentially hurtful encounters) and in many cases to treat him as a much younger child as well. The parent may be so obsessed with the child's limitations that newly developed skills are overlooked. (p. 266)

One of the first steps is to convince the parent that, in some cases, the child is capable, given systematic instruction and some adapted equipment. Table 10.8 provides examples of some activities, one of which uses an adapted tricycle so that the child can maneuver it even with physical handicaps. In this case the tricycle has the handlebars converted to a vertical position, a special seat, and special pedals that allow the child to use it despite his or her physical limitations. The payoff for such activities is not only the strengthening of the motor skills, but the activity can be used to stimulate language and cognition objectives and results in a better self-image as children prove to themselves, to their parents, and to others that they are competent despite certain handicaps.

Learning Environment   To provide for the wide range and combinations of intellectual and physical disabilities found among physically handicapped children, different kinds of educational provisions have evolved. The following types of facilities have been organized for the physically impaired child.

REGULAR SCHOOL CLASSES A large majority of children with mild or moderate physical handicaps attend regular classes with

TABLE 10.8
Developmental Consequences of a Physical Activity

Major Activity	Motor	Language and Cognition	Social-Emotional
1. Instruction in riding and use of an adapted tricycle	Bilateral hand use; reciprocal leg movements	Use of names and functions in talking about the tricycle; imaginary play through assuming roles and taking trips	Satisfaction of successfully riding the tricycle; tricycle offered as a present and source of fun; increased mobility for relating to peers through use of the tricycle; parents view tricycle as an accomplishment rather than a setback to mobility
2. Symmetrical sitting and riding on a rocking horse	Bilateral hand use; bilateral integration of movement	Imaginary play, such as rocking games and "cowboys"; use of action words (e.g., *fast, slow*)	Pleasurable gross motor activity provides an outlet for hyperactivity; opportunity for self-initiated and independent use of rocking horse
3. Finger painting on an easel in a group setting	Bilateral hand use	Experiencing a new medium; sustained attention to a satisfying task; exploration and use of concepts related to color and texture; meaningful play activity fostering creative expression	Opportunity for peer group activity; opportunity to indicate desire to stop activity without resorting to temper tantrums

Source: F. Connor, G. Williamson, and J. Siepp, *Program guide for infants and toddlers with neuromotor and other developmental disabilities.* New York: Teachers College Press, 1978, p. 288. Copyright © 1978 by Frances P. Connor, John M. Siepp, and G. Gordon Williamson. Reprinted by permission of the publisher.

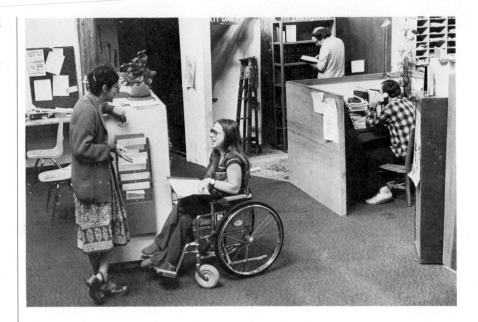

Physically handicapped people can receive invaluable assistance from agencies that help them lead more independent lives.
(Photo: © 1980 Peter Menzel/Stock, Boston.)

nonhandicapped children. Adaptations to their physical conditions are made in the regular class.

HOME INSTRUCTION Home instruction is provided for children who are physically disabled to the extent that they cannot attend a school or live where a school suitable for them is unavailable.

HOSPITAL SCHOOLS Hospital schools generally enroll physically handicapped children during short-term diagnostic and treatment periods. Children with severe physical handicaps are usually admitted to such hospitals.

SHELTERED-CARE FACILITIES Children with severe physical handicaps who cannot be taken care of at home are provided with sheltered-care (residential) facilities and are offered education in these centers.

SPECIAL SCHOOLS OR CLASSES Special schools or special classes in regular schools are one type of facility for the multiply and severely handicapped child. Such facilities are found in separate schools or in a class or section of a regular school. For some activities and for some children integration with ordinary children for part of the day is practical. Such mainstreaming is practiced more widely with preschool children.

RESOURCE AND ITINERANT SERVICES When the child is in a regular grade and the program is mainstreamed, resource rooms and itinerant services are furnished for those children who need supporting help. Medical services in the form of physical therapy, speech remediation, and occupational therapy are also provided.

SUMMARY OF MAJOR IDEAS

1. Multiply handicapped children are those who have more than one exceptionality, each of which would be severe enough to justify special education services.
2. The prevalence of multiply handicapped children is less than 5 percent of the total number of handicapped children, but each child presents a major challenge for special education.
3. Many different types of multiply handicapping conditions affect children, but some combinations are more familiar to the educator. These include (a) mental retardation and cerebral palsy, (b) mental retardation and hearing impairment, (c) mental retardation and severe behavior problems, (d) autism, (e) behavior disturbance and hearing impairment, and (f) dual sensory impairments of vision and hearing.
4. A major attempt is being made to deinstitutionalize multiply handicapped children and to integrate them whenever possible into a mainstreamed or least restrictive environment.
5. A comprehensive system of special education for multiply handicapped children includes (a) a developmental framework, (b) early and continuous intervention, (c) systematic instructional procedures, (d) appropriate curricula to meet the special needs of the handicapped, (e) adjunctive services to provide additional health and social services, and (f) objective evaluation to provide evidence of growth due to special education.
6. A curriculum for multiply handicapped children would consist of some combination of self-help skills, gross and fine motor skills, communication skills, socialization, prevocational and vocational training, functional academics, and recreation and leisure skills.
7. A major adaptation for communication skills development is the augmentative systems for communication allowing children who have trouble speaking to develop receptive language through the use of communication boards.

8. Children with physical handicaps or with other health impairing conditions have major problems with mobility or physical vitality that require environmental and program adjustments.

9. The negative and withdrawal reactions of many peers and adults to physical handicaps create self-image problems for the child with the handicap.

10. Despite federal legislation, many learning environments remain inaccessible to the physically handicapped. Less than 60 percent of school buildings, classrooms, science laboratories, and toilets are currently accessible for the physically handicapped.

11. Preschool programs for physically impaired children focus on parent training and the adaptations of common tools and toys to accentuate early physical and motor development.

12. There are many learning settings for physically handicapped and other health impaired children including home instruction for those who are homebound. Other programs—from mainstreaming to resource rooms to special schools—may be found in various communities in the United States.

UNRESOLVED ISSUES

1. Where Are the Trained Personnel? The educational problems for children with two or more major handicaps are difficult to meet for even the most sophisticated professionals. Few professionals actually receive training in two or more areas. Generally, a teacher of the deaf will try to learn something about mental retardation or a teacher of the visually handicapped will try to gain insight into neurologically impaired children. There are few organized training programs to prepare specialists for children with multiply handicapping conditions.

2. The Cost of Technology. Handicapped children have gained much through the steady progress of technology but the benefits have not been as widespread as needed because of the high cost of the products. Despite a variety of efforts to help those who need such tools for communication or mobility, most handicapped people still have trouble gaining access to the products of modern science and technology.

3. Preschool Programs for the Handicapped. Extensive attempts have been made at the state and federal level to encourage local programs to provide services to handicapped children below the age of 5. The vast organization of the public schools and the mandatory requirements for attendance have made special programs for the handicapped easier to establish for children over age 5. Despite the wide general agreement on the advantages of providing special services as early as possible, there are still many handicapped children who do not have the benefit of a preschool start to master basic social and adaptive skills.

4. Public Acceptance of Physically Handicapped. Although much progress has been made in increasing acceptance of the child with visible handicaps, the negative reaction of many well-meaning people to children with cerebral palsy or muscular dystrophy or similar disorders causes many adaptive problems for these children. Children with handicaps often have to mature into adolescence before realizing that it is not their problem that is causing the reaction but rather the problem of the so-called normal individual. As more information about handicaps becomes known and available to all, such negative reactions to handicapped people are likely to diminish. Acceptance in the workplace also remains a major barrier, even more than the physical barriers that recent legislation has tried to counteract.

REFERENCES OF SPECIAL INTEREST

Cohn, M., & Gross, P. *The developmental resource* (Vol. 2). New York: Grune & Stratton, 1979.

This book deals with one of the most difficult issues in special education. When a child has multiple handicaps and developmental progress has been markedly retarded, teachers have difficulty determining the point in the developmental process at which the child's program should begin and identifying the sequence of events that would follow some kind of developmental pattern. The authors have provided a compendium of developmental skills across the cognitive, social, and other domains and have fixed them at various age levels allowing the reader to see not only the approximate level at which a child is expected to attain various skills but also the developmental order of skills that follow.

Connor, F., Williamson, G., & Siepp, J. (Eds.). *Program guide for infants and toddlers with neuromotor and other developmental disabilities.* New York: Teachers College Press, 1978.

This book is a compilation of the experience and insight gained by professionals in forty-nine centers of the National Collaborative Infant Project. Over four thousand children, half of whom were diagnosed as having cerebral palsy, participated in this effort to produce a program guide for curriculum development for young handicapped children. The book is divided into three parts: (1) the basic foundations for a program serving atypical children and their families; (2) developmental programs in movement, prespeech, language, cognition, and the socioemotional domain; and (3) the curriculum in practical applications.

Doyle, P., Goodman, J., Grotsky, J., & Mann, L. *Helping the severely handicapped child: A guide for parents and teachers*. New York: Thomas Crowell Publishers, 1979.

This book provides parents with very specific advice on how to help their handicapped child acquire a level of self-care at home—feeding, dressing, toilet training, and so forth. Other sections of the book help parents find assistance for their child through the identification of appropriate community agencies, special equipment, and even babysitting. A final section details the legal rights of the handicapped child so that the parents can protect the right of their child to receive a free, appropriate education.

Fredericks, H., & staff of the Teaching Research Infant and Child Center. *The teaching research curriculum for moderately and severely handicapped*. Springfield, Ill.: Charles C Thomas, 1980.

This publication consists of two volumes—*Self-Help and Cognitive* and *Gross and Fine Motor*—that provide eighty-five detailed task analyses of self-help, cognitive, and motor skills. The *Self-Help and Cognitive* volume includes steps in teaching self-feeding, dressing, personal hygiene, personal information, reading, and number concepts. The *Gross and Fine Motor* volume consists of twenty-five task analyses of motor skills. Most of the task analyses have undergone field testing by many teachers.

Haring, N., & Brown, L. (Eds.). *Teaching the severely handicapped* (Vol. 1). New York: Grune & Stratton, 1976.

A good overview of philosophy and practice in education of the severely handicapped. Major sections deal with developmental sequence and curricula, assessment, performance measurement, and intervention strategies. Each chapter is written by specialists in the field and is representative of the optimistic viewpoint that important educational goals can be met for the severely handicapped.

Sontag, N., Smith, J., & Certo, N. (Eds.). *Educational programming for the severely and profoundly handicapped.* Reston, Va.: Council for Exceptional Children, 1977.

This compilation of articles and papers places a heavy emphasis on teaching strategies for the most severely handicapped child. A special section focuses on alternative systems of communication. The need to plan for family involvement and community reintegration is also stressed. A good portrait of the field at the time of publication.

Epilogue

We would like to end this text the way it began, by reflecting on some of the important changes that have occurred in the past quarter century in trying to cope with the educational problems of exceptional children. We would also like to present briefly what current work in the field implies for the future of special education programs.

The truth of the statement "*Today* was *tomorrow, yesterday*" is apparent. The present blends into the future like the flow of a river going downstream. We expect present trends to unfold into the future in some predictable fashion. They reflect not only the growing knowledge about exceptional children but also the new techniques and technology that will aid in their education. Such trends also include the changing attitudes of the children, their parents, and members of the larger society.

Special education has been a field in ferment during the past twenty-five years. There is good reason to believe that changes in special education will continue for some time to come, in part because of the momentum that has built up with recent advances in the field, but also because special education is inextricably linked to the general public education program. The winds of change are being strongly felt throughout the entire American education enterprise. Symbolically, it might be said that when the larger American educational system catches cold, special education gets pneumonia!

TANGIBLE GAINS

Much of this text has been devoted to covering significant advances and improvements in the education of exceptional children over the past quarter century. There are many lists that could be made detailing the most significant of these gains. The following list focuses on a few that seem particularly important.

1. **Public acceptance.** Perhaps the greatest advance has been in the growing public acceptance of the capabilities of exceptional children when they are given appropriate educational opportunities. This public acceptance has brought forth commitment for increased financial support for special education at local, state, and federal levels to provide those resources which, it is hoped, will allow each exceptional child to more closely approach his or her potential.

2. **The law and the courts.** The increasing public acceptance of children with handicaps has been translated into court decisions and laws that confirm the right to education for all American citizens, handicapped or not. It has further confirmed the philosophy that children with handicaps should not be separated from the major flow of society. Such provisions have increased opportunities for exceptional children to practice their social adaptation skills with many different groups and in many different settings in our society.

3. **Diagnosis of learning problems.** During the past twenty-five years procedures for diagnosing special learning problems have become more sophisticated. New tests and performance tasks have enabled educators to be much more specific in observing the strengths and weaknesses of each exceptional child. Through devices such as the *individualized educational plan*, programs are designed that reflect the individual strengths and weaknesses on which the teacher or the therapist should focus.

4. **Technological advances.** The revolution in electronics and computers has had an impact on the field of exceptional children as well as on many other fields in our society. Capabilities exist for successfully producing special communication devices to transform the printed word into tactual stimulation or auditory signals for people with visual handicaps. Telephone lines are used to carry typewriter messages for those who are hearing impaired. Inventions such as communication boards enhance the ability of handicapped individuals to receive and transmit information about their basic needs. Electronics have been used to help orthopedically handicapped children move about more effectively.

5. **Behavior analysis and change.** The rapidly developing techniques of behavior analysis, when combined with detailed task analysis and a program of systematic rewards for effective performance, have brought moderately and severely handicapped chil-

dren into more interactive situations with their teachers, who may have previously underestimated their capabilities or misjudged their motivation. While the nature of their handicaps makes the progress of these children slow, it is clearly possible that progress can be made by using these instructional techniques.

6. **Family and ecology.** We have gradually come to realize that the environment in which we live can have a significant influence on us. The importance of the family and society in general to the development of the exceptional child has led to a whole new series of attempts to train parents and to create a more favorable learning environment for the child. Special education now provides not only direct instruction for exceptional children but also a variety of devices and strategies designed to create enriched and facilitating environments that enable the children to make the most of their capabilities.

7. **Trained cadres of professionals.** The continuing increase in the number of exceptional children who receive special services means a similar increase in the number of professionals who devote their careers to providing those services. The universities of this country, aided substantially by federal grants, train teachers, speech-language pathologists, school psychologists, and other professionals who provide special services for exceptional children. This cadre of trained personnel supplies the professional base for effective programming and hope for developing more sophisticated techniques and procedures in the future.

TARGETS FOR TOMORROW

Despite the tangible gains previously listed, there are, for those who are interested in the exceptional child, many obstacles to overcome. As the "Unresolved Issues" sections in each chapter have revealed, there are still many problems to be solved by you, the readers of this text, who represent the future generation of special educators. The following is a list of some agreed-upon targets for the immediate future.

1. **More effective instructional skills.** Although the courts and the laws can mandate the placement of exceptional children in the mainstream, they cannot mandate effective instruction after children have been placed. We have much to learn about the environmental design and the specific type of instruction and curriculum that will enable the professional to teach with a high degree of competence and thereby make the most of the opportunities created by judicial and legislative actions.

2. **Better working relationships with regular educators.** Integration of handicapped children into the mainstream of society has helped emphasize the need for cooperation between professionals in special education and in regular education. These relationships are often entangled by strong egos on both sides and the kind of professional rivalry that is less than facilitating. With many people of good will striving for ways to create productive working environments for all of the professionals involved, it is likely that we will see more effective cooperative planning in the future. There is little doubt that such cooperation is sorely needed if we are to provide the best of what we know for exceptional children and their families.

3. **Providing vocational education programs.** It has been noted a number of times in this text that the most detailed program descriptions of work with exceptional children have usually been found at the elementary school level. In many respects the most difficult part of the educational program for exceptional children has been at the secondary level where the basic skills that the child has learned have to be translated into vocational and career education programs to help the exceptional individual function in the adult work place. This is especially important in view of disturbing talk concerning the possibility that handicapped people may become a permanent underclass in our society. We need more detailed strategies and curriculum programs for all types of exceptional children at the secondary level and a closer integration between that secondary program and the world of work to which the exceptional child must adapt.

4. **Development of early childhood programs.** As puzzling as the limited development of secondary programs for exceptional children has been, the inability to provide systematic services for handicapped children below age 5 is even more disturbing. While many communities have made attempts in this area, there are few systematic programs and no single responsible community agency to provide special services at a time in the child's life that all professionals agree is crucial to development. Whether the public schools take on these responsibilities or other community agencies accept them, we need to provide more consistent help to these children during their most formative years—years in which a multitude of behavior patterns may emerge to further complicate the job of the special educator.

5. **Wide application of technological advances.** While modern technological advances represent major scientific breakthroughs in improving communications, they often have had limited impact on

the child with handicaps. The reasons for this involve the extraordinary expense of some electronic devices and their bulk and complexity, which makes them difficult to transport and use except in central locations such as special schools. The wide dissemination of both technological and instructional advances will remain a problem until those obstacles are overcome.

6. **Improving measurement instruments.** Much of the knowledge that educational personnel have accumulated about exceptional children and their instruction has been obtained by means of the assessment instruments that are used. These measures not only define the field of interest for professionals but also limit the scope of their work. Definitions of self-concept, intelligence, achievement, and other key educational concepts are generally derived by the instruments that are used to measure such concepts. The ideas or concepts that we have will be no more sophisticated than the instruments we are able to develop to represent such concepts. We need better tools to express the broad social adaptation and self-concept domains of the individual. New and better measures are needed to characterize the growing importance of family-child and societal-family interactions that are the crux of the ecological approach.

7. **Maintaining gains.** Although many gains have been made in the battle for equal opportunity for handicapped children, those gains are not necessarily permanent. The cost of programs for the handicapped and, to a lesser extent, the higher cost of programs for the gifted, may eventually become a sticking point for public support. A recent study by the Rand Corporation showed that the per pupil cost for educating exceptional children is two to five times more than that for the average student. While the cost of special education may be more expensive, the benefits are noteworthy. Through special programs, exceptional individuals have achieved a greater measure of independence and have made significant contributions to society. Nevertheless, further advances in the field of special education require public acceptance that the higher costs are part of society's long-range moral and educational commitments.

8. **Providing resources to promote new advances.** Over the past fifty years, experiences in industry, agriculture, medicine, and other fields have demonstrated rather clearly those elements that are necessary for a discipline, a field of study, or a business to prosper. In each instance, the provision of resources allows for the continuous improvement of the product involved, whether that product is a corn crop, health services, or increased profits for the manufacturer of shoes. These resources include support for *research*

to generate new ideas and concepts, *training* to provide new skills and techniques to practitioners, *development* to organize current knowledge into effective practice, *demonstration* to display to others the best of current practices, and *dissemination* to communicate effective and proven ideas from one place to another. It is not at all clear that the field of special education will receive such support in sufficient degree to allow for continuous improvement in programs that professionals, parents, and interested citizens desire.

As was noted in earlier editions of *Educating Exceptional Children*, our democratic philosophy is based on the belief that "all men are created equal"—equal before the law—so it involves equality of opportunity. This implies educational opportunity for all children—the right of each child to receive help in learning to the limits of his or her capacity whether that capacity is small or great. It is ironic that it took nearly two hundred years for this philosophy to be enacted into law. The intent of PL 94–142, the Education for All Handicapped Children Act, enacted by the U.S. Congress in 1975, matches that of the Declaration of Independence, the cornerstone of our democratic society, as the following paraphrase demonstrates:

We hold these truths to be self-evident, that all children, handicapped and nonhandicapped, are created equal; that they are endowed by their creator with certain inalienable rights, among these are the right to equal education to the maximum of each child's capability. To secure these rights, Public Law 94–142 was established. We, the people of these United States, solemnly declare that all exceptional children shall be educated at public expense, and that their education will be in the least restrictive environment.

As Americans, we live in a society where criticism of our institutions and their practices is an expected and valued social element because self-satisfied institutions or professions can eventually become a danger to their clients. Much criticism is directed toward schools, government, business, the media, labor, churches, and other social institutions. Much of this criticism, we might add, is not without merit and is often well-deserved. Still, it is worthwhile to reflect that some credit is due to a society that is trying very hard to maintain an ideal that all citizens should be given equal educational opportunity and that special provisions will be made for those who are so exceptional that it becomes difficult for them to realize that goal without special help.

Glossary

Adjunctive services Services that supplement or support the basic educational program. Also various diagnostic procedures, medical consultation, paraprofessional aides, and the use of mechanical aids in vision and hearing.

Adventitious Acquired accidentally in contrast to congenital or inherent causes.

Agraphia Impairment in the ability to write.

Albinism Hereditary lack of pigment in the iris, skin, and hair.

Alexia Loss of the ability to read written or printed language.

Amino acid One of a group of acids that are both basic and acid and are obtained from protein by hydrolysis.

Amniocentesis A procedure for analyzing the amniotic fluid (a watery liquid in which the embryo is suspended) of the pregnant woman to determine any genetic defects in the unborn child.

Angular gyrus A cerebral convolution that forms the back part of the lower parietal region of the brain.

Anticonvulsant medication Medication employed to inhibit or prevent the onset of epileptic or other convulsive seizures.

Aphasia Loss or impairment of the ability to communicate by language, spoken or written, or by signs.

Asphyxia Loss of consciousness as a result of too little oxygen. Considered as one possible cause of brain damage at birth.

Aspirate To pronounce a vowel, a consonant, or a word with an initial *h* sound.

Asthma A disease marked by recurrent attacks of wheezing coughs, labored breathing (particularly on expiration of air), and a sense of constriction due to spasmodic contraction of the bronchi.

Ataxia A form of cerebral palsy marked by incoordination in voluntary muscular movements.

Athetosis A form of cerebral palsy marked by slow, recurring, weaving movements of arms and legs, and by facial grimaces.

Audiogram A graphic record of hearing acuity at selected intensities throughout the normal range of audibility, recorded from a pure-tone audiometer.

Audiometer An instrument for testing acuity of hearing.

Auditory association Ability to relate concepts presented orally.

Auditory closure The ability to recognize the whole word or phrase from the presentation of a partial auditory stimulus.

Auditory reception The ability to derive meaning from orally presented material.

Auditory sequential memory The ability to remember a sequence of auditory stimuli.

Aura, epileptic A subjective sensation that precedes and marks the onset of an epileptic attack.

Autism A childhood disorder rendering the child noncommunicative and showing ritualistic behavior or obsession with sameness.

Aversive stimulus A stimulus that a subject will avoid if possible.

Behavior modification Applied behavior analysis, using behavior concepts and laws to deal with problems of education and other life adjustments.

Bilingual Using or able to use two languages.

Bronchiectasis A chronic dilation of one of the two main branches of the windpipe or their subdivisions.

Carbohydrate Any of various neutral compounds as sugars, starches, and cellulose that constitute a major part of human foods.

Cataract A condition in which the crystalline lens of the eye, its capsule, or both become opaque with consequent dimming of vision.

Catastrophic reaction Response to a shock or a threatening situation with which an individual is unprepared to cope. Behavior is inadequate, vacillating, inconsistent, and generally retarded.

Central nervous system (CNS) That part of the nervous system to which sensory impulses are transmitted and from which motor impulses originate; in vertebrates, the brain and spinal cord.

Cephalic Pertaining to the head.

Cerebral dominance An assumption that one cerebral hemisphere generally dominates the other in control of bodily movements. In most individuals the left side of the brain controls language and is considered the dominant hemisphere.

Cerebral dysfunction Refers to a specific learning disability in mental functioning where the suspected cause is in physiological or neurological operation of the brain.

Cerebral palsy Any of the number of abnormal conditions affecting control of the motor system due to brain lesions.

Cerebrospinal fluid The fluid that circulates in certain spaces within the brain and down the central canal of the spinal cord.

Chromosome One of the minute bodies in the nucleus of a cell that contains the genes or hereditary factors.

Cleft palate Congenital fissure of the roof of the mouth, often associated with cleft lip (harelip).

Clonic Pertaining to a spasm (clonus) in which rigidity and relaxation alternate in rapid succession.

Clonus Involuntary rapid contractions and relaxations of a muscle.

Conductive hearing loss A condition that reduces the intensity of the sound vibrations reaching the auditory nerve in the inner ear.

Congenital Present in an individual at birth.

Conservation The ability to retain a concept of area, mass, length, and other features when superficial changes are made in the appearance of an object or scene.

Control group A group of subjects who are similar to those used in an experiment but who do not receive the experimental treatment.

Criterion-referenced test A test designed to measure a child's development in terms of absolute levels of mastery, as opposed to the child's status relative to other children, as in a norm reference test.

Cystic fibrosis A hereditary disease due to a generalized dysfunction of the pancreas.

Decibel A unit of measure of the relative loudness of sound, from the faintest sound that can be heard to a sound that is painful. It is used in measuring the degree of hearing loss.

Diabetes mellitus A disorder of carbohydrate metabolism, characterized by insulin deficiency and an excessive amount of glucose (sugar) in the urine and in the blood.

Diagnostic prescriptive teaching An educational strategy of delineating a child's strengths and weaknesses and then of designing a specific program for teaching on the basis of those findings.

Diplegia Bilateral paralysis affecting like parts on both sides of the body.

Disinhibition Lack of ability to refrain from response to what is perceived, often resulting in hyperactivity and distractibility.

Dysarthria Difficulty in the articulation of words due to involvement of the central nervous system.

Dyscalculia Inability to perform mathematical functions.

Dysgraphia Inability to produce the motor movements required for handwriting.

Dyslexia Impairment of the ability to read.

Edema The presence of abnormally large amounts of fluid in the intercellular tissue spaces of the body.

Electroencephalograph An instrument for graphically recording electrical brain waves.

Embryo The human organism from conception up to the third month of pregnancy.

Encephalitis lethargica An infectious inflammation of the brain (sleeping sickness).

Endogenous Originating from within. A term used to characterize a constitutional condition. Compare *exogenous*.

Epicanthic fold A congenital formation of the eyelid consisting of a vertical fold of skin on either side of the nose.

Epilepsy A group of nervous diseases marked primarily by convulsions of varying forms and degrees.

Etiology The study of causes or origins of a disease or condition.

Exaphoria Insufficient action of certain muscles of the eye so that one eye tends to deviate outward but can be controlled by extra muscular effort.

Exogenous Derived or developed from external causes.

Experimental group A group participating in an experiment that is subjected to whatever is being tested or evaluated.

Familial Occurring in members of the same family, as a familial disease.

Feebleminded An outmoded term used to refer to the entire range of mentally retarded individuals. In England it referred to the higher levels of the mentally retarded.

Fetus The unborn child from the third month of pregnancy until birth.

Figure-ground disturbance The inability to discriminate a figure from its background.

Finger agnosia The inability to recognize or identify the individual fingers of one's own hand when stimulated by touch.

Galactosemia An inherited condition of mental retardation caused by an error in the metabolism of the galactose in milk.

Glaucoma A disease characterized by increased pressure inside the eyeball caused by accumulation of fluid in the front portion.

Gonorrhea An infectious disease of the genitourinary tract, transmitted chiefly by sexual intercourse.

Grammatic closure Ability to make use of the redundancies of oral language in acquiring automatic habits for handling syntax and grammatical infections.

Grand mal An epileptic seizure in which the convulsions are severe and widespread with rather prolonged loss of awareness.

Haptic Pertaining to the sense of touch and kinesthesis.

Hemiplegia Paralysis of one side of the body.

Hemophilia A hereditary condition characterized by delayed clotting of the blood with consequent difficulty in checking hemorrhage.

Hydrocephalus A condition of excess cerebrospinal fluid within the ventricular and subarachnoid spaces in the brain.

Hyperactivity Excessive movement or motor restlessness.

Hyperkinesis Pathologically excessive motion.

Hypertonicity Excessive tension in the condition of a muscle not at work.

Hypoactive Showing diminished motor function or activity.

Idiot An outdated term referring to the most severely retarded for whom total dependency throughout life was expected.

Imbecile An outmoded term used to refer to the moderately retarded (IQ range 25-50), who are roughly equivalent to the subgroup referred to as trainable retarded children.

Incus The central one of three small bones in the middle ear that transmit sound to the inner ear.

Individual education plan (IEP) A formal statement of short-term and long-term objectives and educational services to meet the unique needs of a particular handicapped child.

Insulin A protein hormone produced by the pancreas and secreted into the blood where it regulates carbohydrate (sugar) metabolism.

Interindividual Pertaining to a comparison of one person with another or of one person with a group of individuals.

Intonation Rise and fall in pitch of the voice in speech.

Intraindividual Pertaining to a comparison of different characteristics within an individual.

In utero In the uterus; the period of time in a baby's life from conception until birth.

Keratitis Inflammation of the cornea.

Kynesthesis Sensations from nerve endings in the muscles, joints, and tendons that are stimulated by bodily movements and tensions.

Laterality Awareness of the two sides of the body and the ability to identify left and right. Often used to mean preferential use of one side of the body.

Least restrictive environment The philosophy, supported in some legislation, of bringing the handicapped as close to the normal social setting as possible.

Lipids Any one of numerous fats and fatlike materials that, together with carbohydrates and proteins, form the principal structural components of living cells.

Mainstreaming An administrative procedure for keeping exceptional children in the normal classroom for the majority of the school day.

Malleus The largest and outermost of the three small bones in the middle ear that carry sound to the inner ear.

Malocclusion Abnormality in the coming together of the teeth.

Mastoidectomy Surgical removal of the mastoid cells surrounding the temporal bone.

Megavitamin therapy A treatment program that features an unusually heavy dosage of selected vitamins to modify behavioral and emotional disturbances.

Meningitis Inflammation of the meninges (the membranes covering the brain and spinal cord), sometimes affecting vision, hearing, and/or intelligence.

Metabolism The conversion of digested nutrients into building material for living tissue or energy to meet the body's needs.

Minimum brain dysfunction A poorly defined syndrome often including hyperactivity, distractibility, perseveration, and disorders of perception, body image, laterality, and sometimes symbolization.

Monoplegia Paralysis of one body part.

Moron A term not in current use that referred to the upper range of mentally retarded individuals capable of self-sufficiency under favorable environmental conditions. Roughly equivalent to the group referred to as "educable."

Mosaicism A form of Down's syndrome (mongolism) in which adjacent cells will be found to contain different numbers of chromosomes.

Muscular dystrophy One of the more common primary diseases of muscle. It is characterized by weakness and atrophy of the skeletal muscles with increasing disability and deformity as the disease progresses.

Myopia Nearsightedness in which the rays from distant objects are brought to a focus before they reach the retina.

Nephrosis A noninflammatory, degenerative condition of the kidney.

Neurologic Pertaining to the normal and abnormal functions of the nervous system.

Neurophysiological Pertaining to the physiology of the nervous system.

Normalization A philosophy encouraging environmental design as much like the norm as possible. Even in institutionalized settings it is possible to create more normal living arrangements to aid eventual adaptive behavior.

Obturator Any organic structure or prosthetic device in the body (e.g., the soft palate) that closes or stops an opening.

Open classroom A classroom providing learning centers in open space, allowing children of various levels of ability some freedom of choice, interests, and creativity.

Ophthalmia neonatorum Gonorrheal inflammation of, and discharge from, the conjunctiva of the eye of the newborn baby under two weeks.

Ophthalmologist A physician who specializes in the diagnosis and treatment of defects and diseases of the eye.

Optometrist A person who examines, measures, and treats certain eye defects by methods requiring no physician's license.

Osteomyelitis Inflammation of bone that begins with a hematogenous abcess and, if not checked, may spread through the bone to involve the marrow and other parts.

Otitis media An inflammation of the middle ear.

Otolaryngoscopic Referring to an examination of the ear, nose, and throat.

Otosclerosis The formation of spongy bone in the capsule bone in the ear.

Paraplegia Paralysis of both legs and the lower part of the body; motion and sensation are affected.

Perinatal The period of time closely surrounding the time of birth.

Perseveration Continuation of an activity after cessation of the causative stimulus.

Petit mal Epileptic seizure in which there may be only a momentary dizziness or blackout or some automatic action of which the patient has no knowledge.

Pharynx That part of the throat that leads from mouth and nose to the larynx.

Phenylketonuria (PKU) An inherited error of metabolism resulting in a lack of the necessary enzyme for oxydizing phenylalanine which in turn promotes accumulation of phenylpyruvic acid and mental retardation.

Phonation The production of speech sounds.

Phoneme A speech sound or closely related variants commonly regarded as being the same sound.

Poliomyelitis An acute viral disease characterized by involvement of the central nervous system, sometimes resulting in paralysis.

Postnatal After birth.

Prenatal Occurring or existing before birth.

Proprioceptive Pertaining to stimulations from the muscles, tendons, and labyrinth which give information concerning the position and movement of the body and its members.

Prosthesis An artificial substitute for an absent part of the body.

Prosthodontics Making dental substitutes such as crowns, bridges, and dentures.

Psycholinguistics The study of the process whereby the intentions of speakers are transformed into signals and whereby those signals are transformed into interpretations by hearers.

Psychomotor epilepsy A form of epilepsy in which the seizures consist of purposeful but inappropriate acts; a difficult form to diagnose and control.

Psychopathology The study of the causes and nature of mental disease.

Psychotropic drug A medication used primarily for its behavioral effects; used with children particularly for its influence on attention and hyperactivity.

Recessive trait A trait, controlled by heredity, that remains latent or subordinate to a dominant characteristic.

Reinforcement A procedure to strengthen a response by the administration of immediate rewards (positive reinforcement).

Resonance The vibrating quality of a sound.

Response The activity of an organism or an organ, or the inhibition of previous activity resulting from stimulation.

Retina A layer of light-sensitive cells at the back of the eyeball. These cells receive the visual image formed by the lens and carry the message to the brain via the optic nerve.

Retrolental fibroplasia A disease of the retina in which a mass of scar tissue forms in back of the lens of the eye. Both eyes are usually affected, and it occurs chiefly in infants born prematurely who received excessive oxygen.

Rheumatoid arthritis A systemic disease characterized by inflammation of the joints and a broad spectrum of manifestations often involving destruction of the joints with resultant deformity.

Rh incompatibility The combination of an Rh-negative mother and an Rh-positive father can produce antibodies that can cause serious consequences for the fetus unless the condition is identified and blood transfer procedures are instituted immediately after birth.

Rubella German measles.

Schema A number of ideas or concepts combined into a coherent plan; a model that displays the essential or important relations between concepts.

Schizophrenia A group of psychotic reactions characterized by fundamental disturbances in reality relationships, by a conceptual world determined excessively by feeling, and by marked affective, intellectual, and overt behavioral disturbances.

Sensorimotor Referring to an act whose nature is primarily dependent on the combined or integrated functioning of sense organs and motor mechanisms.

Sensorineural hearing loss A defect of the inner ear or the auditory nerve in transmitting impulses to the brain.

Sound blending Ability to synthesize the separate parts of a word and produce an integrated whole.

Spasticity Excessive tension of the muscles and heightened resistance to flexion or extension, as in cerebral palsy.

Sphincter A ringlike muscle that closes a natural orifice.

Spina bifida A defect of closure in the posterior bony wall of the spinal canal without associated abnormality of the spinal cord or meninges.

Stapes A small stirrup-shaped bone, the inner-most of a chain of three bones in the middle ear transmitting sound to the inner ear.

Still's disease Juvenile rheumatoid arthritis.

Stimulus The physical, chemical, biological, and social events that act on the individual.

Strephosymbolia Reversal in perception of left-right order especially in letter or word order; "twisted symbols."

Stuttering A pattern of speaking in which the even flow of words is interrupted by hesitations, rapid repetition of speech elements, and/or spasms of breathing.

Synergic Acting together or in cooperation.

Syntax That part of a grammar system that deals with the arrangement of word forms to show their mutual relations in a sentence.

Synthesis Process of putting together to form a whole.

Syphilis A contagious venereal disease.

Tachistoscope A machine that exposes visual material for a variable period of time.

Tactile (tactual) Having to do with the sense of touch.

Task analysis A procedure of reducing complex tasks to their simpler components so that they can be taught more easily.

Taxonomy The science of classification of objects or events into natural or related groups based on some factor common to each.

Tonic Characterized by contraction of a muscle sufficient to keep the muscle taut but not sufficient to cause movement.

Total communication The incorporation of appropriate aural, manual, and oral methods of communication to ensure effective communication with and among hearing-impaired persons.

Translocation A type of chromosomal aberration, found in some cases of Down's syndrome (mongolism), in which a chromosome has broken and become fused to another chromosome.

Trauma Any experience that inflicts serious damage to the organism. It may be a psychological as well as a physiological insult.

Triplegia Paralysis of three of the body's limbs.

Trisomy 21 Mongolism caused by having three instead of a pair of chromosome 21.

Uvula The pendent fleshy lobe suspended from the soft palate, above the back of the tongue.

Verbal expression Ability to express one's own concepts verbally in a discrete, relevant, and approximately factual manner.

Visual association Seeing relationships among concepts presented visually.

Visual closure Ability to identify a visual stimulus from an incomplete visual presentation.

Visual fusion The coordination of the separate images in the two eyes into one image.

Visual reception Ability to gain meaning from visual symbols.

Visual sequential memory Ability to reproduce sequences of visual items from memory.

References

CHAPTER 1

Abeson, A., & Zettel, J. The end of the quiet revolution: The Education for All Handicapped Children Act of 1975. *Exceptional Children*, 1977, 114–130.

Cain, L. Parent groups: Their role in a better life for the handicapped. *Exceptional Children*, 1976, *42*, 432–437.

Cansler, D., Martin, G., & Valand, M. *Working with families*. Winston-Salem, N.C.: Kaplan School Supply, 1975.

Dunn, L. M. Special education for the mildly retarded—Is much of it justified? *Exceptional Children*, 1968, *35*, 5–24.

Farber, B. Family adaptations to severely mentally retarded children. In M. Begab & S. Richardson (Eds.), *Mentally retarded in society*. Baltimore: University Park Press, 1976.

Frankenburg, W. Considerations for screening. In N. Ellis & L. Cross (Eds.), *Planning programs for early education of the handicapped*. New York: Walker & Co., 1977.

Gallagher, J. *The search for the educational system that doesn't exist*. Reston, Va.: Council for Exceptional Children, 1972.

Gallagher, J., Forsythe, P., Ringelheim, D., & Weintraub, F. Federal and state funding patterns for programs for the handicapped. In N. Hobbs (Ed.), *Issues in the classification of children* (Vol. 2). San Francisco: Jossey-Bass, 1975.

Gottlieb, J. Mainstreaming: Fulfilling the promise? *American Journal of Mental Deficiency*, 1981, *86*, 115–126.

Hobbs, N. *The futures of children: Categories, labels, and their consequences*. San Francisco: Jossey-Bass, 1975.

Hunt, J. McV. *Intelligence and experience*. New York: Ronald Press, 1961.

Karnes, M., & Teska, J. Children's response to intervention programs. In J. Gallagher (Ed.), *The application of child development research to exceptional children*. Reston, Va.: Council for Exceptional Children, 1975.

Kirk, S. Evolution and present status of early education of the handicapped. *Exceptional Children*, 1982, *29*, 71–78.

Kirp, D., Kurloff, P., & Buss, W. Legal mandates and organizational change. In N. Hobbs (Ed.), *Issues in the classification of children* (Vol. 2). San Francisco: Jossey-Bass, 1975.

Martin, E. W. *The Fourth World: A Challenge for Today and Tomorrow.* Paper presented at the UNESCO World Conference of Actions and Strategies for Education, Prevention, and Integration, Malaga, Spain, November 1981.

Melcher, J. Law, litigation, and handicapped children. *Exceptional Children*, 1976, *43*, 126–130.

National Advisory Committee on the Handicapped. *The unfinished revolution: Education for the handicapped, 1976 annual report.* Washington, D.C.: Department of Health, Education, and Welfare, U.S. Office of Education, U.S. Government Printing Office, 1976.

Pelosi, J., & Hocutt, A. *The Education for All Handicapped Children Act: Issues and implications.* Chapel Hill, N.C.: Frank Porter Graham Child Development Center, University of North Carolina at Chapel Hill, 1977.

President's Committee on Mental Retardation. *The six-hour retarded child.* Washington, D.C.: U.S. Department of Education, Office of Special Education, 1970.

Reynolds, M. C., & Birch, J. W. *Teaching exceptional children in all America's schools.* Reston, Va.: Council for Exceptional Children, 1977.

Robinson, N. Mild mental retardation: Does it exist in the People's Republic of China? *Mental Retardation*, 1978, *16*, 295–298.

Ryan, W. *Blaming the victim.* New York: Random House, 1971.

Stedman, D. Early childhood intervention programs. In B. Caldwell & D. Stedman (Eds.), *Infant education: A guide for helping handicapped children in the first three years.* New York: Walker & Co., 1977.

Turnbull, H., & Turnbull, A. (Eds.). *Parents speak out: Views from the other side of a two way mirror.* Columbus, Ohio: Charles E. Merrill, 1978.

CHAPTER 2

Bailey, D. B., & Harbin, G. L. Nondiscriminatory evaluation. *Exceptional Children*, 1980, *47*, 590–596.

Brookover, W. B., Beady, C., & Flood, P. *Schools can make a difference: As indicated by a study of elementary school social systems and school outcome.* East Lansing, Mich.: College of Urban Development, Michigan State University, 1977.

Hobbs, N. (Ed.). *Issues in the classification of children* (Vol. 2). San Francisco: Jossey-Bass, 1975.

Rutter, M., Maughan, B., Mortimore, P., Ouston, J., & Smith, A. *Fifteen thousand hours: Secondary schools and their effects on children.* Cambridge, Mass.: Harvard University Press, 1979.

Wiederholt, J., Hammill, D., & Brown, V. *The resource teacher: A guide to effective practices.* Boston: Allyn and Bacon, 1978.

CHAPTER 3

Adler, M. A study of the effects of ethnic origin on giftedness. *Gifted Child Quarterly*, 1963, 7, 98–101.

Arnold, A. Leadership: A survey of the literature. In *A new generation of leadership*. Los Angeles: National/State Leadership Training Institute on the Gifted and Talented, 1976.

Astin, H. *Sex differences in mathematical and scientific precocity*. Paper presented at AAAS meeting, Washington, D.C., 1972.

Barbe, W. A study of the family background of the gifted. *Journal of Educational Psychology*, 1955, 47, 302–309.

Bloom, B. *Stability and change in human characteristics*. New York: Wiley, 1956.

Braga, J. Early admission: Opinion vs. evidence. *Elementary School Journal*, 1971, 72, 35–46.

Bronowski, J. *The ascent of man*. Boston: Little, Brown, 1973.

Bruner, J. *The process of education*. Cambridge, Mass.: Harvard University Press, 1960.

Callahan, C. *Developing creativity in the gifted and talented*. Reston, Va.: Council for Exceptional Children, 1978.

Coleman, J., Campbell, E. Q., Hobson, C. J., McPartland, J., Mood, A. M., Weinfeld, F. D., & York, R. L. *Equality of educational opportunity*. Washington, D.C.: U.S. Government Printing Office, 1966.

Eilber, C. Report card: The first year at the School of Science and Math. *Popular Government*, 1981, Fall, 23–26.

Feldhusen, J., & Treffinger, D. *Teaching creative thinking and problem solving*. Dubuque, Iowa: Kendall/Hunt, 1977.

Feldman, D. The mysterious case of extreme giftedness. In A. Passow (Ed.), *The education of the gifted and talented: Seventy-eighth yearbook of the National Society for the Study of Education*. Chicago: University of Chicago Press, 1979.

Fox, L. *Changing times and the education of gifted girls*. Address given at Second World Conference on Gifted and Talented Children, San Francisco, 1977.

Gallagher, J. Teacher variation in concept presentation in biological science curriculum study program. *Biological Science Curriculum Study Newsletter*, 1967, 30, 8–19.

Gallagher, J. *Teaching the gifted child* (2nd ed.). Boston: Allyn and Bacon, 1975.

Gallagher, J. Needed: A new partnership for the gifted. In J. Gibson & P. Chennels (Eds.), *Gifted children: Looking to the future*. London: National Association for Gifted Children, 1976.

Gallagher, J., Aschner, M., & Jenne, W. *Productive thinking of gifted children in classroom interaction*. CEC Research Monograph Series B5. Reston, Va.: Council for Exceptional Children, 1967.

Gallagher, J., Weiss, P., Oglesby, K., & Thomas, T. *Report on education of the gifted* (Vol. 1). Unpublished manuscript, 1982. (Available from Frank Porter Graham Child Development Center, University of North Carolina, Chapel Hill, N.C.)

Gowan, J., & Groth, N. The development of vocational choice in gifted children. In J. Gowan (Ed.), *The guidance and measurement of intelligence development and creativity.* Northridge, Calif.: San Fernando Valley State College.

Guilford, J. P. *The nature of human intelligence.* New York: McGraw-Hill, 1967.

Hollingworth, L. *Children above 180 IQ.* Yonkers, N.Y.: World Book, 1942.

House, E., Kerins, T., & Steele, J. *Illinois gifted program evaluation.* Urbana, Ill.: Center for Instructional Research and Curriculum Evaluation, University of Illinois, 1969.

Jenkins, M. Case studies of Negro children of Binet IQ 160 and above. *Journal of Negro Education,* 1948, *12,* 159–166.

Keating, D. The study of mathematically precocious youth. In J. Stanley, D. Keating, & E. Fox (Eds.), *Mathematical talent: Discovery, description, and development.* Baltimore: Johns Hopkins University Press, 1974.

Kirk, W. D. A tentative screening procedure for selecting bright and slow children in kindergarten. *Exceptional Children,* 1966, *33,* 235–241.

MacKinnon, D. *In search of human effectiveness.* Buffalo, N.Y.: Creative Education Foundation, Inc., 1978.

Maker, C. *Curriculum development for the gifted.* Rockville, Md.: Aspen Systems Corp., 1982.

Mansfield, R., Busse, T., & Krepelka, E. The effectiveness of creativity training. *Review of Educational Research,* 1978, *48,* 517–536.

Marks, W., & Nystrand, R. (Eds.). *Strategies for educational change.* New York: Macmillan, 1981.

Marland, S. (Ed.). *Education of the gifted and talented.* Report to the Congress of the United States by the U.S. Commissioner of Education. Washington, D.C.: U.S. Government Printing Office, 1972.

Martinson, R. A. An analysis of problems and priorities: Advocate survey and statistics sources. In S. Marland (Ed.), *Education of the gifted and talented.* Report to the Congress of the United States by the U.S. Commissioner of Education. Washington, D.C.: U.S. Government Printing Office, 1972.

Mercer, J., & Lewis, J. Using the System of Multicultural Pluralistic Assessment to identify the gifted minority child. In I. Sato (Ed.), *Balancing the scale for the disadvantaged gifted.* Los Angeles: National/State Leadership Training Institute on the Gifted and Talented, 1981.

Montour, K. William James Sidis, the broken twig. *American Psychologist,* 1977, *32,* 265–279.

Oden, M. The fulfillment of promise: Forty year follow-up of the Terman gifted group. *Genetic Psychology Monographs,* 1968, 77, 3–92.

Parnes, S. J. *Programming creative behavior.* Buffalo, N.Y.: State University of New York, 1966.

Passow, A. (Ed.). *The education of the gifted and talented: Seventy-eighth yearbook of the National Society for the Study of Education.* Chicago: University of Chicago Press, 1979.

Passow, A. Differentiated curricula for the gifted/talented. *Proceedings of the First National Conference on Curricula for the Gifted/Talented.* Los Angeles: National/State Leadership Training Institute on the Gifted and Talented, 1982, pp. 1–20.

Perkins, H. V. Classroom behavior and underachievement. *American Educational Research Journal*, 1965, *2*, 1–12.

Plomin, R., DeFries, J., & McClearn, G. *Behavioral genetics: A primer.* San Francisco: W. H. Freeman, 1980.

Plowman, P., & Rice, J. (Eds.). *California project talent.* Final report. Sacramento, Calif.: California State Department of Education, 1967.

Raph, J. B., Goldberg, M. L., & Passow, A. H. *Bright underachievers.* New York: Teachers College Press, 1966.

Renzulli, J. S. *The enrichment triad model: A guide for developing defensible programs for the gifted and talented.* Mansfield Center, Conn.: Creative Learning Press, Inc., 1977.

Renzulli, J. S. *What makes giftedness?* Brief No. 6. Los Angeles: National/State Leadership Training Institute on the Gifted and Talented, 1979.

Renzulli, J. S., Smith, L. H., White, A. J., Callahan, C. M., & Hartman, R. K. *Scales for rating the behavioral characteristics of superior students.* Mansfield Center, Conn.: Creative Learning Press, Inc., 1976.

Reynolds, M. C. A framework for considering some issues in special education. *Exceptional Children*, 1962, *29*, 147–169.

Robeck, M. Special classes for intellectually gifted students. In P. Plowman & J. Rice (Eds.), *California project talent.* Final report. Sacramento, Calif.: California State Department of Education, 1967.

Sears, P. S., & Barbee, A. H. Career and life satisfactions among Terman's gifted women. In J. C. Stanley, W. C. George, & C. H. Solano (Eds.), *The gifted and the creative: A fifty-year perspective.* Baltimore: Johns Hopkins University Press, 1977.

Shaw, M. C., & McCuen, J. T. The onset of academic underachievement in bright children. *Journal of Educational Psychology*, 1960, *51*, 103–108.

Southern Region Education Board. *Southern Region Advanced Placement Program.* Unpublished manuscript, 1981. (Available from Southern Region Education Board, Suite 200, 17 Executive Park Drive, N.E., Atlanta, Georgia 30329.)

Stanley, J. Identifying and nurturing the intellectually gifted. In W. George, S. Cohn, & J. Stanley (Eds.), *Educating the gifted: Acceleration and enrichment.* Baltimore: Johns Hopkins University Press, 1979.

Terman, L., & Oden, M. The Stanford studies of the gifted. In P. Witty (Ed.), *The gifted child.* Lexington, Mass.: D. C. Heath, 1951.

Terman, L., & Oden, M. *Genetic studies of genius.* Vol. 4, *The gifted child grows up.* Stanford, Calif.: Stanford University Press, 1947.

Torrance, E. *Explorations in creative thinking in the early school years. VI: Highly intelligent and highly creative children in a laboratory school.* Minneapolis: Bureau of Educational Research, University of Minnesota, 1959.

Torrance, E. Unique needs of the creative child and adult. In A. Passow (Ed.), *The education of the gifted and talented: Seventy-eighth yearbook of the National Society for the Study of Education.* Chicago: University of Chicago Press, 1979.

Walberg, H. Physics, femininity, and creativity. *Developmental Psychology*, 1969, *1*, 47–54.

Weiss, P. *Attitudes toward gifted education.* Unpublished doctoral dissertation, University of North Carolina, Chapel Hill, 1978.

Whitmore, J. *Giftedness, conflict, and underachievement.* Boston: Allyn and Bacon, 1980.

Williams, F. *Classroom ideas for encouraging thinking and feeling.* Buffalo, N.Y.: Dissemination of Knowledge Publishers, 1970.

Wolf, M. Talent search in the visual and performing arts. In I. Sato (Ed.), *Balancing the scale for the disadvantaged gifted.* Los Angeles: National/State Leadership Training Institute on the Gifted and Talented, 1981.

CHAPTER 4

Abroms, K., & Bennett, J. Current genetic and demographic findings in Down's syndrome: How are they presented in college textbooks on exceptionality? *Mental Retardation,* 1980, *18,* 101–107.

Baller, W., Charles O., & Miller, E. Midlife attainment of the mentally retarded: A longitudinal study. *Genetic Psychology Monographs,* 1966, *75,* 235–239.

Bijou, S. A functional analysis of retarded development. In E. Ellis (Ed.), *International review of research in mental retardation* (Vol. 1). New York: Academic Press, 1966.

Birch, H. G., & Gussow, J. *Disadvantaged children.* New York: Harcourt/Brace Jovanovich, 1970.

Birch, H. G., Richardson, S. A., Baird, D., Horrobin, G., & Illsley, R. *Mental subnormality in the community.* Baltimore: Williams & Wilkins, 1970.

Bradfield, R. H., Brown, J., Kaplan, P., Rickert, E., & Stannard, R. The special child in the regular classroom. *Exceptional Children,* 1973, *35,* 384–390.

Brickey, M., Brauning, L., & Campbell, K. Vocational histories of sheltered workshop employees placed in projects with industry and competitive jobs. *Mental Retardation,* 1982, *20,* 52–57.

Brickey, M., & Campbell, K. Fast food employment for moderately and mildly mentally retarded adults. *Mental Retardation,* 1981, *19,* 113–116.

Budoff, M., & Gottlieb, J. Special class students mainstreamed: A study of an aptitude (learning potential) X treatment interaction. *American Journal of Mental Deficiency,* 1976, *81,* 11.

Cegalka, W. J., & Tyler, J. L. The efficacy of special class placement for the mentally retarded in proper perspective. *Training School Bulletin,* 1970, *67,* 33–65.

Channing, A. *Employment of mentally deficient boys and girls.* Department of Labor, Bureau Publication No. 210. Washington, D.C.: U.S. Government Printing Office, 1932.

Charles, D. C. Ability and accomplishment of persons earlier judged mentally deficient. *Genetic Psychology Monographs,* 1953, *47,* 3–71.

Crissey, M. Mental retardation: Past, present, and future. *American Psychologist,* 1975, *30,* 800–808.

Cromer, R. F. Receptive language in the mentally retarded: Processes and diagnostic distinctions. In R. L. Schiefelbusch & L. L. Lloyd (Eds.), *Language perspectives—retardation, acquisition, and intervention.* Baltimore: University Park Press, 1974.

Cunningham, C., & Sloper, P. *Helping your exceptional baby.* New York: Pantheon Books, 1980.

Doll, E. A. The essentials of an inclusive concept of mental deficiency. *American Journal of Mental Deficiency*, 1941, *46*, 214–219.

Downs, M. The hearing of Down's individuals. *Seminars in Speech, Language, and Hearing*, 1980, *1*, 25–38.

Dunn, L. M. Special education for the mildly retarded: Is much of it justifiable? *Exceptional Children*, 1968, *35*, 5–24.

Farber, B. *Mental retardation: Its social context and social consequences.* Boston: Houghton Mifflin, 1968.

Farber, B. Family adaptation to severely mentally retarded children. In M. Begab & S. Richardson (Eds.), *The mentally retarded and society: A social science perspective.* Baltimore: University Park Press, 1975.

Feuerstein, R., Rand, Y., Hoffman, M. B., & Miller, R. *Instrumental enrichment.* Baltimore: University Park Press, 1980.

Foss, G., & Peterson, S. Social interpersonal skills relevant to job tenure for mentally retarded adults. *Mental Retardation*, 1981, *19*, 103–106.

Francis, R. J., & Rarick, L. *Motor characteristics of the mentally retarded.* Cooperative Research Monograph No. 1. Washington, D.C.: Department of Health, Education, and Welfare, U.S. Office of Education, 1960.

Gallagher, J. J. The special education contract for mildly handicapped children. *Exceptional Children*, 1972, *38*(March), 527–535.

Gampel, D. H., Gottlieb, J., & Harrison, R. H. Comparison of classroom behavior of special-class EMR, integrated EMR, low IQ, and nonretarded children. *American Journal of Mental Deficiency*, 1974, *79*, 16–21.

Gold, M. Research on the vocational habitation of the retarded: The present, the future. In N. Ellis (Ed.), *International review of research in mental retardation* (Vol. 6). New York: Academic Press, 1973.

Goldstein, H. *The social learning curriculum.* Columbus, Ohio: Charles E. Merrill, 1974.

Goldstein, H., Moss, J., & Jordan, L. J. *The efficacy of special class training on the development of mentally retarded children.* Cooperative Research Project No. 619. Washington, D.C.: U.S. Office of Education, 1965.

Goodman, L., Budner, S., & Lesh, D. The parent's role in sex education. *Mental Retardation*, 1971, *9*, 43–45.

Gottlieb, J. Mainstreaming: Fulfilling the promise? *American Journal of Mental Deficiency*, 1981, *86*, 115–126.

Gottlieb, J., Semmel, M. I., & Veldman, D. J. Correlates of social status among mainstreamed mentally retarded children. *Journal of Educational Psychology*, 1978, *70*, 396–405.

Gray, S., Klaus, R., & Ramsey, B. Participants in the early training projects: 1962–77. In M. Begab, C. Haywood, & H. Barber (Eds.), *Psychosocial influences in retarded performance* (Vol. 2). Baltimore: University Park Press, 1981.

Gresham, F.M. Social skills training with handicapped children: A review. *Review of Educational Research*, 1981, *51*(1), 139–176.

Grossman, H. (Ed.). *Manual on terminology and classification in mental retardation.* Washington, D.C.: American Association on Mental Deficiency, 1977.

Gunzberg, H. C. The education of the mentally handicapped child. In A. M. Clarke and A. D. B. Clarke (Eds.), *Mental deficiency: The changing outlook*. London: Methuen and Company, Ltd. 1974.

Halpern, A. S. The impact of work/study programs on employment on the mentally retarded: Some findings from two sources. *International Journal of Rehabilitation Research*, 1978, *39*, 138–146.

Hanson, M. *Teaching your Down's syndrome infant: A guide for parents*. Baltimore: University Park Press, 1977.

Heber, R. F. *Research on the prevention of socio-cultural retardation through early prevention*. Paper presented to Extraordinary Session of the International Union for Child Welfare Advisory Group on Social Problems of Children and Youth, Ostend, Belgium, November 21–25, 1977.

Heber, R., & Garber, H. The Milwaukee Project: A study of the use of family intervention to prevent cultural-familial mental retardation. In B. Friedlander, G. Sterritt, & G. Kirk (Eds.), *Exceptional infant*. New York: Brunner/Mazel, 1975.

Heiss, W., & Mischio, G. Designing curriculum for the educably mentally retarded. In E. L. Meyen, G. A. Vergason, & R. J. Whelan (Eds.), *Strategies for teaching exceptional children*. Denver: Love, 1972.

Heller, K. Effects of special education placement on educable mentally retarded children. In K. Heller, W. Holtzman, & S. Messick (Eds.), *Placing children in special education: A strategy for equity*. Washington, D.C.: National Academy Press, 1982.

Itard, J. M. G. *The wild boy of Aveyron*. Translated from the French by G. Humphrey & M. Humphrey. New York: Appleton-Century-Crofts, 1932.

Johnson, G., & Kirk, S. Are mentally handicapped children segregated in the regular grades? *Exceptional Children*, 1950, *17*, 65–68.

Jones, R. Labels and stigma in special education. *Exceptional Children*, 1972, *38*, 553–564.

Karnes, M. B., & Teska, J. A. Children's response to intervention programs. In J. J. Gallagher (Ed.), *The application of child development research to exceptional children*. Reston, Va.: Council for Exceptional Children, 1975.

Kauffman, J., & Payne, J. (Eds.). *Mental retardation: Introduction and personal perspectives*. Columbus, Ohio: Charles E. Merrill, 1975.

Kennedy, R. *The social adjustment of morons in a Connecticut city*. Hartford, Conn.: Social Service Department, Mansfield-Southbury Training Schools, 1948.

Kirk, S. A. *Early education of the mentally retarded*. Urbana, Ill.: University of Illinois Press, 1958.

Kirk, S. A. Research in education of the mentally retarded. In H. Stevens & R. Heber (Eds.), *Mental retardation: A review of research*. Chicago: University of Chicago Press, 1964.

Kolstoe, O. P. *Teaching educably mentally retarded children* (2nd ed.). New York: Holt, Rinehart and Winston, 1976.

Krupski, A. Are retarded children more distractible? Observational analysis of retarded and nonretarded children's classroom behavior. *American Journal of Mental Deficiency*, 1979, *84*, 1–10.

Lambert, N. M., Windmiller, M., Cole, L., & Figueroa, R. A. Standardization of a public school version of the American Association on Mental Deficiency Adaptive Behavior Scale. *Mental Retardation*, 1975, *13*, 3–7.

Lazar, I., & Darlington, R. Lasting effects of early education: A report from the consortium for longitudinal studies. *Monographs of the Society for Research in Child Development*, 1982, *47*, 2–3.

Lejeune, J., Gautier, M., & Turpin, R. Etudes des chromosomes somatiques de neuf enfants. *C. R. Academie Sci.*, 1959, *248*, 1721–1722.

Lilienfield, A. M. *Epidemiology of mongolism.* Baltimore: Johns Hopkins University Press, 1969.

Lillie, D. Dimensions in parent programs: An overview. In J. Grim (Ed.), *Training parents to teach.* Chapel Hill, N.C.: Technical Assistance Development System, University of North Carolina, 1974.

Mayer, W. (Ed.). *Planning curriculum development.* Boulder, Colo.: Biological Sciences Curriculum Study, 1975.

Meichenbaum, B. *Cognitive behavior modification: An integrative approach.* New York: Plenum Publishing Co., 1977.

Mercer, J. The myth of 3% prevalence. In G. Tarjan, R. K. Eyman, & C. E. Meyers (Eds.), *Sociobehavior studies in mental retardation: Papers in honor of Harvey F. Dingman.* Washington, D.C.: Monographs of the American Association on Mental Deficiency, No. 1, 1973.

Mercer, J. *System of Multicultural Pluralistic Assessment: Technical manual.* New York: Psychological Corporation, 1979.

Mercer, J. R., & Lewis, J. F. *System of Multicultural Pluralistic Assessment.* New York: Psychological Corporation, 1978.

Morgan, S. B. Development and distribution of intellectual and adaptive skills in Down's syndrome children: Implications for early intervention. *Mental Retardation*, 1979, *17*(5), 247–249.

Naremore, R., & Dever, R. Language performance of educable mentally retarded and normal children at five age levels. *Journal of Speech and Hearing Research*, 1975, *18*, 82–95.

Neisworth, J. T., & Smith, R. M. *Modifying retarded behavior.* Boston: Houghton Mifflin, 1973.

Nitowsky, H. Alcohol syndrome. *Rose F. Kennedy Center Notes.* The Bronx, N. Y.: Albert Einstein College of Medicine, Winter 1979.

Permenter, N. Retardate for a week. *Journal of Rehabilitation*, 1973, *39*, 18–21, 41.

Plomin, R., DeFries, J., & McClearn, G. *Behavioral genetics: A primer.* San Francisco: W. H. Freeman, 1980.

President's Committee on Mental Retardation. *The six-hour retarded child.* Washington, D.C.: U.S. Government Printing Office, 1970.

President's Committee on Mental Retardation. *The problem of mental retardation.* Washington, D.C.: U.S. Department of Health, Education, and Welfare, Publication No. (OHO) 75-22003, 1975.

Ramey, T., & Haskins, R. The modification of intelligence through early experience. *Intelligence*, 1981, *5*, 5–19.

Rarick, L., & Widdop, J. H. The physical fitness and motor performance of educable mentally retarded children. *Exceptional Children*, 1970, *36*, 509–520.

Richardson, S. Family characteristics associated with mild mental retardation. In M. Begab, C. Haywood, & H. Garber (Eds.), *Psychosocial influences in retarded performance* (Vol. 2). Baltimore: University Park Press, 1981.

Rie, H. E., & Rie, E. D. *Handbook of minimal brain dysfunctions: A critical view.* New York: Wiley, 1980.

Robinson, H., & Robinson, N. *The mentally retarded child* (2nd ed.). New York: McGraw-Hill, 1976.

Rynders, J., & Horrobin, J. Project EDGE: The University of Minnesota's communication stimulation program for Down's syndrome infants. In J. Hellmuth (Ed.), *Exceptional infant.* New York: Brunner/Mazel, 1975.

Rynders, J., Spiker, C., & Horrobin, J. Understanding the educability of Down's syndrome children: Examination of methodological problems and recent literature. *American Journal of Mental Deficiency*, 1978, *82*, 440–448.

Sameroff, A. & Chandler, M. Reproductive risk and the continuum of child-taking casualty. In F. Horowitz (Ed.), *Review of child development research* (Vol. 4). Chicago: University of Chicago Press, 1975.

Scheerenberger, R. C. A study of public residential facilities. *Mental Retardation*, 1976, *14*, 32–35.

Seguin, E. *Idiocy: Its treatment by the physiological method.* Reprinted 1907. New York: Teachers College Press, 1866.

Semmel, M. I. Barritt, L. S., & Bennett, S. W. Performance of EMR and non-retarded children in a modified cloze task. *American Journal of Mental Deficiency*, 1970, *74* (March), 681–688.

Shonkoff, J. Biological and social factors contributing to mild mental retardation. In K. Heller (Ed.), *Selection and placement of students in programs for the mentally retarded.* Washington, D.C.: National Academy of Sciences, Committee on Child Development Research and Public Policy, 1982.

Shriver, E. *Facts on Special Olympics.* Washington, D.C.: Special Olympics, Inc., 1980.

Simeonsson, R., & McHale, S. Review: Research on handicapped children: Sibling relationships. *Child Care, Health and Development*, 1981, 7, 153–171.

Skeels, H. M. *Adult status of children with contrasting early life experiences.* Monographs of the Society for Research in Child Development, No. 31. Chicago: University of Chicago Press, 1966.

Skeels, H., & Dye, H. A study of the effects of differential stimulation on mentally retarded children. *Proceedings of the American Association on Mental Deficiency*, 1939, *44*, 114–136.

Skinner, B. F. *Science and human behavior.* New York: The Free Press, 1953.

Soloman, A., & Pargle, R. Demonstrating physical fitness impairment in EMR. *Exceptional Children*, 1967, *34*, 163–168.

Sowers, J., Thompson, L., & Connis, R. The food service vocational training program. In G. Bellamy, G. O'Connor, & O. Karan (Eds.), *Vocational rehabilitation of severely handicapped persons.* Baltimore: University Park Press, 1979.

Streissguth, A., Landesman-Dwyer, S., Martin, J., & Smith, D. Teretogenic effects of alcohol in humans and animals. *Science*, 1980, *209*, 353–361.

Tarjan, G., Wright, W. W., Eyman, R. K., & Keeran, C. V. Natural history of mental retardation: Some aspects of epidemiology. *American Journal of Mental Deficiency*, 1973, *77*, 369–379.

Walker, V. *The efficacy of the resource room for educating mentally retarded children.* Unpublished doctoral dissertation, Temple University, 1972.

Welch, E. A. The effects of segregated and partially integrated school programs on self-concept and academic achievement of educable mentally retarded children. *Exceptional Children*, 1967, *34*, 93–100.

Wolfensberger, W. *The principle of normalization in human services.* Toronto: National Institute on Mental Retardation, 1972.

Zane, T., Walls, R., & Thvedt, J. Prompting and fading guidance procedures: Their effect on chaining and whole task teaching strategies. *Education and Training of the Mentally Retarded*, 1981, *16*, 125–135.

Zider, S., & Gold, M. Behind the wheel training for individuals labelled moderately retarded. *Exceptional Children*, 1981, *47*, 632–639.

CHAPTER 5

American Foundation for the Blind. *Facts about blindness.* New York: American Foundation for the Blind, 1976.

Barraga, N. *Visual handicaps and learning: A developmental approach.* Belmont, Calif.: Wadsworth, 1976.

Barraga, N. (Ed.). *Program to develop efficiency in visual functioning.* Louisville, Ky.: American Printing House for the Blind, 1980.

Bateman, B. *Reading and psycholinguistic processes of partially seeing children.* Reston, Va.: Council for Exceptional Children, 1963.

Bateman, B. Visually handicapped children. In N. G. Haring & R. L. Schiefelbusch (Eds.), *Methods in special education.* New York: McGraw-Hill, 1967.

Berla, E. Tactile scanning and memory for a spatial display by blind students. *Journal of Special Education*, 1981, *15*, 341–350.

Birch, J. W., Tisdall, W. J., Peabody, R., & Sterrett, R. *School achievement and effect of type size on reading in visually handicapped children.* (Cooperative Research Project No. 1766.) Pittsburgh: University of Pittsburgh, 1966.

Bliss, J. C., & Moore, M. W. The Optacon reading system. *Education of the Visually Handicapped*, 1974, *6*, 98–102.

Chess, S. The influence of defect on development in children with congenital rubella. *Merrill Palmer Quarterly*, 1974, *20*, 255–274.

Corn, A., & Martinez, I. *When you have a visually handicapped child in your classroom: Suggestions for teachers.* New York: American Foundation for the Blind, 1978.

Cotzin, M., & Dallenbach, K. M. "Facial vision": The role of pitch and loudness in the perception of obstacles by the blind. *American Journal of Psychology*, 1950, *63*, 485–515.

Cratty, B. *Movement and spatial awareness in blind children and youth.* Springfield, Ill.: Charles C Thomas, 1971.

DeMott, R. Verbalism and affective meaning for blind, severely visually impaired, and normally sighted children. *New Outlook for the Blind*, 1972, *66*, 1–25.

Dickman, I. *Sex education and family life for visually handicapped children and youth: A resource guide*. New York: American Foundation for the Blind, 1975.

Fraiberg, S. Parallel and divergent patterns in blind and sighted infants. *Psychoanalytic Study of the Child*, 1968, *23*, 264–300.

Gottesman, M. A comparative study of Piaget's developmental schema of sighted children with that of a group of blind children. *Child Development*, 1971, June, 573–580.

Hatfield, E. Why are they blind? *Sight Saving Review*, 1975, Spring, 1–22.

Hatlen, P., LeDuc, P., & Canter, P. The blind adolescent life skills center. *New Outlook for the Blind*, 1975, *69*, 109–115.

Hayes, S. P. *Contributions to a psychology of blindness*. New York: American Foundation for the Blind, 1941.

Huff, R., & Franks, F. Educational materials development in primary mathematics: Fractional parts of wholes. *Education of the Visually Handicapped*, 1973, *5*, 46–54.

Juurmaa, J. On the accuracy of obstacle detection by the blind. *New Outlook for the Blind*, 1970, *64*, 104–117.

Kephart, J., Kephart, C., & Schwartz, G. A journey into the world of the blind child. *Exceptional Children*, 1974, *40*, 421–429.

Klineman, J. Hidden abilities discovered among multiply handicapped blind children. *Education of the Visually Handicapped*, 1975, *7*, 90–96.

Lowenfeld, B. (Ed.). *The visually handicapped child in school*. New York: John Day Co., 1973.

Lowenfeld, B., Abel, G. L., & Hatlen, P. H. *Blind children learn to read*. Springfield, Ill.: Charles C Thomas, 1967.

Malone, L., DeLucchi, L. & Thier, H. *Science activities for the visually impaired: SAVI leadership trainer's manual*. Berkeley, Calif.: Center for Multisensory Learning, University of California, 1981.

Martin, G., & Hoben, M. *Supporting visually impaired students in the mainstream*. Reston, Va.: Council for Exceptional Children, 1977.

Meighan, T. *An investigation of the self-concept of blind and visually handicapped adolescents*. New York: American Foundation for the Blind, 1971.

Myerson, L. Somatopsychology of physical disability. In W. M. Cruickshank (Ed.), *Psychology of exceptional children and youth* (3rd ed.). Englewood Cliffs, N.J.: Prentice-Hall, 1971.

Napier, G. D. Special subject adjustments and skills. In B. Lowenfeld (Ed.), *The visually handicapped child in school*. New York: John Day Co., 1973.

Newcomer, J. Sonicguide: Its use with public school blind children. *Visual Impairment and Blindness*, 1977, *6*, 268–271.

Orlansky, M. *Encouraging successful mainstreaming of the visually impaired child*. MAVIS Sourcebook No. 2. Boulder, Colo.: Social Science Education Consortium, Inc., 1980.

Pintner, R., Eisenson, J., & Stanton, M. *The psychology of the physically handicapped*. New York: F. S. Crofts, 1941.

Reynell, J. Developmental patterns of visually handicapped children. *Child Care Health and Development*, 1978, *4*, 291–303.

Scholl, G., & Schnur, R. *Measures of psychological, vocational, and educational functioning in the blind and visually handicapped.* New York: American Foundation for the Blind, 1976.

Spungin, S. (Ed.). *Guidelines for public school programs serving visually handicapped children* (2nd ed.). New York: American Foundation for the Blind, 1981.

Stephens, B., & Simpkins, K. *The reasoning, moral judgment, and moral conduct of the congenitally blind.* (Final Project Report, H23-3197.) Washington, D.C.: Office of Education, Bureau of Education for the Handicapped, 1974.

Stephens, B., Smith, R. E., Fitzgerald, J. R., Grube, C., Hitt, J., & Daly, M. *Training manual for teachers of the visually handicapped.* Chicago: Stoelting, 1981.

Tillman, M. H., & Osborne, R. T. The performance of blind and sighted children on the Wechsler Intelligence Scale for Children: Interaction effects. *Education of the Visually Handicapped,* 1969, *1,* 1–4.

Umsted, R. Improving braille reading, *New Outlook for the Blind,* 1972, *66,* 169–177.

Warren, D. *Blindness and early childhood development.* New York: American Foundation for the Blind, 1977.

CHAPTER 6

Altshuler, K. Sexual patterns and family relationships. In J. Rainer, K. Altshuler, & F. Kallman (Eds.), *Family and mental health problems.* New York: New York State Psychiatric Institute, 1963.

Blackwell, P., Engen, E., Fischgrund, J., & Zarcadoolis, C. *Sentences and other systems.* Washington, D. C.: Alexander Graham Bell Association, 1978.

Brackett, D. Assessment: Adaptations, interpretations, and implications. In M. Ross & L. Nober (Eds.), *Educating hard of hearing children.* Reston, Va.: Council for Exceptional Children, 1981.

Brasel, K., & Quigley, S. *The influence of early language and communication environments in the development of language in deaf children.* Urbana, Ill.: University of Illinois Institute for Research on Exceptional Children, 1975.

Calvert, D., & Silverman, R. *Speech and deafness.* Washington, D.C.: Alexander Graham Bell Association, 1975.

Conference of Executives of American Schools for the Deaf. *American Annals of the Deaf,* 1976, *121,* 4.

Craig, W., & Craig, H. Directory of services for the deaf. *American Annals of the Deaf,* 1980, *125,* 179.

Farwell, R. Speech reading: A research review. *American Annals of the Deaf,* 1976, *121,* 19–30.

Frisina, R. *Report of the Committee to Redefine Deaf and Hard of Hearing for Educational Purposes* (mimeo), 1974.

Furth, H. *Thinking without language: Psychological implications of deafness.* New York: The Free Press, 1966.

Gentile, A. *Further studies in achievement testing of hearing impaired students: 1971.* Annual Survey of Hearing Impaired Children and Youth (Gallaudet

College Office of Demographic Studies, Ser. D, No. 13). Washington, D.C.: Gallaudet College, 1973.

Goldin-Meadow, S., & Feldman, H. The creation of a communication system: A study of deaf children of hearing parents. *Sign Language Studies*, 1975, *8*, 225–234.

Hardy, J. B. The whole child: A plea for a global approach to the child with auditory problems. *Education of the deaf: The challenge and the charge.* Washington, D.C.: U.S. Government Printing Office, 1968.

Hicks, D. E. Comparison profiles of rubella and non-rubella deaf children. *American Annals of the Deaf,* 1970, *115*, 65–74.

Jensema, C. The relationship between academic achievement and the demographic characteristics of hearing impaired children and youth. (Gallaudet College Office of Demographic Studies.) Washington, D.C.: Gallaudet College, 1975.

Jordan, I. K., Gustason, G., & Rosen, R. An update on communication trends in programs for the deaf. *American Annals of the Deaf,* 1979, *124*, 350–357.

Kemker, F., McConnell, F., Logan, S., & Green, B. A field study of children's hearing aids in a school environment. *Language, Speech, and Hearing Services in the Schools,* 1979, *10*, 47–53.

LaSasso, C. National survey of materials and procedures used to teach reading to hearing-impaired children. *American Annals of the Deaf,* 1978, *123*, 22–30.

Lerman, A., & Guilfoyle, G. *The development of pre-vocational behavior in deaf adolescents.* New York: Teachers College Press, 1970.

Levitt, H., Pickett, J., & Houde, R. *Sensory aids for the hearing impaired.* New York: Institute for Electrical and Electronics Engineering Press, 1980.

Mahoney, G., & Weller, E. An ecological approach to language intervention. In D. Bricker (Ed.), *Language intervention with children* (Vol. 2). San Francisco: Jossey-Bass, 1980.

Meadow, K. *Deafness and child development.* Berkeley, Calif.: University of California Press, 1980.

Meadow, K. P. Early communication in relation to the deaf child's intellectual, social, and communicative functioning. *American Annals of the Deaf,* 1968, *113*, 29–41.

Moores, D. The vocational status of young deaf adults in New England. *Journal of Rehabilitation of the Deaf,* 1969, *2*, 29–41.

Moores, D. *Educating the deaf: Psychology, principles, and practices* (2nd ed.). Boston: Houghton Mifflin, 1982.

Moores, D. F., Fisher, S., & Harlow, M. *Post secondary programs for the deaf: Monograph VI: Summary and guidelines.* (University of Minnesota Research, Development and Demonstration Center in Education of Handicapped Children, Research Report No. 80.) Minneapolis: University of Minnesota, 1974.

Moores, D., Weiss, K., & Goodwin, M. Early education programs for hearing impaired children: Major findings. *American Annals of the Deaf,* 1978, *123*, 925–936.

Moores, J., & Moores, D. Language training with the young deaf child. In D. Bricker (Ed.), *Language intervention with children.* New Directions for Exceptional Children (Vol. 2). San Francisco: Jossey-Bass, 1980.

Northern, J. L., & Downs, M. P. *Hearing in children* (2nd ed.). Baltimore: Williams & Wilkins, 1978.

Prickett, H., & Hunt, J. Education of the deaf—the next ten years. *American Annals of the Deaf*, 1977, *122*, 365–381.

Quigley, S. P. *The influence of finger spelling on the development of language, communication, and educative achievement in deaf children*. Urbana, Ill.: Institute for Research on Exceptional Children, 1969.

Quigley, S. P., Jenne, W. C., & Phillips, S. B. *Deaf students in colleges and universities*. Washington, D.C.: Alexander Graham Bell Association, 1968.

Quigley, S., & Kretschmer, R. *The education of deaf children*. Baltimore: University Park Press, 1982.

Quigley, S. P., Steinkamp, M. W., Powers, D. S., & Jones, B. W. *Test of syntactic abilities*. Beavertown, Ore.: Donmac, Inc., 1978.

Ries, P. *Reported causes of hearing loss for hearing impaired students: 1970–1971*. (Annual Survey of Hearing Impaired Children and Youth, Ser. D, No. 12.) Washington, D.C.: Gallaudet College, 1973.

Schein, J. D., & Delk, M. T., Jr. *The deaf population of the United States*. Silver Spring, Md.: National Association of the Deaf, 1974.

Schlesinger, H. S., & Meadow, K. P. *Sound and sign: Childhood deafness and mental health*. Berkeley, Calif.: University of California Press, 1972.

Silverman, R. Education of the deaf. In L. E. Travis (Ed.), *Handbook of speech pathology*. New York: Appleton-Century-Crofts, 1967.

Stephens, T., Blackhurst, A., & Magliocca, L. *Teaching mainstreamed students*. New York: Wiley, 1982.

Trybus, R. J., & Karchmer, M. A. School achievement scores of hearing impaired children: National data on achievement status and growth patterns. *American Annals of the Deaf*, 1977, *122*, 62–69.

Vernon, M. Current etiological factors in deafness. *American Annals of the Deaf*, 1968, *113*, 106–115.

Vernon, M. Multiply handicapped deaf children. Reston, Va.: Council for Exceptional Children Research Monograph, 1969.

Vernon, M., & Koh, S. D. Effects fo oral preschool compared to early manual communication on education and communication in deaf children. *American Annals of the Deaf*, 1971, *116*, 569–574.

Wier, C. Habilitation and rehabilitation of the hearing impaired. In T. Hixon, L. Shriberg, & J. Saxon (Eds.), *Introduction to communication disorders*. Englewood Cliffs, N.J.: Prentice-Hall, 1980.

Whorf, B. *Language, thought, and reality*. Cambridge, Mass.: MIT Press, 1956.

CHAPTER 7

Bangs, T. *Language and learning disorders of the pre-academic child with curriculum guide*. New York: Appleton-Century-Crofts, 1968.

Bloodstein, O. *Speech pathology: An introduction*. Boston: Houghton Mifflin, 1979.

Bloom, L., & Lahey, M. *Language development and language disorders*. New York: Wiley, 1978.

Bzoch, K., & Williams, W. Introducing rationale, principles, and related basic embryology and anatomy. In K. Bzoch (Ed.), *Communicative disorders related to cleft lip and palate* (2nd ed.). Boston: Little, Brown, 1979.

Comprehensive Assessment and Service (CASE) Information System. Washington, D.C.: American Speech-Language-Hearing Association, 1976.

Dearman, N., & Plisko, V. *The condition of education.* Washington, D.C.: National Center for Education Statistics, 1981.

Eisenson, J. The nature of defective speech. In W. Cruickshank (Ed.), *Psychology of exceptional children and youth* (3rd ed.). Englewood Cliffs, N.J.: Prentice-Hall, 1971.

Eisenson, J. *Aphasia in children.* New York: Harper & Row, 1972.

Eisenson, J., & Ogilvie, M. *Speech correction in the schools* (4th ed.). New York: Macmillan, 1977.

Freeman, G. *Speech and language services and the classroom teacher.* Reston, Va.: Council for Exceptional Children, 1977.

Gillespie, S., & Cooper, E. Prevalence of speech problems in junior and senior high schools. *Journal of Speech and Hearing Research*, 1973, *16*, 739–743.

Hull, F., Mieike, P., Willeford, J., & Timmons, R. *National speech and hearing survey.* Project No. 50978, Bureau of Education for the Handicapped, U.S. Office of Education. Washington, D.C.: Department of Health, Education, and Welfare, 1976.

King, R., Jones, C., & Lasky, E. In retrospect: A fifteen year follow-up report of speech-language disordered children. *Language, Speech, and Hearing Services in the Schools*, 1982, *13*, 24–36.

McDermott, L. The effect of duplicated and unduplicated child count on prevalence of speech-impaired children. *Language, Speech, and Hearing Services in the Schools*, 1981, *12*, 115–119.

National Institute of Neurological Disease and Stroke. *Human communication and its disorders: An overview.* Bethesda, Md.: Public Health Service, 1969.

Neal, W. Speech pathology services in the secondary schools. *Language, Speech, and Hearing Services in the Schools*, 1976, *7*, 6–16.

Perkins, W. Disorders of speech flow. In T. Hixon, L. Shriberg, & J. Saxon (Eds.), *Introduction to communication disorders.* Englewood Cliffs, N.J.: Prentice-Hall, 1980.

Project Upgrade. *Model regulations for school language, speech and hearing programs and services.* Washington, D.C.: American Speech and Hearing Association, 1973.

Schiefelbusch, R. Synthesis of trends in language intervention. In D. Bricker (Ed.), *New directions for exceptional children*; (Vol. 2) *Language intervention with children.* San Francisco: Jossey-Bass, 1980.

Taylor, J. Public school speech-language certification standards: Are they standard? *ASHA* 1980, *22*, 159–165.

Van Hattum, R. Communication problems associated with cleft palate. In S. Dickinson (Ed.), *Communication disorders, remedial principles and practices.* Glenview, Ill.: Scott, Foresman, 1974.

Van Hattum, R. Services of the speech clinician in schools: Progress and prospects. *ASHA*, 1976, *18*, 59–63.

Van Riper, C. *Speech correction: Principles and methods* (6th ed.). Englewood Cliffs, N.J.: Prentice-Hall, 1978.

Webster, L., & Brutten, G. The modification of stuttering and associated behaviors. In S. Dickinson (Ed.), *Communication disorders, remedial principles and practices*. Glenview, Ill.: Scott, Foresman, 1974.

Winitz, H. Articulation disorders: From prescription to description. In E. Meyen (Ed.), *Basic readings in the study of exceptional children and youth*. Denver: Love Publishing, 1979.

Zemmol, C. A priority system of case load selection. *Language, Speech, and Hearing Services in the Schools*, 1977, *8*, 85–98.

CHAPTER 8

American Psychiatric Association. *Diagnostic and statistical manual of mental disorders: Third edition (DSM-III)*. Washington, D.C.: American Psychiatric Association, 1977.

Axelrod, S. Token reinforcement programs in special classes. *Exceptional Children*, 1971, *37*, 371–379.

Bandura, A. *Principles of behavior modification*. New York: Holt, Rinehart & Winston, 1969.

Barkley, R. A. Using stimulant drugs in the classroom. *School Psychology Digest*, 1979, *8*, 412–425.

Blatt, M. M., & Kohlberg, L. The effects of classroom moral discussion upon children's level of moral judgement. *Journal of Moral Education*, 1975, *4*(2), 129–161.

Block, J. H., & Block, J. The role of ego-control and ego-resiliency in the organization of behavior. In W. A. Collins (Ed.), *Minnesota symposia on child psychology* (Vol. 13). New York: Erlbaum, 1980.

Bower, E. M. *Early identification of emotionally handicapped children in school*. Springfield, Ill.: Charles C Thomas, 1960.

Bronfenbrenner, U. Context of child rearing: Problems and prospects. *American Psychologist*, 1979, *34*, 844–850.

Camp, B. W., & Bash, M. A. *Think aloud: Increasing social and cognitive skills: A problem-solving program for children*. Champaign, Ill.: Research Press, 1981.

Charles, L., Schain, R., & Zelnicker, T. Optimal dosages of methyphenidate for improving the learning and behavior of hyperactive children. *Developmental and Behavioral Pediatrics*, 1981, *2*, 78–81.

Cohen-Sandler, R., Berman, A., & King, R. Life stress and symptomatology: Determinants of suicidal behavior in children. *Journal of Child Psychiatry*, 1982, *21*, 178–186.

Connors, C., & Werry, J. S. Pharmacotherapy. In H. C. Quay & J. S. Werry (Eds.), *Psychopathological disorders of childhood* (2nd ed.). New York: Wiley, 1979.

DeMagistris, R. J., & Imber, S. C. The effects of life space interviewing on academic and social performance of behaviorally disordered children. *Behavior Disorders*, 1980, *6*, 12–25.

Douglas, V. I. Stop, look, and listen: The problem of sustained attentions and impulse control in hyperactive and normal children. *Canadian Journal of Behavioral Science*, 1972, *4*, 259–282.

Dweck, C. The role of expectations and attributions in the alleviation of learned helplessness. *Journal of Personality and Social Psychology*, 1975, *31*, 674–685.

Feagans, L., & McKinney, J. The pattern of exceptionality across domains in learning disabled children. *Journal of Applied Developmental Psychology*, 1981, *1*, 313–328.

Feldhusen, J. S., Thurston, J. R., & Benning, J. J. Sentence completion responses and classroom social behavior. *Personnel and Guidance Journal*, 1966.

Froomkin, J. *Estimates and projections of special target group populations in elementary and secondary schools.* Report prepared for the President's Commission on School Finance. Washington, D.C.: Government Printing Office, 1972.

Galbraith, R. E., & Jones, T. M. *Moral reasoning: A teaching handbook for adapting Kohlberg to the classroom.* St. Paul, Minn.: Greenhaven Press, 1976.

Galvin, J. P., & Annesley, F. R. Reading and arithmetic correlates of conduct-problem and withdrawal children. *Journal of Educational Research*, 1971, *5*, 213–219.

Graubard, P. The extent of academic retardation in a residential treatment center. *Journal of Educational Research*, 1964, *58*, 78–80.

Graubard, P. Children with behavioral disabilities. In L. Dunn (Ed.), *Exceptional children in the schools: Special education in transition* (2nd ed.). New York: Holt, Rinehart & Winston, 1973.

Hetherington, E. M. Divorce: A child's perspective. *American Psychologist*, 1979, *34*, 851–858.

Hetherington, E. M., & Martin, B. Family interaction. In H. C. Quay & J. S. Werry (Eds.), *Psychopathological disorders of childhood* (2nd ed.). New York: Wiley, 1979.

Hewett, F. M. Behavioral ecology: A unifying strategy for the '80s. In R. Rutherford, A. Pietro, & J. McGlothlin (Eds.), *Severe behavior disorders of children and youth*. Phoenix, Ariz.: Arizona State University, 1980.

Hobbs, N. Helping disturbed children: Psychological and ecological strategies. *American Psychologist*, 1966, *21*, 1105–1115.

Hobbs, N. Project Re-Ed: New ways of helping emotionally disturbed children. In Joint Commission on Mental Health of Children, *Crisis in child mental health: Challenge for the 1970s*. New York: Harper and Row, 1970.

Hobbs, N. *Helping disturbed children: Psychological and ecological strategies II. Project Re-Ed, twenty years later.* Nashville, Tenn.: Center for the Study of Families and Children, Vanderbilt University, 1979.

Illich, I. *Deschooling society.* New York: Harper and Row, 1970.

Johnson, R., & Johnson, D. Building friendships between handicapped and nonhandicapped students: Effects of cooperative and individualistic instruction. *American Educational Research Journal*, 1981, *18*, 415–423.

Kelly, T. J., Bullock, L. M., & Dykes, M. K. Behavioral disorders: Teachers' perceptions. *Exceptional Children*, 1977, *43*, 316–318.

Keogh, B. Hyperactive and learning disorders: Review and speculation. *Exceptional Children*, 1971, *38*, 101–110.

Keogh, B. Current issues in educational methods. In J. Millichap (Ed.), *Learning disabilities and related disorders*. Chicago: Yearbook Medical Publishers, 1977.

Knoblock, P. Open education for emotionally disturbed children. *Exceptional Children*, 1973, *39*, 358–365.

Kohlberg, L. Stage and sequence: The cognitive-developmental approach to socialization. In D. A. Goslin (Ed.), *Handbook of socialization theory and research*. Chicago: Rand McNally, 1969.

Kohlberg, L. Moral stages and moralization: The cognitive developmental approach. In T. Lickona (Ed.), *Moral development and behavior: Theory, research, and social issues*. New York: Holt, Rinehart and Winston, 1976.

Kroth, R. L., Whelan, R. J., & Stables, J. M. Teacher applications of behavior principles in home and classroom environments. In E. L. Meyen, G. A. Vergason, & R. J. Whelan (Eds.), *Strategies for teaching exceptional children*. Denver: Love, 1972.

Long, N. J., & Newman, R. G. The teacher and his mental health. In N. J. Long, W. C. Morse, & R. G. Newman (Eds.), *Conflict in the classroom: The education of emotionally disturbed children* (4th ed.). Belmont, Calif.: Wadsworth, 1980.

Maccoby, E., & Masters, J. Attachment and dependency. In P. Mussen (Ed.), *Carmichael's manual of child psychology* (Vol. 2). New York: Wiley, 1970.

McFall, R. M. *Behavioral training: A skill-acquisition approach to clinical problems*. Morristown, N.J.: General Learning Press, 1976.

Montgomery, M. Cultural therapy and practice. In J. Paul & B. Epanchin (Eds.), *Emotional disturbance in children*. Columbus, Ohio: Charles E. Merrill, 1982.

Morse, W. C. The helping teacher/crisis teacher concept. *Focus on Exceptional Children*, 1976, *8* (September), 1–11.

Newman, R. G. Alienation of today's youth. In N. J. Long, W. C. Morse, & R. G. Newman (Eds.), *Conflict in the classroom: The education of emotionally disturbed children* (4th ed.). Belmont, Calif.: Wadsworth, 1980.

Paul, J., & Epanchin, B. (Eds.), *Emotional disturbance in children*. Columbus, Ohio: Charles E. Merrill, 1982.

Quay, H. C. Classification. In H. C. Quay & J. S. Werry (Eds.), *Psychopathological disorders of childhood* (2nd ed.). New York: Wiley, 1979.

Redl, F. *Mental hygiene and teaching*. New York: Harcourt Brace Jovanovich, 1959.

Rhodes, W. C. The disturbing child: A problem of ecological management. *Exceptional Children*, 1967, *33*, 449–455.

Robins, L. *Deviant children grown up*. Baltimore: Williams & Wilkins, 1966.

Rubin, R., & Balow, B. Prevalence of teacher identified behavior problems: A longitudinal study. *Exceptional Children*, 1978, *45*, 102–111.

Salvia, J., Schultz, E. W., & Chapin, N. Reliability of Bower Scale for screening of children with emotional handicaps. *Exceptional Children*, 1974, *41*, 117–118.

Schwartz, J. Childhood origins of psychopathology. *American Psychologist*, 1979, *34*, 879–885.

Seeman, M. Powerlessness and knowledge: A comparative study of alienation and learning. *Sociometry*, 1967, *30*, 105–123.

Sprague, R., & Sleator, E. Drugs and dosages: Implications for learning disabilities. In R. M. Knights & D. Bakker (Eds.), *The neuropsychology of learning disorders*. Baltimore: University Park Press, 1976.

Ullmann, C. E. *Identification of maladjusted school children* (Public Health Monograph No. 7). Washington, D.C.: U.S. Government Printing Office, 1952.

Weinstein, L. *Evaluation of a program for re-educating disturbed children: A follow-up comparison with untreated children*. Washington, D.C.: U.S. Department of Health, Education, and Welfare, 1974. (ERIC Document Reproduction Service No. ED-141-966.)

Werry, J. S. The diagnosis, etiology, and treatment of hyperactivity in children. In J. Hellmuth (Ed.), *Learning disorders* (Vol. 3). Seattle: Special Child Publications, 1968.

Whiting, B. B. *Six cultures—Studies of child rearing*. New York: Wiley, 1963.

Wood, F. H. Defining disturbing, disordered, and disturbed behavior. In F. H. Wood & K. C. Lakin (Eds.), *Disturbing, disordered, or disturbed?* Reston, Va.: Council for Exceptional Children, 1982.

Wood, F. H., & Zabel, R. Making sense of reports on the incidence of behavior disorders/emotional disturbances in school-aged children. *Psychology in the Schools*, 1978, *15*, 45–51.

CHAPTER 9

Adelman, H. S., & Comfers, B. E. Stimulant drugs and learning problems. *Journal of Special Education*, 1977, *11* (4), 377–415.

Barsch, R. *A movigenic curriculum*. Madison: Wisconsin State Department of Public Instruction, 1965.

Barsch, R. *Achieving perceptual motor efficiency: A space-oriented approach to learning*. Seattle: Special Child Publications, 1967.

Bartel, N. R. Problems in arithmetic achievement. In D. D. Hammill & N. R. Bartel (Eds.), *Teaching children with learning and behavior problems*. Boston: Allyn and Bacon, 1975.

Brutten, M., Richardson, S. O., & Mangel, C. *Something's wrong with my child*. New York: Harcourt Brace Jovanovich, 1973.

Bush, W., & Giles, M. *Aids to psycholinguistic teaching*. Columbus, Ohio: Charles E. Merrill, 1969.

Cawley, J. F., & Goodstein, H. *A developmental program of quantitative behavior for handicapped children*. Research report to Bureau of Education for the Handicapped. Washington, D.C.: U.S. Office of Education, 1972.

Cawley, J. F., & Vitello, S. J. A model for arithmetic programming for handicapped children. *Exceptional Children*, 1972, *39* (October), 101–110.

Chalfant, J. D., & Scheffelin, M. A. *Central processing dysfunctions in children: A review of research*. Washington, D.C.: U.S. Department of Health, Education, and Welfare, 1969.

Cox, S. The learning disabled adult. *Academic Therapy*, 1977, *13* (September), 79–86.

Cratty, B. J., & Martin, M. M. *Perceptual motor behavior and educational processes.* Springfield, Ill.: Charles C Thomas, 1969.

Cruickshank, W., & Hallahan, D. *Psychoeducational foundations of learning disabilities.* Englewood Cliffs, N.J.: Prentice-Hall, 1973.

Cruickshank, W., Bentzen, F. A., Ratzeburg, F. H., & Tannhauser, M. *A teaching method for brain-injured and hyperactive children.* Syracuse, N.Y.: Syracuse University Press, 1961.

DeFries, J. C., & Decker, S. N. Genetic aspects of reading disability. In P. G. Aaron & M. Halatesha (Eds.), *Neuropsychological and Neuropsycholinguistic aspects of reading disabilities.* New York: Academic Press, 1981.

Delacato, G. H. *The diagnosis and treatment of speech and reading disorders.* Springfield, Ill.: Charles C Thomas, 1963.

Dunn, L. M., & Smith, J. O. *Peabody language development kits.* Circle Pines, Minn.: American Guidance Service, 1967.

Education for All Handicapped Children Act. Public Law 94–142, Ninety-fourth Congress, November 29, 1975.

Englemann, S., & Bruner, E. *Distar: An instructional system.* Chicago: Science Research Associates, 1969.

Federal Register. Procedures for evaluating specific learning disabilities. 42 (250), Section 121a.541. Washington, D.C.: Department of Health, Education, and Welfare, Office of Education, December 29, 1977.

Fernald, G. M. *Remedial techniques in basic school subjects.* New York: McGraw-Hill, 1943.

Fernald, G. M., & Keller, H. The effect of kinesthetic factors in the development of word recognition in the case of non-readers. *Journal of Educational Research,* 1921, *4* (December), 355–377.

Frostig, M., & Horne, D. *The Frostig program for the development of visual perception.* Chicago: Follett Educational Corporation, 1964.

Gaddes, W. H. *Learning disabilities and brain function: Neuropsychological approach.* New York: Springer-Verlag, 1980.

Gearhart, B. R. *Teaching the learning disabled: A combined task-process approach.* St. Louis: C. V. Mosby, 1976.

Getman, G. H. The visuo-motor complex in the acquisition of learning skills In B. Straub & J. Hellmuth (Eds.), *Learning disorders* (Vol. 1). Seattle: Special Child Publications, 1965.

Gillingham, A., & Stillman, B. *Remedial work for reading, spelling, and penmanship.* New York: Hackett and Wilhelms, 1936.

Gillingham, A., & Stillman, B. *Remedial training for children with specific disability in reading, spelling, and penmanship* (5th ed.). Cambridge, Mass.: Educators Publishing Service, 1965.

Gray, B., & Ryan, B. *A language program for the non-language child.* Champaign, Ill.: Research Press, 1973.

Hallgren, B. Specific dyslexia (congenital word-blindness): A clinical and genetic study. *Acta Psychiatrica et Neurologica,* 1950, *65,* 1–287.

Hammill, D. D., & Larsen, S. C. The effectiveness of psycholinguistic training. *Exceptional Children,* 1974, *41* (September), 5–14.

Hammill, D. D., & Larsen, S. C. The effectiveness of psycholinguistic training: A reaffirmation of position. *Exceptional Children,* 1978, *44* (March), 402–412.

Hammill, D. D., Leigh, L. E., McNutt, G., & Larsen, S. C. A new definition of learning disabilities. *Learning Disability Quarterly*, 1981, *4* (Fall), 336–342.

Hannah, P., Hodges, R., & Hannah, J. *Spelling: Structure and strategies.* Boston: Houghton Mifflin, 1971.

Hegge, T., Kirk, S., & Kirk, W. *Remedial reading drills.* Ann Arbor, Mich.: George Wahr, 1936.

Hermann, K. *Reading disability: A medical study of word-blindness and related handicaps.* Springfield, Ill.: Charles C Thomas, 1959.

Johnson, D. J., & Myklebust, H. R. *Learning disabilities: Educational principles and practices.* New York: Grune & Stratton, 1967.

Karnes, M. *GOAL: Language development.* Springfield, Mass.: Milton Bradley, 1972.

Karnes, M. *The Karnes early language activities (GEM).* Champaign, Ill.: Generators of Educational Materials, 1975.

Karnes, M. *Learning language at home.* Reston, Va.: Council for Exceptional Children, 1977.

Karnes, M., Zehrbach, R., & Teska, J. The Karnes preschool program: Rational curricular offerings and follow-up data. In S. Ryan (Ed.), *A report on longitudinal evaluations of preschool programs* (Vol. 1). DHEW Publication No. (OHD) 77-24. Washington, D.C.: Office of Child Development, Children's Bureau, 1974.

Kavale, K. Functions of the Illinois test of psycholinguistic abilities (ITPA): Are they trainable? *Exceptional Children*, 1981, *47* (April), 496–513.

Kavale, K. Meta-analysis of the relationship between visual perceptual skills and reading achievement. *Journal of Learning Disabilities*, 1982, *15* (January), 42–51.

Kephart, N. Perceptual-motor aspects of learning disabilities. *Exceptional Children*, 1964, *31* (December), 201–206.

Kirk, S. An interview with Samuel Kirk. *Academic Therapy*, 1978, *13* (May), 617–620.

Kirk, S., & Kirk, W. *Psycholinguistic learning disabilities: Diagnosis and remediation.* Urbana, Ill.: University of Illinois Press, 1971.

Kirk, S., Kliebhan, Sr. J. M., & Lerner, J. W. *Teaching reading to slow and disabled learners.* Boston: Houghton Mifflin, 1978.

Kirk, S., McCarthy, J., & Kirk, W. *The Illinois Test of Psycholinguistic Abilities* (rev. ed.). Urbana, Ill.: University of Illinois Press, 1968.

Lerner, J. W. *Learning disabilities: Theories, diagnosis, and teaching strategies* (3rd ed.). Boston: Houghton Mifflin, 1981.

Lerner, J. W., Mardel-Czudnowski, C., & Goldenberg, D. *Special education for the early childhood years.* Englewood Cliffs, N.J.: Prentice-Hall, 1981.

Lombardi, T. P., & Lombardi, E. J. *ITPA: Clinical interpretation and remediation.* Seattle: Special Child Publications, 1977.

Luick, A., Kirk, S., Agranowitz, A., & Busby, R. Profiles of children with severe oral language disorders. *Journal of Speech and Hearing Disorders*, 1982, *47* (February), 88–92.

Lund, K., Foster, G., & McCall-Perez, F. The effectiveness of psycholinguistic training, A re-evaluation. *Exceptional Children*, 1978, *44* (February), 310–321.

McGinnis, M. *Aphasic children.* Washington, D.C.: Alexander Graham Bell Association, 1963.

Meier, J. Prevalence and characteristics of learning disabilities found in second grade children. *Journal of Learning Disabilities,* 1971, *4* (January), 6–19.

Minskoff, E., Wiseman, D., & Minskoff, J. *The MWM program for developing language abilities.* Ridgefield, N.J.: Educational Performance Associates, 1975.

Myers, P. T., & Hammill, D. D. *Methods for learning disabilities* (2nd ed.). New York: Wiley, 1976.

Myklebust, H. R., & Boshes, B. *Minimal brain damage in children.* Final report, Contract 108-65-142, Neurological and Sensory Disease Control Program. Washington, D.C.: Department of Health, Education, and Welfare, 1969.

National Advisory Committee on Handicapped Children. *First annual report, subcommittee on education of the committee on labor and public welfare, U.S. Senate.* Washington, D.C.: U.S. Government Printing Office, 1968.

Orton, S. T. Specific reading disability—Strephosymbolia. *Journal of the American Medical Association,* 1928, *90,* 1095–1099.

Peters, M. *Diagnostic and remedial spelling manual.* London: Macmillan Education Ltd., 1975.

Pittman, J. *The future of the teaching of reading.* Paper presented at the Educational Conference of the Educational Records Bureau, New York City, November 1, 1963.

Raschke, D., & Young, A. A comparative analysis of the diagnostic-prescriptive and behavioral-analysis models in preparation for the development of a dialectic pedagogical system. *Education and Training of the Mentally Retarded,* 1976, *11* (April), 135–145. (a)

Raschke, D., & Young, A. The dialectic teaching system: A comprehensive model derived from two educational approaches. *Education and Training of the Mentally Retarded,* 1976, *11* (October), 232–246. (b)

Ross, A.O. *Psychological aspects of learning disabilities and reading disorders.* New York: McGraw-Hill, 1976.

Schwartz, M., Gilroy, J., & Lynn, G. Neuropsychological and psychological implications of spelling deficit in adulthood: A case report. *Journal of Learning Disabilities,* 1976, *9* (March), 144–148.

Slingerland, B. *A multi-sensory approach to language arts for specific language disability children.* Cambridge, Mass.: Educators Publishing Service, 1974.

Smith, J. O. Effects of a group language development program upon psycholinguistic abilities of educable mentally retarded children. *Special Education Monograph.* Nashville, Tenn.: George Peabody College for Teachers, 1962.

Spalding, R. B., & Spalding, W. T. *The writing road to reading.* New York: Morrow, 1957.

Strauss, A. A., & Lehtinen, L. *Psychopathology of the brain-injured child.* New York: Grune & Stratton, 1947.

Torgesen, J. What should we do with psychological processes? *Journal of Learning Disabilities,* 1979, *12* (October), 514–521.

Valett, R. *The remediation of learning disabilities*. Palo Alto, Calif.: Fearon Publishers, 1967.

Woodcock, R. W., Clark, C. R., & Davies, C. O. *The Peabody rebus reading program*. Circle Pines, Minn.: American Guidance Service, 1967.

Ysseldyke, J., & Salvia, J. Diagnostic-prescriptive teaching: Two models. *Exceptional Children*, 1974, *4* (November), 181–186.

CHAPTER 10

Abeson, A., & Zettel, J. The end of the quiet revolution: The education of all handicapped children act of 1975. *Exceptional Children*, 1977, *44*, 114–130.

Altshuler, K. Z. Identifying and programming for the emotionally handicapped deaf child. In D. W. Naiman (Ed.), *Needs of emotionally disturbed hearing impaired children*. New York: New York University School of Education, 1975.

Balthazar, E., & Stevens, H. *The emotionally disturbed, mentally retarded*. Englewood Cliffs, N. J.: Prentice-Hall, 1975.

Bricker, D., & Carlson, L. An intervention approach for communicatively handicapped infants and young children. In D. Bricker (Ed.), *Language intervention with children* (Vol. 2). New Directions for Exceptional Children. San Francisco, Calif.: Jossey-Bass, 1980.

Bricker, D., & Iacino, R. Early intervention with severe/profoundly handicapped children. In E. Sontag (Ed.), *Educational programming for the severely and profoundly handicapped*. Reston, Va.: Council for Exceptional Children, 1977.

Brown, L., Nietupski, J., & Hamre-Nietupski, S. Criterion of ultimate functioning. In M. Thomas (Ed.), *Hey, don't forget about me*. Reston, Va.: Council for Exceptional Children, 1976.

Connors, C., & Werry, J. Pharmacotherapy. In H. Quay & J. Werry (Eds.), *Psychopathological disorders of childhood* (2nd ed.), New York: Wiley, 1979.

Dantona, R. Services for deaf-blind children. *Exceptional Children*, 1976, *43*, 172–174.

DeWeerd, J. *Handicapped children's early education program*. Washington, D.C.: U.S. Department of Education, Special Education Programs, 1979.

Douglas, H., & Hoffman, H. Socioemotional development. In F. Connor, G. Williamson, & J. Siepp (Eds.), *Program guide for infants and toddlers with neuromotor and other developmental disabilities*. New York: Teachers College Press, 1978.

Fair, D., & Birch, J. Effect of rest on test scores of physically handicapped and nonhandicapped children. *Exceptional Children*, 1971, *38*, 335–336.

Fassler, J. Performance of cerebral palsied children under conditions of reduced auditory input. *Exceptional Children*, 1970, *37*, 201–209.

Fredericks, H., Jordan, V., Gage, M., Levak, L., Alrich, G., & Wadlow, M. *A data-based classroom for the moderately and severely handicapped*. Monmouth, Ore.: Instructional Development Corp., 1975.

Fredericks, H., & Staff of the Teaching Research Infant and Child Center. *The teaching research curriculum for moderately and severely handicapped*. Springfield, Ill.: Charles C Thomas, 1980.

Gallagher, J. J., & Wiegerink, R. Educational strategies for the autistic child. *Journal of Autism and Childhood Schizophrenia*, 1976, 6, 1.

Haring, N., & Bricker, D. Overview of comprehensive services for the severely/profoundly handicapped. In N. Haring & L. Brown (Eds.), *Teaching the severely handicapped* (Vol. 1). New York: Grune and Stratton, 1976.

Haywood, C. What happened to mild and moderate mental retardation? *American Journal of Mental Deficiency*, 1979, 83, 429–431.

Healey, W., & Karp-Nortman, D. *The hearing impaired, mentally retarded: Recommendations for action.* Washington, D.C.: American Speech and Hearing Association, 1975.

Holman, L., & Freedheim, D. Further studies on intelligence levels in cerebral palsied children. *American Journal of Physical Medicine*, 1958, 37, 90–97.

Hopkins, T., Bice, H., & Colton, K. *Evaluation and education of the cerebral palsied child.* Arlington, Va.: International Council for Exceptional Children, 1954.

Luckey, R. E., & Addison, M. R. The profoundly retarded: A new challenge for public education. *Education and Training of the Mentally Retarded*, 1974, 9, 123–130.

McKenzie, H., Hill, M., Sousie, S., York, R., & Baker, K. Special education training to facilitate rural, community based programs for the severely handicapped. In E. Sontag (Ed.), *Educational programming for the severely or profoundly handicapped.* Reston, Va.: Council for Exceptional Children, 1977.

Office of Civil Rights. *State, regional, and national summaries of data from the Fall 1978 civil rights survey of elementary and secondary schools.* Washington, D.C.: U.S. Department of Education, 1982.

Quay, H., Werry, J. (Eds.). *Psychopathological disorders of childhood* (2nd ed.). New York: Wiley, 1979.

Ranier, J. D. Severely emotionally handicapped hearing impaired children. In D. W. Naiman (Ed.), *Needs of emotionally disturbed hearing impaired children.* New York: New York University School of Education, 1975.

Rawls, D., Rawls, J., & Harrison, C. An investigation of six- to eleven year-old children with allergic disorders. *Journal of Consulting and Clinical Psychology*, 1971, 36, 260–264.

Robinson, H., & Robinson, N. *The mentally retarded child* (2nd ed.). New York: McGraw-Hill, 1976.

Roos, P., & Oliver, M. Evaluation of operant conditioning with institutionalized retarded children. *American Journal of Mental Deficiency*, 1969, 74, 325–330.

Rutter, M. Diagnosis and definition. In M. Rutter & E. Schopler (Eds.), *Autism: A reappraisal of concepts and treatment.* New York: Plenum Press, 1978.

Schonell, F. *Educating spastic children.* Edinburgh: Oliver and Boyd, 1956.

Schopler, E., & Bristol, M. *Autistic children in public school.* ERIC Exceptional Child Education Report, Division TEACCH, University of North Carolina, 1980.

Sherr, R. D. Public school programs. In M. A. Thomas (Ed.), *Hey, don't forget about me.* Reston, Va.: Council for Exceptional Children, 1976.

Snell, M. E. (Ed.). *Systematic instruction of the moderately and severely handicapped.* Columbus, Ohio: Charles E. Merrill, 1978.

Sontag, E., Smith, J., & Sailor, W. The severely/profoundly handicapped: Who are they? Where are we? *Journal of Special Education,* 1977, *11* (1), 5–11.

Stephen, E., & Hawks, G. Cerebral palsy and mental subnormality. In A. M. Clarke & D. B. Clarke (Eds.), *Mental deficiency: The changing outlook* (3rd ed.). New York: The Free Press, 1974.

Task Force Report on the Mentally Retarded–Deaf. Washington, D.C.: Office of the Assistant Secretary for Human Development, Office of Mental Retardation Coordination, November, 1973.

Turnbull, H. Law and the mentally retarded citizen: American responses to the declarations of rights of the United Nations and International League of Societies for the mentally handicapped—Where we have been, are, and are headed. *Syracuse Law Review,* 1979, *30,* 1093–1143.

Vanderheiden, G., & Harris-Vanderheiden, D. Communication techniques and aids for the nonvocal severely physically handicapped. In L. Lloyd (Ed.), *Communication assessment and intervention strategies.* Baltimore: University Park Press, 1976.

Watson, J. *How to use behavior modification with mentally retarded and autistic children.* Tuscaloosa, Alabama: Behavior Modification Technology, 1972.

Wolf, J., & Anderson, R. *The multiply handicapped child.* Springfield, Ill.: Charles C Thomas, 1969.

Yoder, D. Communication systems for nonspeech children. In D. Bricker (Ed.), *Language intervention with children* (Vol. 2). New Directions for Exceptional Children. San Francisco: Jossey-Bass, 1980.

Name/Source Index

Abeson, A., 18, 31, 452
Abroms, K., 64, 130
Ackerman, B., 376
Addison, M. R., 434
Adelman, H. S., 379
Adelson, E., 202
Adler, M., 79
Agranowitz, A., 374
Alley, G., 411
Altshuler, K., 240, 428
American Foundation for the Blind, 187
American Psychiatric Association, 326
Annesley, F. R., 332
Arnold, A., 89
Aschner, M., 84, 98
Astin, H., 84
Axelrod, S., 348

Bailey, D. B., 40
Baller, W., 140
Balow, B., 328
Balthazar, E., 421
Bandura, A., 339
Bangs, T., 305
Barbe, W., 79
Barbee, A. H., 84
Barkley, R. A., 360
Barraga, N. C., 182–183, 185, 187, 188,
    222–223, 227–228
Barritt, L. S., 138
Barsch, R., 395, 396
Bartel, N. R., 405
Bash, M. A., 344
Bateman, B., 183, 196–197
Bell, A. G., 7, 255, 256
Bennett, J., 64, 130
Bennett, S. W., 138
Benning, J. J., 332

Berman, A., 336
Bice, H., 420
Bijou, S., 173
Binet, A., 7, 121
Birch, H. G., 133
Birch, H. G., et al., 127
Birch, J. W., 23, 275, 451
Birch, J. W., et al., 197
Blackhurst, A., 233–234
Blackwell, et al., 267
Blatt, M. M., 346
Bliss, J. C., 224
Block, J., 335
Block, J. H., 335
Bloodstein, O., 294, 301–302, 307–308,
    319, 360
Bloom, B. S., 88, 97–98, 115
Bloom, L., 303
Boshes, B., 375
Bower, E. M., 328
Brackett, D., 235
Bradfield, R. H., et al., 151
Braga, J., 105
Braidwood, T., 254
Braille, L., 7, 209
Brantley, J., 356
Brasel, K., 258
Brauning, L., 141
Bricker, D., 431–433, 439, 440
Brickey, M., 140–141
Bristol, M., 424
Bronfenbrenner, U., 338
Bronowski, J., 96, 116–117
Brookover, W. B., et al., 62
Brown, L., 431, 460
Brown, V., 59
Bruner, E., 402
Bruner, J., 95

Williams, W., 296
Williamson, G., 459–460
Winitz, H., 292
Wiseman, D., 398–399
Wolf, M., 80
Wolfenberger, W., 166
Wood, F. H., 323, 328
Woodcock, R. W., 402

Yoder, D., 442–443

Young, A., 393
Ysseldyke, J., 389–390

Zabel, R., 328
Zane, T., 174–175
Zehrbach, R., 398
Zelnicker, T., 360
Zemmol, C., 309
Zettel, J., 18, 452
Zider, S., 174

Subject Index

Aphasia, 143, 281, 397
   childhood/congenital/developmental,
      305–306
   expressive, 397
   receptive, 397
Aphonia, 300. *See also* Communication
      disorders
Applied behavior analysis, for severe/pro-
      found mentally retarded, 422–423
Aptitude-task interaction, *see* Process-task
      training
Aptitude tests, *see* Tests and testing
Arithmetic
   for blind, 222
   diagnosing learning disabilities in,
      403–404
   remedial methods for, 404–405
   for trainable mentally retarded, 171
   see also Mathematics
Articulation
   proficiency and intelligence and, 291
   socioeconomic status and, 291
   in speech production, 287
Articulation disorders, 281, 284, 285,
      288–292. *See also* Communication dis-
      orders
Arts and crafts, for trainable mentally re-
      tarded, 172
Ascent of Man, The, 96
Assessment, 27. *See also* Tests and testing
Association, in intelligence tests, 43
Association for Children with Learning
      Disabilities, 14
Association method, for oral language
      learning disabilities, 397
Asthma, 448, 449, 451–452
Astigmatism, 190
Attention
   disabilities, 374, 384
   educable mentally retarded and, 137
   in learning and behavior disorders, 333
   in multiply handicapped, 440
   see also Memory
Attribute listing, 100–101
Audiometer, pure-tone, 234
Auditory discrimination, articulatory pro-
      ficiency and, 291
Auditory global method, *see* Auditory
      training
Auditory impairments, *see* Hearing im-
      pairments
Auditory method, for teaching language
      to the hearing impaired, 257
Auditory receptive training, for oral lan-
      guage learning disabilities, 397
Auditory training, for hearing impaired,
      260–261
Auditory-vocal disorders, 306

Augmentative systems for communication
      in multiply handicapped, 442–443
   direct selection, 443
   encoding, 443
   scanning, 443
Autism, 423–428

Backward chaining, for moderate/severe
      mentally retarded, 174–175
Baseline, 347, 348
Bausch and Lomb Orthorater, 185
Behavioral characteristics
   of behavior problem children, 331–338
   of communication disordered children,
      286–306
   of hearing impaired children, 244–250
   of gifted children, 71–85
   of learning disabled children, 370–375
   of mentally retarded children, 135–144
   of multiply handicapped children,
      419–431
   of physically handicapped children,
      447–452
   of visually impaired children, 193–199
Behavior modification program
   for behavior problems, 343, 346–348
   for multiply handicapped, 435
   for trainable mentally retarded,
      174–175
Behavior problems, children with,
      322–363
   academic achievement and, 332
   anxiety-withdrawal, 327, 334–337, 345
   behavior modification for, 343, 346–348
   biophysical factors and, 341–342
   causes of, 362
   characteristics of, 331–338
   check lists for identifying, 329–330
   classification of, 326–327
   conduct disorders, 327, 331–334
   countercultural interventions for, 350
   definition of, 322–324
   developmental profiles of, 324–326
   divorce and, 341
   drug therapy for, 359–360
   ecological strategy for, 343, 349, 350,
      353
   educational adaptations for, 342–360
   educational and psychological strate-
      gies for, 342–343
   environmental factors and, 338–341
   factors related to, 338–342
   family and, 341
   helping teacher for, 357–359
   identification of, 329–331
   immaturity, 327, 337–338
   individualized education plan for,
      354–356

Behavior problems (*cont.*)
  interview schedules for identifying, 330
  learned helplessness in, 344–345
  learning environment for, 349–359
  and mental retardation, 421–423
  and multiple handicaps, 343, 346–348
  objective tests for identifying, 330
  observation of, 330–331
  open education for, 354
  operant conditioning and, 346–347
  paraprofessionals used with, 360
  PL 94–112 and, 354
  prevalence of, 327–329
  procultural interventions for, 349–350
  projective tests for identifying, 324, 330
  psychodynamic strategy for, 343
  psychoeducational strategy for, 342,
    354–357
  Re-Ed program for, 350, 352–353
  residential schools for, 350
  self-control taught to, 344
  sex differences in, 341–342
  skills needed by, 343–348
  social environment of, 338–341
  socialized aggression, 327, 338
  societal mental health and, 361–362
  stimulants and, 359
  task analysis, 347–348
  teachers and, 342, 357–359, 361
  token reinforcement and, 348
  of trainable mentally retarded, 174–175
  value decisions in, 345–346
  see also Autism
Behavior therapies, for stuttering, 295
Biological Sciences Curriculum Study,
    154–155
Blind Adolescent Life Skills Center, 217
Blindness, *see* Visual impairments
Bloom's Taxonomy of Educational Objec-
    tives, 97–98
Braille, use of, 209–211, 224
Brain injury, 395
  language development and, 143
  learning disabilities and, 377–378
Brainstorming
  in the enrichment triad, 108–109
  fluency improved by, 98–100
Brown v. *Board of Education*, 21
Bureau of Education for the Handi-
    capped, 17

California Achievement Test, interindi-
    vidual differences in, 40–42
Cannonball theory, gifted and, 77
Captioned Films for the Deaf, 268
Cataracts, 189, 190
Causes of exceptionalities
  changing views on, 8–11
  see also specific exceptionalities

Cawley-Goodstein system, 405
Cerebral palsy, 284, 448, 449, 450, 459
  athetoid, 301
  atoxic, 301–302
  communication disorders with, 284,
    301–303, 313
  mental retardation with, 419–420
  motor development and, 438–439
  rubella and, 302
  spasticity and, 301
  visual impairment with, 187
Ciliary muscles, 187
Civil Rights Act, 415
Class action law suits, 21–22
Classification
  of behavior problems, 326–327
  of communication disorders, 281
  of exceptional children, 37–39
  of hearing impairments, 235–238
  in intelligence tests, 43, 69
  labeling and, 38–39, 64
  of learning disabilities, 370–375
  of mental retardation, 123–125
  in preschool level, 26
  of visual impairments, 182–183
Classification System of Psychopathologi-
    cal Disorders in Children, 326
Cleft lip, 296
Cleft palate, 284, 295–297. *See also* Com-
    munication disorders
College
  gifted and, 105, 112
  hearing impaired and, 265–266
Communication boards, multiply handi-
    capped and, 443
Communication disorders, children with,
    278–319
  aphasia, 143, 281, 300, 305–306, 397
  articulation disorders, 281, 284, 285,
    288–292
  augmentation systems and, 442–443
  behavior therapies for stuttering and,
    295
  case history of, 282
  causal factors in, 283–284
  cerebral palsy and, 284, 301–303, 313
  characteristics of, 286–306
  classification of, 281
  classroom teachers and, 311–312
  cleft palate, 284, 295–297
  consultant services for, 313, 315
  defect assessment of, 283
  definition of, 278–279
  delayed language development in, 281,
    284, 305
  delivery services for teaching, 312–314
  developmental profile and, 279–281
  diagnostic centers for, 314
  diagnostic procedures for, 282–284,
    310–311

Maladjustment, *see* Personal adjustment; Social adjustment

Malnutrition, learning disabilities caused by, 378–379

Manual method, for teaching language to the hearing impaired, 253–254, 255, 257, 258, 259

Map reading, for visually impaired, 215–216

Massachusetts School for Idiotic and Feebleminded Youth, 6

Mathematics, for gifted, 91–92, 93, 103, 105. *See also* Arithmetic

Medical model, 9, 11

Memory
deficits, 373
of educable mentally retarded, 137
in intelligence tests, 43
measuring skills of, 69, 98, 99
see also Attention

Meningitis
hearing loss and, 240, 241, 250–251
multiple handicaps and, 250–251

Mental health, of gifted, 76. *See also* Behavior problems

Mental operations, in intelligence tests, 43

Mental retardation/mentally retarded, 119–179
adaptive behavior and, 123, 127–128
behavioral disturbances and, 421–423
causes of, 128–133
cerebral palsy and, 419–420
characteristics of, 135–144
classification of, 123–125
curriculum content for, 55–56
definition of, 120–123
developmental profiles of, 47, 133–135
employment and, 140–141
environment and, 123, 131, 132–133
family background and, 135–136
fetal alcohol syndrome causing, 132, 133
genetic disorders causing, 128–131
hearing impairment and, 420–421
identification of, 125–126
individual differences in, 46, 47, 49–50
infectious diseases causing, 132
intellectual subnormality and, 121–122
intelligence and, 121–123, 125
language acquisition and use in, 138–139
lead poisoning causing, 132
memory and, 137
motor abilities in, 136–137
personal characteristics of, 139–140
phenylketonuria causing, 131
physical abilities in, 136–137

polygenic inheritance and, 131
preschool programs for, 146
prevalence of, 52, 126–128
public school enrollment of, 53, 54
social characteristics of, 139–140
society's view of, 175–176
socioeconomic status and, 10–11, 127, 132–133, 145–147
toxic agents causing, 132
viruses causing, 132
see also Down's syndrome; Educable mental retardation; Severe/profound mental retardation; Trainable mental retardation

Mentor program, for gifted, 104, 113

Mild mental retardation, *see* Educable mental retardation

Mills v. *Board of Education*, 21

Milwaukee Project, 146

Minicourses, for gifted students, 110–111

Minority group children
courts and, 21
and educable mental retardation, 149–150, 152
as gifted, 79–81
personality and, 339–340
in special classes, 149–150, 152
in special education programs, 10–11

MIT Braille Emboss, 224

Mobility training, for blind, 213–215, 216, 217

Modeling, 159, 339

Model Secondary School for the Deaf, 265

Moderate mental retardation, *see* Trainable mental retardation

Mongolism, *see* Down's syndrome

Monterey system, 397

Montessori materials, 405

Moral development, for value decisions, 345–346

Motivation, in teaching educable mentally retarded, 157

Motor abilities
articulatory proficiency and, 291
blind and, 197–198
educable mentally retarded and, 136–137
multiply handicapped and, 438–439
trainable mentally retarded and, 142–143, 172

Movigenic curriculum, 396

Multidisciplinary approaches, to preschool child, 26

Multiple handicaps/multiply handicapped, 414–447
academic achievement and, 251
adjunctive services for, 433
autism, 423–428